Colección Tamesis

SERIE A: MONOGRAFÍAS, 206

# COMPANION TO SPANISH SURREALISM

'I, Salvador Dalí, come from Spain, which is the most irrational and most mystical country in the world.' Dalí's implicit suggestion is surely that Spaniards make good surrealists – as this volume confirms. Dedicated chapters consider major figures such as García Lorca, Salvador Dalí, Luis Buñuel, Rafael Alberti, Vicente Aleixandre, Luis Cernuda, Joan Miró and Gómez de la Serna; other less mainstream figures are gathered into surveys of work in particular genres. The emphasis throughout is on the theme, topic or aspect of a given figure's work that is typical, illustrative, informative and original, and the intention is to represent the broad evolution of Surrealism, from the early Freudian preoccupation with the unconscious, to the Hegelian metaphysics of 'the surrealist object', finally to the politics of Marxist materialism. The introduction focuses on salient features of Surrealism in Spain, and considers the value of its contribution both in terms of its adherence to French theory and as a distinctive cultural phenomenon.

ROBERT HAVARD is Professor of Spanish, University of Wales, Aberystwyth.

# COMPANION TO SPANISH SURREALISM

Edited by
Robert Havard

TAMESIS

First published 2004 by Tamesis, Woodbridge


ISBN  1 85566 104 7




Tamesis is an imprint of Boydell & Brewer Ltd
PO Box 9, Woodbridge, Suffolk IP12 3DF, UK
and of Boydell & Brewer Inc.
668 Mt. Hope Avenue, Rochester, NY 14620, USA
website: www.boydellandbrewer.com


A CIP catalogue record for this book is available
from the British Library


Library of Congress Cataloging-in-Publication Data

Havard, Robert.
  Companion to Spanish Surrealism / edited by Robert Havard.
     p. cm. – (Colección Tamesis. Serie A, Monografías ; 206)
  Includes bibliographical references and index.
  ISBN 1-85566-104-7 (hardback : alk. paper)
  1.  Surrealism–Spain. 2.  Arts, Spanish–20th century.
  I. Title. II. Series.
  NX562.A1H38 2004
  700'.946'0904–dc22                          2003027668


This publication is printed on acid-free paper

Printed in Great Britain by
Antony Rowe Ltd, Chippenham, Wiltshire

# CONTENTS

vi                                    CONTENTS

# ILLUSTRATIONS

*Plates appear between pages 116 and 117*

Urban Perspective with
Self-Portrait (1929)

Federico García Lorca. By kind
permission of the Fundación García
Lorca, Madrid

The Tilled Field (1923–4)

Joan Miró. © Successió Miró/ADAGP,
Paris, DACS, London 2004.
Photograph by David Heald ©
The Solomon R. Guggenheim
Foundation, New York

Soft Skulls and Cranial
Harps (1935)

© Salvador Dalí. Gala-Salvador Dalí
Foundation, DACS, London 2004

Scarecrows (1929)

Maruja Mallo. Reproduced by kind
permission of the Mallo family.

Four Fishermen's Wives of
Cadaqués (1928)

© Salvador Dalí. Museo Nacional Centro
de Arte Reina Sofía, Photographic
Archive, Madrid. Gala-Salvador Dalí
Foundation, DACS, London 2004

The Great Masturbator
(1929)

© Salvador Dalí. Gala-Salvador Dalí
Foundation, DACS, London 2004

Unsatisfied Desires (1928)

Salvador Dalí. Oil, sand, and seashells on
board; 30 in. × 24½ in., San
Francisco Museum of Modern Art,
fractional gift of Jan and Mitsuko Shrem,
Clos Pegase Winery Collection, ©
Salvador Dalí, Gala-Salvador Dalí
Foundation, DACS, London 2004

The Lugubrious Game (1929)

© Salvador Dalí. Gala-Salvador Dalí
Foundation, DACS, London 2004

The Endless Enigma (1938)

© Salvador Dalí. Gala-Salvador Dalí
Foundation, DACS, London 2004

Impressions of Africa (1938)

© Salvador Dalí. Gala-Salvador Dalí
Foundation, DACS, London 2004

# CONTRIBUTORS

**Dawn Ades** is Professor of Art History and Theory at the University of Essex, Director of the University of Essex Collection of Latin American Art and Director of the AHRB Research Centre for Studies of Surrealism and its Legacies. Her research has been mainly in two areas: Surrealism and Latin American art. Her books include *Dada and Surrealism Reviewed* (1978), *Salvador Dalí* (1982), *Photomontage* (1986), *Marcel Duchamp* (with Neil Cox and David Hopkins) (1999) and *Dalí's Optical Illusions* (2000).

**Andrew A. Anderson** is Professor of Spanish at the University of Virginia. Besides a number of publications on García Lorca, notably *Lorca's Late Poetry: A Critical Study* (1990), he has also written on such topics as Surrealism in Spanish theatre, Italian Futurism and Spain, and Ernesto Giménez Caballero. His current research is concerned with the literary historiography of between-the-wars Spanish poetry and with the ways in which the historical avant-garde manifested itself in Spain.

**Gwynne Edwards** is Research Professor of Spanish at the University of Wales, Aberystwyth. His books on cinema include: *The Discreet Art of Luis Buñuel* (1982), *Almodóvar: Labyrinths of Passion* (2001) and *Indecent Exposures* (1995). His theatre studies include, *Lorca: The Theatre Beneath the Sand* (1980) and *Lorca: Living in the Theatre* (2003). He has translated some forty plays from Spanish, while his interest in Surrealism has continued in his recently completed study, *A Companion to Luis Buñuel*.

**Haim Finkelstein** holds the Evelyn Metz Chair in Art History at Ben-Gurion University of the Negev, Israel. His book *Surrealism and the Crisis of the Object* was published in 1980, while his recent publications include two volumes devoted to Dalí, *Salvador Dalí's Art and Writing 1927–1942* (1996), and a critical edition of his shorter writings, *The Collected Writings of Salvador Dalí* (1998). His current research focuses on the notion of Space in surrealist theory, philosophy and writing, and as effected in the various manifestations of surrealist visuality (art, film).

**Robert Gurney** is an Honorary Lecturer in the Department of Hispanic Studies at the University of Wales, Swansea. In addition to several articles on Larrea, he has published *La poesía de Juan Larrea* (1985), while he has also written on Vicente Huidobro and Pablo Picasso. He is currently working on a second book, *Juan Larrea en Argentina*, parts of which further explore the poet's connections with Surrealism.

**Derek Harris** is a specialist in the 1927 Generation, having published widely on Lorca, Cernuda, Aleixandre and Alberti, all of whom figure in his ground-breaking study of Surrealism in Spain, *Metal Butterflies and Poisonous Lights: The Language of Surrealism* (1998). He also edited several volumes of poetry, including *Luis Cernuda, Un río, un amor, Los placeres prohibidos* (1999).

**Robert Havard** is Professor of Spanish at the University of Wales, Aberystwyth where he teaches Spanish poetry, Surrealism and art. His early work on Machado, Guillén, Salinas and Lorca culminated in *From Romanticism to Surrealism: Seven Spanish Poets* (1988). This has recently been complemented by *The Crucified Mind: Rafael Alberti and the Surrealist Ethos in Spain* (2001). He is currently working on a book on Spanish art.

**Alan Hoyle** Honorary Research Fellow at Manchester University, began researching into Ramón Gómez de la Serna as a Cambridge postgraduate in Madrid in 1966–7, when he met Ramón's widow. The following year he made a draft inventory of the Gómez de la Serna MSS archive at Pittsburgh University. Subsequently, as a lecturer at Manchester University, he has published on Ramón's politics, *greguerías*, novels and avant-garde humour. In 2003 he was awarded a Ph.D. '(Published work)' for *Ramón Gómez de la Serna: towards a Definition of his Art.*

**Patricia McDermott** is Honorary Senior Research Fellow in Spanish at Leeds University and Associate Editor of the *Bulletin of Spanish Studies*. Her research interests cover the twentieth-century novel, poetry, theatre and cultural history. She is currently working on the *auto sacramental* as a dramatic model in twentieth-century theatre; two preliminary essays appear in *The Spanish Avant-garde* and *Changing Times in Hispanic Culture* (both edited by D. Harris).

**Maria T. Pao** is Assistant Professor of Spanish at Illinois State University. She has published articles on Spanish avant-garde texts by Ernesto Giménez Caballero, Federico García Lorca, Agustín Espinosa, and others, and is co-editor of *¡Agítese bien!: A New Look at the Hispanic Avant-Gardes* (2002).

**Jacqueline Rattray** is the current holder of the Queen Sofía Junior Research Fellowship at Exeter College, Oxford. She has completed a doctoral thesis entitled 'The Surrealist Visuality of José María Hinojosa: A Sight for Sore Eyes'. Her current research is concerned with the experimental writings of various Spanish surrealists.

**James Valender** teaches Spanish literature at El Colegio de México. His research interests centre on the poetry of the 1927 Generation and the literature written by Spanish Republicans in exile. He has published essays on

Cernuda, Altolaguirre, Lorca, Concha Méndez and Prados. His edition of Luis Cernuda's *Epistolario* (*1924–1963*) appeared in 2003.

**Jason Wilson** is Professor of Latin American Literature at University College London. He has written extensively on Surrealism, including *Octavio Paz. A Study of his Poetics* (1979) and *Octavio Paz* (1986), as well as articles relating Borges, Cortázar, Carpentier, Alberti and Vallejo to strands of Surrealism. He has taught courses on Hispanic Surrealism over decades and is currently completing a study of the reception and rejection of Surrealism in Latin America.

# ACKNOWLEDGEMENTS

The editor and publishers wish to extend their thanks to the Research Fund of the University of Wales, the Instituto Cervantes and the Queen Sofia Fund of Exeter College, Oxford for assistance with the publication costs of this book.

# Introduction

## ROBERT HAVARD

France is the most intelligent country in the world, the most rational country in the world. Whereas I, Salvador Dalí, come from Spain, which is the most irrational and the most mystical country in the world.[1]

Spanish Surrealism is the subject of this book, though it might be less contentious to unlock adjective from noun and say Surrealism in Spain or even Surrealism and Spain. These problems of nomenclature will need attention, but let us begin with a reassuringly trivial anecdote in support of Dalí's theme of Spanish irrationality with its implicit suggestion that Spaniards make good – or better – surrealists.

A while ago, when taking a coach to Barajas airport, I struck up conversation with a lady who nodded politely, if quizzically, at my banal remarks on the weather and how well Madrid was looking in April. I started to say how clean the streets were when she seized her opportunity to stem my flow: 'Oh, yes, the centre's fine, but you should see where my daughter lives, in Casa de Campo. It's a mess!' Hackles rising, she explained: 'Vans come round on Monday evenings, loudspeakers blaring, reminding people to put their rubbish out for collection next day. What happens? Wagons come down at 8 on Tuesday, just as they said and . . . nothing! No rubbish; pavements empty! They roll through without so much as having to brake.' She sighed in despair: 'On Wednesday people put their rubbish out and there it stays all week, rotting.' A hint of pride was discernible when she added: 'You can't tell us Spaniards what to do. *Hacemos lo que nos da la gana.*'

The idea that Spaniards are a law unto themselves bears twofold on the issue of Surrealism in Spain. Rebellious individualism is one good reason why the likes of Dalí were receptive to surrealist thinking and count among the movement's finest practitioners. Paradoxically, the same individuality

---

[1] With these words Dalí began his lecture 'Phenomenological Aspects of the Paranoiac-Critical Method' at the Sorbonne, 17/12/1955; see Salvador Dalí, *Diary of a Genius*, trans. Richard Howard (London: Hutchinson, 1990), 127.

explains why most who breathed Surrealism's heady air flatly deny it and look upon the surrealist label as a French contagion. Typical is Vicente Aleixandre, perhaps Spain's most surrealist poet, who spent decades in denial before publishing a volume entitled *Poesía superrealista. Antología* [*Surrealist Poetry. Anthology*] (1971). The medium makes a difference. Those who deal in the visual, like Dalí or film-maker Luis Buñuel, had no problem exporting their work to Paris and were quickly accepted in André Breton's coterie. Like Picasso and others before them, they could compete in Paris on their own terms. It was different for those whose mode of expression was verbal. Aleixandre, Cernuda, Alberti and Lorca were poets isolated by language, for the French, like Breton himself, had no Spanish and little knowledge of its culture.[2] Without prospect of input in Paris, Spanish poets were reduced to a passive role *vis-à-vis* the journals and manifestos that emanated from Surrealism's HQ. Unsurprisingly, they felt the surrealist tag compromised their originality. In Spain, fertile as its soil was for seeds that blew south, there was nothing that resembled an organized surrealist movement. Nor did the main avant-garde journal, Giménez Caballero's *La Gaceta Literaria* (1927–32), generate the kind of party mentality that Breton fostered as editor of *La Révolution surréaliste* (1924–9) and then *Le Surréalisme au service de la révolution* (1930–3). Spaniards did their own thing.

All of which makes it difficult to know what Spanish Surrealism or Surrealism in Spain means and amounts to, or indeed what criteria should be used in recognizing, defining and assessing it. The problem is starkly illustrated by the differing approaches of critics Paul Ilie and C.B. Morris.[3] Ilie – somewhat in the spirit of Dalí – suggests there has always been a 'surrealist mode' in Spain, which can be traced back through the likes of Valle-Inclán, Goya, Cadalso and Quevedo. Morris, by contrast, argues that the movement is French-based and the term Spanish Surrealism is a contradiction and no more meaningful than 'Welsh Gongorismo'. Ilie is surely not wrong to speak of surrealist precedents in Spain and to connect it with earlier movements, notably Romanticism, as James Valender does in his essay on Luis Cernuda in this volume. However, to see the surrealist mode as 'a broad aesthetic category' that is perennial in Spain is ultimately unsatisfactory for it downgrades the special circumstance of Surrealism, a movement that emerged from Dada after the First World War and received its decisive impetus from Freud's theory of the unconscious. At the other end of the scale, Morris cannot be wrong to remind us that Surrealism is French-led, though his point of

---

[2] Breton admitted to his 'ignorance parfaite de la culture espagnole' in his lecture, 'Caractères de l'évolution moderne et ce qui en participe', delivered in French in Barcelona, 17/11/1922, *Oeuvres complètes, I* (Paris: Gallimard, 1988), 292.

[3] Paul Ilie, *The Surrealist Mode in Spanish Literature* (Ann Arbor: University of Michigan Press, 1968), C.B. Morris, *Surrealism in Spain, 1920–1936* (London: Cambridge University Press, 1972).

view is purist and exclusive. As Dawn Ades demonstrates in her essay here on Dalí, it is paradoxical that while Surrealism insisted on its internationalism – ideologically, politically and culturally – it jealously guarded its Paris power base. We recall that *Surréalisme* was a term Breton appropriated in 1922 from Apollinaire – who had first used it in 1917 – to designate the still unresolved fermentation of avant-garde ideas in Futurism, Cubism and Dada.[4] Dada held genetic ascendancy as a revolutionary, anti-art movement whose nihilism was a response to the absurdity and institutionalized immorality of the First World War. Its roots were multiple, in Berlin, Zurich and New York, and when it arrived in Paris at the end of the war many of its leading figures – Max Ernst, Man Ray, Hugo Ball, Tristan Tzara – were non-French. Internationalism was also a feature of Cubism – with Picasso and Juan Gris – and of Futurism, led by Marinetti in Italy and Mayakovsky in the USSR. In view of this eclectic patrimony, one may question the validity of circumscribing Surrealism as a French phenomenon, a tendency that reflects the influence Breton exercised as the self-appointed administrator of Surrealism's patent.

Yet the patent was itself modified as Breton issued three separate manifestos on Surrealism (in 1924, 1929 and 1938), each with a different ethos and emphasis. Broadly and in chronological order, these were psychoanalytical (or Freudian), metaphysical (Hegelian) and political (Marxist), though in practice there was much overlapping. What is certain is that Surrealism's evolution in France complicates matters as far as Spain is concerned. How do you track the influence of a changing cultural phenomenon when its receptors may be responding to different messages at different times? A further complication is that the movement in France was not unified or harmonious, but rent with schisms even as it changed. 'Pope' Breton excommunicated dissenters – including Joan Miró, in 1926, and Dalí, ten years later – as he strove to impose order on his cardinals. Besides expulsions, there were defections from Aragon, Desnos, Artaud, Leiris and others, for political and aesthetic reasons, or out of frustration with the overbearing pontiff, while long-standing dissidents like Georges Bataille chose to remain outside. The fact that Surrealism evolved and fragmented in France has not always been taken into account by observers of the Spanish scene. The latter, needing a benchmark against which to measure Spanish achievements, have tended to cling like biblical fundamentalists to Breton's original definition in the *First Manifesto* (1924), which made 'psychic automatism' its *sine qua non*:

> SURREALISM. *n. masc.* Pure psychic automatism through which it is intended to express, either orally or in writing, or in any other way, the

---

[4] Breton first used the term in a brief essay, 'Pour Dada', where he acknowledged that Apollinaire had coined it in his preface to *Mamelles de Tirésias*. See Breton, *Oeuvres*, 239, 1259.

actual way thought works. The dictation of thought, free from all control exercised by reason, without regard to any aesthetic or moral concern.[5]

This is an important definition and it would continue to be so, both because automatism was a central tenet in Surrealism's programme of liberating the psyche and because many surrealists never went beyond it. However, it is not the whole picture, as perhaps the parodic element in the dictionary definition already insinuates. As the 1920s wore on, there was increasing scepticism about the value of works that simply, as it were, discharged the unconscious. As Breton put it in the *Second Manifesto*: 'I doubt that anyone will be surprised to see Surrealism turn its attention, in passing, to something other than the solution of a psychological problem, however interesting that problem may be.'[6] By the end of the decade, Surrealism was receiving new impetus, notably from Dalí's emphasis on controlling the psyche and its discharge. This amounted to the artist becoming analyst as well as analysand in respect of the psychic data he or she used as source material.[7] Impetus also came from the concept of 'the surrealist object', which brought an idealist (Hegelian) aspiration to integrate material reality with subjective reality, an aggregation that constituted a higher, strictly metaphysical or *sur*real elevation.[8] In a parallel sense, the redirection was indebted to Jacques Lacan and his view that 'the unconscious is structured like a language'.[9] Insofar as this posited an ordering rather than a chaotic tendency in the workings of the psyche, it complemented Dalí's theory of 'paranoiac criticism'.

These points implicitly inform two recent critical approaches to the issue of Surrealism in Spain. Derek Harris focuses on linguistic strategies in key poets, notably the extent to which phonemic patterns or concatenation serve to generate lexemes and, in effect, the text itself.[10] His approach has the advantage of preserving 'psychic dictation' as Surrealism's lynchpin while it

[5] André Breton, *Manifestoes of Surrealism*, trans. Richard Seaver and Helen R. Lane (Ann Arbor: University of Michigan Press, 1972), 26.

[6] Breton, *Manifestoes*, 139.

[7] As Breton acutely observed of Dalí, he was 'strong enough to participate as actor and spectator simultaneously' in the events of his unconscious. See 'The Dalí Case', in *Surrealism and Painting*, trans. Simon Watson Taylor (London: Macdonald, 1965), 133.

[8] This is the kind of metaphysical issue that Haim Finkelstein explored in his seminal study, *Surrealism and the Crisis of the Object* (Ann Arbor: University of Michigan Press, 1979), and which is operative in his chapter on Dalí in the current volume.

[9] See Jacques Lacan, *The Four Fundamental Concepts of Psycho-Analysis*, trans. Alan Sheridan (London: Penguin, 1977), 20. The link between Lacan and Dalí is noted, for instance, by Malcolm Bowie, *Lacan* (London: Fontana, 1991), 39, and by David Macey in his introduction to *The Four Fundamental Concepts of Psycho-Analysis*, xv. Dalí writes on Lacan in *The Unspeakable Confessions of Salvador Dalí, as told to André Parinaud*, trans. H.J. Salemson (London: Quartet Books, 1977), 140–1.

[10] Derek Harris, *Metal Butterflies and Poisonous Lights: The Language of Surrealism in Lorca, Alberti, Cernuda and Aleixandre* (Anstruther: La Sirena, 1998).

also embraces Lacanian notions of linguistic structuring as som
emanates willy-nilly from cathartic articulation of the psyche. H
due regard for the French model by including a section on parall
in French poetry, though it is noteworthy that the greater flexibili
ish syntax – via its distinctive verb endings, for instance, and its
of subject pronouns – favours the generation of prized ambiguities
production. By this yardstick, the four poets Harris studies – Lo
Cernuda and Aleixandre – are progressively more authentic in te
surrealist utterance, a point he develops in the present volume
reading of Aleixandre.

A different tack is taken by Robert Havard, who argues the di
of Spanish Surrealism on grounds that the circumstance that pro
Alberti, Buñuel and Dalí was one 'supersaturated with religio
three mentioned were educated by Jesuits (or, in Dalí's case, the
Christian Brothers who were also banned in France), a factor tha
strong presence in them of Surrealism's two most characteristic
namely: the neurotic, provoked by a repressive upbringing, and
dental, an ingrained propensity for biblical/oracular patterns o
articulation. Together the two points echo Dalí's view of Spain
irrational and the most mystical country in the world'. For H
Alberti is the most representative example of Spanish Surreali
he goes the full distance from Freud to Marx, or from autom;
munism, a theme taken up in his essay here, which attempts to l
of intersection in Alberti between subjective and material reali

An important bearing on the distinctiveness of Surrealism
indigenous cultural roots and formative milieu. Alberti asserts
alismo español viene de Goya'[12] [Spanish Surrealism comes fr
it is also clear that there were immediate avant-garde precursor
partook of the same feverish activity and a similar upheaval
occurred elsewhere after 1910. The Spanish patriarch in this s
Gómez de la Serna, not only because he fulfilled an almost Br
holding court at the Café Pombo in Madrid, where he sparked
erated a buzz of cultural subversion, but also for the sheer inve
own work. Ramón's most famous invention was the *greg*
humorous and essentially innocuous observation in image f
Dada's anti-art spirit, as the following example shows:

> Al quitarse el collar y dejarlo sobre el velador, sonaban sus
> tos de los besos muertos.

---

[11] Robert Havard, *The Crucified Mind. Rafael Alberti and the Surre*
(London: Tamesis, 2001), 232.

[12] See Francisco Aranda, *El surrealismo español* (Barcelona: Lum(

[When she took off her necklace and left it on the pedestal table, its pearls clattered like the dead kisses of skeletons.]

Or again:

El gaitero toca con la laringe y los pulmones fuera, convertidos en gaita con flecos.[13]

[The bagpiper plays with larynx and lungs on the outside, changed into a tasseled bagpipe.]

Of particular note in the *greguería* is its tendency to *aggregate*, which is to say, to combine in its single image a sense of material orientation, or 'thingi-ness', with a sense of the human self. In this, it anticipates the metaphysical integration of 'the surrealist object'. The same principle applies throughout Ramón's work, including his novels, which makes him the logical point of departure here. Type-casting Ramón as a *precursor* does him less than justice, no doubt, as Alan Hoyle's essay suggests, but his resistance both to Freudian and Marxist thinking precludes his assimilation as a full-blown surrealist. This is decidedly not the case – at least as far as Freud is concerned – with Hinojosa, Giménez Caballero and Larrea, who are the subjects of the chap-ters that follow. In her comparative treatment of Hinojosa and the Catalan artist Joan Miró, both of whom were Paris-based, Jacqueline Rattray reminds us of the strong presence of Spaniards in the French capital where they tended to gather for *tertulias* [informal debates] at La Rotonde café in Montparnasse. Taking her starting point from an early edition of *La Révolution surréaliste* (1925), which showed an illustration of Miró's *The Tilled Field* alongside a photograph by Hinojosa, Rattray examines the practical dynamics of automa-tism via examples of oneiric and hallucinogenic imagery in both poet and painter. Freud – whose work was translated into Spanish from 1922 – or rather, Freudianism, comes into its own in Giménez Caballero's collection of short stories on taboo subjects, *Yo, inspector de alcantarillas* [*I, Sewer Inspec-tor*] of 1928, a title indicative of the scatological content of the unconscious in the view of an author with serious religious hang-ups. With surprising results, Maria T. Pao examines Giménez Caballero's use of a cathartic, con-fessional mode that reflects the power both of psychoanalysis and of the Catholic Church, which held him equally in thrall. Juan Larrea's formation owed more to the image-based experimentation of *Ultraísmo* and *Crea-cionismo*, two ephemeral but important movements of the late 1910s. He is treated last in this group because the subject of Robert Gurney's essay is a later, unfulfilled collaboration with Luis Buñuel. Gurney's approach is based on a series of interviews he conducted with the still largely unrecognized Basque writer whom Buñuel greatly admired.

---

[13] Ramón Gómez de la Serna, *Obras selectas* (Madrid: Editorial Plenitud, 1947), 586, 565.

With Luis Buñuel, whose first three films are examined here by Gwynne Edwards, we encounter our first internationally renowned surrealist and reach the high ground of Surrealism in Spain where Dalí, Alberti, Cernuda, Aleixandre and, perhaps more controversially, Lorca are also to be found. Four of these figures – Buñuel, Dalí, Lorca and Alberti – were associated with the Residencia de Estudiantes in Madrid, an enlightened university centre which, pointedly, had no chapel, though its doors were open to foreign visitors like the communist Louis Aragon who lectured there on Surrealism's revolutionary mission in April 1925.[14] From the late 1910s, the *Resi* brought together young provincials from all parts of Spain, fostering diverse cultural interests and a collective dynamic. There would be collaborations, between Lorca and Dalí, for instance, on the play *Mariana Pineda*, and between Buñuel and Dalí, on the film *Un Chien andalou*.[15] A mutually beneficial liaison also arose between two non-resident associates of the group, Rafael Alberti and the young artist Maruja Mallo, a prototype feminist and 'sinsombrerista' [literally *hatless* person]. The epiplasmic, junk objects in Alberti's surrealist volumes – starting with *Sobre los ángeles* [*Concerning the Angels*] (1927–8) – are paralleled by Maruja Mallo's crude, almost colourless paintings of thistles, fossils, footprints and *Scarecrows*, the last being the title of a canvas that André Breton bought at her 1932 Paris exhibition. Madrid's Prado Museum was a constant source of inspiration, counting among its influential holdings hallucinatory works by Hieronymus Bosch – virtually naturalized as *el Bosco* – and Pieter Breughel, as well as Goya's *Black Paintings*. At the cutting edge were art groups such as that in Vallecas led by Benjamín Palencia and Alberto Sánchez whose materialist ethos appealed to Maruja Mallo and Rafael Alberti, a painter before he became a poet. The city was growing apace in the 1920s and shedding its own provincial air, this process being accelerated by Giménez Caballero's founding of the *Cineclub Español* in 1928, one year after he launched *La Gaceta Literaria*. Buñuel, who had left for Paris in 1925, regularly sent back films and articles on films to the club and journal, serving as one of many who brought a cosmopolitan culture closer to Spain. Dalí became an envoy too, though his messages went more often to Catalonia, to the Sitges journal, *L'Amic de les Arts*, launched in 1926, and to the Dalmau gallery in Barcelona where he exhibited, as did Lorca in 1927. Dalí's contribution to Surrealism, rich in both output and theory, warrants two chapters in the present volume. In the first of these Dawn Ades shows the importance to Dalí's surrealist trajectory of certain little known, anti-art paintings of 1927–8, while in the second Haim Finkelstein explores the metaphysics of 1930s paintings that evince Dalí's 'paranoiac-critical method'. Lorca also

---

[14] Parts of Aragon's lecture were published in *La Révolution Surréaliste* in June 1925.
[15] Dalí designed the sets for Lorca's play *Mariana Pineda*, premiered in Barcelona in 1927, while Buñuel and Dalí worked closely together on the scenario of *Un Chien andalou* in 1929.

receives two chapters, though in his case because his work is important in at least two different genres, namely poetry and film/drama. In addition, since views differ as to the validity of applying the term surrealist to Lorca, it is fitting that such differences be voiced here by Andrew A. Anderson and Patricia McDermott.

Lorca illustrates another problem of assessment that stems from the belated start and brief time-span of the surrealist impact on his work. For all its psychosomatic features, his best-known volume of poems, *Romancero gitano* [*Gypsy Ballads*] of 1928, cannot be called surrealist. Indeed, it is largely because his friends Dalí and Buñuel dismissed it as old hat and provincial that Lorca felt the need to redirect his work and, with this in mind, escape Spain. There had been harbingers in 'Oda a Salvador Dalí' [Ode to Salvador Dalí] (1926), written when Lorca was most infatuated with the Catalan painter; but radical change only came when he went to New York in 1929–30. There his poetry shed the traditional idiom of *Romancero gitano* just as the coloured Andalusian pieces he had exhibited in Barcelona only two years previously gave way to stark line-drawings that expressed his deeply troubled self. In *Perspectiva urbana con autorretrato* [*City-scape with Self-Portrait*], for instance, the poet's sense of oppression in the alien metropolis is caught by the geometry of the towering blocks that bear down on him or his wispy, Miró-like innocence. It is also reflected in the incarcerated zoo animals far removed from their natural habitat, one of which kicks out in frustration with its hind legs. At the same time, nature encroaches in the form of vegetal images to the bottom left and top centre, prophesying the return of nature or 'la llegada del reino de la espiga' [the coming of the kingdom of the ear of corn], when 'la Bolsa será una pirámide de musgo' [the Stock Exchange shall be a pyramid of moss],[16] which is the apocalyptic, yet ultimately positive, message of *Poeta en Nueva York*. There is, in short, a perfect correspondence between poem and drawing, though the latter was a medium that Lorca perhaps found freer from logical constraints.[17] What is clear is that Lorca became aware of new possibilities of expression by the late 1920s and this is reflected in *Poeta en Nueva York*. As a poetic mode, it was relatively short-lived, but this does not diminish its intensity. Indeed, there is a growing consensus that this is the period of Lorca's greatest achievement.

---

[16] Federico García Lorca, *Obras completas* (Madrid: Aguilar, 11th edn, 1966), 526, 487.

[17] See Martha J. Nandorfy, *The Poetics of Apocalypse: Federico García Lorca's 'Poet in New York'* (Lewisburgh: Bucknall University Press, and London: Associated University Presses, 2003), 239. Nandorfy draws attention to Lorca's letters to Sebastián Gasch in which he spoke of 'writing and sketching poems' and of resolving some of his problems 'with pencils': 'Estos dibujos son poesía pura o plástica pura a la vez. Me siento limpio, confortado, alegre, *niño*, cuando los hago. Y me da horror la *palabra* que tengo que usar para llamarlos' [These drawings are pure poetry or pure plasticity at one and the same time. I feel clean, comforted, happy, like a *child*, when I do them. And I hate to have to use a *word* to give them a title]. *Obras completas*, 3 (Madrid: Aguilar, 1993), 953, 970.

Lorca's *Perspectiva urbana con autorretrato* [*City-scape with Self-Portrait*]

The same sudden, radical change was made by Rafael Alberti whose Gón-
gora-inspired *Cal y canto* [*Lime and Lyric*] of 1927 was followed by his first
surrealist volume, *Sobre los ángeles* [*Concerning the Angels*] of 1928, which
the poet always felt received disproportionate attention from critics. No doubt
many found his subsequent *Sermones y moradas* [*Sermons and Dwelling
Places*] (1928–9) too puzzling if not unintelligible, while his 1930s work,
written after he had turned red, was often unfairly dismissed as propaganda.

Abruptness of change applies also to Luis Cernuda, another who attended the celebrations in Seville in December 1927 marking Góngora's tercentenary. His volume *Perfil del aire* [*The Slender Air*] of that year reflects the formal virtues he admired in the Cordovan poet. Yet Cernuda was soon writing *Un río, un amor* [*A River, a Love*] (1929), which had been inspired by his reading of French surrealist poets, notably Paul Éluard. The same pattern of change from tight form to free structure is seen in Vicente Aleixandre whose crafted *Ámbito* [*Ambience*] (1924–7) is followed by the prose-poems of *Pasión de la tierra* [*Earth Passion*] of 1928, which launched a surrealist mode he sustained longer than any other Spaniard. Even Salvador Dalí's conversion to Surrealism was relatively late and abrupt, being prompted in no small part by Joan Miró who first visited him in Figueres in September 1927. Impressed by two of Dalí's recent paintings, the Tanguy-like *Honey is Sweeter than Blood* and *Apparatus with Hand*, Miró persuaded Dalí that his future lay in conquering Paris, while Dalí, for his part, was already under the spell of Miró's work and anti-art theories, as Dawn Ades shows. In short, the compressed period 1927–9 was critical for virtually all those leading Spanish writers and artists who made the transition to a surrealist mode of expression. By that time, moreover, they were all approaching or had reached the age of thirty and had a significant prehistory as creative figures. This may help explain the distinctive Spanish quality in their work that made it much more than a variation in design or a model made under licence.

By contrast, and perhaps surprisingly, Latin American writers seem to have had a more direct link with Paris, as Jason Wilson explores in a final essay, it being arguable that Surrealism's impact in that continent was longer lasting than in Spain. Fittingly, Breton's *Third Manifesto* was written in Mexico City with Leon Trotsky, in 1938, by which time political events precluded any possibility of Spain developing a surrealist movement, the diaspora of its intellectuals – mostly to Spanish America – having begun. Wilson's chapter forms a coda that signposts the directions Surrealism took in that continent and is a final reason for eschewing the geographically precise title Surrealism in/and Spain for the more accommodating 'Spanish Surrealism'.

# 1

# Ramón Gómez de la Serna: Precursor

## ALAN HOYLE

The latest supplement to Rico's history of criticism has a whole section devoted to Ramón Gómez de la Serna and the Avant-Garde separate from one on the 1927 Generation from Vanguard to Surrealism.[1] This indicates the preeminence of Ramón (his preferred nomenclature, which I shall use) as a prolific and pioneering writer, and as a showman of the avant-garde in his famous *tertulia* at the Café Pombo in the centre of Madrid, whose Saturday night spectacle and banquets attracted foreign visitors such as Valéry Larbaud and occasionally members of the younger generation such as Salinas, Buñuel and Lorca. Fernando Vela, in the same year (1924) that he wrote the first Spanish review of Surrealism, described Ramón in Pombo cultivating 'el pensamiento asociativo, que es lo que da una visión mágica del mundo, una visión juvenil' [associative thought, which is what gives a magical vision of the world, a youthful vision].[2] His best-known invention, the *greguería*, a short aphoristic prose poem combining metaphor and humour, was the principal vehicle for that associative thought, which according to Cernuda taught his generation a new way of looking at the world, but fell short of Surrealism because it was not dictated by the subconscious.[3] Too many have followed Cernuda into thinking that with the advent of Surrealism Ramón was left behind as an epitome of the so-called dehumanized, ludic art of the 1920s. For example, Harris has a footnote merely acknowledging Ramón as a precursor whose *greguerías* 'can be seen as having certain pre-surrealist qualities', but whose main role is seen as the initiator of the Spanish avant-garde through his translation of Marinetti's Futurist manifesto in 1909.[4]

---

[1] C.B. Morris, 'Ramón y la vanguardia', in Francisco Rico (ed.), *Historia y crítica de la literatura española. Epoca contemporánea: 1914–1939. Primer suplemento*, vol. 7/1, ed. A. Sánchez Vidal (Barcelona: Crítica, 1995), 132–46.

[2] Fernando Vela, *El grano de pimienta* (Buenos Aires: Espasa-Calpe, 1950), 86.

[3] Luis Cernuda, *Prosa completa*, ed. D. Harris and L. Maristany (Barcelona: Barral, 1975), 412 and 406–7.

[4] Derek Harris, *Metal Butterflies and Poisonous Lights: The Language of Surrealism in Lorca, Alberti, Cernuda and Aleixandre* (Anstruther: La Sirena, 1998), 45 and 19–20.

The question of Ramón's relationship to Surrealism has been tackled already by some critics. Cardona (1957) proclaims the affinity highlighting *El Incongruente* [*The Incongruent One*] (1922) as a true surrealist novel and better than Breton's *Nadja*.[5] Ilie (1968), however, thinks it an 'abortive attempt at a surrealist novel'.[6] Umbral (1978) argues perceptively that Ramón was the only great prose writer of the avant-garde and, though he employs a surrealistic free association, his revolution in language is both more coherent and more optimistic than the Freudian concept of Surrealism.[7] Soldevila-Durante seems to prefer for Ramón the term *hiperrealismo* [*hyper-realism*] used by Dámaso Alonso to denote a general tendency (including Surrealism).[8] Although he finds surrealistic anticipations in Ramón's early *Prometeo* [*Prometheus*] period, as well as knowledge of the surrealists in Ramón's 1931 essay in *Ismos* [*Isms*], Soldevila concludes, rightly, that Ramón does not share their use of the subconscious, their violence or, surely wrongly, their concept of *amour fou* [*mad love*].[9] So the four critics find some parallels with Surrealism but not a full convergence, thus confirming the position taken by Guillermo de Torre in his 1957 prologue (comparing Ramón with Picasso), which links the 'micropsicología' [micropsychology] of the *greguería* with Cubism and claims that the later novels of the nebula (barely mentioned by Soldevila) are imaginatively much richer than anything produced in the wake of Surrealism.[10] An extravagant claim perhaps, but one that is supported by two other views that add a double perspective often missing in the standard picture of Spanish Surrealism: from ex-surrealists and from Latin America.

The Mexican Paz has expressed his unconditional admiration for Ramón: 'Para mí es el gran escritor español' [For me, he is the great Spanish writer].[11] Though an ex-disciple of Breton, Paz has his own idea of Surrealism as the second stage of the avant-garde taking Romanticism and the religion of analogy to an extreme beyond the first stage, which is characterized by analogy plus the irony (humour and prose) that comes from the contradiction of death. Rather than Freudian pessimism and Breton's exaltation of Sade and sin, Paz emphasizes a Rousseauistic innocence, Fourier's philosophy of love, and dreams as the

[5] Rodolfo Cardona, *Ramón: A Study of Gómez de la Serna and his Works* (New York: Torres, 1957), 18–23 and 96–102.

[6] Paul Ilie, *The Surrealist Mode in Spanish Literature* (Ann Arbor: University of Michigan Press, 1968), 156.

[7] Francisco Umbral, *Ramón y las vanguardias* (Madrid: Espasa-Calpe, 1978), 67, 156–66 and 59–62.

[8] Rosa Chacel in fact associates Ramón with 'hiperrealismo' and 'rehumanización' in her 'Evasión', *Diario 16 (Culturas)* (2 July 1988), v.

[9] Ignacio Soldevila-Durante, 'Ramón Gómez de la Serna: *Superrealismo* and *Surrealismo*', in *The Surrealist Adventure in Spain*, ed. C.B. Morris (Ottawa: Dovehouse, 1991), 62–79.

[10] Guillermo de Torre, 'Prólogo. Ramón y Picasso: paralelismos y divergencias', in Ramón Gómez de la Serna, *Obras completas*, II (Barcelona: AHR, 1957), 16 and 18.

[11] Octavio Paz, 'Una de cal . . .', *Papeles de Son Armadans*, 140 (1967), 186.

erotic expression of the body freed from linearity and installed in the present, expressing a sense of '*otredad*' [otherness].[12] This revisionist view, if correct, brings, as we shall see, Ramón closer to at least one form of surrealist practice.

The other writer is the Chilean Neruda, whose surrealist volume *Residencia en la tierra* [*Residence on Earth*] published in Madrid in 1935 was a landmark, according to Paz. Despite what the latter calls his Stalinism,[13] Neruda did not allow Ramón's increasing conservatism to prevent him from supplying a prologue to Ramón's posthumous second edition of selected work, in which he said the following: 'Así también la gran figura del surrealismo, entre todos los países, ha sido Ramón. Es verdad que sobrepasa a tal escuela, porque es anterior y posterior, y porque su tamaño caudaloso no cabe en una escuela de tantos pisos' [So also the great figure of Surrealism, among all the countries, has been Ramón. It is true that he goes beyond that school, because he comes before and after, and because his enormous abundance cannot fit inside a school with so many floors]. This challenge to the experts in Spanish Surrealism has largely been ignored. Whether Ramón is a major surrealist is open to argument; that he precedes and extends its confines I hope to show in this study, as well as providing some support to Neruda's additional assertion that Ramón revolutionized the Spanish language and changed reality: 'con su tinta bautismal inauguró de nuevo el mundo' [with his baptismal ink he inaugurated the world again].[14] To do so, I shall examine the first two of the three phases of Ramón's work implied by Neruda, beginning with the middle one which runs parallel to the Surrealism of the 1920s.

It could well be argued that his novel of 1922, *El Incongruente*, supports Ramón's claim, made in 1931, that he had been practising 'super-realismo' [super-realism] for many years.[15] Whatever terms might be used to define his most characteristic work of the 1920s (hyper-realism etc.), the key, as I have argued elsewhere,[16] to the *greguería* and Ramón's approach to the absurd (*incongruencia*) is to define it as a clear poetic juxtaposition of two comically incongruous things, producing an incongruity that also involves a double congruence: a poetic, irrational one and a rational, comic one. Though Ramón was resistant to Surrealism's use of the Freudian subconscious, the

12 Octavio Paz, *Los hijos del limo: del romanticismo a la vanguardia* (Barcelona: Barral, 1974), 164, 176, 83, 135, 84, 109, 103–4, 179, 203 and 207; and 'André Breton o la búsqueda del comienzo', in his *Corriente alterna* (Mexico: Siglo XXI, 1967), 52–64.

13 Paz, *Los hijos del limo*, 189–90 and 178.

14 Pablo Neruda, 'Ramón', prologue to Ramón Gómez de la Serna, *Obras selectas*, 2nd edn (Barcelona: AHR, 1971), 7–8.

15 'La novela para mí desde hace muchos años ha sido este super-realismo, esta suposición atestiguada de la libertad en la tierra' [For me the novel has been for many years this super-realism, this attested imagining of freedom on earth], *Ismos* (Madrid: Biblioteca Nueva, 1931), 354.

16 'El problema de la greguería', *Actas del IX Congreso de la Asociación Internacional de Hispanistas*, ed. S. Neumeister (Frankfurt: Vervuert, 1989), II, 283–92.

incongruous/congruous structure of his imagery can be understood partly in terms of Freud's analysis of humour. If the poetic dips into the irrational (intuitive or unconscious), the comic adopts the perspective of commonsense reason, and by humouring it, what rationality normally represses is allowed pleasurable expression.[17] Gustave the Incongruent embodies this poetic humour for he is a whimsical mixture of *enfant terrible* and childhood innocent, Romantic outsider-cum-proto-surrealist and a Chaplinesque victim of comic absurdity, all of which come to a fitting and original climax when he enters a cinema in the centre of Madrid to discover his future soulmate sitting by chance next to him, as they watch a magical projection of their own selves coming together in the film on the screen. The finale forms a visually striking four-part analogy, whose Romantic, pre-surreal perfection resulting from Destiny or Chance is compromised by an avant-garde irony and humour that recognizes the implausibility of the event, while allowing the pleasure of seeing desire satisfied and celebrated as a miracle of the quotidian. The whole of the novel is a succession of chance encounters between desire, or imagination, and reality, which are made available to Gustavo because of his incongruence, his disconnection from normal thought and behaviour. Such as when he stands outside a block of flats staring at the balconies waiting for a woman to give him succour, and inevitably out leans 'una rubia oxigenada' [a peroxide blonde] (IX, 627).[18] Another example is when he discovers a whole village of wax mannequins, fulfilling temporarily his dream of the ideal, silent, living doll by his side so as to avoid the institution of marriage desired by real women. Ramón, famously, had his own real-life mannequin imported from Paris to sit on his settee. But aside from his celebrated cult of eccentricity, it was the arresting quality of his texts that led to the translation of this novel into French in 1927, just before Breton's *Nadja*. I quote a passage from each for comparison:

> Tout récemment encore, comme un dimanche, avec un ami, je m'étais rendu au 'marché aux puces' [. . .] (j'y suis souvent, en quête de ces objets qu'on ne trouve nulle part ailleurs, démodés, fragmentés, inutilisables, presque incompréhensibles, pervers enfin au sens où je l'entends et où je l'aime, comme par exemple cette sorte de demi-cylindre blanc irrégulier, verni, présentant de reliefs et des dépressions sans signification pour moi [. . .] que j'ai ramené chez moi [. . .])   (59)

> [Quite recently again, probably one Sunday, with a friend, I had gone to the 'flea-market' [. . .] (I go there often, in search of those objects you can't find

---

[17] The function of the joke is to 'proteger de la crítica las conexiones verbales e ideológicas productoras del placer' [protect from criticism the verbal and ideological connections that cause pleasure], Sigmund Freud, *El chiste y su relación con lo inconsciente*, trans. Luis L. Ballesteros y de Torres (Madrid: Alianza, 1990), 116.

[18] The numbers in parenthesis preceded by a volume in roman numerals here and subsequently refer to Ramón Gómez de la Serna, *Obras completas*, ed. Ioana Zlotescu (Barcelona: Círculo de Lectores/Galaxia Gutenberg, 1996–).

anywhere else, out of fashion, in pieces, unusable, almost incomprehensible, perverse in fact in the sense that I understand it and which I love, like for example this sort of half-cylinder, which is white, irregular-shaped, varnished, and presenting reliefs and depressions without any meaning for me [. . .] and which I've brought back home [. . .])]

Il commençait [son rêve] vieillard et finissait enfant; tout alors était inverti: il n'atteignait à la sagesse que dans son enfance, et regrettait plus que jamais de devoir mourir, car si son enfance le voyait mourir de vieillesse, la mort ne constituaient pas moins pour lui un malheur subit puisqu'il n'avait vécu qu'un jour et qu'il achevait sa vie par son commencement, en retournant se perdre dans le ventre maternel où il mourait [avant] d'être conçu.[19]

[He'd begin [his dream] an old man and end it an infant; so everything was reversed: he reached wisdom only in his infancy, and regretted more than ever having to die, because if his infancy saw him dying of old age, death represented no less for him a sudden misfortune since he had only lived a day and he completed his life by its beginning, going back to losing himself in his mother's womb where he died [before] being conceived.]

Ramón's well-known obsession with objects and, in particular, with the flea-market of the Rastro, is echoed in the first passage, while the second reminds us of the surrealist obsession with dreams. However, surprisingly perhaps, the first is Breton's and the second is Ramón's – from a chapter entitled 'Ses rêves' [His Dreams] in a slightly mangled translation. The paragraph on dream, death and time's reversal is a good example of the sort of neo-baroque conceit that Ramón was so frequently capable of creating. With its baroque reversal, the passage makes a coherent, if complicated, sense of an apparently absurd dream depicting the ultimate absurdity of life contradicted by death. Most of Gustavo's dreams, we are told, are too disturbingly absurd or painfully macabre to be included, thus leaving him free to concentrate on the pleasurable incongruities of his real-life day-dreaming. Ramón deliberately chooses to avoid the murky depths of the unconscious exposed in dreams and later in many surrealist paintings and films.[20] The absurdity of Gustavo's disconnection from the congruence of commonsense thought and behaviour is more humorously poetic than surrealist absurdity would be, but, cut loose from conventions of social responsibility, he is in the same state of availability (*disponibilité*) to the vagaries of chance as one of the surrealist precursors, Gide's Lafcadio, but without his gratuitous violence. Ramón's character does

---

[19] *Nadja* (1928, revised by author, 1963), in *Oeuvres complètes*, I, ed. M. Bonnet (Paris: Gallimard, 1988), 676. The first part appeared in the magazine *Commerce* in Autumn 1927. *Gustave l'Incongru*, trans. J. Cassou and A. Wurmser, 2nd edn (Paris: Kra, 1927), 160.
[20] One of the interludes in the 1917 volume of *Greguerías* is significantly entitled 'El sueño anodino'.

not subvert reality with the unconscious, but rejects the normal consciousness of reality: 'El había desmentido de tal modo todas las cosas, y suponía de tal modo que las unas podían ser igual que las otras, que [. . .] en relación con él, todo desvariaba [He had denied everything so much, and assumed to such an extent that things could be the same as each other, that [. . .] in relation to him, everything went haywire] (IX, 606). I shall later try to locate the source of this, one that might be shared by Surrealism.

After the discovery of the half-cylinder in the flea-market (analysed by Cardinal as an example of Objective Chance),[21] the Breton passage has on the next page a girl stall-holder who happens to be a fan of Shelley, Nietzsche and Rimbaud, though not of the pessimism in Aragon's *Le Paysan de Paris*. Breton's search for a marvellous sense of surreality through his adulterous dalliance with the enigmatic Nadja is confidently optimistic, but goes awry when she ends up in a madhouse, which Breton callously exploits to proclaim a revolutionary 'émancipation' [emancipation] of everybody including lunatics (B, 741).[22] The book ends with the oft-quoted maxim, 'La beauté sera CONVULSIVE ou ne sera pas' [Beauty will be convulsive or not at all]; but less quoted is its cryptic illustration by a newspaper report about an interrupted message from a plane that, we infer, must have crashed. This aesthetic of enigmatic violence is foreshadowed by an equally unexplained report that the tower of the manor-house where the narrator is staying, coming just after the anticipated apparition of Nadja, blows up in a 'neige de plumes, qui tombe de ses colombes' [snow of feathers falling from its doves], covering the courtyard in 'vrai sang' [real blood] (B, 682).[23] This disturbing and seemingly relished conjunction of violence and beauty is not seen in Ramón's search for the surreal (in his terms, for erotic congruence through incongruence).

Curiously, what the two novels do share is the absence of the Freudian unconscious to be found in dreams. Even if Breton explicitly states his admiration for psychoanalysis and its study of dreaming, he specifically states he does not want to be judged by psychoanalysis for his ideas, and that what he is narrating are his own 'méditations' and 'rêveries' (B, 653). So, if one defines Surrealism by its exploitation of the usually understood Freudian influences, we would be in the odd position of calling *Nadja* the work of a surrealist (*the* surrealist) but not a surrealist work. In fact that is virtually intimated in the author's comparison of the arrangement of his material to a surrealist, i.e. automatic, text that produces the unequalled pleasures of the unexpected and incommunicable but has been made

[21] Roger Cardinal, *Breton: 'Nadja'* (London: Grant & Cutler, 1986), 15 and 23.

[22] This and subsequent quotations of Breton, indicated in parenthesis by B plus numbers, refer to *Oeuvres complètes*, I.

[23] The editor suggests ingeniously that the dead doves and the plane crash are secretly coded metaphors for the disaster of madness befalling Nadja (B, 1541–2 and 1563–4). However, their literal reality remains inexplicably, tragically, violent.

communicable by having its terms 'mûrement réfléchis, et pesés' [maturely reflected on and pondered].[24] The consequence of this is another curiosity, particularly in view of those who would define such a work by its surrealist use of language: the prose discourse in *Nadja* is conventionally correct, urbane and coherently composed, much less surreal that the image-packed incongruousness of Ramón's narrative, though the latter, as we know, replaces solemnity with playful humour.[25]

Cardinal's study of Objective Chance in *Nadja* suggests to me a different Freudian angle than the usual one to reveal an interesting similarity between surrealist practice and Ramón's. After an unsubstantiated attempt at a Hegelian explanation of the random interaction of subject to object as 'a systematic dialectical process', Cardinal persuasively argues that Breton adopts the Freudian model of the pleasure principle thwarted by the reality principle, 'with a simple reversal'. Desire is fulfilled when the pleasure and reality principles meet. It is only conscious reason that prevents us seeing this happen.[26] Although again the precise source is unspecified, I would suggest that Freud's psychoanalysis of humour brings Breton and Ramón remarkably closer, for in it Freud sees joking (and wit in general) as a conscious transaction with rationality in order to release the pleasures of the irrational, with a consequent bilaterality of sense/nonsense that can be seen as the congruent incongruence of the *greguería*. Freud, moreover, compares joking to the pleasure principle of child's play and, very significantly, to dreaming, with the difference that dreams evade the censorship of reason by displacement of desire into an expression that is uncommunicable because unintelligible. Breton's 'rêveries' are communicable as a conscious form of day-dreaming, whose hidden intellectual, even playful wit is not the same but is analogous to Ramón's creative humour, just as jokes are for Freud analogous to dreams.[27] There is another, unexpected coincidence here. Freud refers to the intellectual errors committed unconsciously in dreaming and consciously in joking as 'psychical automatism'. This may or may not be the specific source for Breton's famous definition, but what is clear is that Freud has derived it from Bergson's analysis of laughter as 'automatism'.[28] For Bergson that means an unconscious distraction from rational adjustment to the real world. As I have argued elsewhere, Bergson's *Le Rire* also sees art as a conscious adoption of a wilful distraction from normality, comparable to Quixotic madness, conceptual play,

---

[24] The 1963 edition changes the original phrase, 'texte "surréaliste"', to 'texte "automatique"' (B, 1528–9).

[25] For the criteria of Freud or language, see respectively Dennis and Harris in Morris, *The Surrealist Adventure*, 84 and 166.

[26] Cardinal, 22.

[27] Freud, *El chiste*, 148–54, 160–1 and 184.

[28] Freud, *El chiste*, 186, 188 and 202. My translation is the same as the English *Standard Edition*.

and dreaming.[29] Bergson's vitalism probably inspired parallel though different effects in Ramón and Surrealism. But its concept of the inner life as *durée* or flux is the link that connects with the principal common source we will eventually arrive at.

Another of Ramón's novels, published the year before the surrealist manifesto, *El secreto del Acueducto* (1923), illustrates this conscious distraction in the protagonist who conducts a double love affair with the Segovian aqueduct and his niece. His relationship with his surroundings is an extension of his sexual drive: 'La sexualidad es la vida [. . .] La llamada sexual hay que arrojarla contra las cosas. ¡Dichosos los que saben transformarla!' [Sexuality is life . . . The sexual flame must be thrown against things. Happy those who know how to transform it!] (IX, 932). Reminiscent of Freud and D.H. Lawrence, the novel's impassioned, imagistic perception of reality is also comparable to what Cardinal describes in *Nadja*: when Breton responds, say, to a shop-sign, he employs a 'logic of non-rational association' that 'places him in an intimate, libidinal relation to phenomena'.[30]

A similar phenomenon occurs in Ramón's major novel of the period, *El novelista* (1923–5), with its use of a syncopated succession of typically arresting images to describe a pleasurable version of 'palomares' [dovecotes], seen as convents of cooing passion, hidden 'pozos' [wells] of desire in the dry, repressed landscape of Castile (X, 344). Ramón shares Surrealism's Romantic wish to liberate sexual desire, but instead of plunging into the unconscious to find the absolute of surreality as preached by Breton's manifesto, Ramón creates a paradise of the senses through heightened, high-tempo, impassioned perception. His novelist-protagonist asserts that writing should be an affirmation of life, not as a disease to be cured by doctors or travel, but as a sensation of well-being, 'sana y rauda en su pura contemplación' [healthy and rapid in its pure contemplation] (X, 312), and that in his fiction he walks through a 'realidad supuesta como por una novela de magia' [an imagined reality as if through a novel of magic] (X, 310). Although magical could certainly be applied to Ramón's specially intensified realism, another term to define it was used by Ortega in his *La deshumanización del arte* [Dehumanization of Art] (1925).[31] In the section on supra- and infra-realism, as well as calling the supra-realism of metaphor the most radical instrument of dehumanization, or 'evasión de lo real' [escape from the real], he says that Ramón, like Proust and Joyce, practises 'infrarrealismo', which reverses the normal hierarchy to foreground the usually unnoticed, supposedly unimportant, details of life.[32] Though Ortega

---

[29] I discuss this aspect of Freud and Bergson in my *El humor ramoniano de vanguardia* (Manchester: Department of Spanish & Portuguese, 1996), 11–12 and 16.

[30] Cardinal, 24. See my 'Towards an Understanding of *El secreto del Acueducto*', in *Studies on Ramón Gómez de la Serna*, ed. N. Dennis (Ottawa: Dovehouse, 1988).

[31] Domingo Pérez Minik, an ex-Tenerife surrealist, uses the term 'magical realism' for Ramón in *Novelistas españoles de los siglos XIX y XX* (Madrid: Guadarrama, 1957).

[32] José Ortega y Gasset, *Obras completas* (Madrid: Alianza), III (1983), 374.

doesn't mention it, the Spanish gallicism, *surrealismo*, could phonetically mean 'sub-realism' and could have been used to describe the way in which the three writers use metaphor to reveal what lies beneath the cloak of realism.[33]

Ortega's main term, 'dehumanization', which is better understood by the other synonym he uses, *estilización* [stylization], became a stigma attached to the non-committed art of the 1920s by those who preferred the so-called 'rehumanized' art of the 1930s. Surrealism's second manifesto, as we know, tried to erect a bridge from one to the other. But dehumanization helps to beg a major question: to what extent does Ramón share with Surrealism a sub-version of conventional morality especially in terms of social responsibility to others? It is also raised by a puzzling coincidence of terminology. In the first surrealist manifesto Breton says that a spirit of *'démoralisation'* has taken up residence in the château of Surrealism, by which he means unscrupulousness towards others (B, 322). Now if we turn to one of Ramón's many manifestos, his prologue to the first volume of *Greguerías* (1917), it begins, 'Desmoralizo a mi alma' [I demoralize my mind/soul] (IV, 41), with the capital D being typographically highlighted in the subsequent volume, *Greguerías selectas* (1919).[34] The obvious meaning is that his soul feels dispirited at the prospect of having to give a rational explanation for his new genre of writing, but then he launches into an extensive and enthusiastic one, which retrospectively, if one worries long enough about the prominence of that first word 'Desmoralizo', raises the possibility that it could also mean 'de-moralize', that is, to strip morality from his mind, because his *greguerías* flaunt their irresponsibility, their refusal to conform to socially useful descriptions of the world.

What is clear is that the rest of the prologue exults in the *greguería*'s sub-version of conventional thinking through a 'descomposición del espíritu' [decomposition of the mind], 'para que todo resulte muy deshecho, un poco bien deshecho' [so that everything ends up undone, a bit well undone] (IV, 705 and 703). Logical categories are deliberately confused because they are only conventions, i.e. lies: 'La Greguería se ampara de la confusión que necesita [. . .] porque s[ó]lo para presentarse ante los examinadores se necesita llevar bien claras y aprendidas las mentiras' [The Greguería cloaks itself in the con-fusion it needs [. . .] because only when sitting before the examiners does one need to have the lies clear and well-learnt in one's head] (IV, 46). Emptied of these categories, the mind acquires a bizarre freedom, especially in visual con-templation, 'un modo de ver, sin pretensiones, pero sin indiferencia y sin reser-vas' [a way of looking, without pretensions, but also without indifference and reservations] (IV, 706). Not only does this influence the 1927 Generation's way

---

[33] According to Giménez Caballero, as cited by Dennis in Morris, *The Surrealist Adventure*, 98.

[34] It is not highlighted in the *Obras completas* (IV, 701). This first paragraph was omitted from later volumes.

of looking, it could be that the concepts of confusion and de-moralization anticipate similar terms in Dalí,[35] and as a project of radical deconstruction, are derived, as I shall argue, from a source that is shared, though less directly, by Breton's Surrealism.

Before that, I want to emphasize that the *greguería* and its programme of active, even hyper-active, contemplation is not amoral, but contains an explicit alternative morality that distinguishes it from the more destructive freedom of surrealist thinking. It demands a moral reversion of consciousness, of the soul, to its 'bondad' and 'credulidad nativa' [natural goodness, and credulity] (IV, 46). This Rousseauistic view of an intrinsically innocent human nature is reinforced by a cult of contemplation and humility redirected towards heightening and finding transcendence in the trivial objects of immediate reality, relinquishing a rational control over it. This attitude is influenced by some sort of Buddhism – the *greguerías* are likened to prayers offered to Buddhist deities such as 'Arroz-Puro' [Pure-Rice] (IV, 44) – and is allied to a secular, neo-baroque emphasis on mortality that prompts a joyful attentiveness to details – 'Yo me siento morir alegremente y así [. . .] me fijo en las cosas' [I feel myself happily dying and so [. . .] I fix my attention on things] (IV, 707). The ambiguity of Ramón's subversive ethic can also be seen in his use of the term 'perderse': 'ellos no se atreven a perderse por la voluntad, por la armonía que pueda haber en perderse con intensidad, y, sin embargo, se perderán por la muerte' [they don't dare lose themselves through their own volition, for the harmony there may be in losing oneself with intensity, and, nevertheless, they will be lost through death] (IV, 43). It evokes the idea of sinful perdition, but the total loss of self in death stimulates a losing of the self in the perception of material reality to find salvation in a new consciousness of being alive, fragmented into a succession of passing, heightened moments, or enjoyable epiphanies, that require the coining of the new term *greguería* to define them.[36] One example given of what is meant is the (rather Proustian) childhood memory of watching in wonder the strange 'escala de polvo' [ladder of dust] in the 'materialidad' [materiality] of the shaft of sunlight slanting through a chink in the window shutter (IV, 48).

These sensations and impressions usually remain unconscious, unexpressed, hidden by the normal consciousnesss of a reality that is ordered and stabilized by a goal-directed reason, employing concepts fixed permanently by language. Ramón derides as puritanical the need for clear, unchanging definitions that stop us seeing 'cómo se descompone la vida *detrás de la vida*' [how life decomposes behind life] and impose on objects a 'rigor excesivo de

---

[35] Dalí said his notorious Barcelona lecture had 'miras altamente desmoralizadoras y confusionistas' [highly demoralizing and confusion-creating purposes], as translated in Ian Gibson, *The Shameful Life of Salvador Dalí* (London: Faber & Faber, 1997), 250.

[36] Wylie Sypher, *Loss of the Self in Modern Literature and Art* (New York: Knopf & Random House, 1962) mentions Zen Buddhism but not Ramón or Surrealism.

cosas inmortales y divinas' [excessive rigour of things inmortal and divine] (IV, 708). So, abstract concepts with the permanence and moral authority of a divine absolute are undermined, 'decomposed', in the underlying sensory flux. Moreover, the centrality of man in this moral order is denied by the assertion that he is living 'al margen de la creación' [on the margins of creation] (IV, 706) and that he should embrace his insignificance in order to provoke humility and a reorientation of mind: 'No los principios abstractamente revolucionarios, sino la trivialidad admitida' [Not abstractly revolutionary principles, but triviality accepted] will create 'la libertad espiritual' [freedom of the spirit], thus solving life's insoluble problems, paradoxically, 'por la franca disolución, por la incongruencia y las pequeñas constataciones que apenas parecen tener que ver con ellos' [by their blatant dissolution, by incongruence and the tiny, true observations that scarcely seem relevant to them] (IV, 45). With another play on his favoured *d* words (dissolution/de-solution) Ramón pinpoints the procedure behind the *greguería*: a dissolution of the system, disconnection from it to find new, logically absurd connections ('*incongruencia*'), and confirmation of the discoveries ('*constataciones*'), however small or limited, through their successful definition in words, usually in the affirmative form of an aphoristic generalisation involving an image. Here are two examples:

> ¡Oh, si en vez de Jesús hubiese sido Jesusa! ¡Qué senos de crucificada habría habido, qué senos más supremos! (IV, 406)

> [Oh, what if Jesus had been female! What breasts there would have been on every crucifix, the most supreme breasts of all!]

> Todas las carnes muertas parecen dolerse aún, cuando el carnicero las corta, todas menos la del jamón . . . El jamón está satisfecho de haber mejorado con la muerte y la salazón, está satisfecho de ser rico jamón, y le gusta repartirse en lonchas finas, revelando además su belleza veteada e inconfundible. (IV, 81)

> [All meats seem to be still in pain, when the butcher cuts into them, all of them except cured ham . . . Cured ham has the satisfaction of having improved with its death and the salting, it is satisfied to be delicious ham, and it likes to be divided up into fine slices, revealing moreover its unmistakable veined beauty.]

The second one typically shows a metaphorical transference of life to the inanimate, as well as a lucid restoration of the distinction between subject and object, unlike a surrealist image that goes the whole hog into the irrational such as Magritte's well-known still-life, 'The Portrait' (1935), which depicts an eye (whose eye?) staring at the observer out of the plate of ham.

The activity of 'Surréalisme' in its definition as pure psychic automatism (B, 328) has exercised critics as to how far this is in practice totally uncontrolled by reason. Breton's insistence that the brilliant spark produced by a Reverdy image is the result of irrational surrealist activity, with reason playing a limited yet – one notes – a crucial role, 'se bornant à constater, et à apprécier le phénomène lumineux' [restricting itself to confirming and appreciating the luminous phenomenon] (B, 338), is, it seems to me, anticipated in 1917 by Ramón's rational expression (*constatación*) of the irrational impression that results from voiding the mind of its normal categories to be able to think by free association, allowing the mind 'su propia extensión, su vacío, su espontánea confesión, su tontería destilada, [. . .] su independencia' [its own extension, its emptiness, its spontaneous confession, its distilled foolishness, its independence] (IV, 46). Though Breton emphasizes Freud's work on dreams, he specifically links surrealist activity to the spontaneous waking confessions of the patient on the couch, what he calls '*pensée parlée*' [spoken thought] (B, 326). But he seems to have no intention of simulating neurotic responses in the way Dalí later claimed to do. In fact, what strikes me is the irony of the contradiction in surrealist theory between dream and reality which Breton wishes to resolve by seeking precisely what he says is unattainable: the absolute of surreality. Dreaming may eventually give access to this 'grand Mystère' [great Mystery] (B, 319), but in reality what the surrealists too often come up with are the disturbing products of nightmare (the mooncloud = eyeball-razor analogy in Buñuel's *Un Chien andalou*), and, as if to compensate for the absolute remaining a distant dream, Breton's idea of 'le merveilleux' [the marvellous] (B, 319) is stated to be attainable here and now, at least through literature. And soon the marvellous, rather than in dreams, becomes rooted in the everyday, as we have seen in Breton's *Nadja*, and as we see in Aragon's *Le Paysan de Paris* (1926), whose preface (to what he calls a modern mythology) steers towards the waking dream of the senses, the marvellous errors of which – like experiencing light as a 'matière à miracle' [matter for miracle] – are to be defended against the forces of rational habit, redefining the focus of Surrealism as the miracle of the 'merveilleux quotidian' [quotidian marvellous].[37] This, I would suggest, is very near to the daily miracles of Ramón's *greguerías*, except that they are also, in his neobaroque fashion, his 'cenizas cuotidianas' [daily ashes] (IV, 48). In later practice, as we know, the surrealist image is often pushed beyond the limits of intelligibility, whereas the *greguería* strives always to make its incongruity in some way congruent with a reality some readers can try to recognize and share.

    The best ones are small miracles of subtle sensation defined with daring, precision and wit. They also form the basis of Ramón's other works, such as *Senos* [*Breasts*] (1917), a book that sublimates the erotic into a virtuoso display of imaginative observation, creating, to use Barthes' phrase, a *texte de*

[37] *Le Paysan de Paris* (Paris: Gallimard, 1966), 14 and 16.

*jouissance*,[38] with all the usual tropes (synecdoche, metonymy, metaphor) employed to define and celebrate the marvellous in the quotidian, for example:

> Es grato ver pasar los senos frente a la ventana del café, hacia el jardín público, cruzándose con los que van hacia el centro populoso de la ciudad, más engolados, cubiertos por el más hermético peto. Todos han salido para adornar la ciudad, para poner inquietud en ella, para cumplir algo así como un deber cívico.   (III, 669)

> [It is so pleasant to see breasts passing by the café window, towards the public gardens, alongside those going the other way towards the crowded city-centre, more haughtily high-necked because more covered up by the most hermetically protective bodices. All of them have come out to adorn the city, to unsettle it, to fulfil, as it were, a civic duty.]

Or if we want one a bit more surreal, but still typically down-to-earth, there is this:

> Nos hemos imaginado la escena de un seno que cayese y le hemos visto envolverse en sí mismo y rodar sutilmente cerrado en una redondez blanda y compacta, como cuando una gota de agua se cae en el polvo y se hace una bolita así.   (III, 668)

> [We have imagined the scene of a breast falling off and we have seen it wrap itself up in itself and roll subtly enclosed in a soft, compact roundness, as when a drop of water falls into the dust and turns into a little ball just like it.]

The pleasurable transcendence of these trivia, the marvellously defined absolutes of their passing moments, would be invisible to the *greguería*'s antithesis, the 'abstractly revolutionary principles' of, say, Marxist-Leninism or feminism. Those haughty bourgeois bosoms going to the city-centre would, in 1917 and for two decades after, often be in the line of fire. And feminists would undoubtedly see in the second passage a glaring example of dehumanization of women reduced to a double object under the male gaze – first the breast, one of them, and then the demeaning ball of dust.

Another of the five books Ramón had become famous for by 1920, the one on the circus, celebrates the childish innocence of the not so everyday. However, the first one, *El Rastro* (1914), explores the permanent and marginal reality of the Rastro flea-market. It still has the solid blocks of discursive prose that the *greguería* was designed to break up; but it is important because its subject matter and philosophy are intrinsic to Ramón's writing and will take us back to his early formative period. The exploration of the graveyard of objects

---

[38] Roland Barthes, *Le Plaisir du texte* (Paris: Seuil, 1973), 36 and 83, also alluded to by Nicolás (III, 52).

that is the Madrid market consolidates what I have called, rather vaguely, the
discovery of an 'almost phenomenological' view of the self and the objects of
consciousness.[39] Relevant to this must be both Ortega and Bergson, but not, I
would have thought, the abstract and obscure rationality of Hegel's
*Phenomenology of Spirit*, referred to in Breton's second manifesto. However,
a quotation from Hegel – 'Tened el valor de equivocaros' [Have the courage to
make a mistake] (IV, 43) – which precedes the passage already quoted in the
*Greguerías* prologue on losing oneself, makes me wonder whether Ramón's
loss of self owes something to the Hegelian 'self-estrangement' in 'other-
ness';[40] and whether that phenomenology of consciousness, like the structure
of metaphor I have used Ramón's incongruence terminology to define, is a
dialectical process in which the congruence remains in tension with the incongruity between self and reality, poetic identity and comic difference.
Interestingly, Breton's reference to Hegel has been seen as the clue to a tran-
scendentalism in Surrealism's concept of mind (what Ramón would later call
higher congruence).[41] However, since I think Breton is quoting Hegel in order
to justify extending the psychological revolution into the social, of relevance
here might be Short's comment that the surrealist use of the Hegelian dialectic
to reach a 'certain point of the mind' where all contradictions cease, lacks the
rigour of Hegel's Absolute Idea, achieving only 'a sort of syncretism, a balance
of opposites, or what Sartre called a perpetual 'papillotement' [flickering]
between subject and object, real and imaginary'.[42] Perhaps Ramón's dialectic
of incongruity is much more clearly aimed at experiencing and expressing on
a daily basis the latter phenomenon of oscillation between self and other
because of Ramón's emphasis on, and acceptance of, the relativizing force of
time as a constant passing present, each moment of which is disconnected from
the others. Hegel's, like all other Romantic absolutes, was dissolved for Ramón
at an early stage in the junkyards of the Rastro.
     In the Rastro he urges an iconoclastic loss of self in objects: 'Sumerjámonos
en las cosas, consiguiendo así [. . .] la ironía de uno mismo [. . .] la
idiotez inevitable y liberadora' [Let's submerge ourselves in things, thus

---

[39] In my 'Ramón Gómez de la Serna (188[8]–1963): Introduction, Selection and
Translation', *Aura: A Journal of the Avant-Garde* (Manchester: Department of French), 1,
no. 3 (1995), 52. Jean-Antoine Diaz, 'La phénoménologie du Rastro par Ramón: une
esthétique de l'occasion, une culture du fragment', *Ramón Gómez de la Serna: Etudes*, ed.
E. Martin-Hernandez (Clermont-Ferrand: University of Blaise-Pascal, 1999), 61–76,
contains some insights derived from Nietzsche via Habermas (p. 75 especially), obscured,
ironically, by the postmodern flux of critical theory.

[40] G.R.G. Mure, *The Philosophy of Hegel* (London: Oxford University Press, 1965), 34
and 13.

[41] Robert Havard, *The Crucified Mind: Rafael Alberti and the Surrealist Ethos in Spain*
(London: Tamesis, 2001), 8–9.

[42] Robert Short, 'Surrealism', in *French Literature and its Background: 6: The
Twentieth Century*, ed. John Cruickshank (London: Oxford University Press, 1970), 123.

achieving . . . the irony of oneself . . . the inevitable and liberating idiocy].[43]
The apocalyptic chaos of objects, demonstrating through death a constant
'cambiar de dueño de todo' [change of owner of everything] (III, 712), teaches
a radical lesson of self-abasement, and yet simultaneously one of liberation
from the dominant system of language fixed to the conventional concepts of
things. So that each object, removed from its proper place and jumbled up
randomly next to other objects, releases a 'delirio de palabras' [delirium of
words] (III, 78); objects become ' "¡Maravillosas asociadoras de ideas! . . . " '
[marvellous associators of ideas] (III, 75). Wandering around 'al azar, perdidos, buenos' [at random, lost, good] (III, 212), we are also told to direct our
gaze at everything with a new concentration and relaxation, like the little
Buddhist statues who best epitomize the philosophy of the Rastro, viewing it as
a 'nirvana real' (III, 211), that is, a Nirvana grounded in reality. The Rastro
encourages a special kind of contemplation, cured of conceptual abstractions,
a 'mirada' [looking] that enables, we are told, the best artists to find the
'fórmula de paz, libertad y conformidad' [formula for peace, freedom and con-
formity] (III, 217). As well as an aesthetic, the Rastro is also a strange ethic of
rebellion; for the spiritual exercise of contemplation is concentrated on the
passing present of time, this 'escape del presente' [escaping of the present],
which because it is ungraspable, takes us out and away from ourselves,
'desmoraliza, llena de abandono toda obra artística' (III, 784) [de-moralizes,
fills with abandon every work of art], translatable, I think, with the hyphen of
ambiguity to include the stronger idea of moral perdition because of the clari-
fication that moralities ('morales'), economics, and aesthetics threaten to close
'ese frente abierto a la muerte, a la vida, al abismo, a lo inconcebible' [that front
open to death, life, the abyss, the inconceivable] (III, 785). The Rastro flea-
market represents not simply a baroque-cum-dadaist apocalypse, but also a
descent into consciousness, the pre-formed, deprogrammed self's consciousness of reality, to explore as yet unconceptualized sensations, to be expressed
in words newly liberated from their normal functions (comparable to, but less
superficial than, Marinetti's liberation of words from syntax in 1912–13).

The artistic, psychological and social clear-out performed by dropping into
the Rastro, is developed in semi-fictional form the same year (1914) with the
creation of *El Doctor Inverosímil* [*The Improbable Doctor*], emphasizing
the therapeutic project of anti-realism. It anticipates the surrealist desire to
cure the psyche of its conventionalism, but, despite Ramón's later claim to
have anticipated Freud, instead of using a Freudian therapy of the subconscious, Ramón's doctor diagnoses the problems of consciousness, its lack of
awareness of its unconscious relationship to surrounding objects. In other
words, this first attempt at a novel or anti-novel (in the loose unstructured

---

[43] *Obras completas* (Barcelona: AHR, 1956), I, 62; which I prefer to the later version
(III, 81). Nicolás sees in *El Rastro* the seed of Dada and the surreal (III, 44). Zlotescu also
sees a close affinity between *ramonismo* and Surrealism (III, 26 and 30).

format of a casebook) takes back into society the attitude of mind formulated
in the Rastro. The eccentric doctor's whimsical, holistic, alternative medicine
stresses the importance of looking, that is, not a vacuous, mindless staring –
one must avoid 'que las miradas se pierdan' [looks being lost] (IX, 101),
which is a wasteful loss of self – but instead an active, fully conscious, mind-
and heart-focused perception – '¡Ni una mirada que no vea lo que mira!' [Not
even one look that doesn't see what it watches!] (IX, 132). Madness for the
doctor is a degeneration of brain matter, causing 'inconsciencia' [uncon-
sciousness] (IX, 225), that is, lack of conscious awareness, and in no way
gives access to the non-existent soul. The Nietzschean laughter of the patient
aware of his own incipient madness directed at those who believe the soul is
anything but 'masa encefálica' [encephalic mass] (IX, 170) leads us back to
the origins of Ramón's writing.

The double meaning of the title of the 20-year-old Ramón's first real book,
*Morbideces* [*Morbidezza*] (1908), contains its thesis: the sickness of having to
think is cured by the sensory pleasure of not thinking. Therapy for the neurosis of pure reason is to attain a state of 'éxtasis descerebrado' [debrained
ecstasy] (I, 463, 503), disappearing into 'nirvana' (I, 507), and purging perception of its mental categories to become a 'cristal hialino' [transparent glass]
that puts the self in direct contact with things outside (I, 469). The ambiguity
of the title corresponds to the ambiguity of the author's position, 'como
inadaptado y como adaptado' [as maladjusted and as well-adjusted] (I, 512):
his rebelliousness is mitigated by a desire for a quiet life. Though both
thinkers are mentioned critically, Nietzsche is behind the anti-rationalism, and
Schopenhauer is behind the Buddhist redirection of perception (I, 470), while
the language of adaptation shows the influence of Darwinism, through both
Haeckel and 'Dar[ví]n' [*sic*] (I, 469).[44] No one yet has looked at Ramón's
incongruent/congruent position from a Darwinian viewpoint. As well as the
need to compromise for survival in the real world, evolutionary theory emphasizes the crucial role of chance to produce the necessary variations to create
innovatory change. Initially Ramón sometimes called his *greguerías* (as well
as 'incongruities', or 'looks') 'variations'. How relevant might this be for
Surrealism? Or for Nietzsche?

In his Ateneo lecture of 1910, 'El concepto de la nueva literatura' [The
Concept of the New Literature], Ramón emphasizes the decisive impact of
Nietzsche who, he says, 'nos ha hecho entrar en posesión de nosotros mismos'
[has made us enter into possession of ourselves] (I, 152). Above all, the new
art is about a rebellious 'personalismo' [individualism] (I, 173), regarded as far
more important than any collective, political change, a message underlined by
quotations from Rémy de Gourmont and Oscar Wilde, the latter (though no one
has yet noticed) from his decidedly unorthodox essay, 'The Soul of Man
under Socialism'. This radical revolution of individual consciousness is then

---

[44] Original spelling in *Morbideces* (Madrid: Imprenta 'El Trabajo', 1908), 29.

explored in Ramón's *El libro mudo (secretos)* [*The Mute Book (Secrets)*] (1910) consisting of a struggle in monodialogue to find the words to express the inner self silenced by conventional reason, and to adopt an extreme of willed absurdity: 'Ramón [. . .] un gran olvido y una gran absurdidad para todas las cosas . . . Así todo será analogía y proteísmo' [a great forgetfulness and a great absurdity for everything . . . So all will be analogy and proteanism] (I, 738). This is described at the end as a 'muerte civil' [civil death] (I, 743), dropping out of normal life, losing his 'apellido' [surname] (I, 740), and gravitating towards the Rastro with its lesson of nihilism and a radical 'trasmutación de todos los valores' [transmutation of all values] (I, 725). The strong Nietzschean echoes here include the call for a 'verdadero desarme ético universal' [real, universal, ethical disarmament] (I, 632); but the removal of moral restraints, inviting the sort of violent cruelty on display in Marinetti's manifesto and Lautréamont's *Maldoror*, both translated in *Prometeo*,[45] is significantly modified in Ramón's case by his recommendation, 'No ser crueles pero ser absurdos' [Not to be cruel but to be absurd], and to indulge in a 'juego prohibido, jovial y destructor – blandamente destructor' [prohibited game, jovial and destructive – softly destructive] (I, 696).

A clue to this gentle, non-violent subversion of normality, employing contemplation as its main weapon is to be found in Ramón's pseudonymous other self, Tristán, who provides the prologue to this work.[46] The name is obviously Wagnerian, but it is the Wagner closest to Schopenhauer's philosophy of pessimistic renunciation, and probably it is the Nietzsche closest to both, for the latter quotes Tristan and Isolde in *The Birth of Tragedy*. The suicidal love-death owes much to Schopenhauer's ideal of self-immolation, which in its most extreme form is suicide, but in its practical form is through contemplation – 'ser s[ó]lo una mirada' [to be only a look] – a pantheistic, Buddhist 'mirada en blanco' [looking with the mind blank] (I, 686–7), which by the end becomes more focused – 'el absurdo es el blanco' [the absurd is the aim] – and more active, full of 'voluntariedad' [wilfulness] (I, 742). Ramón's Tristán represents the height of his Schopenhauerian tendency, which is crucially being modified by a Nietzschean affirmation of the self through a new perception of reality, and of morality, visible for example in Nietzsche's *The Genealogy of Morals: An Attack*, which opposes to Schopenhauer's disinterested, castrating contemplation a 'seeing' that is 'essentially perspective' and multiple, with as many 'different eyes' as possible.[47]

[45] Lautréamont in *Prometeo*, no. 9 (July 1909), 69–78, and Marinetti, no. 6 (April 1909), 65–73.

[46] Zlotescu, in her indispensable study of 'El ciclo de "Tristán" ', especially *Morbideces* and *El libro mudo* (I, 381–414), suggests another reason for the pseudonym: a private association of Ramón and Carmen de Burgos with Wagner's lovers (I, 391).

[47] Friedrich Nietzsche, *The Birth of Tragedy and The Genealogy of Morals*, trans. F. Golffing (New York: Doubleday, 1956), 255 (third essay, sect. xii). Wagner's opera is quoted in sect. xxii of *The Birth of Tragedy*, 132–3.

This is an interesting juncture because an aesthetic of visual perception partly derived from Schopenhauer's negation of 'will' in favour of a loss of self in a Platonic absolute 'idea' (which Ramón could still admire in Juan Ramón Jiménez, one of his contributors in *Prometeo*), is being transformed into a Nietzschean affirmation of the biological self in a contingent reality freed from all absolutes. This anticipates not only the later divorce between Juan Ramón's pure poetry and the 27 Generation's move towards the impurities of Surrealism and commitment, but also the later nostalgia for a lost absolute in both Ramón's and the surrealists' campaign of constant metamorphosis.[48]

The radical tendency emerges more fully from the book of Nietzsche's that probably had the most influence on Ramón – *The Will to Power* (1901) with its draft subtitle, *'Attempt at a Revaluation of all Values'* (xvii).[49] Ramón's passing reference to 'la voluntad de poder' [the will to power] in his Ateneo lecture (I, 154) shows that he was well aware that the term applied to the human drive to control reality through reason for the purposes of evolutionary survival. Later post-Hitler associations of Nietzsche with a violent will to dominate simply ignore the fact that the book is a massive attack on rationality's imposition of an entirely conventional and therefore false, but necessary, order – 'a system of systematic falsification' (315) – on the underlying chaos that Nietzsche calls the 'flux of becoming', which normal language is 'useless for expressing' (380). For example, the grammatical concept of 'I' is a fiction or convention that prevents the self from 'vanishing in the multiplicity of change' (270). 'We are always unconscious of the real activity of the outer world' (265), because it is turned into a mental construct by habitual associations and familiar language. The simplified phenomena of the apparent world 'adapted' to our needs hide the 'unformulable' 'chaos of sensations' that constitute '*another kind* of phenomenal world' (307), one which 'is essentially a world of relationships', with 'a differing aspect from every point', 'the sum' of which 'is in every case quite incongruent' (306).[50] This perspectivist phenomenalism, therefore, denies the existence of any real absolute perspective, or world 'in-itself', understood, that is, in terms of Kant's noumenal (essentialist) reality. And it is Kant's invention of this 'transcendental world' on

---

[48] For Schopenhauer's ideal of absolute perception in which the individual '*loses* himself' [original italics], see especially *The World as Will and Idea*, trans. R.B. Haldane and J. Kemp (London: Routledge & Kegan Paul), I (1883) (book iii, sect. 34), 231.

[49] The numbers in parenthesis refer to Friedrich Nietzsche, *The Will to Power*, trans. W. Kaufmann and R.J. Hollingdale (New York: Random House, 1968). Gonzalo Sobejano, in his *Nietzsche en España* (Madrid: Gredos, 1967), documents Nietzsche's influence on Ramón's physiological vitalism and the Dionysiac intoxication with concrete reality of the *greguería* (593), but misses the epistemological, and therefore literary, impact of *The Will to Power*.

[50] I have yet to ascertain whether the term 'incongruent' is the same in the Spanish (or even French) translation that Ramón must have used.

moral grounds that is especially criticized for introducing '*Moral values even in the theory of knowledge*', used ultimately as 'a justification of God' (310). Artists and philosophers, says Nietzsche, should negate the truth of the rationally and morally ordered world in order to accept the world of change '*to create a world* as it ought to be' (317), and to counter convention with 'the will to power as art' (419), combining a Dioynisian '*sexuality, intoxication, cruelty*' (421) with an 'Apollinian' clarity and simplicity (539–40) of vision (420). After the denial of reason, 'we dare to be absurd, childish, lyrical' (524), and as part of the reversal of values, 'we regard as important the lowly things that have at all times been despised' such as 'the body' and the 'smallest world' of our immediate vicinity (524). We 'pagans in faith', he concludes, are the ones 'who dare to live in a dismoralized world' imagining higher creatures 'beyond [Christianity's] good and evil' (533).

This, it seems to me, is the precise source for the incongruent antirationalism in Ramón and possibly for Surrealism's onslaught on reason.[51] At the very least, it provides a better translation for the 'spirit of dismoralisation' in Breton's first manifesto, and some support for the ambiguity of Ramón's de-moralization of his mind to explain his *greguerías*, meaning both demoralize and dismoralize. However, a major difference is that Surrealism went much further 'beyond good and evil' by incorporating, however unconsciously or indirectly, the Dionysian destructiveness into Breton's 'convulsive beauty'. Whereas Ramón delved much more into that unconscious chaos of sensations emanating from the lowly reality surrounding the self, and employed an Apollinian clarity to reconcile his own will to artistic power with the will to power of conventional knowledge. Ramón tries to adapt his incongruent vision to normal reality, in terms of intelligible communication with others, and confine it to his immediate milieu, so that a Darwinian adaptability in an evolving, creative present, plus a Schopenhauerian softness and serenity, modifies his Nietzschean, hard-headed radicalism. In contrast, Breton's Surrealism is much more intellectualist, trying to use Hegel's dialectic of reason to bridge the contradictions, not only between Freud and Marx, but also between the Romantic absolute and the Nietzschean flux.

To complete this genealogical convergence, I shall quote Nietzsche's conveniently compressed essay 'On Truth and Lie in an Extra-Moral Sense', beloved of deconstructionists, such as De Man, who bolsters my feeling that Ramón's phenomenology comes not from Husserl, Ortega or Hegel, but from Nietzsche's critique of the phenomenalism of consciousness as a metaphysical construct, which is, De Man says, 'a prefigurative critique of what later became known as phenomenology'.[52] The main theme of Nietzsche's essay certainly prefigures something that Ramón and Breton made the centre of

---

[51]  Anna Balakian dismisses Nietzsche as 'too destructive and egocentric' for Breton, *Surrealism: the Road to the Absolute* (London: Allen & Unwin, 1972), 124.

[52]  Paul De Man, 'Nietzsche's Theory of Rhetoric', *Symposium* (Spring 1974), 37.

their poetics: the 'fundamental impulse of man' is the 'formation of metaphors' (188).[53] These express the sensations that then become ossified into concepts, forming a towering edifice like a 'columbarium' (which may be tomb, or is it a dovecote?) (187). That edifice has to be deconstructed by the philosopher-artist, because men lie 'unconsciously', out of habit, and *by this very unconsciousness, by this very forgetting*', arrive 'at a sense of truth.' Art liberates this impulse towards metaphor to express 'that other perceptual world of first impressions' and 'sensations' (181) by breaking up the edifice then rearranging it 'ironically', and because these 'intuitions' have no words made for them, 'when man sees them he is dumb, or speaks in forbidden metaphors and in un-heard of combinations of ideas' (190). The metaphorical impulse longs to reshape 'the existing world of waking man as motley, irregular, inconsequentially incoherent, attractive and eternally new as the world of dreams is. For indeed waking man *per se* is only clear about his being awake through the rigid and orderly woof of ideas' (188). In such passages this essay seems to me to confirm the Nietzschean source for Ramón's artistic fixation on the incongruous, unconscious, chaos of impressions between the self and reality. But it also helps pinpoint the issue where his relationship with Surrealism is most problematic: dream in what senses? Ramón's metamorphosis of waking reality gives it a deliriously dream-like appearance, at the same time as he carefully avoids staring through what Nietzsche calls 'a crevice in the chamber of consciousness' into the darker depths of man's 'pitiless' and 'murderous' nature, where man is 'as it were, hanging in dreams on the back of a tiger' (176). Surrealism would ride on the back of this tiger, the Dionysian underworld of unconscious drives that anticipates the Freudian unconscious, while also attempting to create a less turbulent, Apollinian, dream-vision of a marvellous surreality.

Ramón was now ready to embark on his Nietzsche-inspired immersion in the external day-dreaming reality of unconscious sensations, manifested by his call on the first page of *Tapices* [*Tapestries*] for 'delirio' [delirium], but first a 'perdición completa, magnánima' [complete, magnanimous perdition], followed by the word and 'una especie de lógica' [a sort of logic], resulting in a pre-surrealist activity that produces the first *greguerías*, such as 'Mi carne está llena de sillas y escarabajos' [My flesh is full of chairs and beetles] (I, 904), and the gregarious name of which indicates his wish to unite the esoteric with the language and everyday reality of the tribe. Ramón's normal self, lost in the solipsistic introverted muteness of *El libro mudo*, loses itself another way in the external world to become an extroverted *mirador* [observer] (I, 905), taking his eccentric personality into the streets and into the café Pombo in the heart of Madrid, projecting avant-garde art into life,

---

[53] The numbers in parenthesis refer to 'On Truth and Falsity in their Ultramoral Sense' (1873), trans. M.A. Mügge, in *The Complete Works of Friedrich Nietzsche*, ed. O. Levy (Edinburgh and London: Foulis), II (1911).

changing reality with an even more radical and sustained 'reversal of consciousness' than that attributed by Shattuck to Apollinaire.[54] Accompanying this was a surprising reversal of terminology, for he had first used the word *greguería* in 1908 with its normal dictionary meaning to describe the restrictive effect of the city's system of signs and values – 'su greguería se impone sobre el ciudadano [. . .] le estrecha de deberes' [its clamour imposes itself on the citizen . . . constrains him with duties] (I, 489). By 1912 he was applying it to his personal revaluation of urban life, uncovering the latent moments of epiphany, such as 'En el verano, la ciudad está llena de timbres . . . ' [In summer the city is full of door-bells] (I, 933), thus anticipating the surrealist quest for revelation within the city and what Cardinal calls Breton's pleasurable reversal of the reality principle.

Gathering round himself a group of adepts, such as Bergamín and Gutiérrez Solana, both depicted in the latter's painting of the Pombo *tertulia* (now at the Reina Sofía Museum), Ramón issued his first 'Proclamation' from Pombo in 1915, advocating a literature violently independent of commercial classifications, 'el libro libre en que se libertase el libro del libro' [the free book in which the book would be liberated from the book] (III, 16), and, with Pombo as a refuge from the violent passions engendered in neutral Spain by the world war, defending thought as a pleasurably absurd diversion against the disapproval of the intellectual establishment, including, incidentally, professors and students of foreign languages (who, he jests, can say the same banality in several different ways). In fact, his scorn for the university academy made his activities far less intellectually pedantic and authoritarian than, say, Breton's. As Gibson rightly observes, with the 'metaphorical shock tactics' of the *greguería* 'Ramón's was the light touch missing in the somewhat puritanical Residencia de Estudiantes, and it is not surprising that Buñuel became a regular of Pombo'.[55] Furthermore, Ramón's humorous anti-intellectualism was tolerated by the one academic he did admire, Ortega, who provided him with an outlet in the *Revista de Occidente* for, among other things, two essays in the 1930s that are significant for Ramón's evolving response to the success of the surrealist phenomenon. His third phase as a commentator on and participant in Surrealism deserves a study all of its own.

[54] Roger Shattuck, *The Banquet Years. The Origins of the Avant-Garde in France: 1885 to World War I*, rev. edn (London: Cape, 1969), 315.

[55] Gibson, 96. Agustín Sánchez Vidal, 'De Ramón al surrealismo', *Insula*, no. 502 (October 1988), 13–14, emphasizes that Buñuel was a regular attender for six whole years.

# 2

# A Delicious Imaginary Journey with Joan Miró and José María Hinojosa

## JACQUELINE RATTRAY

In the fifth edition of *La Révolution surréaliste* (15 October 1925) there is a double-spread that succinctly evokes the whole spirit of the surrealist revolution. Opening the section entitled 'Rêves' [Dreams] – a noteworthy choice of title, situating dreams as one of the fundamental mechanisms for surrealist exploration – there is a painting by Joan Miró, entitled 'Terre labourée' [The Tilled Field] (see Plate Section). This picture provides a visual epigraph for the dream texts by two French surrealists – Michel Leiris and Max Morise – that follow. Separating two of these texts is a photograph of a Spanish street scene, 'Vue de Malaga'. The photograph is published anonymously and some sixty years would pass before the name of the likely photographer became known. The critic Alfonso Sánchez Rodríguez has recorded that, in 1985, when the journal *Puertaoscura* was launched in Malaga, an inaugural poster was produced to mark the occasion. The image used was the same photograph that had appeared in *La Révolution surréaliste* in 1925. This time, however, the caption in the lower part of the poster credited the work. The anonymous photographer was actually a surrealist poet from Malaga, José María Hinojosa.[1] The following discussion will bring together the famous Catalan surrealist painter and the little-known Andalusian poet through the meeting point of Paris and Surrealism. The focus will be on some of Hinojosa's surrealist texts, which he began to write while living in Paris and which have been compared to some of Miró's paintings of the time. In accordance with surrealist theories, this argument will be engaged with questions relating to artistic process rather than common manifestations of artistic production.

Time has revealed a meaning to the layout of that double-spread in *La Révolution surréaliste* that is more profound than the editors in Paris could ever have imagined. Miró's painting, which had been purchased from him by the leader of the surrealist movement, André Breton, stands at the head of the

---

[1] Alfonso Sánchez Rodríguez, 'Una aproximación al "Caso Hinojosa"', unpublished thesis (Estudi General de Lleida, 1990), 34.

page and leads the way for the whole section. *The Tilled Field* (1923–4) shows
an oneiric depiction of Miró's Catalan landscape, and the painting is full of
images that have evolved into some of his personal motifs.[2] Scattered throughout the picture there are animals that have been distorted, mutilated or juxtaposed in terms of scale. In the foreground is a tree, personified through the
addition of an eye and an ear. Miró has spoken of this tree as 'something
human. A beautiful tree breathes and listens to you.'[3] In the background there
is a farmhouse, recognisable from his earlier work *The Farm* (1921–2).[4] And
to the left is another tree-like object, which would later become the geometrical sign representing the human figure in *Catalan Landscape (The Hunter)*
(1923–4). From this human-tree symbol, three flags are hung – those of Spain,
Cataluña and France – all of which have personal significance for Miró.

In terms of Miró's artistic development, *The Tilled Field* is a significant
marker for two main reasons. One was that, with this painting, Miró now
found himself embraced by the surrealist group in Paris – he later claimed that
Breton and Éluard 'only became aware of my existence when my painting
freed itself into poetry and dreams with *The Tilled Field, Harlequin's
Carnival* and the others that followed'.[5] Breton would later refer to Miró as
'perhaps the most surrealist of us all', even though Miró himself was always
reluctant to become a committed member of the surrealist group in Paris.[6] The
second significant factor is that, through this painting, Miró entered into a
whole new domain of pictorial expression. While he was working on *The
Tilled Field*, he wrote to his friend J.F. Ráfols comparing his feelings to those
of an intrepid explorer: 'I confess that I am often gripped by panic, the kind
of panic that is felt by an explorer travelling through virgin territory.'[7]

In contrast to the buzzing activity contained in *The Tilled Field*, the anonymous photograph shows a desolate street scene, a scene empty of life and yet
pregnant with expectation. In the centre of the shot, a solitary lamp-post
casts its shadow against a highly textured wall, reminding the viewer of the

[2] For a more detailed reading of this painting, see Jacques Dupin's *Joan Miró: Life and
Work*, trans. Norbert Guterman (New York: Abrams, 1962), 136–52 and Janis Mink's *Miró*,
(Cologne: Taschen, 2001), 37–53.

[3] Arthur C. Danto, 'Miró's "little miracles"', *Art News*, 92, 8 (Oct. 1993), 138–43 (142).

[4] This painting was famously sold to Ernest Hemingway. For an account of the
circumstances of the sale, see William Wiser, *The Crazy Years: Paris in the Twenties*
(London: Thames & Hudson [1983], 1990), 151–2.

[5] Gérard Durozoi, *History of the Surrealist Movement*, trans. Alison Anderson
(Chicago & London: University of Chicago Press, 2002), 116–19 (116).

[6] Miró's refusal to toe the surrealist party line would culminate in his expulsion in
1929. See the chapter 'Juan Miró' [sic] in Gérard Xuriguera, *Pintores españoles de la
Escuela de París*, trans. Antonio Urrutia (Madrid: Ibérico Europea de Ediciones, 1974),
59–67 (63).

[7] Sarane Alexandrian, *Surrealist Art* (London: Thames & Hudson [1970], 1993), 71.
The whole letter is published (with a slightly different translation) in Margit Rowell (ed.),
*Joan Miró: Selected Writings and Interviews*. (New York: Da Capo Press, 1992), 82.

surrealist technique taken from Leonardo da Vinci's perceptual process of staring at a wall until images and shapes start to appear before the eyes. With
regard to Hinojosa's contribution, ironically it is quite appropriate that his
photograph should have been published anonymously. Historically, his importance has been overlooked within the overall development of Surrealism in
Spain – the reasons for which are complicated and multiple – and his name has
been most remembered for the 'conspiracy of silence' that has surrounded him
from critics, literary historians and, crucially, by his fellow poets and artists
of the time.[8] The process of re-establishing this figure is now well under way –
primarily owing to the work of Julio Neira and Sánchez Rodríguez.[9] And their
work has culminated in two new editions of Hinojosa's work – his *Epistolario*
(1997) and his *Obra completa (1923–1931)* (1998).[10]

The graphic meeting between Miró and Hinojosa, displayed in the pages of
*La Révolution surréaliste*, marks an early point of contact between the artist
and the poet. This, however, was not their only encounter. Another similar
meeting can be found in the Catalan journal, *L'Amic de les Arts* (June 1928).
Here an article by J.V. Foix, 'Presentació de Joan Miró' [Introducing Joan
Miró], appears next to a review of Hinojosa's work by Lluís Montanyà, 'Punts
de vista sobre el superrealisme: *La Flor de California* de José María
Hinojosa' [Points of view about Surrealism: *The Flower of California* by
José María Hinojosa].[11] The subject of Montanyà's review is one of the
better-known of the six books that Hinojosa published in his relatively
short-lived literary career. The title, *La Flor de California* (1928), is inten-
tionally mispronounced to force the rhyme with the poet's own name, José
María. The work is comprised of two distinct sections – seven dream narratives and seven oneiric texts. Both parts share similar themes and imagery that
explore some typically surrealist concerns – anticlericalism, black humour,
objective chance, and images of fragmented bodies, eye mutilations, subterranean dream-worlds, etc. The primary difference between the two sections
lies in their use of language. Where there is a degree of coherence to the

---

[8] See Sánchez Rodríguez, 'Donde arraigue el olvido, la *arriesgada* reivindicación del
poeta surrealista José María Hinojosa', *Palabras del 27* (Malaga), 5 (Dec. 1990), 25–6.
Also Francisco Aranda, *El surrealismo español* (Barcelona: Lumen, 1981), 156.

[9] Bibliographies of critical works relating to Hinojosa can be found in Sánchez
Rodríguez's *José María Hinojosa:. ensayo bibliográfico* (Malaga: Centro Cultural de la
Generación del 27, 1994) and Neira's *Viajero de soledades: estudios sobre José María
Hinojosa* (Seville: Fundación Genesian, 1999).

[10] Both editions are published by Fundación Genesian of Seville. All references to
Hinojosa's poetry are to this, the first non-facsimile edition of his *Obra completa*.
Hereafter page references will be cited in the text.

[11] *L'Amic de les Arts* (Sitges), 26 (30 June 1928), 198–200. A Spanish translation
of Montanyà's review – 'Puntos de vista sobre el superrealismo: *La Flor de California* de
José María Hinojosa' – is published in *Remolino de voces: La recepción de José María
Hinojosa (1927–1929)* (Malaga: Centro Cultural de la Generación del 27, 1995), ed. and
intro. Sánchez Rodríguez, 59–61.

bizarre dream narratives of the first part, the style of the oneiric texts in the second comes closest to automatic writing. In his review, Montanyà comments on the visual quality of Hinojosa's texts and remarks that: 'Lo forman una serie de visiones algo apocalípticas, de una apocalipsis moderna, filtrada por Picasso y Chirico, con cables a Joan Miró' [They form a series of somewhat apocalyptic visions, of a modern apocalypse filtered through Picasso and Chirico with cables to Joan Miró]. As if to highlight the point, an illustration by Miró, *The Dialogue of Insects* (1925–6), appears midway through Montanyà's review.

As well as these artistic–literary meetings between Miró and Hinojosa, there are also biographical points of reference. During the 1920s, both were living in Paris where they were part of the Spanish group that used to meet at 'La Rotonde' café in Montparnasse.[12] This large gathering included writers, film-makers, musicians, intellectuals and painters.[13] Other than Miró, some of the more famous members of this group were Luis Buñuel and Salvador Dalí.[14] The importance of the 'Rotonde' meetings was more than purely social. Here, the group would debate new ways of artistic exploration; books, manifestos and journals would be shared among the participants; drawings would be sketched and literature discussed. It was at the 'Rotonde' that Hinojosa, as well as a number of the other Spaniards, became acquainted with the French surrealists – Breton, Aragon, Péret, Unik, etc.[15] A further biographical reference is that Hinojosa – who, owing to his wealth, was nicknamed the 'bohemian with a current account'[16] – actually owned paintings by Miró in his private art collection. Other treasures included works by artists such as Juan Gris, Pablo Picasso, Salvador Dalí and Francisco Bores.[17] Tragically, all of these works are thought to have been destroyed when the family home in Malaga was burnt at the onset of the Spanish Civil War.

Paris was an important site for both artists in terms of the friendships that were made and in their artistic development. During the time that coincided

[12] For Miró's recollections of Paris (which omit any mention of Hinojosa), see the chapter 'Joan Miró: En aquel París que era una fiesta' in Lluis Permanyer, *Los años difíciles de Miró, Llorens Artigas, Fenosa, Dalí, Clavé, Tàpies* (Barcelona: Lumen, 1975), 7–26, and Mercedes Guillén, *Conversaciones con los artistas españoles de la Escuela de París* (Madrid: Taurus, 1960), 17–24. Hinojosa's impressions of Paris are emotionally revealed through his letters: Hinojosa, 1997, 49–53, 63–6 and notes on. 125–7, 132–5.

[13] The 'Rotonde' group constituted one stage of the 'Escuela española de París'. An overview of three distinct stages to the 'Escuela de París' is defined in the introduction of Xuriguera, 1974, 9–18.

[14] Buñuel refers to Joaquín Peinado and Hernando Viñes as his closest friends, although he makes no reference to Hinojosa in relation to the 'Rotonde' group. See the chapter 'Paris (1925–1929)' in Buñuel, *My Last Breath* (London: Vintage, 1982), 78–91 (80).

[15] Neira, 1999, 207.

[16] Neira, 1999, 8.

[17] Neira, 'José María Hinojosa: Vida y Obra', unpublished doctoral thesis (Universidad de Extremadura, 1981), 68.

with Hinojosa's stay in Paris (1925–6), Miró was undergoing a phase of transition in his style of painting, a change that was largely propelled by his connections with the surrealist group.[18] Miró has stressed the importance of poetry as a means for going beyond the strictly plastic, recalling that: 'I went quite a bit that year [1925] with poets because I felt that it was necessary to go a step beyond the strictly plastic and bring some poetry into painting.'[19] At this time, Miró had just finished *Harlequin's Carnival* – a painting that he later 'illustrated' with a poetic text[20] – and had started working on his 'dream paintings'.[21] *Harlequin's Carnival* marks the climax of the phase that had been initiated with *The Tilled Field*, and the 'dream-paintings' the beginning of the next.[22] The first of these two phases is characterised by paintings that retain some degree of recognisable reality. By contrast, in the dream-paintings, the world depicted departs from the constraints of external, concrete forms and enters into the interior realm of dreams and the imagination.[23] These later canvases explore the space between verbal and visual representation and can be defined as 'hybrid' works.[24] In these dream-paintings, the viewer is often confronted with a mixture of both painted forms and words. Miró called these paintings 'picture-poems', a definition corroborated by his assertion that: 'I make no distinction between painting and poetry.'[25] Taking his interest in language a step further, Miró also turned his hand to automatic writing.[26] The year of Miró's first known poetic experiments was 1928, which, incidentally, was the same year that Hinojosa's collection of surrealist texts was first published. As if in return, the paintings of Miró appear as literary subtexts for another reader of

[18] At this time he had a studio at the Rue Blomet where André Masson was his neighbour and Michel Leiris an almost daily visitor. Miró's biography is documented in Rowell, 1992, 21–39.

[19] Quoted in David Burnett, 'The Poetics of the Paintings of Miró', *Artscanada*, 238–9 (Dec. 1980–Jan. 1981), 6–11 (9).

[20] The text, originally published in *Verve* (Paris) (Jan.–Mar. 1939), is re-edited in Rowell, 164.

[21] Miró was also working on three smaller paintings: *Landscape, Head of a Catalan Peasant* and *Dialogue of the Insects* (Winter 1924–5). Dupin, 1962, 148, 157.

[22] Mink, 42 and Dupin, 152.

[23] See the section 'Dream Painting and the Comprehension of the Void (1925–1927)' in Dupin, 153–74.

[24] This definition of the picture-poems as 'in-between' or 'hybrid' works is presented by Katharine Conley in her essay 'Anamorphic Love: The surrealist poetry of desire' in *Surrealism: Desire Unbound*, ed. Jennifer Mundy (London: Tate Publishing, 2001), 101–23 (105).

[25] Burnett, 6. For a further discussion of Miró's word-images, see John C. Welchman, 'After the Wagnerian Bouillabaisse: Critical Theory and the Dada and Surrealist Word-Image', in Judi Freeman (ed.), *The Dada & Surrealist Word-Image*. (Cambridge, Mass.: MIT Press, 1989), 57–95 (87), and Elza Adamowicz, *Surrealist Collage in Text and Image: Dissecting the exquisite corpse* (Cambridge: Cambridge University Press, 1998), 8–9.

[26] *Joan Miró: 1893–1993*, exhibition catalogue, Fundació Joan Miró (Boston, New York, Toronto and London: Bullfinch Press, 1993), 192.

Hinojosa's *La Flor de California*, the poet-painter José Moreno Villa. In a letter
that forms the preface to *La Flor de California*, Moreno Villa writes:

> Sería perfecta si yo pudiese escribirla [esta carta] como dictada por el
> volante misterioso de los sueños, porque así pertenecería al género que tú
> persigues, cuya técnica pones de manifiesto en los *Textos Oníricos* [. . .] Y
> recuerdo que comprendí mejor los cuadros de Bores o de Miró cuando leí
> tus narraciones y que, también éstas se me iluminaron al ver aquéllos.
>
> (Hinojosa, 1998, 148)

> [It would be perfect if I could write this [letter] as if dictated by the mys-
> terious driver of dreams, because that way I would belong to the genre that
> you pursue, whose technique you make manifest in the *Oneiric Texts* [. . .]
> And I remember that I understood the paintings of Bores or of Miró better
> when I read your narratives and that these [texts] also illuminated me upon
> seeing those [paintings].]

   In agreement with Moreno Villa's observations, Miró's techniques in painting can be used to illustrate Hinojosa's process of automatic writing. In *La
Flor de California*, the oneiric texts display a number of traits that are general characteristics of automatic writing, as well as manifesting a variety of
concerns particular to Hinojosa. Many of these texts actually give voice to the
theory of automatism that is primarily laid out by Breton in the *First
Manifesto of Surrealism* (1924). Before proceeding to offer a close,
Miróesque reading of one of Hinojosa's oneiric texts, some of the main characteristics of automatic writing will be discussed by looking at just the opening phrases of other texts in this collection.
   The practice of automatic writing involves entering into a particular mental
state before even taking pen to paper. The writer empties their mind of preconceived ideas and then, opening the floodgates to the subconscious, lets the
mental images rush out. During this process, the writer effectively becomes a
transcribing vessel for these images, tracing the actual functioning of thought.
Conscious control of poetic construction is repressed and the writer proceeds
without turning back to correct or amend sentences. Breton has commented on
the experience when words seize control of the writing process, noting that:
'the first sentence will come spontaneously, so compelling is the truth that with
every passing second there is a sentence unknown to our consciousness which
is only crying out to be heard'.[27] For Miró, the experience of commencing a
painting is one that he describes in poetic rather than visual terms: 'The painter
works like the poet: the word comes before the thought.'[28] In a well-known
interview entitled, 'I Work Like a Gardener' (1959), Miró elaborates on his

---

[27] André Breton, *Manifestoes of Surrealism*, trans. Richard Seaver and Helen R. Lane
(Ann Arbor: University of Michigan Press, 1969), 30.
[28] Rowell, 216–24 (219).

method of working: 'I work in a state of passion and excitement. When I begin a painting, I am obeying a physical impulse, a necessity to begin.'[29] The experience of being overwhelmed by thoughts expressed by Breton's theory and Miró's practice is also described by Hinojosa at the beginning of 'Oneiric Text II'. Here the poet-protagonist speaks of how 'Envuelto en un rumor de olas atajo en mi cerebro todos los pensamientos que pretenden escaparse por la escotilla . . . ' [Enveloped in a murmur of waves, I intercept in my brain all the thoughts which try to escape through the floodgates] (Hinojosa, 1998, 179). For the reader of this text, the intellectual response is one of containment followed by a haphazard unleashing of images and ideas. One critic has described this experience of reading automatic texts as invoking a logic of 'breach and broach'.[30] Although the goal of automatism is to explore and record the anarchic world of the subconscious, the inherent paradox is that irrational images can only be externalised through the medium of language – a conscious system of rational thought. The main difference between the more conventional, controlled use of language and a surrealist use of language is that words are now given an active role; they are no longer required to merely reflect reality but to reconstruct the world that we perceive through language.

The first image of the automatic text will often serve as the stimulant for the stream of images that follow, bursting out in a long, unpunctuated flow of words. The text remains only loosely moored to the constraints of conventional writing by punctuation, for, as Breton notes, 'the fact still remains that punctuation no doubt resists the absolute continuity of the flow with which we are concerned'.[31] This insurgent flow of images stimulates an auto-generation of further images through various chains of association. The progression of disconnected images originating from a spontaneous source is another primary concern of Miró's. He has recorded that:

> I start my paintings under the influence of a shock that I feel and that takes me out of reality. The cause of the shock can be a little thread coming loose from the canvas, a drop of water falling, this print that my finger leaves on the shiny surface of this table. Anyway, I need a starting point, even if it's only a grain of dust or a flash of light. This shape generates a series of things, one thing giving birth to another thing. In this way, a bit of thread can set off a world.[32]

Miró's desire for a chance happening before starting to paint should not lead us to the conclusion that his paintings are 'automatic' in the sense of being

[29] Rowell, 246–53 (249).

[30] See Johnny Gratton's 'Runaway: Textual Dynamics in the Surrealist Poetry of André Breton', in Ian Higgins (ed.), *Surrealism and Language* (Edinburgh: Scottish Academic Press, 1986), 30–45.

[31] Breton, 1969, 30.

[32] *Joan Miró: 1893–1993*, 425.

undertaken without any preconceived ideas – his sketchbooks reveal that he made a number of preparatory drawings before setting to work on the canvas.[33] This method of painting introduces one of the central concerns in the debate surrounding Surrealism and painting during the 1920s – i.e. that pictorial representation necessarily entails a greater degree of conscious control than writing.[34] This, however, does not detract from the overall effect of Miró's paintings, nor of the oneiric quality they evoke for the viewer.[35] At the beginning of Hinojosa's 'Oneiric Text V', a process is described that conveys this Miróesque concern with provoking accidents.

> Voy cuidadosamente ensartando en un hilo blanco todas mis ideas y cuando ya tengo una buena ristra de ellas las balanceo en el espacio y al romperse el hilo caen sobre mi cabeza hechas copos de nieve.   (Hinojosa, 1998, 182)

> [I carefully string together all of my ideas on a white thread and when I have a good string of them I balance them in space and when the string breaks they fall on my head as snowflakes.]

As well as presenting the reader with a reified image, this opening sentence demonstrates the auto-generation of language through the chains of associations that follow. This particular oneiric text goes on to describe an adventure to the North Pole and the path unfolds though colour references to white – bones, spermatozoa, snow, polar bears, teeth.

The metaphor of a journey, especially in relation to dream-exploration, is a recurrent image across the whole range of surrealist manifestations. It is also a central concern of both Miró and Hinojosa's work. In Surrealism, the type of metaphorical journey embarked upon does not normally follow a conventional, linear path. It is rather a synaesthetic exploration towards an unknown destination. This path of poetic discovery had already been taken up by that famous surrealist predecessor, Arthur Rimbaud, who led the way under the famous slogan: 'the poet makes himself a seer by a long, prodigious and rational disarrangement of *all* the senses'. Miró's admiration for poets such as Rimbaud is not discerned by looking for specific signs or forms in his paintings. His interest lay rather in Rimbaud's challenge to poetry which opened up wider questions relating to language, truth and meaning. For Miró, the possibility for exploring parallel issues is seen through the function and

[33] See Stanley Meisler, 'For Joan Miró, poetry and painting were the same', *Smithsonian* (Washington, D.C.) (Nov. 1993), 62–75 (66).

[34] The argument was quickly resolved – as the historical development of Surrealism has revealed – and surrealist poetry would even be overtaken by painting in the most famous manifestations of Surrealism.

[35] René Passeron observes that Miró's paintings can be seen not so much as condensed dreams as machines for making people dream. *Phaidon Encyclopedia of Surrealism*, trans. John Griffiths (Oxford: Phaidon, 1978), 205–11 (209).

spatial structure of his paintings.[36] As well as the comparison to the intrepid explorer noted earlier, Miró has compared working on his paintings to the undertaking of an adventure.[37] In Hinojosa's writing, including some of his earlier books, the theme of travelling is very much apparent.[38] In both sections of *La Flor de California* – the dream narratives and the oneiric texts – a number of bizarre journeys take place involving different modes of transport. The first of Hinojosa's oneiric texts displays both the characteristic form and content of the surrealist journey: 'Viajero sagrado por los ríos lechosos, sin remos ni miosotis para acortar las distancias. . . ' [Sacred traveller of the milky rivers, without oars or miosotis to shorten the distance]. As is suggested in this opening part to the first, long sentence, this text goes on to reveal an obvious intertextuality with Rimbaud's famous poem of unguided sailing, 'Le Bateau ivre' [The Drunken Boat].

In his Miróesque evaluation of Hinojosa's *La Flor de California*, Moreno Villa comments on the structural dimension of Miró's painting as being characterised by a certain fluidity.[39] The language Moreno Villa employs is full of Rimbaldian connotations – of sensory disarrangement and of an hallucinogenic, almost mystical, experience:

> Hay una fluencia de líneas en este cuadro que, durante algún tiempo es sorda, pero que de repente cuaja en una forma conocida, en un elemento vivo e iluminado. Hay lo mismo en tus narraciones, líneas que se alargan o enrolan por alusiones o relaciones de aparente sin sentido, mudas, y que, de pronto, cuajan en una frase sencilla, iluminada. . .

> [There is a fluency of lines in this painting that, for some time is deaf, but that suddenly gels in a known form, in a living and visionary element. There is the same in your narratives, lines that grow or enlist allusions or connections that seem meaningless and that suddenly gel in a simple, visionary phrase.]

In surrealist manifestations, fluidification is one technique which is explored as a means to derealise the world of reality – the obvious example comes from another Catalan surrealist, Salvador Dalí, and his famous melting watches. In the opening sentence to 'Oneiric Text IV', the poet-protagonist relays a state

---

[36] This area is explored at length in Burnett, 1981.

[37] Rowell, 258.

[38] Hinojosa's third book of poems is named after the idea of a compass rose, *La Rosa de los Vientos* [*The Rose of the Winds*] (1927). For further information on this book in relation to other poets of the time, see Neira's article 'La rosa de los vientos en la poesía española de los años 20', *Anuario de Estudios filológicos de la Universidad de Extremadura* (Cáceres), VII (1984), 263–80, re-edited in Neira, 1999, 151–76.

[39] Jacques Dupin has also commented on the fluidity of Miró's painting. See his article 'La transmutación' in the exhibition catalogue *Joan Miró: Años 20. Mutación de la realidad* (Madrid: Museo español de arte contemporáneo, 1983), 30–48 (30).

of corporeal fluidification: 'Mi cuerpo inundado de agua del mar transita por todos los recovecos . . . ' [My body flooded with sea-water goes through all the nooks and crannies] (Hinojosa, 1998, 181). Language allows the reader to follow the image of the submerged body before dissolving into the surreal concept of the poet-protagonist himself as free-flowing matter. The body flows into the surrounding environment in a way that liberates the visualising possibilities for each reader as the image defies the logical constraints of form.

The unfolding of an automatism-effect world, linked to some of Miró's pictorial techniques, becomes apparent within a close reading of Hinojosa's 'Oneiric Text III' (Hinojosa, 1998, 180). Long sentences overflow through a lack of punctuation, language auto-generates and words reflect upon one another. Within the following, Miróesque reading of the text, sentences will be quoted and discussed in whole in order to minimise the disruption to the flow. Like many of Hinojosa's other oneiric texts, this text is full of linguistic ambiguities and subtle nuances which add layer upon layer to the reader's interpretation. There is also a self-conscious realisation regarding these aspects of language which will be discussed later on.

'Oneiric Text III' opens with an image of confusion and disorientation that sets the tone for the progression of the sentences: 'Atormentado por las luces desconfié desde entonces de su buena intención y rehuía su encuentro cuando desbocado buscaba los acuarios en los pliegues de la madrugada' [Being tormented by the lights, I no longer trusted their good intentions and shied away from meeting them when, unleashed, I looked for the aquariums hidden in the folds of the early morning]. At first, the reader is struck by the description of the light as disagreeable and untrustworthy. Normally, the reader would interpret or decode the reference to light as a positive symbol of illumination. However, Surrealism typically subverts traditional symbols and their expected meanings to find hidden or suppressed potential. The textual dynamics of 'breach-and-broach' in automatism, mentioned earlier, is presented over the duration of this sentence. At the opening of this text, there is a feeling of restlessness and frustration. This emotion is contained for a while and then, through the word 'desbocado' [unleashed], is quite literally released. The polysemy of this word superimposes different images upon the reader's visualisation. 'Desbocado' conveys the idea of pent-up energy suddenly being set free, as in the image of a horse bolting away. There is also the figurative meaning of letting out a stream of insults. In addition there is the idea of a stream running over and this image of fluidity overflows into the adjoining reference to aquariums. With echoes of both Rimbaud's sensory disarrangement and Moreno Villa's observation of phrases that gel in Hinojosa's oneiric texts, morning is given a tangible quality, having folds in which the poet-protagonist searches. Before this first sentence has reached its end, the self-generating process has set in, and seemingly unrelated images find themselves linked together.

The next sentence both condenses and elaborates some of the ideas expressed in the opening sentence. The language used reflects the emotional response to the lights and continues with the theme of untrustworthiness. Words can be picked out that link back and carry forward the idea of the energetic chase suggested through 'desbocado'.

> No pude dar alcance a mi buena intención y rodeado mi cuerpo de aristas que engranaban en las esquinas fui recorriendo la ciudad con una marcha a la deriva mientras se desperezaban los árboles despertados por un grito que brotaba en espiral del cielo y venía a clavarse en el sexo de la Tierra deján-dola embarazada de ecos.

> [I couldn't catch up with my good intentions and, with my body surrounded by edges that interlocked at the corners, I drifted around the city while the trees stretched themselves out, woken up by a shout that rose in a spiral from the sky and then plunged itself into the sex of the Earth leaving it pregnant with echoes.]

Another element of sensory disarrangement enters the text with a reified force. This description of sharp angles that interlock at the corners gives geometrical form to the physical image. But the logic of the image of the body surrounded by 'aristas' [edges] presents a physical image that is problematic for the reader to visualise. Language creates a double-image, superimposing literal and figurative meanings. And, by coincidence, this double-image is able to translate into English through the idiomatic idea of time knocking the rough edges off one's character. Given that these edges are present in this scene, the implication is of a regression in time, back to another surrealist paradise: childhood. Both form and content of this sentence convey the idea of rambling: images proceed in a seemingly disconnected flow and the poet-protagonist now finds himself turned into a traveller. He speaks of drifting aimlessly around the city, a reference that the reader can easily identify with that favourite practice of the surrealists in *flâneur*-like wanderings. Then in a characteristically Miróesque image, the trees are personified and sound is reified. The sexualising of the Earth adds another Miróesque touch to this picture, when the natural world becomes mythologised, as well as metamorphosed, into a woman in the final part of this sentence.

As has been witnessed previously, this text proceeds with a 'breach-and-broach' effect for the reader. The next sentence, although comparatively short, is full of overlapping images. 'El aire áspero que refrescaba mis pupilas pedía con insistencia la transfiguración de la carne' [The jagged air that refreshed my pupils insistently asked for the transfiguration of my flesh]. With the tactile description of the air as 'áspero' [rough, harsh, jagged], the reader can link this image back to the earlier description of the folds in the morning. Also contained in this signifier, is the idea of jaggedness, which re-evokes the sight of the body surrounded by sharp angles. The overall image of the air demanding the transfiguration of the flesh, carries blasphemous implications that will be explored later on. The attack on vision and perception is a familiar surrealist trait, emblematically portrayed through various examples of eye-mutilation imagery. The hallucinogenic power of Surrealism is another attribute shared by the works of Miró and Hinojosa. Miró maintained that his hallucinations were caused through exhaustion or exaltation, but most memorably through hunger, and that his only 'food' was the surrealist poetry that he read.[40] For Hinojosa, his poetry reveals a number of naturally occurring substances that intoxicate his images – in this case, the air and tiredness. Here, the traveller's vision undergoes a process of distortion, caused initially by the jagged air and the morning mist, before his tiredness takes control:

> La niebla deshojaba las perspectivas con un rumor desorientado y mi cansancio llegó al límite al verme rodeado de ardillas que con sus ardides me impedían asomarme a los balcones de la calle empinada con dirección al Vaticano.

> [The mist pulled the leaves off the perspectives with a disorientated murmur and my tiredness reached the point that I saw myself surrounded by squirrels who, with their tricks, prevented me from coming out on to the balconies overlooking the steep street towards the Vatican.]

Miró's pictures are frequently populated with animals engaged in childlike antics, such as the playful squirrels here in Hinojosa's world. Childlike humour is a characteristic of both Miró and Hinojosa's surrealist adventures but, as the target of comedy becomes more apparent, their paths start to diverge. Generally, in Surrealism there is a strong element of anticlericalism – a theme epitomised in that well-known photograph of Benjamin Péret insulting a priest. Miró, however, was less concerned with ridiculing religion and seemingly more at ease with his spiritual roots. One critic notes that 'Miró's personal religion was comparable to a kind of peasant syncretism: a mixture of devout Christianity (Catholicism), animism or pantheism in regard to nature, and an identification as well to cosmic forces.'[41] In the case of Hinojosa, and in particular in *La Flor de California*, there is an anti-religious presence, which takes a particularly Catholic slant, as the following sentence reveals: 'El Papa me recibió en pijama y santificó todas las fiestas algo extrañado de ver mi piel rosada' [The Pope received me in his pyjamas and sanctified all the festivities, finding it somewhat strange to see my pink skin]. This iconoclastic humour is followed by a couple of seemingly unrelated questions. The reader shares in the alienating experience of the traveller's self-doubt when he asks: '¿Qué de particular tenía mi piel rosada? ¿Es que

---

[40] Danto quotes Miró as having remarked that: ' "I was carried away by the new ideas they [the surrealist poets] brought and especially the poetry they discussed. I gorged myself on it all night long." Poetry was all Miró was able to gorge himself on at this time, for he was exceedingly poor, and so hungry that he was subject to hallucinations.' Danto, 141–2. See also Dupin, 162.

[41] Rowell, 3.

la araña se descuelga del cielo y pica en cualquier parte?' [What was so strange about my pink skin? Is it that the spider lowers itself from the sky and nibbles on whatever part?] The uncomfortable scene can easily be pictured of the Pope and the traveller looking at one another with an air of disbelief. The simple linguistic device of introducing questions within the text forces the reader to engage more directly with the scene. What is actually being said by the content of these questions is of secondary importance to the effect they produce.

In trying to make sense of this scene, the reader may feel the need to employ a psychoanalytical reading of this oneiric text and its component dream symbols. The obvious Freudian interpretation to make would be to translate the spider as a psychoanalytical symbol for the female genitalia, a reading that would link this 'Freudian' spider back to the impregnating of the Mother earth at the beginning of the text. However, the temptation to decode all such images in Surrealism should be avoided, as Miró himself has argued on occasions. Surrealism's relationship with psychoanalysis is more problematic than is often assumed. Rather than adhering to every psychoanalytical dictate Surrealism takes and adapts selected elements of the theory. To apply the decoding mechanism of Freudian dream-analysis to surrealist manifestations will inevitably lead to a misinterpretation of the text/painting. Resisting the desire to look for symbolic function, the reference to the spider here simply brings the flow of language back to images associated with the natural world. Insects appear in a number of surrealist manifestations with differing effects. Miró's own fascination with insect-like creatures in his paintings was simply for the emotion of disgust they can provoke from the viewer.

The text makes explicit the return to the natural world in the following sentence. The images reflect upon the earlier description of the trees, the wandering traveller, and the interlocking edges in the natural world. Like Miró's geometrical forms, upon which paintings such as the *Tilled Field* and *Harlequin's Carnival* are structured, the world of Hinojosa's text here is one of angles and lines:

> Perdido en este bosque de ángulos rectos tropecé con la bisectriz olvidada que me condujo entre voces amigas a la cumbre del Mont Blanc desde donde volaron mis cabezas en varias direcciones disfrazadas de buenas palabras para convencer a los murciélagos de la conveniencia de que hablasen el esperanto o cualquier otro lengua parecida.

> [Lost in this forest of right angles I bumped into the forgotten bisector that conducted me between friendly voices to the summit of Mont Blanc from where my heads flew in a number of directions disguised as good words in order to convince the bats that it would be useful if they spoke Esperanto or whatever other similar language.]

The bisector, a line that cuts a right-angle in two, is a recognisable geometrical concept, but here it is made to perform a different function. This forgotten bisector becomes a guiding path for the lost traveller. In this scene, the world described takes on the atmosphere of a fairytale. The genre of fairytales, particularly distorted fairytales, is frequently used by surrealist explorers. Such a fairytale land is often evoked by Miró, along with other childlike concerns such as the animals already noted, as a means for uncovering a more menacing view of the world.[42] In Hinojosa's world there is the sinister feeling of being lost in the woods, which is contrasted with the optimism of escape. The initial sense of alienation is lifted by reference to friendly voices and by giving the reader a familiar geographical point of reference, Mont Blanc. At this point in the text, Hinojosa also addresses more philosophical problems of communication between languages. This is a recurring theme in some of the other the oneiric texts – in 'Oneiric Text IV', for example, the poet-protagonist expresses a desire for a universal language through a modernisation of the Tower of Babel myth. In contrast to the frustration expressed by Hinojosa, for Miró, the potential for additional meaning across different languages is seen as liberating rather than restrictive. Miró has spoken of his thought processes in poetry as well as in painting, as being formulated instinctively in French rather than in his native Catalan.[43]

The text is edging towards its conclusion in an image of quite explicit sexualised content: 'La ciudad disparó sus calles en el vacío en apoteosis final mientras dos verdaderos enamorados se cobijaban bajo la parra moscatel unidos por un beso condensado en éxtasis' [In a final apotheosis the city shot its streets into the void while two real lovers took shelter under the muscatel vine joined by a kiss condensed in ecstacy]. The reference to these lovers as being 'real' lovers implies that the city shooting its streets into the void can be seen as unreal or metaphorical lovers. The use of 'apotheosis' suggests a climactic experience with the conjoining, religious implication of mystical sensuality. However, the fact that the city is the personified object of this heightened experience brings a sense of the everyday to the scene, which denies religion its mysterious and mystical power. This description overlaps with the next erotic image where both pairs of lovers come together and the personal and the universal mix: 'Los enamorados transcribían exactamente las palpitaciones lunares y siempre que comenzaban a contar no pasaban del uno' [The lovers exactly transcribed the lunar palpitations and whenever they began to count they didn't get past the number one]. These images used by Hinojosa bring together two of Miró's underlying concerns with sexuality and the cosmic world. There is, however, one important difference between the poet's and painter's approach in this respect. One critic has noted how 'Miró's

[42] For a discussion of the use of fairytales in Surrealism with particular reference to Miró and poetry, see Adamowicz, 'Writing Miró: Blue Tales for Adults', *New Comparison* (Lancaster), 31 (Spring 2001), 89–111.

[43] See the interview, 'Alcanzar el máximo de pureza' in Georges Raillard's *Conversaciones con Miró* (Barcelona: Granica Editor S.A., 1978), 89–106 (99–100).

canvases from the mid-1920s breathe a guiltless eroticism, with scenes of coupling and frank depictions of sexual organs'.[44] This 'guiltless eroticism' in Miró can be discerned through a notable lack of specific religious reference in his paintings – as has been noted, Miró's personal spirituality was reconciled through a type of pantheism. For Hinojosa, on the other hand, his depictions of eroticism tend to be framed within the context of explicit blasphemy, and unconsciously or not, point to his underlying Catholic guilt. Correspondingly, his portrayals of sexual activity or carnal desire never reach fulfilment.

After the explicit but frustrated depiction of metaphorical intercourse in the previous images, a final image of death brings this text to its close. This image can be read as both a confession of the poet's Catholic guilt as well as evoking the idea of the *petit mort* following the sexual adventures of the lovers. 'Aquella mañana de bramidos encandiló mis oídos, que se rindieron a la menor indicación del silencio a la muerte' [That morning of roars bewildered my ears, which surrendered themselves to the slightest indication of silence to death]. This concluding image to the text brings a return to morning, to light, the ending of dreams and the silencing of the nocturnal world of surrealist exploration. The reader is returned full-circle to the opening depiction of this text – where the narrator spoke of being tormented by the lights – and the whole reading–visualising process can begin again. This circularity highlights the Miróesque structure to Hinojosa's text when we consider Miró's own feelings about his work: 'In my paintings, there is a kind of circularity system. If even one form is out of place, the circulation system stops, the balance is broken.'[45]

Having examined the poetic force steering both Miró and Hinojosa's manifestations of Surrealism, one striking characteristic is not only the similarity in technique but the differences of individual expression. The question of individual expression within the wider concerns of the surrealist revolt opens up further issues related to the political orientation of Surrealism and of the path that Surrealism followed (for a while) with the communist party. This need to give voice to the personal as well as the collective is evident in the introductory example taken from that double-spread of *La Révolution surréaliste*. These pages bring together an international community within an interdisciplinary microcosm, and yet the very personal attributes of the individual activists are still very much apparent. As well as the problematic relationship between Surrealism and Marxist politics there is an equally complicated link with psychoanalysis. Dreams are valued by the whole variety of Surrealist explorers for their collective individuality: we all know what it is to dream and yet dreams, by their very nature, are exclusively personal. Rather than seeking to decode dreams, Surrealism celebrates the creative potential they offer

---

44  Jennifer Mundy, 'Letters of *Desire*' in Mundy (ed.), 2001, 10–53 (33–4).
45  Rowell, 249.

the individual poet or artist and for the response they provoke from the reader or spectator. The dynamism, sensory disarrangement, fluidification and mental exploration that Moreno Villa feels in response to both Miró's and Hinojosa's work are all part of this creative process. In summing up his response, Moreno Villa describes the whole pictorial-poetic experience as one that takes him on a type of visual voyage. He writes: 'Cada cuadro y cada narración de esos vuestros es, pues, un delicioso viaje imaginativo' [Each painting and each narrative of yours is, well, a delicious imaginary journey].

# 3

# Juan Larrea and The Film Buñuel Did Not Make

## ROBERT GURNEY

In 1948, following a private showing of *Un Chien andalou* [*An Andalusian Dog*] in his house in Mexico City, Buñuel invited the Spanish poet Juan Larrea to write a surrealistic film script based on a 300–400 page novel, *Ilegible, hijo de flauta*, [*Illegible, Son of Flute*], which Larrea had begun in 1927–8 and which was lost in his sister's country house in Vallecas, near Madrid, during the Spanish Civil War. The script falls into three main parts: (1) The Old World, which is in decay, where the main address is Desengaño 27 [Disillusionment 27], an apparent reference to their disappointment with their fellow poets of the Spanish Generation of '27; (2) The Journey, characterised by rail and sea disasters, and (3) The New World, where miraculous things take place. Buñuel was unable to make the film. He tried again in 1957, asking Larrea to write some more scenes, which Larrea did, helped by his daughter, Luciana Larrea. Buñuel objected to a crowd scene, a gathering of Jehovah's Witnesses in a large stadium, presumably because the special effects required would have taken too much time and money. Buñuel clearly could not afford to pay thousands of extras, so trick photography – borrowing shots from a football match, for example – would have been needed, even if he had been able to work out a way of making an establishing shot (a wide angle shot encompassing the entire scene, the crowd plus the two protagonists crossing the arena, to be shot from above or from ground level and absolutely essential to build the mood or atmosphere). There was clearly no way of avoiding this shot in a professionally made film and, unfortunately, no way of achieving it easily and cheaply. It is possible, too, that Buñuel, in the wake of the McCarthyite era, of which, it can be argued, he had, perhaps, at MOMA, been an early victim, felt that it was better to let sleeping dogs lie and not include what might be taken as a reference to the witch-hunts of McCarthyism (the crowd shouts 'Kill them', as Avendaño and Ilegible cross the arena). Larrea dug his heels in and the project foundered.

In 1963 Buñuel 'returned to the charge' with a plan to film *Ilegible* together with, possibly, Jensen's *La Gradiva*, Fuentes' *Aura* and Cortázar's *Las Ménades*. Larrea agreed that Buñuel could cut the 1957 script down considerably, which would, no doubt, have meant removing some or all of the eight scenes added in 1957. The project foundered on the question of finance and censorship. In 1980, with Buñuel's agreement to do what he liked with the script, Larrea published in *Vuelta* a version that is longer than that of 1948 but a little shorter than that of 1957.[1] The key dates, then, in the history of this unrealised film, are 1927–8, 1948, 1957, 1963 and 1980.

At no point in the interviews I had with him in Córdoba, Argentina, in 1972, did Larrea link Avendaño with Buñuel, although, as will be seen, he accepted some similarity between himself and Ilegible. Francisco de Avendaño's play *Comedia Florisea* (1551) centres on a pair of characters, Muerto [Dead Man], a victim of misfortune, and Floriseo, a victim of unrequited love, who decide to commit suicide but who are mocked by a shepherd before they can carry out their plan. Avendaño may be a reference to this Golden Age play, although Larrea did not mention it. Ilegible and Avendaño owe more to Don Quijote and Sancho Panza. The script ends with Ilegible pointing at what turns out to be a mirage – a huge female figure, like an immense Venus de Milo or the Statue of Liberty – which, on closer inspection, is just a windmill: 'Pero al mirar de nuevo hacia el sol ya no se ve la mujer sino un molino de grandes aspas semejante a los famosos de la Mancha' [But on looking again towards the sun a women is no longer seen but a windmill with great sails similar to the famous ones of la Mancha].

The aim of this chapter is to suggest possible origins of *Ilegible, hijo de flauta*. It will consider the concept of transformation, which Larrea gleaned from Arabic literature and other sources, and seek to establish that the transformations and metamorphoses that Larrea and Buñuel cultivated in this unrealised screen play, or cinematic story ('relato fílmico', as Larrea described it in *Vuelta*), have their origins in Larrea's complex poetry and in his highly surrealist imagination, evidence of which can be found in an early unpublished story that Larrea called, in Basque, *Jaungoikua* [*God, Lord of the Heights*]. The main sources of information are Larrea's quite detailed testimony relating to *Ilegible, hijo de flauta*, given in the course of thirty-five interviews (unpublished), which he granted me at his home and his university office in 1972, and a literary correspondence (also mainly unpublished) I had with him between 1969 and 1978.

Buñuel had a high regard for Larrea's poetry. For Buñuel, writing to José (Pepín) Bello Lasiera in 1928, he was *number one*. Having dismissed Lorca and Alberti, he writes:

> Nuestros poetas exquisitos, de elite antipopulachera, son: Larrea, el primero; Garfias (lástima de su limitación y escasez de imaginación, sus

---

[1] *Vuelta* (Mexico) (Feb.–Mar. 1980), 4–13 and 18–24. Some of the details in this paragraph derive from Larrea's article, '*Ilegible, hijo de flauta*: complementos circunstanciales', in *Vuelta* (Mar. 1980, 24–5).

funciones serían divinas si sólo tuviera la mitad de fantasía de Federico);
Huidobro; a veces el histrión de Gerardo Diego;[2]

[Our exquisite poets, forming an elite that rejects writing for the masses,
are: Larrea, whom I place first; Garfias (pity about his limited and meagre
imagination, his functions would be divine if only he had half of Federico's
imagination); Huidobro; occasionally our play-actor Gerardo Diego;]

The two poets listed without reservation are Larrea and Huidobro. Buñuel
puts them in an élite that does not pander to the lower tastes of the public,
revealing that at that time he shared a belief that art and literature form the
space where artists and intellectuals communicate. It was their domain.
Sánchez Vidal has suggested that Buñuel had been absorbing Larrea's images
as early as 1919.[3] When Larrea and Buñuel discussed the possibility of making of a film together in 1948, in Mexico City, they agreed that they had the
same 'façon d'imaginer', or ways of imagining.

For example, when one places the cow-in-the-bed scene in Buñuel's *L'Âge
d'or* [*The Golden Age*] (1930) alongside Larrea's 1919 image of an embalmed
ox in his bedroom frightening away the hours, which are like flies, with its
tail, one can see a possible connection:

> En mi cuarto
>    un buey embalsamado
>       se espantaba las horas con el rabo
>             '*Cosmopolitano*'[4]

[2] Ian Gibson, *Lorca–Dalí. El Amor que no pudo ser* (Barcelona: Plaza y Janés Editores, 1999), 215.

[3] A. Sánchez Vidal, 'Juan Larrea y Luis Buñuel: Convergencias y divergencias en torno a *Ilegible, hijo de flauta*', in *Al Amor de Larrea*, ed. J.M. Diaz de Guereñu (Valencia: Pre-Textos, 1985), 121–44. *Actas de las Primeras Jornadas Internacionales Juan Larrea* (San Sebastian and Bilbao, July 1984). In the same book see also R. Gurney, 'Larrea y la poesía francesa anterior al surrealismo (de Nerval à Valéry)', 11–38.

[4] J. Larrea, *Versión celeste* (Barcelona: Barral Editores, 1970), 61. See also the analysis of *Cosmopolitano* and its connections with Huidobro's *Ecuatorial* in R. Gurney, *La poesía de Juan Larrea* (Lejona, Bilbao: Servicio Editorial / Argitarapen Zerbitzua, Universidad del País Vasco / Euskal Herriko Unibertsitatea, 1985), 131–64. A more recent edition of Larrea's poetry is J. Larrea, *Versión celeste* (Madrid: Cátedra, 1989). The present paper is the beginning of a much-delayed response to S. Laemmel-Serrano, *Juan Larrea ou Le suicide en poésie* (Berne: Peter Lang, 1995). A useful introduction to the topic is D. Bary, '*Ilegible, hijo de flauta*: guión cinematográfico de Juan Larrea y Luis Buñuel', in his *Nuevos Estudios sobre Huidobro y Larrea* (Valencia: Pre-Textos, 1984), 167–77. Also relevant are D. Bary, *Larrea, Poesía y Transfiguración* (Madrid: Editorial Planeta / Universidad Complutense, 1976) and J.M. Diaz de Guereñu, *La poesía de Juan Larrea. Creación y sentido* (San Sebastián: Cuadernos Universitarios Mundaiz, 1988). For an introduction to the death-of-the-self phenomenon in Western culture, see A. Sánchez-Vidal, 'Extrañamiento e Identidad de "Su Majestad el Yo" al 'Extasis de los objetos' ", in V. García de la Concha, *El Surrealismo* (Madrid: Taurus, 1982), 50–73. Also relevant is

> [In my room
>         an embalmed ox
>                 frightened away the hours with its tail]
>                                 [*Cosmopolitan*]

What does Larrea's image mean? During the 1972 Córdoba interviews he said that he did not mean anything in his poetry and he spoke of feelings rather than thoughts. This was taken to suggest that he did not mean just one thing but presented an image that can have a different meaning for each reader. It is also a reference – Larrea used words very carefully – to the demise of the bourgeois self, which is a major theme in his poetry and in *Ilegible*. When, aligning himself with Rimbaud, he told me in Interview 2, 8 July 1972, 'Escribía a lo *Bateau Ivre* . . . No quiero decir nada en mi poesía' [I was writing in a *Bateau Ivre* style . . . I do not mean anything in my poetry], the emphasis, I felt, in English, would have been upon the 'I'. The meaning is coming from somewhere else. He was in the tradition of the inspired poet. His images first flowed automatically but were then worked on by a subtle intelligence, a controlled automatism. The original meaning, however, flowed from a dimension that was similar to that where Jung posited a collective unconscious and which was inspired, to Larrea's mind, by a higher intelligence. 'Alguien nos toca' [Someone is playing us], he said to the late writer José Manuel Castañón, as the latter told me, when we stood next to Antonio Machado's grave during a commemorative ceremony in Collioure Cemetery, France, on 18 December 1999.

Buñuel used a real cow for his scene. A live one, rather than a stuffed one, was, presumably, the only one available. Larrea uses 'un buey', a castrated ox, a symbol of great strength in the Basque Country, where there is a competition called 'los bueyes', a trial of strength, in which oxen drag giant stones along behind them with ropes. Yet Larrea's ox is dead. An ox can also suggest dumbness in Spanish – 'habló el buey y dijo mu' [when the ox opened its mouth, it spoke nonsense] – which suggests a rejection by Larrea, in his use of the image of an ox, of what he perceived as the moribund, cliché-ridden *modernismo* being written in Spanish poetry, by himself and others, prior to his intense *ultraísta–creacionista* breakout of 1919. The ox, flicking its tail mechanically, can be taken as a metaphor for the state of Larrea's lyrical activity, heavy with fatigue, prior to his contact, in May 1919, with Huidobro's *creacionismo*. The verb is in the past tense: 'un buey . . . *se espantaba* las horas con el rabo' [An

*Luis Buñuel. Obra literaria*, Introducción y notas de Agustín Sánchez Vidal (Zaragoza: Ediciones de Heraldo de Aragón, 1982), *Ilegible, hijo de flauta*, 286–91. On Larrea's Surrealism, see R. Gurney, 'Juan Larrea, Unrecognised Father of Spanish Surrealism?', *Proceedings of the First Conference of Hispanists in Poytechnics and Other Colleges*, ed. R. Gurney (London: Middlesex Polytechnic/Instituto de España, 1978), 21–36. For a recent overview of Larrea's life and work, see M.-F. Iglesia Lesteiro, *Juan Larrea. Vida y poesía* (Bilbao: Bilbao-Vizcaya Kutxa, 1997).

ox *frightened* away the hours with its tail]. Rubén Darío had died in 1916. The ox has had embalming fluid put into its veins, a technique used in preparing the dead for burial. It has been mummified, like an exhibit in a natural history museum. Yet this stuffed ox is not completely dead, for its tail is still moving, still able to flick its tail at flies. It still has this residual nervous reaction and is able to pass the time flicking at the hours that congregate in a circle on its rear end. The suggestion of a clock's pendulum, which, in its movement, resembles a flicking tail, is also made. A Freudian interpretation would refer to onanism, and to a feeling of great heaviness and to a feeling of exasperation at the passing of time, alleviated by the movement of the tail ('rabo' also has a vulgar meaning in Spanish). The overriding feeling, however, is one of discomfort, of something being completely wrong. An ox should not be in a bedroom. The room is too small for such a creature. This is how Larrea felt in 1919. He had a room in the family home in the centre of Bilbao, where he used to go to get away from the rest of the family in order to write. He was going nowhere. He was 24 and his family were still frustrating his attempts to form heterosexual relationships. He felt that he was hardly alive. Buñuel's cow in the bed has been interpreted as a reference to the police ('une vache' = 'un agent de police'):[5] 'The cow suggests both the police, who are arresting the hero, and her mother,' according to Durgnat.[6] The feeling behind the image, though, is more one of frustration, of something that it is not at all right, something grotesque. Larrea described the grotesqueness of his life in 1919 in terms of an ox in his bedroom. That was his language. That was how he communicated. Buñuel, feeding on this material, injects it, transformed, into his film in order to describe frustration. If Sánchez-Vidal is right, Buñuel was listening to Larrea's language at an early stage in his development.

The impact of Larrea's 1919 image in 'Evasión' [Breakout]

> Acabo de desorbitar
> al cíclope solar[7]
>
> [I have just gouged out
> the solar cyclops' eye]

upon the opening of Buñuel's *Un Chien andalou* [*An Andalusian Dog*] has been noted by critics, by Aranda (1975), for example: 'In fact the image of the cut eye dates as far back as a poem by Larrea of 1918'.[8] The poem was written in May 1919, Larrea told me in Córdoba. It opens with a reference to Ulysses' escape from a cave by blinding the one-eyed giant Polyphemus,

[5] G. Sandry and M. Carrère, *Dictionnaire de l'argot moderne*, cinquième édition (Paris: Au Quais de Paris, Editions du Dauphin, 1957).

[6] R. Durgnat, *Luis Buñuel* (Berkeley: University of California Press 1977), 41.

[7] *Versión celeste*, 49.

[8] F. Aranda, *Luis Buñuel: A Critical Biography* (London: Secker and Warburg, 1975), 67.

whose eye is compared with the sun. Larrea was announcing his intention to
write a poetry of the imagination, an imagined poetry, one which did not
describe the outside world, when he put out the sun's light. The moon is cut
into by a cloud and moonlight begins to be obscured, just before the eyeball
is sliced in *Un Chien andalou*.

In an unpublished essay, Eduardo Fermín Partido (1993) reminds us that
the image of the lacerated eye became a commonplace in Spanish Surrealism.
Starting with Larrea in 1919 it was repeated by Hinojosa, Lorca, Maruja
Mallo, Dalí, Espinosa and Alfonso Ponce de León. Fermín also recalls that
Guillermo de Torre, in his *Historia de las literaturas de vanguardia* [*History
of Avant-Garde Literatures*] (1974), had traced the image back to that of a
child with its cheek torn out by a shaving knife and to that of a face bleeding
as a result of a wound by a penknife in *Les Chants de Maldoror* [*The Songs
of Maldoror*] by Isidore Ducasse, 'le comte de Lautréamont', the 'father of
Surrealism'. It should not be forgotten, however, that Homer, whose story of
Ulysses and Polyphemus inspired Larrea, had described the gouging out of
the cyclops' eye and that Góngora associated the eye of Polyphemus with the
sun:

> de un ojo ilustra el orbe de su frente
> Emulo casi del mayor lucero
>
> [he lights the orb of his forehead with an eye
> That almost emulates the greatest star]
>
> 'La fábula de Polífemo y Galetea'
>
> [The Fable of Polyphemus and Galatea][9]

How does one respond to Buñuel's letter to Pepín Bello of 1928 in which
he states Larrea was the *first*? Does one take it at face value or does one consider the context? At the time Buñuel was annoyed with Lorca. He was trying
to get Lorca away from Dalí. It is possible, in the light of this, that Buñuel
was simply trying to annoy Lorca and others. It is also possible that he
believed what he was writing. He was not the only one to respond to Larrea
in this way. Rafael Alberti, in a letter to Gerardo Diego of 10 March 1932,
used similar words: 'Larrea, lo mejor. Muchos poemas desconocidos para mí.

---

[9] E. Fermín Partido, 'Juan Larrea en Luis Buñuel: símbolo y "horizonte poético" en
*Ilegible, hijo de flauta* y *Un Chien andalou*', unpublished doctoral cycle paper
(Universidad Autónoma de Barcelona, 1993). See also the destroyed eye in Victor Brauner,
*Self-Portrait*, oil, 1937 and the dagger in the eye in Picasso's *Sketch with pen*, 4 June 1938,
in J. Larrea, *Del surrealismo a Machupicchu* (México: Editorial Joaquín Mortiz, 1967), 48.
Gregorio San Juan, in a personal communication, 2001, feels there is a connection between
the putting out of the solar cyclops' eye with a rejection of the father by Larrea. See also
Luis de Góngora, *Antología poética*, ed. Antonio Carreira (Castalia, 1985), 172.

Lo mejor' [The best, Larrea. Many poems unknown to me. The best]. He was referring to Larrea's poems in Diego's 1932 anthology.[10]

During the interviews I had with him on Buñuel, Larrea made the statement: 'Chacun à son language' [Each person has his or her own language]. In a letter to Gerardo Diego he wrote that, although he could not understand all of Huidobro's poetry, he could *feel* it, adding that comprehension was not necessary for the aesthetic sensation.[11] Larrea could respond to Huidobro's image-based language and, in turn, Buñuel could read both Huidobro's and Larrea's. There were currents of images flowing between Huidobro and Larrea and, it seems, between Huidobro and Larrea and Buñuel. Buñuel was sensitive to Larrea's images between 1919 and 1928. The *Ilegible* project, which was in Buñuel's thoughts over at least a fifteen-year period, from 1948 until 1963, indicates that, at a later stage, Larrea's work was again in his thoughts. The film *La Voie Lactée* [*The Milky Way*] (1969), for example, which Larrea disliked intensely, owed much to Larrea's ideas.

J.F. Aranda, in a letter he wrote to me on the 18 February 1985, made a number of interesting points:

> But, of course, Buñuel wanted desperately to film *Ilegible, hijo de flauta* during 15 years. If he did not, he told me, it was due to Larrea's lack of ductility in conforming himself to the demands of a film script. The evolution of their discussion and the very slow replies of Larrea can be followed partially in Larrea's letters to C.B. Morris (*Surrealism and Spain*) and my own book, *Os poemas de Luis Buñuel*.
>
> It is clear that Buñuel wanted to film *Ilegible* for these obvious reasons: a) because it is a very good film subject (I suppose you know it; it is now published, unabridged, in Spain, Mexico and France.) b) because it was the only film script dealing with the Spanish Civil War which is surrealistic. c) because he liked Larrea and wanted to pay him a homage. I have read letters of Buñuel to his family in 1947–48 saying this.

Elsewhere in the letter Aranda stated that:

> Buñuel admired Larrea for his honesty and integrity, which were things he most admired in people, and for his republican position and the important activity of Larrea as a leader of the Spanish exiled in Mexico. Buñuel was politically very attached to them.

---

[10] G. Morelli, 'Recepción de la antología *Poesía española* de Gerardo Diego en España (y en Italia)', in *Gerardo Diego y la Vanguardia Hispánica*, ed. José Luis Bernal (Universidad de Extremadura: Servicio de Publicaciones, 1993), 67. Actas del Congreso Internacional *Iberoamérica y España en la Génesis de la Vanguardia Hispánica* (*El modelo vanguardista de Gerardo Diego*) (Cáceres: Universidad de Extremadura, 1993).

[11] *Juan Larrea: Cartas a Gerardo Diego, 1916–1980*, Edición a cargo de E. Cordero de Ciria y J.M. Diaz de Guereñu (San Sebastián: Cuadernos Universitarios Mundaiz, 1986), 93.

Aranda also argued that Buñuel considered Larrea to be a surrealist. Referring
to what he calls Larrea's 'very bad reputation among the fanatical surrealists',
he writes:

> They [the fanatics] say he never was one, or that he was a 'traitor'. However,
> it is obvious that Buñuel (who was a very orthodox surrealist and very faith-
> ful to Breton's main directions) did not think so.

Aranda goes on to explain that the surrealists' aversion to Larrea derived from
Larrea's attacks on Breton and his 'subconscious Basque mysticism'. The latter, Aranda argued, was not a problem for Buñuel who had said, 'after all there
is not so much difference between religious and unreligious people'. Aranda
added:

> [. . .] both are victims of their manias and obsessions, he thought, amused,
> as a scientific observer . . . There was no friction of this kind between them.

Regarding Buñuel's statement that for him Larrea was 'el primero', he writes:

> Buñuel wrote he was *the first*. That means: the best, the most intelligent, but
> also the first serious surrealist poet. His possible rivals were beaten, accord-
> ing to Buñuel, because Hinojosa was not good enough and García Lorca not
> surrealist enough. At that time Buñuel was not orthodox enough in
> Surrealism to appreciate Larrea's 'deficiencies'. Because, as you will agree,
> all the poetry of Larrea has a proportion of Creationism, anyway.

Aranda was echoing in this last point, concerning Larrea's Creationism, an
argument put to him in a letter by the author of this chapter. Regarding the
possibility of Larrea having a later influence on Buñuel he writes:

> As for Buñuel, well yes. I do not think that Larrea had any influence on him
> *after 1928*.

And:

> No, Larrea was not 'responsible for a change in Buñuel in Mexico' as you
> suggest. Buñuel *did not* change. He, as a film author, introduced along his
> Mexican career his own themes little by little, as he was gaining authority
> among Mexican film producers, as an efficient and quick professional.

Aranda admitted that there might be a small influence of Larrea and Bergamín
in *The Exterminating Angel*, as there was, he argued, of Lorca in *Simón del
desierto* [*Simon of the Desert*], but they were 'rather remote influences'.
Larrea, it should be noted, was involved in *Los olvidados* [*The Forgotten
Ones*], to an extent that has not been publicly acknowledged.

Sánchez Vidal, on the other hand, perceives an influence of Larrea, particularly of *Ilegible, hijo de flauta*, on Buñuel's post-1948 work:

> [. . .] the great influence of *Ilegible* which should not be understated in the films of Buñuel and which proves to be the loose or itinerant structure which provides the backbone of the trilogy of his maturity: *La Voie lactée*, *Le Charme discret de la bourgeoisie*, and *Le Fantôme de la Liberté*. Great celebration of chance, mystery and freedom, this triptych reintroduces the flow of poetry of *Un Chien andalou* in order to explore more deeply themes already introduced in his first film, and in *L'Age d'or*, *El ángel exterminador* and *Simón del desierto* by means of an expository system of great rigour and (at the same time) freedom only achievable in the light of the picaresque (*Gil Blas*), the *Manuscript found in Saragossa* (book by Potocki and film by Has), *Le coeur du mystère*, by Caillois, and of course, *Ilegible, hijo de flauta*.[12]

The distant origin of the poetic film script *Ilegible, hijo de flauta* lies in Arabic literature. Central to *A Thousand and One Nights* is the concept of transformation. Human beings turn into animals and vice versa. People become cats and mules. They mutate. Wondrous things happen suddenly by magic. In 'The Fisherman and the Jinee', one of the *Arabian Nights* tales, a sorceress turns people into fish and a city into a lake. Later, again by magic, the fish become people and the lake a noisy city again. In 'Julmar the Mermaid and her Son Badar Basim' a queen is transformed into a white bird. In the same story a sorceress sows seeds, which miraculously become wheat, instantly, as happens at the end of *Ilegible*, when the protagonists cast seed as if they are feeding birds.[13] Pedro Calderón de la Barca's play *La vida es sueño* [*Life is a Dream*] (1636) is another source. Among the characters who emerge from a box Ilegible and Avendaño find on the beach in the New World are Basilio, Segismundo in chains, Estrella, etc., 'Todos ellos con las cuencas de los ojos vacías' [All of them with their eye-sockets empty]. At the heart of the protagonists' quest in *Ilegible* there is a female figure who mutates, becomes old, becomes lifeless, a statue, before becoming young again. The idea of transformation is central to *Ilegible*. And it is central to a surreal short story that Larrea wrote in 1915 or 1916. The story bears the title 'God'. Written in Spanish, it had a Basque title, *Jaungoikoa*. Larrea recalled the story during the interviews in Córdoba, Argentina, in 1972. Larrea dated another tale, which he felt was prophetic, the 'Gerardo Diego story', as he called it, in which the fortunes of two characters are transformed and reversed, to 1915–16, and appeared

---

[12] *Al Amor de Larrea*, 137. Translations are mine unless otherwise stated.
[13] R. Burton (trans.), *Arabian Nights: A Selection* (Harmondsworth: Penguin Books, 1997). Also consulted: N.J. Dawood, *Tales from the Thousand and One Nights* (Harmondsworth: Penguin Books, 1973).

to imply that both stories belong to that period. *Jaungoikoa* was a story 'avec un horizon biblique' [with a biblical framework], Larrea stated (French was the main language of our conversations in Argentina). The story revolved around a character called 'Jaungoikoa', which means *God* in Basque, or, more precisely, *The Lord on High*, 'Jaun' meaning *Lord* (like a count or marquis) and 'goiko' *in the sky, in heaven, on high* or *in the highest*. The 'a' at the end of the word is the article. It had a Middle Eastern setting, which may have been Palestine (Larrea could not remember exactly). It centred on a man who was very fat. Larrea had known a villager in those days who drove into Bilbao in a horse and cart and whom the people called 'Jaungoikoa'. To a child's eye, no doubt, the obese peasant on the cart would have seemed high up.

There was a great famine in the country. People began to look around for food. They began to entertain thoughts of eating the fat man. 'Jaungoikoa', God, was very fat. They began to chase him. The only solution he could think of to save himself was to jump into a deep ravine. Down and down he rolled but he was not killed: his fat saved him. When he arrived at the bottom of the ravine, he looked up and saw his pursuers above him, like ants. And he was down there. There was nothing in there to eat, just grass. He began to grow very thin. He saw a cave entrance but it was too narrow. He sensed, however, that there were things in there to eat. He kept on losing weight until he could squeeze through the opening. He finally got into the cave, which, once he was inside, he saw was an Aladdin's cave of wonderful things to eat. He ate everything but then became so fat that he could not get out. Even if he had been able to get out, he would not have managed to climb back up the side of the ravine. While he was in there, he found another hole at the back of the cave but in order to get through he had to lose weight again, which he did. In there he found 'des choses inimaginables' [things beyond his wildest dreams], including 'de la viande de sirène' [manatee meat]. He ate and he ate. He ate everything up and grew very fat. He was a revolting figure. He even ate his own excrement. He grew so fat he rose like a balloon up to the roof of the cave. In the roof there was a hole and through this hole came light and the sound of music – sounds of marvellous things. And he stayed like that, as if for ever, as if almost in heaven but not able to enter. He could hear celestial things but he stayed like that for ever.

When asked what happened to Jaungoikoa, Larrea replied, 'Oh, he probably died'. Musing on the phenomenon of a balloon heading off towards the ceiling, he added, 'The reader must decide for himself what happened to him.' He went on, 'Jaungoikoa, a reference to God, a bit religious, but more ironic. He was called Jaungoikoa, God, out of irony. He was the opposite of God, that fat fellow in Bilbao. He absolutely filled the cart. Goodness knows how he got in and out of it. "Ahí pasa Jaungoikoa" [There goes God], we used to shout and sing.' The use of 'we' suggests Jaungoikoa's procession into Bilbao took place when Larrea was a child, in the years at the turn of the century, 1903–5, perhaps.

At this point in the interview, the thirtieth, the idea was put to Larrea that a similar process of transformation is to be seen in *Ilegible*. Just as Jaungoikoa changes shape, becomes thin, then fat, then thin, then fat again, so the female figure Ilegible and Avendaño pursue, the object of their desire, changes: she goes from beautiful to old, back to desirable and then, in the New World, to inspiring. Ilegible himself undergoes transformations too, usually related to the female figure's mutations. She kisses him passionately at the moment of a shipwreck, having been, until then, a beautiful but lifeless figure thrown up by the sea. As a result, white feathers are seen emerging from his hands. The question was put to Larrea, bluntly, 'Did she represent Spain?' Larrea replied that he had not thought of Spain. He explained that *Ilegible* was 'comme un rêve' [like a dream]; it was 'une oeuvre poétique' [a poetic work]. 'It is like life', he continued, 'You find that thing among the Arabs. Transformation. In Arabic literature there are transformations, *A Thousand and One Nights*, for example. Yes, she was "comme la vie" [like life], "une représentation de la Vie" [a representation of Life], "une objectivation féminine"' [a feminine objectivisation]. She represented the way Larrea felt about life and the way life, Life, as he called it, felt about him. If he felt outside or absent from it, on the margins of a meaningful universe, *she* is described as absent. In his poetry, much of which belongs to a period when Larrea felt, to echo Rimbaud, that 'la vraie vie est ailleurs' [true life is elsewhere], particularly before 1929, she is often described as absent. It is when *she* is felt to be absent that strong feelings surface in Larrea's poetry. As Peter Evans states: 'In Lacan's reformulation of Freud, though, desire is caused above all by a lack, an absence of the object of desire' [. . .].[14] Larrea continued, 'She does nothing. She hardly speaks. She does not do anything. She is just there. She is a feminine projection of life, of ideal life, an ideal projection of life. I found her in the depths of myself. She is 'une idée idéale' [an ideal idea]. I found her 'au fond de moi-même' [deep within myself], 'une chose qui sort de temps en temps' [a thing that comes out from time to time].' *Ilegible, hijo de flauta* presents a female figure whose presence and, often, whose absence permeate the *Versión celeste* poems, but who is, as is natural within the context of a screenplay, more tangible than in the poems, although even in them, she is, for the reader, visualisable. In *Ilegible* she appears, as has been noted, in one of her guises as the Statue of Liberty, with the rays of a star radiating out from her head. In psychological terms, she can be linked with his childless aunt, his father's sister, Micaela Larrea Fagoaga, to whom he was lent as a child, from the ages of four to seven, and who remained the focus of his affection even beyond her death, in his arms, in 1925, an event reflected in *Ilegible*. Micaela was Larrea's *qualitative* mother, to use Larrea's term, as opposed to his *quantitative* or biological mother, Felisa Celayeta Larrea, to whom he felt less close.

[14] P.W. Evans, *The Films of Luis Buñuel, Subjectivity and Desire* (Oxford: Clarendon Press, 1975), 103.

At this point the question was put to Larrea, alluding to Jung's theory of archetypes: 'Is she the *anima*?' Larrea replied in the affirmative, although he immediately added, seeming to backtrack slightly, that his interpretation was not the same as Jung's. Elsewhere in the Córdoba interviews Larrea stated that he had deliberately avoided reading Jung in the 1920s, fearing that his work would have too strong an impact upon his inner experience.

Larrea then turned to the Peruvian poet César Vallejo. There was a similar manifestation in a story by Vallejo. Larrea searched for the story in his library but could not, at that moment, lay his hand on it. It was, Larrea said, a true story. In it Vallejo wakes up calling for his sister and he has a vision. There was, as a result of this vision, 'un éclatement de sa personnalité' [his personality burst into life]. It was an experience of feeling intensely alive. Incidentally, Larrea spoke of his experiences, on arriving in Mexico in 1939, as 'un éclatement' [bursting into life]: 'Vallejo sees a cone of shadow and deep within it a naked woman. 'My sister', he calls out. It is the same thing. It is the *Anima Mundi*, 'comme la Vierge' [like the Virgin] but naked, on another level, 'la femme idéale' [the ideal woman]. There was the same way of experiencing reality in Vallejo.'

Larrea was then invited to comment on the image of the moon-maiden who is dawn out of her cave, barefoot, in the long poem '*Cosmopolitano*'. She appears just after an image of an old woman at the very beginning of the poem:

> Mil agostos te he visto, frutecida
> > Ciudad.
> > > Ciudad de hojas caducas
> > > como mujer en rústica.
> y he cedido tu acera a la luna descalza
> cuando con una brizna
> > > un reflector díscolo
> la sacó de la cueva núbil y expatriada.
>
> > Mis alas se otoñaron hace tiempo.[15]

> [A thousand Augusts I have seen you, fruit-laden
> > City.
> > > City of falling leaves
> > > like a paperback peasant woman
> and I have made way on your pavement for the barefoot moon
> when with a filament
> > > a mischievous searchlight
> drew her out of the nubile cave where she was in exile.
> > My wings were tinged with autumn some time ago.]

The image of the moon coming down into the old city of '*Cosmopolitano*' (1919) led Larrea to refer to 'The City of Jerusalem which is like a woman, the wife of "Yahvé", of God, as in the *Song of Songs*. There is the same connection

15 *Versión celeste*, 57.

of Man and Women on an ideal plane.' It has to be remembered, when referring to Larrea's commentary, that in 1972 he was viewing his past work through the prism of a 'vision of a transformed universal consciousness' to use David Bary's phrase (personal communication, 13.02.03). Neverthless, the *Ilegible, hijo de flauta* project evolved in Larrea's mind over a period of time, including the years in exile when his later philosophical ideas were taking shape. Larrea recalled his poem '*Adolescence en soi*' [Growing pain] at this point:

> Mes lèvres n'ont jamais cessé de renaître de leurs cendres
> entre elles se sont glissées quelques veilles d'ardeur
> quelques feuilles quelques fleurs -quelques tombeaux ouverts-
> mais le jour qu'on doit réduire à son plus pur battement
> n'est jamais arrivé
> le jour où elle aurait dû avoir mille raisons
> pour triompher des cris qui poussent au parvis de son nom
> est toujours resté dedans
>
> Pourtant mon silence gardait les formes dociles des maillots roses
> elle n'aurait eu qu'à dire me voici
> front par éclairs trottoir d'ombre me voici
> elle n'aurait pas eu à s'en repentir
> ce fleuve qui coule insensible aux embûches des lauriers
> cherchant une ancre de solitude une épaule gracieuse
> cette eau obligée à serrer ma soif d'airain contre son coeur
> aurait reflété l'iris de son château de charmes
>
> Dans l'intime horizon des heures qu'il faut perdre
> les croupes de mes nuits plus douces que des éléphants fondus
> à tour d'aile orphelines et veuves sans limites
> auraient promené largement ses yeux
>
> Mais elle restée dedans
> dedans
> comme un temps de cerises dans la poitrine gelée du temps
>
> Pourtant j'aurais si bien su amadouer la glace
> rompue au beau milieu du soir par son sourire
> j'aurais tant aimé remplir d'oeillets ses manques de mémoire
> et flotter sur ses yeux mi-tendres mi-verts
> comme une solitude acquise par la voie des airs [16]

[*Growing Pain*

> My lips have never ceased to rise again from their ashes
> between them have slipped some eager sleepless nights
> some leaves some flowers – some open graves –
> but the day which one must reduce down to its purest beating
> the day when she ought to have had a thousand reasons

---

[16] *Versión celeste*, 150.

for gloating over the shouts which spring up on the forecourt of her
    name
has always stayed inside

Still my silence kept the flexible forms of rose-coloured swimsuits
all she had to say was here I am
forehead glittering pavement in the shade here I am
she would have had no reason to rue the day
this river which flows barely perceptibly into the ambushes of the
    laurels
seeking an anchor of solitude a graceful shoulder
this water obliged to press my thirst for bronze for a solid resting
    place against her heart
would have reflected the iris of her house of charms

Within the intimate confine of the hours one has to waste
the haunches of my nights sweeter than melted elephants
a flurry of orphaned girls and widows without number
would have drawn her eyes into a long lingering gaze

But she stayed inside like cherry time in the frozen bosom of time

Yet I would have been able to stroke and warm so well the glass of ice
broken right in the middle of the evening by her smile

I would have liked so much to have filled her forgetfulness with
    carnations
and to have fluttered over her eyes half-tender half-green
like a loneliness acquired by way of the breezes]

Larrea commented that this was a very Romantic poem, from a certain point
of view. He felt it was quite successful: 'dans ce genre-là, assez réussi'. He said
he was speaking to a woman, a feminine presence, an ideal woman, something
that fluctuates, the Beloved who has never appeared: 'Je m'adressais à une
femme, à une présence féminine, une femme idéale, une chose qui flotte:
l'*Amada* qui n'a jamais apparu.' He remembered the empty pedestal of
'*Comospolitano*' at this point: the pedestal was empty. She had not arrived:

>           Aquel pedestal vacío.
>                       NO
>                 no es tampoco el mío.
>           Pero es el de mi amada.[17]

>           [That empty pedestal.
>                       NO
>                 it is not mine either.
>           But it is that of my beloved.]

---

[17]  *Versión celeste*, 62.

Returning to '*Adolescence en soi*', Larrea commented on the religious tone of the poem lent to it by the image, 'au parvis de son nom' [on the forecourt of her name]. *She* has stayed inside (the cathedral). She has never come out. There is an item of clothing put out for her, a bathing costume, 'un maillot', as if there were a beach nearby, with which to cover her nudity, just as the nakedness of the female figure pulled out of the sea during the journey to the New World is partially covered by one of the men on board *Favorables* (a reference to favourable winds), as the ship was called in the 1980 *Vuelta* version of *Ilegible*, after the little magazine *Favorables París Poema* that Larrea and Vallejo launched in Paris in 1926. In the 1948 version, which Larrea called the 'Prados version', because it had been discovered in Prados's Washington papers, the ship was called *Insaciable*. It was partly the little magazines, *Grecia*, *Cervantes*, *Litoral*, *Favorables París Poema*, *Création* (edited by Huidobro in Paris), *Verso y Prosa* and *Carmen*, which provided the means by which poets like Larrea could reach other poets they had not yet met, although in Larrea's case it was often others who launched his poems for him. The 'maillot' was put there so that she could get dressed, he added. He also commented on the laurels, 'things of glory', and the anchor image, which, he said, recurs in his poetry. He equated the anchor with a graceful shoulder. The shapes are similar and a shoulder is a part of the body one can rest one's head on and where one can feel secure. The poem ended, he added, with the verse he had used in a letter to one of his translators, to the poet Luis Felipe Vivanco, to describe the solitude in which he and his grandson lived in Córdoba after the death of his daughter and son-in-law in an aircraft accident in Sao Paulo in 1961: 'comme une solitude acquise par la voie des airs' [like a loneliness acquired by way of the breezes].

Larrea was pressed to define more precisely the feminine presence in his poetry: It is, he replied, the Other he addresses. 'C'est le fond de soi-même' [It is the very depths of oneself]. It is the bedrock of oneself ('c'est le fond de soi-même'). It is a metaphysical principle but with the shape of a woman. He added that at that time she was not *thought*, not thought of as a metaphysical principle but *felt*, as a feeling, 'un sentiment', 'comme une représentation de la vie absolue' [like a representation of absolute life]. He went on to meditate upon the ways he had attempted to describe a feeling that something was missing from his life by referring to an absent figure. In Goethe, he said, it is the Eternal Feminine, which pulls us upwards, with which *Faust* ends. Some critics have seen this a reference to the Virgin Mary. In Verlaine there is a sonnet, which he had known by heart since the age of sixteen, '*Mon rêve familier*'. Larrea recited the poem from memory at this point. It describes a dream of an unknown woman who loves and understands the poet. She is never the same, always different ('Et qui n'est, chaque fois, ni tout à fait la même'). The poem '*Adolescence en soi*' had the same sentiment. Larrea referred again to archetypes and to a work by Jung. He was searching in his library for the work on transformations of the libido and a reference, in Jung, to a sea-journey and

The Mother. Verlaine's poem, referred to above, is at the end of the chapter.
Larrea argued that Jung defined the *anima* as an archetype of life, linking it
with the mother. For Larrea the *anima* is the Beloved, the eternal feminine.
He rejected Jung's linkage of it with Mother. Larrea did not mention Medium,
Whore etc. For him it was the *Amada*, the Loved One or Beloved, which could
be another thing, he admitted. Larrea was not at ease with Jung.

Curiously, however, a section of an Introduction to the 1948 screenplay,
'Algunos símbolos del film *Ilegible*', associates *her* with *mother*, with Mother
Earth (in 1972 he used the expression 'Anima Mundi' to describe her):

> Se sale del Finisterre, del fin de la tierra, en busca de una realidad distinta
> (mujer flotante, Venus, Libertad, Madre Tierra) y se viene a parar a otro
> lugar diferente, a COLUMBIA, el lugar de la paloma, del ser alado, donde
> la imaginación creadora despliega sus alas poéticas.
>
> [They depart from Finisterre, from the end of the earth, in search of a dif-
> ferent reality (floating woman, Venus, Liberty, Mother Earth) and they
> come to the end of their journey in another different place, COLUMBIA,
> the place of the dove, of the winged being, where the creative imagination
> spreads its poetic wings.]

and:

> La persona que parecía llamada a ser la esposa del protagonista se convierte
> en madre. Esta madre es la libertad futura que lleva consigo la promesa de
> un nuevo día, de una nueva luz, de una nueva conciencia, de la ruptura del
> *yo* particular que es *cadena* que nos tiene presos.
>
> [The person who seemed destined to become the wife of the protagonist
> becomes mother. This mother is future freedom which brings with it the
> promise of a new day, a new light, a new consciousness, the smashing of
> the individual ego which is the chain which holds us prisoner.]

It is not clear how much of this section (all of it, some of it, none of it?) was
written by Buñuel. If Buñuel did not adapt it, he may have put the reference
in to Mother and Mother Earth. It had been included as a marketing device,
as a way of selling *Ilegible* to a potential buyer.

Larrea stated in the Córdoba interviews, referring to the film script itself,
'C'est presque tout moi' [It is almost all me], i.e. most of *Ilegible* was written
by him. He also revealed that 'illisible' [illegible] is what was written on official forms in France if a person's signature could not be deciphered or if the
person could not write his name. The official term, was, he said, 'illisible', 'un
homme illisible' [illegible, an illegible man]. José Bergamín, according to
Larrea, considered the title to be the most beautiful he had heard. Such a man,
Larrea added, was anonymous. The question was put to Larrea that he was
Ilegible. Not happy at first with the question, he agreed eventually that he had

'cette pousée pour l'anonymat' [that desire for anonymity], which he shared with Vallejo, which is implicit in the title. A skeleton in the family cupboard was the question mark over the legitimacy of his father, picked up in *Ilegible* in the reference in the text to 'hijo de puta' [son of a whore], 'fils de pute', 'fils de flûte' – 'flauta' [flute] can have a vulgar meaning in Spanish. Other matters concerning illegitimacy were on his mind when he wrote the novel upon which the film script was based. He had a beautiful daughter. Her mother was Blanca Rodríguez with whom Larrea had an affair, in Madrid, between 1923 and 1925. Larrea had begged Blanca not to tell his mother but she did, which led, no doubt, to a further cooling of his relationship with his mother.

To conclude, *Ilegible, hijo de flauta* has its origins, by Larrea's own admission, in the idea of transformation that he gleaned from *A Thousand and One Nights*. The surreal, magical world of these tales was absorbed into, for example, a story Larrea wrote in approximately 1915–16. Larrea's surrealistic imagination appealed to Buñuel, in all probability from 1919 onwards. The theme of the female figure, with whom the poet seeks a dialogue and who is constantly changing, runs throughout Larrea's poetry and provides a central core to Larrea and Buñuel's script. The concept of the eternal feminine in Larrea bears a resemblance to Jung's idea of the *anima*, although Larrea was keen to point out that their ideas were not identical.[18]

---

[18] This chapter is based on a paper given at the Buñuel 2000 conference at Senate House, the University of London in 2000.

# 4

## To Tell the Truth: Giménez Caballero's
## *Yo, inspector de alcantarillas*

### MARIA T. PAO

By the time Ernesto Giménez Caballero (1899–1988) published his most notorious work *Yo, inspector de alcantarillas* [*I, Sewer Inspector*] (1928), he had already established himself as a protagonist on Madrid's literary scene. In addition to writing essays and reviews for important periodicals, including *El Sol, La Libertad*, José Ortega y Gasset's *Revista de Occidente* and *Revista de las Españas*, he had founded, with Guillermo de Torre, the important cultural review *La Gaceta Literaria* (1927–32). He had published two collections of essays, *Los toros, las castañuelas, y la Virgen* [*Bulls, Castanets, and the Virgin*] (1927) and *Hércules jugando a los dados* [*Hercules Playing Dice*] (1928), and he had composed a series of posters blending graphic art and literary criticism, collected in *Carteles* [*Posters*] (1927). The same year that *Yo, inspector de alcantarillas* appeared, its author hosted a visit by the futurist F.T. Marinetti, undertook a European lecture tour in which he spoke on Spanish art and literature, and founded Cineclub Español, the nation's first film society.

Giménez Caballero's interest in Surrealism dovetailed with his familiarity with psychoanalysis – he had reviewed Freud's *Totem and Taboo* and *Group Psychology and the Analysis of the Ego* – and his awareness of mystic tradition and Catholic ritual. In 'Eoántropo: el hombre auroral del arte nuevo' [Eoanthrope: The Dawn-Man of New Art] he associated Surrealism's valoration of the dream with psychoanalysis: 'Si Freud y la moderna psiquiatría han emocionado la atención del arte con su interpretación de los sueños, mucho más la han conmovido con esa imagen obsesionante de lo que con el nombre de Libido dejaron vagar monstruosamente por los subterráneos más desconocidos del hombre' [If Freud and modern psychiatry have excited the attention of art with their interpretation of dreams, by releasing the obsessive image of Libido to wander monstrously through the most unknown areas of the human underground, they have stirred art even more].[1] At the same time,

---

[1] Ernesto Giménez Caballero, 'Eoántropo: el hombre auroral del arte nuevo', *Revista de Occidente*, 19 (1928), 309–42, 329.

in 'Por ejemplo: el superrealismo' he posited that 'Un poema de San Juan de la Cruz es un texto *surrealista*' [A poem by St John of the Cross is a *surrealist* text].[2] Not surprisingly, psychoanalysis and aspects of Catholicism – particularly confession – represent crucial dimensions of Giménez Caballero's book, informing its Surrealism in a daring way.

The author's personal favorite, *Yo, inspector de alcantarillas* has been considered 'el primer libro superrealista español' [the first Spanish surrealist book][3] and its unique themes and motifs appear in later vanguard works, such as Maruja Mallo's paintings of *Cloacas y campanarios* [*Sewers and Campaniles*] (1932), Rafael Alberti's *Sobre los ángeles* [*Concerning the Angels*] (1929) and *Sermones y moradas* [*Sermons and Dwelling Places*] (1935), and *Crimen* [*Crime*] (1934) by Canaries author Agustín Espinosa. With a cover by Mallo depicting a green–grey figure evoking a joined couple or a splitting amoeba, *Inspector* opens with a first-person narrator describing his descent into 'el reino de los epiplasmas' [the kingdom of epiplasms] (12), where 'vertían las ciudades (animal, vegetal, mineral, hombre) sus últimas substancias disueltas en fango' [cities (animal, vegetable, mineral, human) spilled their final substances dissolved in mud] (13).[4] In this sewer of the subconscious mind, he encounters fellow inspectors: surrealists André Breton, Paul Éluard, Max Ernst, Man Ray and Joan Miró, but also Freud, given as 'el neurópata famoso en la ciudad lejana' [the famous neuropath in the distant city] (9), and Spanish mystic St Teresa.

In the texts that follow – a combination of formally conventional narrations and more experimental vignettes and word games called 'Fichas textuales' [Textual Index Cards], and 'Composiciones' [Compositions] – anonymous, first-person protagonists tell their stories. These unremarkable narrators include a retired civil servant, a railroad-crossing keeper, a muleteer, priests, nuns, a poet, a young engineer and children of bourgeois families. In their tales, however, the theme of sexual perversion stands out, with depictions of pedophilia, incest, fetishism, masturbation, sado-masochism, chastity and attempted bestiality,[5] which contrasts sharply with the book's second focus – the rite of confession as purification and as transgression's apparent antidote. The discussion below will argue that sexual transgression as presented in *Inspector* exceeds the attempts at comprehension and codification inherent in

[2] Ernesto Giménez Caballero, 'Por ejemplo: el surrealismo', *La Gaceta Literaria*, 58 (15 May 1929), 3.

[3] Miguel A. Hernando, 'Primigenia plasmación del superrealismo castellano: *Yo, inspector de alcantarillas*', *Papeles de Son Armadans*, 236–237 (1975), 137–59, 144.

[4] Ernesto Giménez Caballero, *Yo, inspector de alcantarillas* (Madrid: Biblioteca Nueva, 1928); page numbers appear intratextually.

[5] In his discussion of perversion, Roger Scruton lists these along with necrophilia and homosexuality (*Sexual Desire: A Philosophical Investigation* [London: Weidenfeld and Nicolson, 1986], 284–321). Freud had defined perversion as sexual activity without reproductive function.

psychoanalysis and confession. The work upholds the surrealist investigation, here *inspection*, of the human psyche, while at the same time questioning the movement's belief in an authentic self accessible through language. As they endeavor to tell the truth about themselves, the protagonists of Giménez Caballero's book remain somehow unsatisfied.

Along with Surrealism, Freudian psychoanalysis, too, sought the deep roots of the self through words – in its case, talk therapy – and found a model in Catholic confession. Michel Foucault refers to the *scientia sexualis* emerging in the nineteenth century that adapted to scientific discourse, but kept 'as its nucleus the singular ritual of obligatory and exhaustive confession, which in the Christian West was the first technique for producing the truth of sex'.[6] Just as the analysand reveals his past, trusting the analyst to make sense of his narration and reconstruct a comprehensible ego, in confession, the penitent details his transgression for a listener authorized to understand and absolve. Both processes involve 'a narrator disclosing a secret knowledge to another, as a speaker to a listener, writer to a reader, confessor to confessor'.[7] *Inspector* evinces these procedures of disclosure and interpretation, a secular examination of conscience deployed in the name of surrealist self-exploration, through its first-person narrators who foreground the *telling* of their stories and their desire to be understood, if not by their reader (-listener-analyst-confessor), then at least by themselves.

The protagonist of 'Esa vaca y yo' [That Cow and I], a retired city worker with a compulsion to drink milk straight from a cow's teats, struggles to explain himself, plainly articulating the strategy of 'contar' [tell] and 'comprender' [understand] in psychoanalysis and confession: 'Como creo yo que no es un vicio ni una aberración excesiva, cuento este episodio, con un ansia de ser comprendido' [Since I think that it's not a vice or an excessive aberration, I'm telling this story with the longing to be understood] (54). In 'Infancia de Don Juan' [The Childhood of Don Juan], subtitled 'Cuadernos de un jesuíta' [A Jesuit's Notebooks], the now-adult priest explicitly calls his written recollections of his childhood friendship with the boy Don Juan, eventually expelled from their monastery school for masturbating before the altar, an 'examen de mi conciencia' [examination of conscience] (62). As in 'Esa vaca y yo', the narrator of 'Infancia' expects comprehension to follow confession: '¿Y por qué la he de contar? . . . No sé. Pero noto que se me salva algo, escribiendo esto, algo que no veo claro' [And why do I have to tell it? I don't know. But I notice that it rescues something in me, writing this, something that I don't quite understand] (66).

---

[6] Michel Foucault, *The History of Sexuality* (New York: Vintage Books, 1990), 68.

[7] Dennis A. Foster, *Confession and Complicity in Narrative* (Cambridge: Cambridge University Press, 1987), 2. The author uses 'confessor' from its Latin origins as both speaker–penitent and listener–priest; the present article will follow Foster's example.

Confession adheres to a codified set of expectations, a kind of role-playing, that informs the communication between writer and reader as well as between patient and therapist. 'Apertura y extinción de luces' [Lights On, Lights Off] reveals confession not only to be a ritual of mental surveillance, but an act rendering its audience incapable of accessing the truth. The story's narrator has spent his life replaying in his memory a scene of confession from his childhood in an attempt to remove the final blemish from his 'historia moral' [moral history] and 'echarlo por la alcantarilla' [throw it into the sewer] (101): when asked if he had looked at pictures of nude women, he lied to the priest. Throughout the text the narrator alludes repeatedly to the 'escena' [scene] of his transgression. When he rehearses it a final time, he prefaces it with the build-up of an actor taking the stage: '¡Ya era el momento! ¡Ojo! ¡Las frases auténticas! ¡Los clisés, límpidos! Sí, era el momento, ¡eh!' [It was finally time! Careful! Genuine statements! Crystal-clear clichés! Yes, it was time; come on!] (105). With this, the narrator foregrounds the theatricality of confession as a formulaic representation convincingly mouthed. He finally achieves his goal, feeling 'casi limpio' [almost clean], when he makes a confession of his confession to a maid. The sin that he discloses, much bigger now than boyhood curiosity, is that of having beaten the system. The transgression that the very procedure of confession effected through its scripted phrases ('"¿De veras?" – insistió el cura, más por costumbre de insistir, que por habilidad; por amor de insistencia' ['Really?', insisted the priest, more from the habit of insisting than from confessional skill; from the love of insistence] [105]) opens a 'mundo nuevo [..d]e triunfo. De poder' [a new world of triumph. Of power] (106). 'Apertura y extinción de luces' demonstrates how methods meant to extract the truth provide the means of their own subversion. In the case of confession this occurs because the listener – equivalent of the analyst or the reader – becomes contaminated, too.

Dennis A. Foster explains confession's complicity with the formation and apprehension of the self as 'a mode by which people enter into the discourse of their culture, where they step beyond the reiteration of stories and into interpretation. It represents an attempt to understand the terms and the limits by which the people are defined, both as they listen to the confessions of others and as they recount their own transgressions'.[8] But as another human being, the listener-priest becomes likewise 'infected with the doubt and loss evoked by the narrative of confession'[9] and the distinction between penitent-confessor and confessor-priest loses definition.

'Confesionario' [Confessional] dramatizes the failure of confession to provide tidy reconciliation, suggesting that in trafficking in transgression it becomes tainted itself. Presented as a sick patient, the confessional, with its 'pus periférico' [peripheral pus] (193) teems with bacteria, and the very object

---

[8] Foster, 7.
[9] Foster, 3.

designed to separate sinner and priest– the dividing screen – represents the vehicle of contamination: 'Por la porosidad de esa retícula se sumergieron las huestes bacilares. Los intestinos del confesionario están escarificados de inmundicias micropsíquicas' [Troops of bacteria sank through the porosity of that reticle. The confessional's intestines are scarified by micropsychic filth] (194). Most significant, the conversation between the interlocutors evokes sexual congress, a union of sewer mouths: '¡Y cuánta angustia y cuánto espasmo! A través de la celosía romboidal, la voz del sacerdote, como un sexo, y el de ella, como otro, que se buscan estérilmente' [And what anguish and spasm! Through the rhomboid screen, the voice of the priest, like one sex organ, and her voice, like another, seek each other sterilely]. In addition to suggesting the fruitlessness of the confession to restore either the self to wholeness or to union with God, the adverb 'estérilmente' [sterilely] deployed in a sexual context evinces perversion in which intercourse has no reproductive aim, dedicated instead to 'cuánta agüilla, y cuánta materia, y cuánta granulación, y cuánta flora indistinta de morbidez' [so much liquid, and so much material, and so much granulation, and so much hazy, sickly flora] (194).

This allusion to decomposing matter, the state of indistinction between liquid and solid, provides the matrix of the clandestine sexual self: the inspecting narrator sinking into the sewer of the subconscious finds 'materia, materia, materia, materia' [material, material, material, material]; the protagonist of 'El Redentor mal parido' [The Accursed Redeemer], a mule who harbors a secret lust for her owner, 'caía despanzurrándose, voluptuosamente' [would fall, voluptuously, turning inside out] in her 'cuadra rica, bien estercolada, obscura, fétida, picante' [paddock – rich with manure, dark, stinking, pungent] (17); incest in 'Uno y su hermana' [One and His Sister] is depicted as a pulsing organic thing – 'lo que llevaba dentro pululando' [what was pullulating inside him] (147); and 'Monjas' [Nuns] delivers a scene of female masturbation where 'sintió que su dedo se introducía en una hendidura trémula, ardiente, mojada y roja. Y tras su dedo, se introdujo ella misma, toda ella misma. Y una obscuridad absoluta la envolvió' [she felt her finger penetrate a trembling fissure, burning, wet, and red. And after her finger, her whole self followed. And an absolute darkness enveloped her] (177).

While these images of sticky matter evince the unformed desires that lie beneath socialized consciousness, they also exceed the metaphoric by foregrounding the link between transgressive sexuality or eroticism, as identified by dissident surrealist Georges Bataille, and mysticism. Eroticism dissolves the boundaries of the self, merging the one into the other. Bataille observes, 'The desire of the senses is the desire, if not to destroy oneself, at least to be consumed and to lose oneself without reservation.'[10] Moreover, the same impulse to undo, to transgress the limitations of individual identity and attain continuity drives mysticism. In this way, '[t]he lowliest and least cultured

10  Georges Bataille, *The Accursed Share* (II–III, New York: Zone Books, 1993), 113.

human beings have an experience of the possible – the whole of it even – which approaches that of the great mystics in its depth and intensity'.[11]

The characters of *Inspector* similarly achieve a kind of transcendence not through abstinence or asceticism but through sensory excess and revelling, animal-like, in 'those unstable, fetid and lukewarm substances where life ferments ignobly'.[12] The protagonist of 'Esa vaca y yo' [That Cow and I] finds himself transformed in a filthy stable, 'entre el estiércol, y la paja, y la hierba, borracho de este olor nauseabundo y fuerte, que me trasfigura [sic], que me transe' [amid the manure and the straw and the grass, drunk on this strong, nauseating odor that transfigures me, that carries me away] (52). As he feels the milk 'correr por mi garganta, gotearme por la barbilla' [run down my throat, drip down my chin], he reflects that 'en el viejo Oriente la vaca tenía un sentido divino, importantísimo, *místico*' [in the East the cow had a *mystic*, supremely important, divine meaning] (53) and he finds in material excess 'el consuelo que otros hallan [. . .] en una religión' [the solace that others discover in a religion]. In 'Infancia de Don Juan' the narrator loses himself when he comes into contact with the sexually precocious Juan, an experience cast in religious terms: 'yo me confundía con él, me transubstanciaba' [I blurred into him, he transubstantiated me] (63); 'él me empujaba [. . .]. Mis acercamientos a Dios me eran perceptibles' [he pushed me. My nearing God was perceptible to me] (73). Finally, in parsing Juan's masturbation before the altar, 'Infancia' arrives at the intersection of sexual transgression and mysticism and begins to intimate why confession (and psychoanalysis, too) fails as a tool for understanding the self:

> Nadie había comprendido aquel acto enorme de protesta, de rebeldía, de soledad enérgica, de perturbación, que no de masturbación, frente a la divinidad, que simboliza para él la opresión de todo el colegio sobre su vida.
> Nadie, nadie comprendió aquella afirmación de poder a poder, de radicalismo místico. Sacrilegio que era, en rigor, un sacrificio . . .                    (72)

> [Nobody had understood that huge act of protest, of rebellion, of energetic solitude, of agitation, not simply masturbation, before the divinity, that symbolized for him the oppression of the whole school upon his life.
> Nobody, nobody understood that statement of one power to another, of mystic radicalism. A sacrilege that was, in truth, a sacrifice . . .]

The potency of Juan's act lies in its transgression of human and church law. His expenditure of self, in non-procreative ejaculation and the sensory overflow of orgasm, violates the precepts aimed at continuing the species and those meant to ensure the union of the individual with the divine through corporeal renunciation. Rather, Juan's transcendence, a 'radicalismo místico'

---

[11] Bataille, 13.
[12] Bataille, 81.

[mystic radicalism], occurs through the sexualized body. It is the body – its abandonment of borders in erotic encounters, its liquid discharges, and its eventual dissolution in death effecting the individual's transition from discontinuity to continuity – that ultimately renders confession impotent as a mechanism of revelation and comprehension.

Confession's attempt to locate the truth of the self in the activities of the body represents the point of its undoing, something that one-time surrealists Antonin Artaud and Bataille recognized. As early as 1925 the former asserted, 'There is for me an evidence in the realm of pure flesh which has nothing to do with the evidence of reason. [. . .] The truth of life lies in the impulsiveness of matter. The mind of man has been poisoned by concepts.'[13] Later, Bataille would deplore the submission of animal flesh to 'a human order – where [. . .] work, science and bureaucracy change us into abstract entities'. He continues, 'Who would refuse to admit finally that voluptuousness, in its abasements, has a value incomparable to the interests of reason?'[14] The invocation of reason implicit in the interpretive procedures of confession and psychoanalysis is foiled by their methods and participants:

> A confession is both a challenge and a temptation to a rational reader. Reason [. . .] is a faith in the explicability of the world and, more importantly, in the existence and coherence of the thinking self. The confessor is a kind of madman, someone whose deviance into sin suggests the fragility, possibly the illusion, of reason's grasp on knowledge. The desire to understand such tales is motivated in part by the pleasure of mastery, but linked to that pleasure is an obligation: you cannot count on knowing yourself if you cannot make sense of this other.[15]

Foster observes that psychoanalysis similarly finds itself at a loss and notes that Freud's admitted inability to decipher some of his patients' stories suggests 'the ultimate inadequacy of his psychoanalysis either to understand or to cure'.[16] Eluding containment by reason, transgressive desire seeks 'the totality in which man has his share by *losing himself*. For an embrace is not just a fall into the animal muck, but the anticipation of death, and of the putrefaction that follows it.'[17]

Faced with the ultimate dissolution of human existence, the scientific discourse of psychoanalysis and the ritual of confession, both designed to sound the depths of the individual, capsize. *Inspector* reveals this failure when the

---

[13] Artaud's 'Manifeste en Langage Clair' appeared in *La Nouvelle Revue Française* on 1 December 1925; reprinted in *Selected Writings* (New York: Farrar, Straus and Giroux, 1976), 108–9.

[14] Bataille, 119, 181.

[15] Foster, 5.

[16] See Foster, 5–6.

[17] Bataille, 119.

narrator of 'Infancia de Don Juan' finally has to concede, 'Es muy difícil buscar explicaciones a ciertas cosas del alma' [It's very difficult to seek explanations for certain aspects of the soul] (73). The amateur psychologist of 'Datos
para una solución' [Data for a Solution] undertakes a taxonomy of his subject
'con metodología cartesiana' [with Cartesian methodology] (78), while at the
same time, he aims, confessor-like, to inspect the latter's deep self using comparable instruments of calculation: '¡Hermosas tablas logarítmicas las
trazadas tras un reportaje así del alma!' [What lovely logarithmic charts are
drawn up after such an account of the soul!] (80). But in ordering 'estos datos
arbitrarios' [these arbitrary data] (97) he is forced to acknowledge, 'He con-
struído una concavidad' [I've constructed a concavity] (98), a hollow inad-
equate to 'la imagen vital' [the vital image] of the man he tried to configure.
Ending, 'A ver si estos extractos han servido – de veras – para una solución
conjunta y valedera' [Let's see if these extracts have been of use – really – for
a valid and unified solution], the answer seems to be no.

   In 'Apertura y extinción de luces' the narrator ponders his ambiguous
feelings: '¡Qué sufrimiento! Pero ¡qué gozo! Porque la tabla sentimental del
subconsciente está hecha a base de planeados contradictorios. De corrientes
opuestas (refrigeración–calefacción, negro–blanco, luz–opacidad)' [What suffering! But what pleasure! Because the sentimental chart of the subconscious is
made of contradictory plans. Of opposite currents (refrigeration–heat,
black–white, light–darkness)] (103). The failure of his analyses to yield a consistent picture of the self also is reflected in the *composición* titled 'Tablero
negro y blanco' [Black and White Board]. Here the two columns that evoke a
mostly 'logical' associative exercise ('noche' [night] – 'alba' [dawn], 'agua'
[water] – 'llama' [flame], 'no' [no] – 'sí' [yes]) also present 'lágrima' [tear] gen-
erating 'apetito' [appetite] and 'caricia' [caress] resulting from 'enfermedad'
[disease] (207). Like the 'tablas logarítmicas [. . .] del alma' [logarithmic charts
of the soul] and the 'tabla sentimental del subconsciente' [sentimental chart of
the subconscious], 'Tablero negro y blanco' 'tends to spell out – in black and
white, as it were – an abortive attempt to trace a meaningful psychological
profile'.[18]

   Finally, the narration 'Lectura oblicua' [Oblique Reading] speaks directly to
the impossibility of reading the other and, it implies, one's own self. The protagonist examines his attraction to a prostitute who resembles the woman he
loves and concludes that it represents '[u]n caso típico de *sustitución*' [a typical case of *substitution*] (111). The woman, too, has found that men frequently
have approached her because 'les recordaba *a otras*' [she reminded them
*of others*] (115). By the end of the encounter, however, the narrator accepts
her 'yo personal y sin mezcla' [personal and unadulterated 'I'] (115):

   [18] Nigel Dennis, 'Ernesto Giménez Caballero and Surrealism: a Reading of *Yo,
inspector de alcantarillas* (1928)', in *The Surrealist Adventure in Spain*, ed. C.B. Morris
(Ottawa: Dovehouse Editions, 1990), 94.

'Y comenzaba a ver, a *leer*, aquella mujer que tenía presente, por un lado contrario a la primera y alucinante lectura. Comenzaba a deletrear otra persona:
otra leyenda, otro anuncio de *yo*' [And I began to understand, to *read* that
woman before me, on the one hand a reverse of my first, deluded reading.
I began to spell out another person: another inscription, another announcement
of 'I'] (114). But then he equates his reading with 'esas lecturas oblicuas
hechas en anuncios y carteles de las grandes ciudades, de las entradas a las
grandes estaciones: si se viene del sur, al norte se lee una cosa en los listones
blancos de madera; y si se viene del norte al sur, se lee otra sobre los mismos
listones' [those oblique readings of announcements and billboards in big cities,
at the entrances to big train stations: if you come south to north you read one
thing on the white strips of wood; and if you come north to south, you read
another on those same strips] (116). He concludes,

> Un deseo oblicuo. Una satisfacción oblicua. Una mujer oblicua. Un yo que
> era un tú. Un sur que era un norte. Una dislocación de puntos cardinales.
> Una cara, en cruz. Un haz en envés. Eso. Un cartel indistinto y equívoco de
> gran ciudad: una lectura oblicua.    (116)

> [An oblique desire. An oblique satisfaction. An oblique woman. An 'I' that
> was a 'you'. A south that was a north. A dislocation of cardinal points.
> A heads that was a tails. A face in reverse. That's it. An incorrect, confus-
> ing big-city billboard: an oblique reading.]

Efforts to 'deletrear' [spell out, decipher] another person, or even oneself,
result in disorientation; reading becomes akin to sounding out discrete syllables while the word itself remains elusive.

The concepts of spelling out, reading, and interpretation have additional
implications for the kinds of stories told by the narrators of *Inspector* and the
motives of their telling. The protagonists, as observed earlier, insist on con-
fessing, on telling the truth. If only they can explain their secrets they might
be understood. On a fundamental level confession and its heir, psychoanalysis, speak to the need for human connection, comprehension, and acceptance.
This leads to another dimension of Giménez Caballero's book: all his
anonymous characters reveal a deep loneliness. In 'Datos para una solución',
whereas a dog is named Rafael (90), the human under observation is known
only as 'don Tal' [Mr Somebody-or-Other] (91). He attends a *tertulia* every
afternoon, but even though the participants '[s]e contaban entre sí cosas
intimísimas' [told each other extremely intimate things] (94), 'no obstante, se
sintieron siempre desconocidos' [nevertheless, they always felt like strangers]
(95). Family members never visit the narrator of 'Esa vaca y yo', the other
boarders 'nunca me saludan' [never greet me] (49) and, 'después de tanta
soledad' [after so much loneliness] (53), he finds companionship with a cow.
If he tells his embarrassing story, it is 'con una ansia de ser comprendido, de
ser sonreído, con menor brutalidad que la que me dedican mis compañeros'

[with the longing to be understood, to be smiled at, with less brutality than that given to me by my peers] (54). In 'Infancia de Don Juan' the narrator and his friend also suffer from isolation and incomprehension. The former refers repeatedly to his 'soledad' [loneliness] (59, 60, 63, 65) both as a boy and as an adult. He suspects, moreover, that the adolescent Juan 'debió ser también un incompleto, un insatisfecho, un desarmónico, un poco miserable' [must also be incomplete, unsatisfied, out of tune, a little wretched] (63), and he calls his friend's masturbation an act of 'soledad enérgica' [energetic solitude] (72). Although '[n]adie había comprendido aquel acto enorme de protesta' [nobody had understood that huge act of protest], Juan's classmate, now the adult priest, was able to decode the episode, a recognition of meaning unattainable by the narrator himself since 'sé que nadie aquí me entiende' [I know that nobody here understands me] (73).

The urge to be understood by others has a parallel in the desire to comprehend oneself, as the narrator of 'Aventura con Hermafrodita' [An Adventure With Herm-Aphrodite] perceives:

Hay hombres [. . .] que al llegar a la madurez hojean sus vidas como ficheros puros. [. . .]
    Es una necesidad incalculable de clasificación y de recuentos. Por una urgencia de contabilidad provisoria, como esperando un balance general y final de algo. (Una confesión posible y próxima de lecho de muerte.)
                                                                    (155–6)

[There are men who, when they reach maturity, page through their lives like absolute card indexes.
    It's an incalculable need to classify and tally up. Through an urgency to make a provisory accounting, as if expecting a final general balance of something. (A possible death-bed confession.)]

Whether the image pertains to oral confession, the confidences in a diary, a spelling out of identity, notations in a psychologist's chart, or the card catalogue of a life, *Inspector*'s narrators rely on words to reveal truths about themselves and to interpret others. André Breton, too, considered unrestricted language, 'which I am trying to render forever valid, which seems to me to adapt itself to all of life's circumstances', the most effective tool for knowing the self.[19] Sexual transgression, however, cancels the potency of that means.

Bataille observes that the Marquis de Sade attained 'superhuman solitude in the very bosom of humanity' because the perversion and violence he advocated 'is the opposite of the solidarity with other people implicit in logic, laws, and language'; the language that de Sade utters 'repudiates any relationship

---

[19] André Breton, *Manifestoes of Surrealism* (Ann Arbor: The University of Michigan Press, 1972), 33.

between speaker and audience'.[20] Transgressive sexuality 'is defined by secrecy' and may as well not exist insofar as 'our existence is present for us in the form of speech and language'; thus, 'Erotic experience will commit us to silence.'[21] In a related fashion, the protagonists of *Inspector* divulge confidences involving sexual deviance and mystic union – conditions that erase the boundaries of human, animal, and divine and exceed the limits of language – but do not ultimately succeed in their quest for understanding.

If the dominant branch of Surrealism believed in the investigation and recovery of the authentic self through language, Artaud and Bataille, members eventually expelled by Breton, belie that notion. *Yo, inspector de alcantarillas*, in suggesting that all individuals retain a dimension rooted in bodily sensation that escapes containment in language, belongs to this second group. Its protagonists, despite their efforts to tell their secret truths and ascertain the truths of others in their desire for human connection, necessarily must resign themselves, like the young don Juan, to acts of 'energetic solitude'.

[20] Georges Bataille, *Erotism* (San Francisco: City Lights Books, 1986), 189.
[21] Bataille, *Erotism*, 252.

# 5

# Luis Buñuel: The Surrealist Triptych

## GWYNNE EDWARDS

Between 1929 and 1933 Luis Buñuel made three films, all of which can be seen to characterise key aspects of Surrealism. The first of these, *Un Chien andalou* [*An Andalusian Dog*], scripted in close collaboration with Salvador Dalí, received its première in 1929. The second, *L'Âge d'or* [*The Golden Age*], was shown a year later, and, despite the presence of a few Dalinian elements, was largely the work of Buñuel. And the third, *Terre sans pain* [*Land without Bread*], also known as *Las Hurdes*, entirely Buñuel's work, was completed in 1933. As far as Surrealism in general is concerned, Robert Havard has recently argued that it 'moved through three key phases: the psychoanalytical, the metaphysical and the political. Putting it another way, it passed successively under the spell of Freud, Hegel and Marx.'[1] The first of these three phases was concerned, above all, with the revelation of the unconscious mind, in relation to which the studies of Sigmund Freud were highly influential, and had been defined by André Breton in his *First Manifesto* of 1924:

> SURREALISM. *n.masc.* Pure psychic automatism through which it is intended to express, either orally, or in writing, or in any other way, the actual way thought works. The dictation of thought, free from all control exercised by reason, without regard to any aesthetic or moral concern.[2]

The second stage, signposted by Breton's *Second Manifesto* of 1929, stemmed from the belief that psychical or psycho-neurotic material was insufficient on its own, and that there was a need for conceptual substance of the kind suggested by the Hegelian ideal of transcendence via the union of opposites.[3] In short, the notion of subject – object integration and of the surrealist object came into being, a process whereby the artist was able to project his

---

[1] Robert Havard, *The Crucified Mind: Rafael Alberti and the Surrealist Ethos in Spain* (London: Tamesis, 2001), 3.

[2] André Breton, *Manifestoes of Surrealism*, trans. Richard Seaver and Helen R. Lane (Ann Arbor: University of Michigan Press, 1972), 3.

[3] Havard, 8.

fetishes onto concrete objects and thereby structure his neuroses into an artistic whole. Breton praised in particular Salvador Dalí's 'paranoia-critical method', in which the painter was able to participate in the events of his unconscious as actor and spectator simultaneously, deeply involved in them but maintaining an essential critical detachment.[4] The third phase of Surrealism was, in a way, a logical step from the second, for the latter's emphasis on Hegelian materialism linked naturally with the doctrine of dialectical materialism associated with Marx, and turned many of the surrealists – Dalí was a notable exception – to Communism and a desire to carry the revolution of the first phase of Surrealism into the political arena. Nevertheless, as Havard has pointed out, the three phases mentioned above 'are not isolated categories, nor are they chronologically discrete; for one thing, Freud was never discarded, and, for another, Marx was there from the start'.[5] The surrealist journey implied by these phases, as well as their interplay and interrelationship, are to be seen very clearly in what I have termed Buñuel's surrealist triptych.

*Un Chien andalou* was the result of a visit that Buñuel made to the Dalí home in Figueras in the early months of 1929, where, in less than a week, they had put their heads together and produced a script. Buñuel has described how the idea for the film revolved around two dreams, one his own, the other Dalí's:

> When I arrived to spend a few days at Dalí's house in Figueras, I told him about a dream I'd had in which a long, tapering cloud sliced the moon in half, like a razor-blade slicing through an eye. Dalí immediately told me that he'd seen a hand crawling with ants in a dream he'd had the previous night.[6]

Furthermore, both men adopted the policy that no material dictated by reason should be included in the script:

> Our only rule was very simple: no idea or image that might lend itself to a rational explanation of any kind would be accepted. We had to open all doors to the irrational and keep only those images that surprised us, without trying to explain why. The amazing thing is that we never had the slightest disagreement; we spent a week of total identification.[7]

In its emphasis on dream and the choice of images devoid of rational explanation, *Un Chien andalou* can thus be placed in the first phase of Surrealism, though its date of 1929, by which time Dalí was practising his

---

[4] André Breton, 'The Dalí Case', in *Surrealism and Painting*, trans. Simon Watson Taylor (London: Macdonald, 1965), 133.

[5] Havard, 3.

[6] Luis Buñuel, *My Last Breath*, trans. Abigail Israel (London: Vintage, 1994), 103–4.

[7] Buñuel, 104.

'paranoia-critical method', suggests that it was influenced too by the greater element of control and detachment associated with the second phase.

The two dream images that inspired *Un Chien andalou* occur at the beginning of the film and some four minutes into it respectively, and, although described by Buñuel as having occurred to himself and Dalí separately, lay at the heart of a sexual neurosis deeply embedded in the psyche of both men, which explains, no doubt, their agreement as to their inclusion. The initial sequence in which a man (played by Buñuel) appears on a balcony, sharpening a razor, watches a thin cloud approaching a full moon, and, as the cloud pierces the moon, draws the razor across the left eye of a young woman, is, of course, open to different interpretations. In one sense Buñuel assaults the viewer's sensibilities, shocking him or her, in true surrealist fashion, out of complacency and issuing a warning that this is not to be a conventional film.[8] On the other hand, the images have clear sexual implications, for the perfect circle of the moon, repeated in the form of the eye, evokes the hymen intact, while the long thin cloud and the razor suggest the male sexual organ at the moment of penetration. In this context it is important to bear in mind the sexual anxiety that affected both Buñuel and Dalí and that in both cases was connected with their formative years.

Between the ages of 8 and 15 Buñuel attended the Jesuit Colegio del Salvador in Zaragoza, an institution where the pupils were indoctrinated into believing that sex was a bad thing and where they were left, even if they only indulged in daydreams, with a terrible sense of guilt:

> 'they' [the teachers] never ceased to remind us that the highest virtue was chastity, without which no life was worthy of praise . . . . In the end, we were worn out with our oppressive sense of sin, coupled with the interminable war between virtue.[9]

It was a part of his education that left an indelible mark and that led him, crucially, to equate sexual intercourse with death:

> . . . I also have always felt a secret but constant link between the sexual act and death.[10]

As for Dalí, the influence of a smothering, over-protective mother, combined with an education similar to Buñuel's – at a school run by Marist brothers – ensured that he too would be riddled with sexual anxieties, and it is extremely

---

[8] Henry Miller, *The Cosmological Eye* (London, 1945), 57, famously observed: 'Afterwards they showed *Un Chien andalou*. The public shuddered, making their seats creak, when an enormous eye appeared on the screen and was cut coldly by a razor, the drops of liquid from the iris leaping onto the metal. Hysterical shouts were heard.'

[9] Buñuel, 14.

[10] Buñuel, 15.

doubtful that he ever succeeded in having a normal sexual relationship with his wife.[11] For both men, then, the sexual act was associated with anxiety, fear, guilt, and even horror. And if it is argued that in the opening sequence of *Un Chien andalou* it is the female who suffers, not the male, it can also be suggested that the violence perpetrated on her – the equivalent of rape – is an act of revenge, the fantasy of a male who lives in fear of the female sex, as other images in the film suggest.

The second key image of the hand and the ants emerging from a hole in the palm was, as we have seen, Dalí's suggestion. The hand appears in many of his paintings in the late 1920s – *Apparatus and Hand* (1927) and *The Lugubrious Game* (1929) are two examples – and is invariably associated with masturbation, which the priests, and no doubt parents, warned against as being not merely sinful, but as leading to blindness and insanity.[12] As well as this, of course, masturbation, if performed alone, involves fantasy and avoidance of sexual contact with a woman of flesh and blood, again pointing, perhaps, to the emotional immaturity from which Dalí undoubtedly suffered. In the sequence in question the close-up of the young man's hand, initially motionless, suggests emotional and sexual paralysis. The hole in the palm – in one sense evoking the Crucifixion – reinforces the notion of a damaged individual, and the crawling ants, often seen in Dalí's paintings to be close to or covering the mouth – see *The Dream* (1931) – point to decay and death on the one hand,[13] but also, in the sense that the young man is about to respond to the young woman who stands watching him, to new activity and the awakening of sexual desire. Needless to say, the hand in its masturbatory association was also central to Buñuel's formative years, and its centrality to the film was therefore something with which he could readily identify.[14]

The two central images of the eye and the hand are, in the light of the sexual implications described above, the source of every other image in the film, according in their interconnection with Jean Epstein's statement that 'When sleep frees it from the control of reason, the activity of the mind is not anarchic. One finds in it an order which consists above all of associations that are similar, close to each other . . . '[15] This view is, of course, quite similar to Dalí's 'paranoia-critical method', described by Carlton Lake in the following way: 'Basically, it involved setting down an obsessional idea suggested by the unconscious and then elaborating and reinforcing it by a perverse association of ideas and a seemingly irrefutable logic until it took on the conviction of

---

    [11]  See Meryle Secrest, *Salvador Dalí: The Surrealist Jester* (London: Weidenfeld and Nicolson, 1986), 188.
    [12]  Havard, 44.
    [13]  Secrest, 130.
    [14]  Havard, 43.
    [15]  See Agustín Sánchez Vidal, *El mundo de Luis Buñuel* (Zaragoza: Caja de Ahorros de la Inmaculada, 1993), 41.

inescapable truth.'[16] To this extent, if *Un Chien andalou* points to the influence of the first phase of Surrealism in its drawing upon the unconscious
mind, it also relates to the second phase both in the way that the two initial
images suggest others, and in the way that private fetishes are projected onto
objects which, linking with each other, form an artistic whole.

The sexual implications of the two central images are projected first of all
onto the figure of the young man, the cyclist, initially seen riding his bicycle
along a deserted street. His mechanical movements and his expressionless
face point to a lack of emotion or an arrested development, an aspect of his
character underlined by the frilly trimmings, suggestive of a baby, worn on
his head and around his shoulders and waist. In this context it is worth recalling that, as an adolescent, Dalí was still regarded by his parents as 'the child'
and described by his father as 'too much of a baby for his age'.[17] When the
young man then falls from the bicycle and lies inert and expressionless at the
side of the road, completely unresponsive to the young woman's kisses and
embraces, his lack of sexual drive is indeed proven. Furthermore, the box that
he carries around his neck, and that is soon afterwards opened by the young
woman, is seen to contain a tie whose limp form, reminiscent of Dalí's limp
watches in *The Persistence of Memory* (1931) and *Soft Watches* (1930), is a
clear pointer to the painter's obsession with his possible impotence. With
regard to the frilly trimmings, the word which is used in the film script – *man-
teles* – actually had a religious connotation, alluding to the religious surplice
worn by bishops and prelates over the cassock, and brings to mind too the
choir-boy clothing worn by both Buñuel and Dalí during their schooldays.[18]
In other words, the garment worn by the cyclist has a dual function, for it suggests infantilism but at the same time links it to religious indoctrination at
school, a process that had a profoundly damaging effect upon Buñuel and Dalí
alike.

The emotional infantilism of the young man is underlined on several subsequent occasions. After his failed attempt to possess the young woman, the
camera focuses in close up on his hand, this time trapped between the door-
frame and the door. The crawling ants here point not to sexual activity but to
emotional putrefaction, for the young man is then seen to have reverted to his
earlier state, his prostration on the bed and the restitution of the frilly trimmings indicative of his baby-like state. Later on, when the young woman
enters his room in search of him, he initially seems more adult and eager to
meet her, his bold striped tie the very opposite of the limp tie mentioned earlier. But, seeing her in front of him, he quickly loses confidence, places his
hand over his mouth in a gesture of guilt or fear, and, when he removes it, is
seen to have no mouth. The mouth, not so much absent as tightly closed, is to

---

[16] Carlton Lake, *In Quest of Dalí* (New York: Putnam, 1969), 68–9.
[17] Secrest, 58.
[18] Havard, 168.

be found in many of Dalí's paintings of the late 1920s and early 1930s – *Illumined Pleasures, The Lugubrious Game, The Great Masturbator, The Enigma of Desire* (all 1929) – and undoubtedly refers to the painter's sexual anxiety. The point is clearly made in the film when the young woman, angered by the young man's lack of passion, draws attention to her own mouth and thus her powerful sexual drive by ostentatiously applying her lipstick.

Allusions to the causes of Buñuel and Dalí's sexual inhibitions, indicative of how they continued to haunt both men in adult life, are to found in two episodes in particular. In the first of these the young man attempts to pursue the young woman and is literally stopped in his tracks by a number of objects attached to the ropes with which he intends to secure her: a cork, a melon, two priests, and two grand pianos on which are placed two dead and rotting donkeys. Some of these objects are particularly associated with Dalí. In several paintings the cork – *Female Nude* (1928) – and the melon are symbolic of the vagina and female breasts respectively. When Dalí was a child, his father had attempted to reveal to the boy the horrors of venereal disease by leaving an open medical book on top of a piano, thereby unintentionally instilling in him a horror of sex.[19] Dead, putrefying donkeys are to be found in his paintings of the 1920s – *Honey is Sweeter than Blood* (1926), *The Donkey's Carcass* (1928). But many of these images were also meaningful for Buñuel. Grand pianos are in many of his films synonymous with bourgeois culture. The childhood memory of a dead, putrefying donkey stayed with him for the rest of his life.[20] And the significance of priests for both Buñuel and Dalí has already been mentioned. In all the objects attached to the rope there is, then, a multiplicity of overlapping meanings, all of them deeply etched upon the psyche of both men, while the ropes may be seen as a kind of umbilical cord that ties them inescapably to the anxieties shaped by their past.

A second episode, again connected with Buñuel and Dalí's childhood and adolescence, occurs not long after the arrival of the newcomer who divests the young man of his frilly trimmings. The camera reveals a school desk, exercise books, a pen and an ink-well, and the newcomer punishing the young man by making him stand facing the wall, holding books above his head. Here, clearly, is a deep-rooted memory of the schools attended by Buñuel and Dalí and of the punishments handed out for indiscretions, which included masturbation, vividly described by Buñuel and hinted at as the young man's indiscretion by the newcomer's vigorous handling of a cocktail shaker.[21]

While the young man is the film's principal focus of attention, two other young men are his complete opposite. The first of these is the newcomer, an energetic, active individual who, as already mentioned, obliges the young man to rise from the bed and dispense with the frilly trimmings, seeking literally

---

[19] Sánchez Vidal, 247–8.
[20] Buñuel, 11.
[21] Buñuel, 27–8.

to shake him out of his lethargy. The second is the bold and good-looking male with whom the young woman, having turned her back on the first young man, finally goes off, his boldly striped sweater reminiscent of the striped tie seen earlier in the film. The newcomer, identical in appearance to the young man and in that sense his twin, may well have something to do with Dalí's elder brother who, idolised by his parents, had died at the age of twenty-one months. He was also called Salvador, and so the second son was regarded as his replacement. In response, the latter resolved to be as different from him as possible, but the dead brother continued to be an obsession, haunting him for many years. In *Un Chien andalou* the young man's murder of the newcomer may thus be seen as wish fulfilment. At the same time, though, the newcomer and the second young man can be seen as a wish fulfilment of a different kind, for they embody the sexual drive and dominance in which both Buñuel and Dalí were decidedly lacking.

In the light of their sexual inhibitions, the portrayal of the young woman in *Un Chien andalou* is truly revealing. Initially, she sits quietly, reading a book, which is seen to contain a reproduction of Vermeer's *Lacemaker*, but then, suddenly preoccupied by thoughts of the young man, she throws the book away, rushes downstairs, and begins to kiss and embrace him as he lies inert in the road. In this context, the significance of the *Lacemaker* for both Buñuel and Dalí needs to be considered. The painting hung on the wall of Dalí's father's study. He frequently saw it too in Pepín Bello's room at the Residencia de Estudiantes in Madrid, and in 1926 he painted his own version of it – *Girl in Figueras* – using his sister, Ana María, as his model. He seems to have been fascinated in particular by the contrast in Vermeer's original between the young woman's stillness and the threat of pain embodied in the needles she uses to make lace.[22] As for Buñuel, he too was familiar with the painting at the Residencia, and images of women who are sewing and embroidering are to be seen in many of his films, as is the case in *Tristana, Belle de jour* [*Daytime Beauty*], and *Cet obscur objet du désir* [*That Obscure Object of Desire*], to mention only three. For Buñuel sewing and embroidery symbolised, among other things, domesticity and fidelity, but he was also aware that a woman could be unfaithful, her quiet domestic appearance concealing strong and potentially dangerous sexual needs. It was no coincidence that, fearful of such a potential in his wife, Jeanne, he should have encouraged her to devote herself to such domestic tasks, thus avoiding possible temptation.[23]

In the sense that the young woman in *Un Chien andalou* is initially tranquil but then sexually aggressive, she embodies the two contrasting sides of woman, which both Buñuel and Dalí associated with the *Lacemaker*, and which, in

[22] Sánchez Vidal has a particularly interesting section on Dalí's fascination with the Vermeer painting. See 156–9.

[23] See Jeanne Rucar de Buñuel, *Memorias de una mujer sin piano* (written by Marisol Martín del Campo) (Madrid: Alianza Editorial, 1990), 108–9.

Spain and other Mediterranean countries, have their extreme forms in the virgin and the whore. The sudden transition from the one to the other is suggested too at other moments in the film. When, later on, the young woman enters the room in search of the young man, she stands quite still, observing the death's head moth and then the young man standing before her. But then, when his mouth suddenly disappears, pointing to his sexual impotence, her tranquillity becomes aggression, she provocatively lipsticks her own mouth, sticks out her tongue at him, and abandons him, walking out in search of someone who can satisfy her obvious emotional and sexual needs. These, furthermore, have been highlighted earlier in the film in the sequence that 'exteriorises' her deep-felt desires, a sequence in which, in the form of the androgynous figure, she prods the severed hand – synonymous with a limp penis and thus with the young man – in an attempt to bring it to life. Quite clearly, this young woman is possessed of the sexual drive that both Buñuel and Dalí feared in women and that for both men was embodied in the image of the praying mantis.

In this context Jean François Millet's *Angelus* had a particular fascination for Dalí. The painting depicts two peasants at prayer after a day's work in the fields: a male figure holding his hat in front of him at more or less waist level, and a female standing facing him, her head bowed and her hands clasped at her breast in prayer. It is, of course, a painting full of religious feeling, but Dalí's fevered imagination, combined with his deep-seated sexual anxieties, saw it very differently. For him the man's hat concealed an erection, while the woman was the virgin in waiting, her still, prayer-like posture evocative of the praying mantis, which, after mating, devours the male. Dalí's obsession with Millet's painting is reflected in his own numerous treatments of the theme in which the role of woman as deadly predator is very clear: *Homage to Millet* and *Cannibalism of the Religious Mantis of Lautréamont* (both 1934) are good examples. Furthermore, the mantis was also, no doubt, associated with the suffocating attentions of his mother, which had destroyed him in a rather different way.[24] As for Buñuel, insects in general were always a source of fascination, examples of which may be seen in many of his films, and one of his favourite books was *Souvenirs entomologiques*, by the famous French entomologist, J.H. Fabre, which he regarded as 'infinitely superior to the Bible'.[25] Of particular relevance, though, is the fact that not only did he consider copulation to be the closest thing to death, as we have already seen, but that in this context he often thought of those female creatures that devour the male after mating: the black widow spider and the praying mantis.[26] In this respect, Dalí and Buñuel both saw woman as predatory and destructive, and it is therefore no coincidence that *Un Chien andalou*, in which the young woman is shown

---

[24] On the significance of Millet's *Angelus* in Dalí's work, see Secrest, 132–3, and Sánchez Vidal, 110–20.

[25] Buñuel, 217.

[26] Sánchez Vidal, 110.

to be sexually aggressive, should end with a shot in which the young woman and the young man, dying and positioned opposite each other, bring to mind Dalí's interpretation of Millet's *Angelus*, as well as Buñuel's correlation of love and death. And, as well as this, the death theme is emphasised by the use in the film of music from Wagner's *Tristan and Isolde*, the lovers whose passion proved fatal. Not only did Buñuel greatly admire Wagner's music, but Dalí in 1944 designed the set for a stage-production of the opera in which Isolde is very much a variation of the praying mantis.

The dominant images of *Un Chien andalou*, many of them common to both Buñuel and Dalí, are very clearly of the neurotic and obsessive kind that belong to the world of the unconscious and are the stuff of dreams or day-dreams, floating to the surface when reason is not fully in control. In this respect, the cinematic techniques employed by Buñuel – Dalí played no part in the actual filming of the script – further underline the film's dream-like character. Titles alluding to time – ONCE UPON A TIME, EIGHT YEARS LATER, AROUND THREE O'CLOCK IN THE MORNING, SIXTEEN YEARS EARLIER, IN THE SPRING – have a disconcerting effect and create precisely the kind of illogical time-shifts we experience in dreams. More important still are the unexpected changes in location that are created by dissolves – the young woman walks out of the room onto a beach, the newcomer, killed by the young man, falls to the ground in the room, which at once becomes a park – and the transformations of one thing into another – the young woman's breasts into her buttocks. But if these effects suggest the fluidity and the chaotic nature of dream, the network of closely associated images discussed previously give *Un Chien andalou* a coherence, an artistic structure that corresponds to the ideas outlined in Breton's *Second Manifesto* of 1929 and to his advocacy of Dalí's 'paranoia-critical method'. It is no coincidence therefore that, even if Buñuel and Dalí decided to introduce images that had no rational explanation, they made decisions and choices between different images and in that sense exercised a degree of control over their material.

*L'Âge d'or*, shot and premiered in 1930, a little more than a year after *Un Chien anadalou*, has much in common with the earlier film but is also in many ways different. The relationship with the latter is suggested both by the fact that the new film was to be called *La bestia andaluza* [*The Andalusian Beast*], and by the importance given to sexual instinct and desire. This said, Buñuel's plans to write the script once more with Dalí came to nothing, for by this time the painter was distracted by his relationship with Gala, his wife-to-be, and when Buñuel stayed with him in Cadaqués at the end of 1929, they could agree on nothing.[27] Consequently, the film became almost entirely Buñuel's and the emphasis shifted somewhat from *Un Chien andalou*'s concern with the unconscious to a closer examination of the social, cultural and religious

[27] Buñuel, 115.

institutions – much more in the background in the earlier film – that deny desire
and instinct their free expression. The title, *L'Âge d'or*, brings to mind Don
Quixote's eulogy of a past age when men and women lived in harmony with
each other and with Nature. In Buñuel's film, the young man and the young
woman, played by Gaston Modot and Lya Lys, embody natural instinct seeking its own satisfaction and thus in rebellion against a morality created in the
passage of time by social and religious pressures. In this respect *L'Âge d'or* is
clearly in accord with the surrealists' aim – Buñuel was by now a member of
the Paris group – of social revolution, which was, of course, just one step
removed from political revolution, as he later observed:

> All of us were supporters of a certain concept of revolution, and although
> the surrealists didn't consider themselves terrorists, they were constantly
> fighting a society they despised . . . The real purpose of Surrealism was not
> to create a new literary, artistic, or even philosophical movement, but to
> explode the social order, to transform life itself. Soon after the founding of
> the movement, however, several members rejected this strategy and went
> into 'legitimate' politics, especially the Communist Party, which seemed to
> be the only organization worthy of the epithet 'revolutionary'.[28]

While *L'Âge d'or* corresponds to the second stage of Surrealism, and still contains elements from the first, it also anticipates the third.

The documentary opening sequence, depicting the activities of scorpions
and providing information about them in the form of titles, indicates that in
*L'Âge d'or* Buñuel's approach to his subject matter is to be more objective
than was the case in *Un Chien andalou*, particularly in relation to his scrutiny
of bourgeois society, which, like insects, will be placed under his microscope.
The initial sequence is, indeed, the rest of the film in embryonic form, for the
poisonous scorpion attacks any creature that invades its territory no less
aggressively than, as we shall see, the bourgeoisie rejects anyone who flouts
its values and conventions: in this particular case the two young lovers. At the
same time, though, the scorpion also anticipates the lovers in the sense that
they, like it, follow their natural instincts. And, from a structural point of view,
this opening sequence is the first of five, reminiscent of the five sections of
the scorpion's tail, which, like the film's epilogue, ends with a vicious and
deadly sting. Already, there is an objectivity, the sense of an overall control
and structure, which distinguishes *L'Âge d'or* from *Un Chien andalou*.

In the film's second section the scorpions become the bandits, the latter like
the insects in the sense that they too are aggressive and dangerous. And by
implication the bandits, an outsider group, are, of course, the surrealists – it
is no coincidence that their leader is played by Max Ernst – rebels against
social and moral convention. Their heroic spirit is suggested by the music

---

[28] Buñuel, 107.

from Beethoven's *Fifth Symphony* that accompanies the early part of the sequence, but there is also an ominous note in the fact that they, already marginalised, are helpless in the face of so-called civilised society, represented firstly by the archbishops in the rocks and then by the group that arrives by boat and contains priests, nuns, soldiers and civic dignitaries: the church, the army and civic administration combined. These are the reactionary forces, which, as *Un Chien andalou* suggests, stifle emotional development and maturity, and which in *L'Âge d'or*, ultimately frustrate the expression of natural instinct.

Buñuel's aggressive surrealist attack on the bourgeois enemy, developed in greater detail in the film's central section and so often a feature of his later films, has a strong comic edge. The small man with the big moustache, dressed in morning coat and top hat, sporting his medals, and preceding the laying of the foundation stone of the great city of Rome, cradle of civilisation, with a grandiloquent speech, is the personification of pomposity, his self-importance rendered absurd by the emptiness of his words. Similarly, the evocation of the grandeur of Rome and of the Vatican – the Catholic Church hand in hand with the moneyed classes – is undermined when the camera pinpoints a window of the Vatican advertising a room for rent. And the dignity, philistinism and bizarre habits of the bourgeoisie are mocked in three visual 'gags': an elegantly dressed man nonchalantly brushes clouds of dust from his clothes as he emerges from a restaurant; a second casually kicks a violin along the pavement to the accompaniment on the sound-track of Beethoven's *Violin Concerto*; and a third, balancing a flat stone on his head, walks past a statue, oblivious to the fact that it too has a similar stone on its head.[29]

The surrealist assault on bourgeois values is, though, mainly embodied in the two lovers – new forms of the scorpion and the bandits – whose ecstatic groping of each other disrupts the laying of the foundation stone. In action, thought and expression they are not so much rounded characters as pure desire personified, as Buñuel once noted of the young man: 'the hero is animated by egoism, which imagines all attitudes to be amorous, to the exclusion of control or of other sentiments'.[30] Consequently, the young man in particular charges through the film like some runaway stallion, his only objective the consummation of his desire. And in this context love and passion are shown to be everything – visionary, inspiring, motivating, life-enhancing – that bourgeois society is not, and capable, for much of the time, of surmounting the obstacles placed in their way.

Separated and dragged away by outraged onlookers, reminiscent of the fate of the androgen in *Un Chien andalou*, the lovers conquer time and space, their passion for each other unaffected. Indeed, objects suggestive of bourgeois

---

[29] Buñuel, 116.
[30] See Francisco Aranda, *Luis Buñuel: A Critical Biography*, trans. David Robinson (London: Secker and Warburg, 1975), 27.

commercialism – adverts for hand-cream and silk stockings, a female portrait in a shop window – are used by the hero to his own advantage, fuelling his erotic thoughts, while the girl lies on the sofa at home, thinking of him, her head thrown back, and doubtless masturbating. Her rubbing of her nails with a nail-file continues this idea, as do other later moments: her rubbing of her ring, the servant's rubbing a carafe of wine. In the case of the lovers, Buñuel both uses external reality to highlight their inner lives and to show how true passion transcends it, the sequence in which the young woman gazes into the mirror but sees only the reflection of her imaginings being the perfect example. In contrast, the bourgeois world in which the couple are placed is entirely devoid of an inner life, its emphasis entirely on surface elegance.

The dinner party at the country house outside Rome allows Buñuel, as he would do in later films such as *El ángel exterminador* [*The Exterminating Angel*], *Viridiana*, and *Cet obscur objet du désir* [*That Obscure Object of Desire*], to pinpoint and to mock bourgeois superficiality. The elegant drawing-room, immaculately clad guests, polite introductions and forms of address are the essence of this world, and, with it, a self-sufficiency and complacency oblivious to all outside it. The latter is made very evident when the guests are seen to be so absorbed in their conversation that they fail to notice the cart full of drunken peasants as it trundles through the drawing-room; ignore the screaming servant as she runs from the burning kitchen; and express a condescending disapproval of the gardener's shooting of his son. In many ways Buñuel strikes a comic note, both here and in the earlier sequence where the young woman finds a cow rather than a poodle lying on her bed, and this is continued in conjunction with the arrival of the young man who, longing to be alone with the girl but distracted by her mother's inane prattling, slaps the latter across the face and is immediately thrown out. These are delightful comic elements, but they do not conceal the fact that the bourgeoisie, for all its apparent foolishness, rejects all threats to its survival no less than the scorpion rids itself of intruders. It is as if, for all his aggression, Buñuel was well aware that the surrealists' attack on bourgeois social and moral values was doomed to failure, as the latter part of the film suggests.

Alone at last in the garden, the lovers attempt to indulge their passion for each other. Once more love is shown at its most ecstatic and frenzied – in the lovers' embraces and expressions; in their devouring of each other – the young woman eats her lover's fingers; in his anguished face covered in blood; and in his vision of themselves in old age and still in love. But if this part of the film suggests the ecstacy and rapture of love, it also reveals the obstacles that stand in the way of its consummation. The garden chairs, for instance, could not be less suited to the accommodation of embracing bodies. The lovers' first kiss is rudely interrupted by the orchestra, even though the music is, ironically, the love theme from *Tristan and Isolde*. The young man is suddenly summoned to the telephone to take a call from the Minister of the Interior – another nice irony in the sense that the latter disrupts the lovers' 'interior' life.

And finally, the appearance of the orchestra conductor in the garden leads to the girl's abandonment of her lover, as though the arrival of this father figure, whom she now embraces, reminds her of the wrongful nature of her erotic desire and draws her back to bourgeois respectability.

Passion, attempting to sweep aside conventional social and moral values, is thus constrained and finally thwarted, the young man driven to an assault on bourgeois objects, which expresses his frustration but which is also an admission of defeat. The elegant bedroom, symbol of sexual respectability, becomes the focus of his revenge, the elongated form of the plough he wields the phallus that scatters bourgeois refinement – pillows, chairs, ornaments – in its path. But if he succeeds in hurling objects, including an archbishop, through the window, it is significant that the archbishop survives, as do the bourgeoisie, the shocks and assaults to which it is subjected. Buñuel may have delighted in lambasting the powers that be, but he was well aware of their resilience.

The final section of *L'Âge d'or*, rather like the opening of *Un Chien andalou*, is designed to subvert audience expectations. Titles, which describe the activities of the four men, including their leader the Duke of Blangis, who are about to leave his castle after an orgy of 120 days, lead us to expect utterly depraved criminals, but the first to emerge is a figure remarkably like Jesus Christ, hands held in front of him in the traditional pious manner. Furthermore, when a young woman, one of the revellers' victims, appears and begs for help, the Christ figure takes her into the castle where, to judge by her screams, he murders her. In this context, it is important to bear in mind that Buñuel detested the notion of divinity personified in a human being, regarding it as a violation of Nature.[31] The identification of the Sadian Duke of Blangis with Christ is thus Buñuel's irreverent comment on the traditional view, as well as, no doubt, a statement to the effect that the greatest crimes have often been committed in the name of religion. It is significant in this respect that the very last shot of *L'Âge d'or*, accompanied by jolly music, should consist of a cross decorated with female scalps.

As the preceding discussion suggests, *L'Âge d'or* differs in several respects from *Un Chien andalou*. Although it is composed of five separate sections of different length and content and may in that respect seem disconcerting, it has little of the dream-like character of the earlier film, even if the sexual drives of the two lovers can be related to the workings of instinct and the unconscious. Rather, the film has a thematic and, in part, a narrative coherence, an objectivity that points to a clear-sighted, clinical viewpoint. This is very much in line with Buñuel's mature films and, in terms of Surrealism, not only thoroughly representative of its second stage but well on the way to the third.

The third stage, as has been suggested earlier, was distinguished by a more political emphasis, and this, as far as Buñuel was concerned, was perfectly in

---

[31] Sánchez Vidal, 146.

tune with his strongly left-wing beliefs. He has observed that he and his friends did not develop a genuine political consciousness until 1927–8: 'Up until that moment, we paid only minimal attention to the infant Communist and anarchist publications, although they did introduce us to Lenin and Trotsky.'[32] Nevertheless, Buñuel's anti-bourgeois feelings had been awakened many years before this by his own privileged background, an attitude that fitted well with his pugnacious character. Later, his association with the Paris surrealist group, some of whom would join the Communist Party, led him to join the Association of Writers and Artists for the Revolution, even though he claims not to have been a member of the Communist Party itself. By his own admission, nevertheless, his sympathies with Communism remained strong until the end of the 1950s.[33]

*Terre sans pain*, also known as *Las Hurdes*, the part of Extremadura depicted in the film, was shot over a period of four weeks in April and May 1933. By this time the region was generally regarded as perhaps the most poor and backward in the whole of Spain. Following a debate in the Cortes, the King, Alfonso XIII, visited the area in June 1922, and again in 1930, and was visibly shocked by what he saw: small, cramped houses with no chimneys or sanitation; people riddled with physical and mental ailments; a land that produced virtually no food. In 1927 the French scientist, Maurice Légendre, published a study of the region: *Las Hurdes, étude de géographie humaine*, a work that greatly impressed Buñuel. When he arrived there to begin shooting, it was no coincidence that his team consisted of Ramón Acín, Rafael Sánchez Ventura, both anarchists; Eli Lotar, a Trotskyite; and Pierre Unik, a communist. In making the film, Buñuel's purpose was, in true surrealist fashion, to shock and create outrage – not through the presentation on screen of disturbing images released by the unconscious, but through the depiction of a terrible reality which people either ignored or of which they were unaware.[34]

The film's title is immediately followed by its description as a documentary: *Documentaire de LUIS BUÑUEL*, and this by titles, before any pictures are seen and the voice-over begins, the latter describing Las Hurdes as a sterile and inhospitable region where man always struggles to survive. As far as documentary itself is concerned, we have already seen that Buñuel uses it to begin *L'Âge d'or* and that the film in general, like many of his later films, becomes a kind of documentary in which he examines the customs and behaviour of the bourgeoisie much as a scientist would study insects. In the case of *Terre sans pain*, he similarly places the region and the people of Las Hurdes under the microscope, but from the outset his method is, in typical surrealist fashion,

---

[32] Buñuel, 55–6.
[33] Buñuel, 166.
[34] For a detailed study of the film, including the translation of the French commentary into Spanish, see Mercé Ibarz, *Buñuel documental: Tierra sin pan y su tiempo* (Zaragoza: Prensas Universitarias de Zaragoza, 1999).

subversive. If, for example, the initial titles indicate that Las Hurdes is an inhospitable place in which life is a struggle, this in no way prepares one for the horrors that lie ahead. On the contrary, it creates a curiosity in the audience – particularly a bourgeois audience in the 1930s – to see, perhaps, how the other half lives, much as the almost fairytale opening of *Un Chien andalou* – 'ONCE UPON A TIME' – lulls the spectator into a false sense of security.

This tactic is continued in the opening sequence in which a map of the area is shown, accompanied both by the pleasant sound of Brahms' *Fourth Symphony* and the voice-over, which informs us that, before proceeding to Las Hurdes itself, we will pause in La Alberca, a prosperous town with a rich history. A series of shots then reveals typical narrow, winding streets, a sturdy church tower, and, among other things, a traditional ceremony in which the newly married men of the town take part. This, announces the voice-over in a totally calm and objective fashion, involves ripping the head off chickens strung by a rope across the road. It is the film's first shock, reminiscent of the slicing of the eyeball in *Un Chien andalou*, and reinforced here by the narrator's calm voice, which reminds us that he, and we, have to be objective. But the subsequent shots of men, women and children decked out in traditional costume are insufficient to remove from our minds the image of the fluttering, decapitated chicken. Buñuel has surreptitiously exploded his first bomb. This is no ordinary documentary.

From La Alberca, Buñuel takes us – the narrator's address to the film's audience ensures that we are participants in the journey – to the valley of Las Batuecas. Shots of the abandoned Carmelite convent, of lush vegetation, of rushing streams, and of wild life, are once more reassuring, but, as soon as we are introduced to Las Hurdes proper and to the village of Aceitunilla, these pleasant images are swept aside by others of abject misery and degradation, the viewer exposed to horrors he could hardly have anticipated. In contrast to the rushing stream seen earlier, a mere trickle of water runs through the village and is used for all purposes. The camera moves from a ragged woman washing clothes to a pig drinking from the same stream, to a small girl helping a baby to drink, to a mother washing her child, and to a group of children softening stale crusts in the filthy, infected water. In the village school undernourished, barefooted and unsmiling children, their heads shaved in many cases in an effort to rid them of lice, sit at their desks in a wretched schoolroom. On the wall a painting of a young woman in aristocratic dress provides an ironic contrast, while the words written on the blackboard by one of the children – 'Respetad los bienes ajenos [Respect other people's property]' – invites us to ask what respect is shown by the world at large to these poor children.

In the villages of Martilandrán and Fragosa further horrors are revealed. The people are dressed in rags, pigs roam the streets, a small child with an infected mouth and throat dies two days later. In Fragosa the inhabitants live in cramped houses little better than caves, where the absence of chimneys

means that the rooms are filled with smoke, and where they and their animals
sleep on the floor on the rotting leaves of strawberry trees. Illness and disease
abound, both on account of undernourishment and of the presence in summer
of mosquitoes, whose effect is seen in one particular shot of a young man
uncontrollably trembling. As well as this, hunger, poverty and inbreeding produce the dwarves and cretins, the worst affected of the humans who inhabit
Las Hurdes, close-ups of whom turn the last sequences of the film into a portrait gallery of terrible degradation. In this context it seems inevitable that the
film should also emphasise towards its conclusion the death of a small child
whose tiny body is transported by land and water for two days to the nearest
cemetery where the crosses are little more than two sticks of wood.

The journey into Las Hurdes is, in effect, a journey into a hell on earth in
which the inhabitants of the region are shown to be not so much a little lower
than the angels as on a par with and just as helpless as their wretched animals.
The point is effectively made in two telling sequences: in the first a goat stum-
bles on a steep slope and falls to its death; in the second a donkey transport-
ing honey is stung to death by swarms of bees. The people of Las Hurdes can
no more help themselves than can these beasts. Furthermore, no one else
seems willing to offer assistance or compassion. In this respect it is significant that in the villages of Las Hurdes there are so many reminders of the
church: in the form of buildings, inscriptions above doors, and a Christian burial. But in practical terms the church, more concerned with souls than with
physical welfare, has done nothing. The abandoned convent of Las Batuecas
is, perhaps, Buñuel's biting comment on the church's lack of concern with
these people.

*Terre sans pain* is, then, very different indeed from the traditional documentary, its power to shock as great, in a different way, as that of Buñuel's
first two films. In that sense, as well as in its oblique attack on the powers that
be which have ignored Las Hurdes, it is essentially surrealist, more political
in its implications than the earlier films but fully in accord with the beliefs of
those surrealists whose aim it was to attempt to change society. In order to
achieve maximum effect, Buñuel, indeed, carefully structured his material,
not only slowly exposing his audience to increasing horrors, but, as Robert
Havard has suggested, 'staging' certain episodes to that end.[35] In this respect,
therefore, this film shares that element of control that characterised Dalí's
'paranoia-critical' method, which we have already seen to be a feature of both
*Un Chien andalou* and *L'Âge d'or*. Driven on this occasion not by a desire to
reveal the unconscious nor to show natural instinct and desire thwarted by
bourgeois constraints, but by a strong sense of outrage that approaches the
political, *Terre sans pain* can thus be seen as a fine example of the third stage
of Surrealism. When the film had its première at the Palacio de la Prensa in

[35]  Havard, 207–8.

Madrid in 1933, many in the audience disliked what they had seen. Gregorio Marañón, who had accompanied the King to Las Hurdes eleven years earlier, complained that it showed Spain in a bad light, and, most ironic of all, it was banned by the Republican Government. To that extent Buñuel had certainly made his point.

# 6

# Dalí's Anti-paintings of 1928

## DAWN ADES

Just before he officially became a surrealist, Dalí produced a group of large, apparently abstract and in some cases almost bare, canvases that have received little attention from critics or historians. The lack of interest is unsurprising, not just because of their odd and intransigent character, but also because they seem to be an irrelevant interruption in what was an otherwise coherent move, from the 'breakthrough' paintings of 1927, like *Honey is Sweeter than Blood* and *Cenecitas* [*Little Ashes*], to the great pictures of 1929 that mark his entry into the surrealist movement, such as *First Days of Spring, Accommodations of Desire, Lugubrious Game* and the *Great Masturbator*. The contrast between the highly complex, psychoanalytically derived iconography of these paintings and the vacuity of what for the moment I will call the anti-paintings is striking. The former were to re-establish, with a new confidence and brilliance, the idea of a 'dream painting', sidelined within Surrealism since 1924 and the first debates about a putative surrealist painting. The anti-paintings are part of a wider group of experimental works including sand paintings and collage-objects, which accompanied Dalí's passionate, often critical and exploratory early approach to the movement on which he was to have such a far-reaching impact. They cast an interesting light on attitudes to Surrealism in Spain in the second half of the 1920s, and also highlight the complex relationship between Surrealism, abstract art and Miró's claim to 'assassinate painting'.[1]

It is a familiar paradox that, while Surrealism insisted ideologically on its internationalism and opposed the national in both politics and culture, it was directed from Paris, which remained its centre. Artists, writers and critics at a distance from Paris installed their 'power stations'[2] on its current, and groups

---

[1] Miró's denunciation of painting spread widely by word of mouth. It was first quoted by Maurice Raynal in his *Anthologie de la peinture en France de 1906 à nos jours* (Paris, 1927), and then by Tériade in the newspaper *L'Intransigeant*, 7 May 1928. See William Jeffett, *Dalí and Miró circa 1928* (St Petersburg, Florida: Salvador Museum Exhibition Series, 2003), 11.

[2] Walter Benjamin, 'Surrealism: The Last Snapshot of the European Intelligentsia' (1929), in *Reflections* (New York, 1986), 177 ('Intellectual currents can generate a sufficient

were formed in Prague, London, the Canaries, Japan and Belgium among other places, some even with their own review. The question of Surrealism in Spain, though, has been particularly contentious, and Spanish historiography has variously denied its existence or argued that there was a native and original Spanish Surrealism owing nothing to France. The so-called Generation of 1927 'systematically refused to identify themselves with the French section of the movement – a fact corroborated by Dámaso Alonso, who himself never accepted the existence of Surrealism in Spain and thus fed the myth of a literary independence which obviously had no foundation'.[3] Lucía García de Carpi argues that

> In the light of the studies carried out in the last few years there is no doubt as to the existence of surrealist literature and plastic art in Spain. But we might also point out that . . . the fallacy has been gaining ground in Spanish historiography that an 'autochthonous' Spanish Surrealism completely unconnected with the French movement existed, so that the denial of the existence of any kind of manifestation of Surrealism in Spain has turned directly into the justification of its existence in terms of telluric determinism or as an irrefutable psychological group disposition.[4]

Recognising the role of Surrealism among Spanish writers, intellectuals and artists is obviously crucial for a proper investigation of the Spanish avant-garde before the Civil War. But the traffic was not one-way – in the visual arts especially, a number of Spanish artists made vital contributions that helped shape the movement at its core. In different ways Picasso, Miró, Dalí and Oscar Domínguez were major innovative presences at its very heart, active participants in its evolution.

The exhibition *El Surrealismo en España* at the Museo Nacional Centro de Arte Reina Sofía, Madrid (1994–5) is evidence of the large number of artists in Spain who 'tuned in' to Surrealism. It included forty-seven artists of Spanish origin whose work was deemed to have entered the orbit of Surrealism.[5] This happened in several waves and was most noticeable in the early 1930s, after Dalí's acceptance into the movement. Ángel Planells, José Caballero and Joan Massanet, for example, drew on Dalí's model for their dream-laden landscapes. The selection of artists, set against the ongoing debates about Surrealism in Spain, raises some interesting issues.

head of water for the critic to install his power station on them. The necessary gradient, in the case of Surrealism, is produced by the difference in intellectual level between France and Germany.')

[3] Lucía García de Carpi, 'La respuesta española' [Itineraries of Surrealism in Spain], *El Surrealismo en España* (Madrid: Museo Nacional Centro de Arte Reina Sofia, 1994–5), 428.

[4] García de Carpi, 428.

[5] Research on the work and careers of many of these artists is still in an embryonic state.

Their credentials vary considerably: some were fully fledged members of the movement, others had peripheral or temporary affiliations or could be seen broadly as fellow travellers. A few adopted a mode closely associated with Surrealism, as in the cases of Alfonso Buñuel and Adriano del Valle whose collages of engravings are clearly inspired by Max Ernst. The perennial conundrum remains of how to define a surrealist in this context. The diversity in medium (paintings, collages, photomontages, objects, sculpture) and style (from virtual abstraction to highly polished figuration), both confirms the problem of using them as a defining characteristic and runs true to Surrealism in the sense that visual Surrealism cannot be restricted to nor identified with any one style.

Surrealism occupies a peculiar position in relation to avant-garde art of the first decades of the twentieth century. Given that it was initially concerned with language and with poetry, and announced its commitment to automatism in terms of the verbal (though allowing for other modes of automatic practice), the question of its translation into the visual was a matter for extensive debate and diverse solutions. Surrealism came at the visual from a different angle from that of the Fauves, the Cubists, de Stijl or the Purists. The question was made more complex by the previous example of Dada, which had opened up radical questions about the differentiation of art and life, which it deplored. Surrealism was to operate an open-ended approach to the visual arts, larded with a heavy dose of Dada, welcoming the popular, championing the object, curious about the non-Western. The crucial point is that no single style can be identified as surrealist, at least in its early years. The attitude to painting, however, was ambivalent. Although Breton intended the series of articles 'Le Surréalisme et la peinture', which he launched on taking control of *La Révolution surréaliste* in 1925, to affirm painting as a surrealist activity, in the face of attacks by more radical members of the movement, he still referred to it as 'that lamentable expedient'.[6] Painting's value lay in its power over our imagination, in what it 'looked out onto', in revelation and surprise, rather than in any inherent qualities in the medium as such. If for Breton the visual image was a conduit for the imagination, precious for its capacity to make palpable what 'can be', others stressed its faculty for disorientation, potentially more threatening. Breton later described automatism and the 'fixing' of dream images as the two routes followed by surrealist artists but deplored the danger of the latter becoming routine.[7] The 'fixing' of dream images, though with a pedigree stretching back to de Chirico and Max Ernst, really became central to Surrealism with the arrival of Salvador Dalí in 1929.

[6] André Breton, 'Le Surréalisme et la peinture', in *La Révolution surréaliste*, no. 4 (15 July 1925), 29, trans. S. Watson Taylor in *Surrealism and Painting* (Icon Editions, 1972), 6.

[7] André Breton, 'Artistic Genesis and Perspective of Surrealism' (1941) in *Surrealism and Painting*, 68.

This was preceded by the intensive experiments of the first five years of the movement, with Miró's automatism, like that of Ernst and Masson, opening up new practices and new forms of art. However, in 'Le Surréalisme et la peinture' Breton placed Picasso at the head: not any Picasso but the Cubist Picasso of works like *Man with Clarinet*. The new freedom in dealing with reality that the Cubist disintegration of form and its reconstitution in terms of association and metaphor had achieved was taken by Breton as an example of the way the imagination can operate its desire on the real world. Breton always hoped to be able to accept Picasso as 'one of us', and Picasso was at various points in his career to come close to Surrealism, especially in the early 1930s.[8] His constructions, objects and the extraordinarily minimal canvases of the second half of the 1920s continued to challenge the 'lamentable expedient' of painting in the surrealists' eyes. But Picasso, intense though his influence was on Surrealism, kept his distance from the movement. Undoubtedly his work played a part in the dissemination of Surrealism in Spain, though it is not easy and perhaps impossible to separate this from the more general spread of avant-garde practices. Miró, on the other hand, was a member of the movement in Paris from its inception, and was to be a crucial link between Paris and Catalonia.

Although no time period defines the work included in the exhibition *El Surrealismo en España*, the vast majority of the works date between 1927 and 1937, in other words from the moment of intense engagement with avant-garde modes, including Surrealism, to the victory of Franco's nationalists. The only artists represented with work after 1940 were Eugenio Granell (who met Breton in the Caribbean in 1941) and Esteban Frances. Frances, who like Rodríguez Luna left for Mexico after the Civil War, moved subsequently to New York, and their work can be situated in the context of Surrealism in America. The catalogue is reticent on the post-Civil War careers of those artists like Adriano del Valle whose links to the avant-garde 'became weaker due to his being accepted by officialdom'.[9] There is a disturbing if superficial similarity between the works José Caballero produced for Franco's *Laureados de España* and surrealist dream landscapes. Other artists like Alberto Sánchez explicitly rejected 'Paris' (not, admittedly, necessarily the surrealists alone) in favour, like Rodríguez Luna – whose drawings belong in the great satirical anti-war tradition of Goya and Grosz – of a committed art. Alberto wrote in the mid-1930s: 'Today we are at the crossroads. We can now see most of the artists from the great epoch of Paris enveloped in capitalist droolings . . . Ours is another path, a path that will make us alive. Let us make a social art.'[10] Earlier, in 1927, Alberto Sánchez had formed with Benjamín Palencia the 'School of Vallecas', which sought a close relationship with

---

[8]  See Elizabeth Cowling, ' "Proudly we claim him as one of us": Breton, Picasso and the surrealist movement', *Art History*, 8, 1 (March 1985).

[9]  García de Carpi, 511.

[10]  García de Carpi, 508.

nature and the earth. Their interest was centred on the Castilian landscape, which they represented 'not as seen by the eye but as touched by the hand'.[11] The organic morphology of Palencia's work offers interesting comparisons with Arp and Miró, as well as Picasso. But on the whole there is little coherence and no core to this group of artists gathered under the umbrella of Surrealism in Spain. The most powerful voices were closely identified with Paris Surrealism, its manifestos, exhibitions and reviews. Despite the fact that certain special conditions nourished the ground for Surrealism, such as the close association between poets and artists at the Residencia in Madrid, the outcome was not the founding of a sister movement in Spain.

Nonetheless, several of the Spanish artists such as Miró had a double role, within Paris Surrealism as well as at home. There is also often a disjunction between the inscription of an artist as 'surrealist' in, respectively, the context of the Paris centre and of their local avant-garde. Maruja Mallo, for instance, friend of Dalí from the Residencia days and fellow student at the Academy in Madrid, featured, like Dalí, in the pages of *L'Amic de les Arts* (September 1928). The critic Sebastiá Gasch writes of her work: 'No insisterem novament sobre l'amagada substancia de les coses, la realitat profunda, la superrealitat, el lirisme de la realitat, l'essencia de les coses, l'anima dels objectes' [We will not insist on the hidden substance of things, the deep reality, the surreality, the lyricism of reality, the essence of things, the soul of the objects].[12] Two paintings by Maruja Mallo, metaphysical still-lifes, with uncanny dummies and the accoutrements of the 'anti-artistic' as Dalí was to define it, are reproduced. Gasch here clearly associates her work both with Surrealism and with Franz Roh's 'Post-Expressionism' or magic realism, which focused on the uncanny in post-war figuration.[13] These early works by Maruja Mallo are rarely mentioned in connection with Surrealism, however, and her relationship with the movement is largely discussed in terms of the pictures that were exhibited in Paris in 1932, like *Espantapájaros* [*Scarecrows*].[14] This painting was bought by Breton, who was intrigued by her dark vision, and he kept it for the rest of his life.

In the case of Dalí, affiliation to Surrealism from the perspective of Paris Surrealism is registered with his new 'dream' paintings and the film *Un Chien andalou* of 1929. The new recruit was prominently announced in the final issue of *La Révolution surréaliste*, which published details of Dalí's painting

[11] García de Carpi, 503.

[12] Sebastià Gasch, 'Els Pintors Nous: Maria Mallo', *L'Amic de les Arts* (Sitges), no. 28 (31 September 1928 [*sic*]), 220.

[13] Franz Roh's influential 1925 study of post-war metaphysical and new objectivity painting, Nach-*Expressionismus; magischer Realismus: Probleme der neuesten europäischen Malerei*, was translated in the *Revista de Occidente* in 1927 as *Realismo mágico: Post-expresionismo*.

[14] Mallo exhibited her paintings *Cloacas y campanarios* at the Galerie Pierre in Paris in 1932.

*Accommodations of Desire*, and the scenario of the film jointly signed by Buñuel and Dalí. These interventions were welcomed as indicating a new direction in surrealist practice; the publication in the succeeding surrealist journal *Le Surréalisme au service de la révolution* of his text, 'L'Âne pourri', which was part of the 1930 book *La Femme visible*, challenged surrealist automatism and introduced a new mode of enquiry: paranoia. However, the fully accomplished and apparently fixed pictorial mode of Dalí's 1929 paintings was the culmination of a long process of exploration and experiment that took place within the framework of an extensive critical analysis of surrealist ideas within the Catalan and Spanish avant-garde over the previous four or five years; it was also strikingly different from the abstraction of the 'anti-paintings'.

\* \* \*

The avant-garde reviews in Catalonia and in Spain, which proliferated in the second half of the 1920s, were very alert to Surrealism and to a large extent the gateway through which its ideas, with varying degrees of sympathy, passed. The 'little magazine' was the platform shared by writers, intellectuals and artists; it was 'a vehicle which not only provided the arena for aesthetic experimentation but also made possible the theoretical background against which the creative artists worked'.[15] The review with which Dalí had the closest contact was the Catalan *L'Amic de les Arts*, whose editorial board he joined in November 1927. This well-illustrated, large-format review had wide contacts with the European avant-garde. Here one can trace not just a diversity of attitudes to Surrealism among the review's regular contributors but also the other currents that rub up against it and were to inform Dalí's highly individual approach to Surrealism. Works by both Dalí and Miró are reproduced regularly virtually from the inception of the review in 1926. Miró's career and his involvement with Surrealism are closely followed, and Gasch, who became the sternest opponent of Surrealism, expresses outrage in August 1926 at Miró's expulsion from Surrealism following his collaboration on the sets of the ballet *Romeo and Juliet*.[16] His colleague Montanyà regarded it as a symptom of post-war spiritual disorder, but paid careful attention to recent publications such as Aragon's *Paris Peasant* ('a jumble of excellent things and detestable things').[17] In the special issue devoted to Miró in June 1928, Montanyà again analysed Surrealism's origins and efficacy: 'els superrealistes tenen el mèrit d'haver viscut i d'haver comprès amb mes d'intensitat que els altres la desorientacio espiritual de la post-guerra' [The surrealists

[15] Paul Ilie, *The Surrealist Mode in Spanish Literature* (Ann Arbor: University of Michigan Press, 1968), 10.
[16] Sebastià Gasch, 'L'obra actual del pintor Joan Miró', *L'Amic de les Arts* (August 1926), 16.
[17] Luis Montanyà, 'Superrealisme', *L'Amic de les Arts*, no. 10 (31 January 1927), 3.

have the merit of having lived and understood with greater intensity than others the post-war spiritual disorientation].[18]

Between 1927 and 1929 Dalí published numerous prose texts, poems, and theoretical articles on film, photography and the newest painting. It was against this background that he produced the 'anti-paintings'. Of particular significance in their evolution was Dalí's interest in the two much-quoted pronouncements by Miró: 'I want to assassinate painting', and 'Painting is in a state of decadence since the time of cave painting'.[19] Dalí grappled with these in several texts but did not associate them directly with Miró's own work. It is important, however, to distinguish between this denunciation of painting and the concept of the 'anti-artistic'. Although both come broadly within the sphere of the anti-art ideas circulating since Dada, the latter has a quite specific meaning within the Catalan avant-garde, and is associated with the embrace of modernity. Gasch, who, like Dalí, was directly involved with the 'anti-artistic', insisted on the difference between the anti-artistic and Dalí's anti-paintings. He published an article in 1929, 'Pintura i anti-pintura' [Painting and anti-painting] in which he distanced himself from the work and ideas of his friend Dalí while at the same time honestly attempting to explain them. For Gasch, Dalí's work lies outside the art/anti-art discourses; they are outside art altogether. Dalí's canvases, in Gasch's opinion, 'are not painting. They are *hechos* [acts] – not antiartistic – but purely and simply extra-artistic.'[20]

The 'anti-artistic' was characterised by a rejection of artistic traditions and of bourgeois sentimentality. Dalí's writings of early 1928 are peppered with the term ('Art films, anti-artistic films'; 'Review of anti-artistic trends . . . ') and it is summarised in the *Manifesto* he wrote with Sebastià Gasch and Luis Montanyà. Initially untitled and published as a separate single sheet in March 1928, it was reprinted in April by Lorca in his review *Gallo*, no. 2 where it was described as 'El manifiesto anti-artístico catalan'. The choice of yellow paper (hence the nickname *manifest groc*), may have been linked to Dalí's pungent imagery in his lecture to the Ateneo in Sitges, in March 1928, the same month the manifesto was published, which attacked the art of the past, whose value was, he argued, purely archaeological. 'Our artists love all that which time or the antiquarian's hand have left on the adored object, that characteristic yellowish tone: so repugnant, so similar to the one which, in the final analysis, street corners take on after dogs have repeatedly gone and pissed on them.'[21]

---

[18] Luis Montanyà, 'Panorama: punts de vista sobre el superrealisme', *L'Amic de les Arts*, no. 25 (31 May 1928), 200.

[19] Miró's second slogan was also quoted by Tériade, 1928 (see note 1).

[20] Sebastià Gasch, 'Pintura i anti-pintura', *La Veu de Catalunya* (13 June 1929), quoted in Fèlix Fanés, *Salvador Dalí: La Construcción de la imagen 1925–1930* (Electa, 1999), 121.

[21] Dalí, 'Per al "meeting" de Sitges' [text of his lecture at the Ateneo El Centaure in Sitges], *L'Amic de les Arts*, no. 25 (31 May 1928), 195. Partial translation in *Oui: the Paranoid-Critical Revolution, Writings 1927–1933 by Salvador Dalí*, ed. Descharnes, trans. Yvonne Shafir (Boston: Exact Change, 1998).

The artistic was identified with the *putrefact*,[22] while hygiene (the 'sterile' was the opposite of the *putrefact*) characterised this new 'post-machinist' state of mind. Cinema, jazz, sport, photography, motor shows, beach games, modern architecture are among the manifestations of modern life that Dalí and his co-signatories support, while the sentimental in music and art, the imitation of the classical, the Sardana and other picturesque forms of Catalan culture are denounced. Barcelona's Gothic Quarter should be torn down in favour of 'les primers arquitectures clares i joviales del ciment' [light and jovial architecture in reinforced concrete].[23] Dalí's insistence on the value of the strictly object-ive fact is one of the most striking aspects of his notion of the 'anti-artistic'.

> Telephone, wash basin, refrigerators white and shining with ripolin, bidet, little phonograph . . . objects of authentic and very pure poetry.
>
> All this aseptic, anti-artistic and joyful precision, this distilled product of a miraculous mechanical era in which, for the first time in the history of mankind, we can attain numerical perfection in standard objects as a result of the most economical and necessary practical logic, is replaced by artis-tic taste with all the anguish and confusion of arbitrary, bloated, sad, badly made, unusable, dirty, anti-poetic objects: pure, macabre refuse from epochs that are for the most part absurd and uncomfortable . . . [24]

There is an evident debt to Purism and the machine aesthetic as well as to *Neue Sachlichkeit*, Dada and, in such texts as 'Photography: pure creation of the mind', to Moholy-Nagy's 1926 Bauhaus book *Painting Photography Film*. Even when Dalí makes the decision to affiliate himself more directly to Surrealism, these traces remain and were to inform his rejection of the 'passive' modes of automatism.

Dalí's prolific contributions to the final, auto-destructive issue of *L'Amic de les Arts* in March 1929 maintained an ambivalent tone towards Surrealism, which is approved of fully but not exclusively and on his own terms. In a letter to Lorca in September 1928 he had asserted his priorities in relation to Sur-realism, and his need for autonomy:

> Surrealism is *one* of the means of Escape
> But it's Escape itself that is the important thing

[22] On the *Putrefact* as elaborated by Dalí and Lorca, see Dawn Ades, 'Morphologies of Desire', in *Salvador Dalí: The Early Years* (London: South Bank Centre, 1994), 137–40; *Los putrefactos por Salvador Dalí y Federico García Lorca: dibujos y documentos* (Barcelona: Centre Cultural Caixa Catalunya, Apr.–June 1998); Rafael Santos Torroella, *'Los Putrefactos' de Dalí y Lorca* (Madrid: Publicaciones de la Residencia de Estudiantes, 1998).

[23] Dalí, 'Per al "meeting" de Sitges', 195.

[24] Salvador Dalí, 'Poetry of Standardized Utility', *L'Amic de les Arts*, no. 23 (31 March 1928), 176–7; trans. based on those of John London in *Salvador Dalí: The Early Years*, 223 and Shafir in *Oui*, 43.

I'm beginning to have my own modes apart from Surrealism, but
the latter is something alive.
As you can see, I no longer talk about it as I used to . . . [25]

Dalí's statement on the front page of *L'Amic* put the fight against 'the can-
cerous artistic process first', and then announced: 'At this moment, I repeat,
SURREALISM AS A FUNCTION OF REALITY, as living ANTI-ARTISTIC
FACT, as MORAL SUBVERSION, is the only ANTI-IMAGINATIVE
MEANS, through its unlimited, mechanical faculties of accommodation and
speed capable of the most fertile and vertiginous possibilities in the field of
knowledge . . . '

In the same issue of *L'Amic de les Arts* Dalí's 'Review of anti-artistic
trends' covers surrealist objects and dream objects; hysteria; documentaries;
rubber sound; sexual surveys; wireless imagination; books. (The only book
named is Benjamin Péret's *Le grand Jeu*, which he and Buñuel used to read
to each other and weep with laughter.[26]) Of these 'trends', several are explicitly surrealist: the surrealist object, which Dalí describes in the very terms
Breton had used in his *Introduction to the discourse on the paucity of reality*,
a passage which continued to haunt him: 'These new objects could be considered dream objects and would fulfil, as Breton says, the perpetual desire
for verification; it would be necessary, he adds, to manufacture, as far as possible, a few objects which we could only approach in dreams and which seem
indefensible if considered in relation to utility . . . '[27] Dalí was to elaborate on
the object in his famous article in *Le Surréalisme au service de la révolution*
in 1931,[28] but in 1928 it was still a virtual idea, although he had made some
experiments with collage-objects. Hysteria and sexual surveys are drawn from
*La Révolution surréaliste*, whose penultimate issue had included two remarkably frank conversations about sexuality, sexual habits and preferences.[29]
Buñuel later noted the impact open discussion of such things as masturbation

[25] Letter to Federico García Lorca, September 1928. Rafael Santos Toroella (ed.),
'Salvador Dalí escribe a Federico García Lorca (1925–1936)', *Poesía. Revista ilustrada de
información poética*, nos 27–8 (Madrid, April 1987), 88–94.

[26] Luis Buñuel, *My Last Breath* (London: Jonathan Cape, 1984), 110.

[27] *L'Amic de les Arts*, no. 31 (31 March 1929), 10. Breton wrote in *Introduction to the
Discourse on the Paucity of Reality*: 'To satisfy this desire for perpetual verification, I
recently proposed to fabricate, insofar as possible, certain objects which are approached
only in dreams and which seem no more useful than enjoyable. . . Perhaps in that way I
should help to demolish these concrete trophies which are so odious, to throw further
discredit on those creatures and things of "reason".' Trans. Bravig Imbs in F. Rosemont
(ed.), *What is Surrealism?* (London: Pluto Press, 1978), 26.

[28] Salvador Dalí, 'Objets surréalistes', in *Le Surréalisme au service de la revolution*,
no. 3 (December 1931), 16.

[29] 'Recherches sur la sexualité', in *La Révolution surréaliste*, no. 11 (15 March 1928).
The first two soirées only were published. See *Investigating Sex: Surrealist Discussions
1928–1932*, trans. Malcolm Imrie (London: Verso, 1992).

had had upon him, and surely the same was true of Dalí.[30] It is tempting to ascribe the newly explicit sexual imagery in his paintings of 1928 to the 'Recherches sur la sexualité'.

Other 'anti-artistic trends', however, maintain the views expressed in the *Manifest groc*. 'Rubber sound' refers to Jazz (specifically Red Nichols), and 'Documentaries' encompassed 'phonograph, photography, film, literature, microscope etc.' Scientific, hygienic, objective, these were the 'anti-artistic' modes he favoured. 'Wire-less imagination' is glossed with a short comment on Breton, although the term in fact derives from the Futurist Marinetti's 1913 manifesto 'Destruction of Syntax – Imagination without strings – Words-in-freedom'.[31]

Not a single painting was included in this final issue of *L'Amic*, only photographs. Dalí had long praised the 'Clear objectivity of the little camera' and contrasted the 'unconscious calculations of the machine' with the 'murky subconscious processes'.[32] His concept of this 'pure objectivity' builds in part on Moholy-Nagy's idea that photography can make visible things normally invisible to the human eye.[33] Dalí implies that the photograph can produce imagery as startling and unexpected as that produced by automatic writing (or other kinds of automatism). 'A simple change of scale provokes unusual resemblances, and existing, though unimaginable, analogies.'[34] Dalí was to elaborate on this theme in his 1933 essay for *Minotaure*, demonstrating it with Brassaï's photographs of the Paris metro, which produce phallic forms and the praying mantis, and Man Ray's of Barcelona art nouveau architecture shot to resemble waves.[35] Objects of vastly different sizes can be brought together in the photographic image, dramatic close-ups, camera angles and changes in scale producing disconcerting effects ('In a wide and limpid cow's eye, we see a minuscule post-machinist landscape . . . ').[36]

Given Dalí's public expression of a preference for photography and film, why had his work became increasingly abstract, reaching its most extreme point in the anti-paintings, which seem about as unlike a photograph as one

[30] Buñuel, 102.

[31] F.T. Marinetti, 'Destruction of Syntax – Imagination without strings – Words-in-Freedom' (1913), in *Futurist Manifestos*, ed. U. Apollonio (London: Thames & Hudson, 1973), 95. Dalí was certainly aware of Marinetti's visit to Barcelona in February 1928, where he lectured and gave extensive press interviews. For the influence of Futurism on Dalí see Fanés, 107, 112.

[32] Salvador Dalí, 'Photography: Pure Creation of the Mind' ['La fotografía, pura creació de l'esperit'], *L'Amic de les arts*, no. 18 (30 September 1927), 90–1, trans. in *Early Years*, 216.

[33] László Moholy-Nagy, *Painting Photography Film*, Bauhaus Books, vol. 8, 1925 (London and Bradford: Lund Humphries, 1969), 28.

[34] Dalí, 'Photography: Pure Creation of the Mind'.

[35] Salvador Dalí, 'De la beauté terrifiante et comestible, de l'architecture Modern style', *Minotaure*, no. 3–4 (Paris, 12 December 1933).

[36] Dalí, 'Photography: Pure Creation of the Mind'

can get? I would suggest that in the group of canvases under discussion by Dalí, the 'assassination of painting' takes the form of turning painting against itself. It is neither a matter of the 'anti-artistic' nor of the 'an-art' or 'extra-artistic' Gasch proposed in relation to Dalí's work. It is not a question of rejecting painting for an alternative medium but of a violent attack on its very body. The alternative between figuration and abstraction is not pertinent – a more fundamental exposure of the medium is at stake.

Abstraction, at this moment, for Dalí, was a complex affair. In his vivid if contradictory writings, abstraction is not seen as an antithesis to Surrealism, especially as his preferred artists, Miró and Arp, seemed so easily to straddle both. He had written in 'New limits of painting' of the 'abstract, spiritualist and anti-naturalist art that we ourselves defend'.[37] The kind of work he had in mind was Miró's *Painting (Circus Horse)* 1927 (reproduced in *L'Amic* in June 1928) or Arp's reliefs. In the case of Miró in particular the 'abstract' is not a function of any aesthetic ideology. It is not 'pure', but built upon a simplification or reduction of the object via the spontaneous or automatist gesture. In practice, he seems to be attending closely to Miró's work in terms of its implications for painting itself rather than what it might reveal about an unconscious subject. In his theoretical texts he dwells on the visual and poetic possibilities of 'anti-naturalist' art on one hand and on the other its capacity to challenge vulgar conceptions of the real.

One of the most interesting but difficult texts is 'New Limits of Painting'. Its title deserves attention because Dalí is not simply making a survey of contemporary painting. He is exploring the question of limits: if all the old rules governing the painter's art have been superseded, what is in their place? Dalí sees clearly that there is no such thing as complete freedom; he examines the analogy with music, adopted by many apologists for abstraction (and perhaps making an incidental critique of the Gasch's idea of *totalismo*, a version of the *gesamtkunstwerk*). The piano (he claims to quote Ozenfant) is an admirable discipline. It produces a limited choice of necessary and sufficient sounds from the infinity of different possible sounds, while the painter struggles with the equivalent of seventy-five thousand different sounds. But the ensuing discourse about linear, picturesque, tactile elements etc. is not the answer. The most recent limits that have appeared in painting can be derived from 'the latest plastic surrealist creation and even . . . contemporary Cubism' (at the opposite pole from Purism.) But the very openness of this can give fright. There is popular art, the *trouvaille*, and what he calls 'liberating disequilibrium within abstraction'.[38] Dalí evades in his allusive and fragmented text any simple division between abstraction and figuration, but is aware of the

---

[37] Salvador Dalí, 'Nous limits de la pintura' [New limits of Painting], *L'Amic de les Arts* (February 1928), 168. 'Nous limits' appeared in three instalments, in February, April and May 1928.

[38] Dalí, 'Nous limits', 168.

confused and unmarked terrain facing the modern painter. The oppositions he hints at are not determined by this division. Though still half in love with the 'terrible calm' and 'bloody perspectives' of de Chirico, the 'cold geometry' of Morandi and the mathematical abstraction of Cubism, it is the formless and mobile that paradoxically offer the 'new limits'. He acknowledges the surrealist origins of Miró's 'abstraction': 'When inspiration and even the purest subconscious have revealed our individual truths, an organic world full of significant attributions invades the artist's figures. At that moment the most emotive and disturbing facts, slumbering in the deepest of our horrors and our most intimate joys, acquire the supreme taste of light.'[39]

Despite this clear reference to the link between automatism and the subconscious, and the oblique reference to abstraction ('an organic world'), Dalí does not pursue further the question of automatic practices in painting. The 'anti-paintings' are like a battleground of competing ideas about painting as Dalí seeks to find a bridge between the objective disruption of reality and 'the deepest horrors and intimate joys'. The objects that inspired these emotions in Dalí were, as is clear form the poems, especially those that are formless and related to putrefaction and waste.

The slippery morphology of the paintings and collage-objects responds to a passage from Breton's 'Surrealism and Painting' that struck Dalí with special force: the invocation of Arp's relief *Nature morte: table, montagne, ancres et nombril*:

> There is nothing gratuitous about Arp's strange insistence that the word should be conjugated thus: *un nombril, des ombrils*. Who knows, it is perhaps precisely a patch of shadow (*ombre*) he means to convey by the little rings that are such a frequent feature of his reliefs of animals, plants and stones? *Ombril*, a strange word, a slip of the tongue to which I would unhesitatingly apply the epithets tragic, snake in the grass, idea . . . In reality, if we know by now what we mean by that, a nose is not only perfectly at ease by the side of an armchair, it even takes the exact shape of the armchair. What difference is there basically between a pair of dancers and the dome of a beehive?[40]

In his text 'Reality and Surreality' (*L'Amic*, October 1928), Dalí grapples with this question.

> Far from all aesthetics . . . we can establish normal cognitive relations which are removed from our habitual experience. There is really no relationship for

[39] Dalí, 'Nous limits' (April 1928), 186 [A més, en el moment en que la inspiració I encara el mes pue subconscient han actuat per la revelació de les nostres veritats individuals, un mon organic ple d'atribucions significatives ha envait les figuracions dels pintors. En aquests moments els fets mes emotius I tornadors adormits en el mes pregon de les nostres mes intimes horrors I elegries adquireixen el maxim gust de la llum.]

[40] Breton, 'Surrealism and Painting', 47.

us between a beehive and a pair of dancers; or rather, as André Breton would say, there exists no essential difference between these two elements. Indeed, in reality, the poetic relationship between the rider and the reins is analogous only to the one that exists, or could exist, between Saturn and the tiny little larva locked within its chrysalis.[41]

The final sentence is unmistakably Dalí, and the way in which the 'actual' size of an object bears no relation to what we perceive (Saturn is quite as tiny as a butterfly larva, if we do not know our relative position spatially) was one of the fundamental aspects of Dalí's optical illusions, as well as a provocative idea in terms of assumptions about reality. Indeed it is Breton's challenge to narrow definitions of the real that attracted Dalí to Surrealism at this moment.

Miró, for Dalí, offered the purest example of the real as opposed to the stereotype. 'Miró's paintings lead us, by way of automatism and surreality, to appreciate and to establish (in an approximate way) reality itself, thus corroborating the thought of André Breton, for whom surreality could be contained within reality and vice versa.'[42] Miró 'gives back to the line, to the point, to the thinnest lamination, to the figurative sign, to colours, their purest elementary magical possibilities'.[43] These magical possibilities involved transformation, shifting from part to whole, perceptual shifts from huge to tiny, as well as metaphorical condensation within a single configuration.

Dalí's anti-paintings are clearly influenced by the kinds of surrealist abstraction he admired in Arp and Miró. They combine aspects of Miró's 'sign-language' and open fields with Arp's biomorphism, but do not seem to be the result of procedures like the former's automatism. The randomly distributed shapes in these canvases are too eccentric and also too specific to be fully explicable in these terms. To describe these paintings as 'intransigent' might seem strange, but it is deliberate. One of these works was included in the exhibition *Dalí: The Early Years*.[44] In the course of installing this exhibition, *Sun, Four Fishermen's Wives* proved impossible to incorporate into the display, both its size and its utterly different appearance fighting against the otherwise integrated suites of paintings. In the end an entirely new wall was built within the final room, with this work alone hung on it. Of course, various explanations can be advanced to account for this painting's incompatibility with the rest of the works in the exhibition: the stylistic divergence with what had gone before

[41] Salvador Dalí, 'Reality and Surreality', *La Gaceta literaria*, no. 44 (15 October 1928), trans. in *Oui*, 63.

[42] Salvador Dalí, 'Joan Miró', *L'Amic*, no 26 (30 June 1928), trans. in *Oui*, 53. For a detailed discussion of this period, see William Jeffett, *Dalí and Miró c. 1928* (Salvador Dalí Museum Exhibition Series, 2003).

[43] Dalí, 'Joan Miró'.

[44] *Salvador Dalí: The Early Years*, exhibition catalogue, ed. Michael Raeburn (London: South Bank Centre, 1994). Hayward Gallery, London; Metropolitan Museum of Art, New York; Museo Nacional de Arte Reina Sofía, Madrid; Palau Robert, Barcelona.

and was to come, the possibility that it was a failed experiment, or perhaps that it was unfinished. I would argue that the awkwardness of this work is, as with the rest of this group of paintings, deliberate – that they are neither unfinished nor in essence failed experiments (though he might have come to see them as such).[45] Those works seem unfinished or abandoned because of the areas of blank canvas, inconsistent surfaces, the unbalanced composition and uncertainty as to their correct orientation, not to speak of the curious sign-shapes themselves. Despite their abstract appearance these are still closely linked to Dalí's obsessive search for ways of representing sex, which oscillated between a codified eroticism and the frankest possible representation of sexual activity. The anti-paintings are the sign of 'our amorous simplifications'.[46]

They constitute odd scenarios, with shapes that often appear incomplete, cut-off fragments, sometimes anatomical, which cluster at the edges of an otherwise bare canvas, or multiply and swarm into the centre. The intrusion, characteristic of graffiti, of hybrid signs that challenge the purity of the pictorial image appear. On the barest canvases the few traces of forms underline absence and vacuity. Some of the marks resemble graffiti not just in their random placement but in their repetition and subsequent deformation. There is transitory reference to the calligraphic and even some visual similarity to the Andalusian Arabic script.[47]

About eight of these large canvases, ranging from one to two metres in size, survive. Nothing in the picture provides a sense of scale or an illusion of space: unusually for Dalí there is no horizon line and nothing to indicate perspective. The forms, which are quite repetitive, are rudimentary, painted in flat colours (red, black or occasionally blue) without modelling. Beside the 'sand paintings', which overlap with the anti-paintings, at least two include collage elements: feathers are pasted onto *Fishermen in Cadaqués*, and string is incorporated in *Fishermen in the Sun*. Unlike the use of collage in the 1929 paintings such as *Lugubrious Game*, where Dalí has done his utmost to disguise any difference between the painted and the ready-made images, in these works the collage is clearly extraneous, material substance, an addition or challenge to the pictorial.

Several are untitled or have the vague designation 'abstract composition'. However, those that do have titles introduce an unusual variant on the common theme of 'bathers' or 'figures on a beach': *Fishermen and Fisherwomen* or *Fishermen's wives*. The title of one at least of these paintings has altered over time: *Four Fishermen's Wives of Cadaqués* was previously known

[45] *Sun* or *Four Fishermen's Wives of Cadaqués* was shown at the 1979–80 retrospective at the Centre Pompidou, Paris, from the artist's private collection. Most of the surviving canvases of this group emerged after his death in a poor condition and needed extensive restoration, suggesting he cared little for their fate.

[46] 'Nous limits' (May 1928), 186.

[47] *Gallo*, no. 2 (Granada, April 1928), 11.

as *Sun* (Pompidou 1979), and then as *Sun, Four Fisherwomen of Cadaqués* (Descharnes).[48]

The history of the anti-paintings is woven together with the sand paintings and collage-objects of 1928. The imagery in a small group of Dalí's 'sand paintings', on the theme of the 'Bather', had become increasingly sexually explicit. This venerable excuse for painting the nude had become the vehicle for highly suggestive images, which represented male and female bodies singly or together, convulsed with desire. This obsessional subject stretches back to much earlier beach scenes with prostrate bodies, such as *Women Lying on the Beach*, 1926.[49] In the sand paintings naked pink shapes balance precariously between inventive formal distortion, symbolism and the representation of sexual activity.

In the autumn of 1928 Dalí sent his painting *Unsatisfied Desires* (also known as *Two Figures on a Beach*) to the Autumn Salon at the Sala Peres in Barcelona. Two pink anatomical forms, disturbing lumps of erect flesh, confront each other on an empty beach, which is literally represented with sand and little pebbles. Towering into the sky is the rough outline of an enormous and unmistakably phallic big toe. This picture was rejected by the director Maragall, because, apparently, of its unacceptably explicit representation of sexual organs. Dalmau[50] agreed to hang it at the inaugural exhibition at his gallery in October, together with *Female Figure and Masculine Figure on a beach* and the collage-object, *Female Nude*. However, he too got cold feet and, taking a cue from Dalí's *Female Nude*, a curvilinear lump of cork, hung a piece of cork over the male figure in *Unsatisfied Desires*. 'Nada tan lógico' [Nothing so fitting], as Gasch wrote to Miró in commenting on the incident, 'como pegar un trozo de corcho sobre el miembro PIRAMIDAL' [as sticking a piece of cork on a PYRAMIDAL limb].[51] Dalí immediately withdrew the work.

*Female Nude*, a curvilinear piece of cork casting a painted shadow, and *Anthropomorphic Beach*, whose ingredients were oil, cork, stone, red sponge and polychrome finger carved of wood, were Dalí's first ventures into the realm of the object. The cork is a 'found' object, filched from the cork floats used by the Port Lligat fishermen to suspend their nets. *Female Nude*, in its first state, was attached to a much larger support, within which it was asymmetrically positioned, which brings it closer to the anti-paintings. They make an interesting comparison with Miró's more or less contemporaneous series of 'Spanish Dancers' (Spring 1928); like these, the objects are assembled on canvas, thus remaining within the pictorial frame. The *Spanish Dancer*,

[48] Robert Descharnes, *Salvador Dalí: The Paintings* (Cologne: Taschen, 1994).
[49] Reproduced with the title *Figures ajagudes a la Sorra* in *L'Amic*, no. 11 (February 1927).
[50] Dalí had his first one-man exhibition in 1925 at the Gallery Dalmau in Barcelona.
[51] Gasch, letter to Miró, October 1928, quoted in Fanés, 125.

acquired by Breton in July 1928,[52] consisted solely of a feather and a hat-pin piercing a small piece of cork balanced precariously in the upper centre of the canvas. The contrast between the extreme simplicity of the objects and the multiplicity of their associative and metaphorical possibilities enchanted Breton. The objects, pearly grey pin, slightly bedraggled but gracefully curved feather, are what they are; they do not obviously symbolise anything else, and yet they are intensely poetic. The first of Miró's *Spanish Dancers*, however, which incorporated sandpaper, hair, string, nails and an architect's triangle, had, like Dalí's *Anthropomorphic Beach*, a much more explicit sexual symbolism. The triangle evidently stands for the female sex. Whether or not it could be said to symbolise it is another matter; the triangle is a sign already often used by Miró to represent parts of the body. Dalí's objects, like the paintings, alternate between highly abstracted anatomies and direct references to sex. He underlines the crudely phallic character of the finger in *Anthropomorphic Beach* by painting hairs on its base.[53] The red sponge would seem to stand for the female sex, though the curving black shapes are ambivalent. The gender of the nudes and bathers is curiously indeterminate, however.

It is highly unlikely that Dalí was chastened by the Maragall/Dalmau scandal and withdrew into the 'safer' territory of abstraction; his continuation along this route rather absorbs the difficulty of representing the erotic impulse into the problem of painting itself. The occlusion of the representation of sex becomes one with the disintegration of form. Dalí was certainly conscious of a crisis at this moment, not just in his own work but in painting itself. This was not a purely negative recognition of the supercession of a particular mode of art. Uncertain of the future and recognising that nothing remained of the past, Dalí is nonetheless convinced that only in that arena where painting is attacked on its own ground has it any chance of surviving.

> Necessarily disordered forces fight amongst themselves today in the most lively domains of painting. This is a passionate period, because psychologically it is beginning to arouse everyone at the very moment its most radical assassination is being carried out. You could say that nothing remains from earlier painting; not a single one of the concerns of early painters makes the hand of contemporary artists move. I believe that it is not even daring to encourage and affirm all of our affection in this total assassination of painting, and, indeed, of art in general. If it were not so, we would find outside of art suggestions and facts sufficient to move us more effectively than time-proven mechanisms. The assassination of art, what a beautiful

[52] From Miró's Paris dealer, Galerie Pierre.
[53] Salvador Dalí, ' . . . L'alliberament dels dits . . . ' *L'Amic*, no. 31 (March 1929), 6. Dalí illustrates his text with photos of isolated thumbs and fingers; he discusses their sexual symbolism and mentions Freud's reference to the 'flying phallus' of ancient civilisations. See Ades, 'Morphologies of Desire'.

eulogy! The Surrealists are people who honestly commit themselves to that.
I am not of the same mind.[54]

One of the very few references traceable to the anti-paintings in Dalí's volu-
minous memoirs fleetingly records that, after painting the seminal *Honey is
Sweeter than Blood*, he also produced 'a sun dripping with light and bathing
women fit to eat. This ardent work alternated with intense meditation.'[55] This
is a rare hint of the crisis Dalí was undergoing at the time. It also expresses
with unusual clarity the combined impulses of eroticism and violence
(bathing women fit to eat). The poem 'With the sun' makes an interesting
comparison with the painting originally known as *Sun*, in terms of the slip-
page between the images and the dwelling on formless waste:

> With the sun there is a little drop of milk standing on the anus of a
>     sea shell
> With the sun two tiny toothless sharks are born from my
>     underarms . . .
> When it's sunny, I make lovely castles
> With cork painted red
> With coloured feathers
> With saliva
> With hair from my family's ears
> With the vomit of happy animals
> With the beautiful frames of artistic canvases
> With the faeces of female singers, female dancers, goats,
>     chrysanthemum lovers, dried animals . . . [56]

A striking shape painted in brilliant, flat, red in *Sun, Four Fisherwomen of
Cadaqués* reappears in various sizes in *Fishermen in the sun, Untitled* and
*Fishermen in Cadaqués*. A roughly blocked 'U' divided by a half-closed circle
and two smaller circles, it seems to have originated as a pair of breasts, or
rather as two pairs of breasts, male and female, which float beside a rectangular
patch of sand in the now-lost painting *Male and Female Figures on the Beach*,
which was reproduced in *La Gaceta Literaria* in February 1929. Floating pairs
of female breasts, painted with meticulous realism, appear in the sky in
*Cenecitas* [*Little Ashes*] and other earlier pictures. In *Male and Female Figures
on the Beach*, the sand rectangle is invaded by a white form like a convulsed
hand, which creates a negative/positive effect of interlocked limbs or fingers.
This switch between ground and figure, shifting from negative to positive,
resembles Arp's woodcuts and reliefs of the early 1920s. ('Arp's reliefs', as

54 'Nous limits', 195.
55 *The Unspeakable Confessions of Salvador Dalí* as told to André Parinaud (London:
Quartet Books, 1971), 75.
56 'With the sun', *La Gaceta literaria*, no. 54 (15 March 1929), trans. *Oui*, 73.

Breton wrote, 'have the weightiness and lightness of a swallow', Dalí noted in
'New limits of painting'.[57]) This becomes one of the devices by which Dalí
explores the alarming idea of intercourse and its no safer alternative, masturbation. In *Sun, Four Fisherwomen of Cadaqués* Dalí sets in play a visual
negative/positive switch, which underlines the ambiguity of the form; as the
image oscillates, breasts, eyes, faces, genitals or crabs seem to appear.

The most radical in terms of their bareness and grossly rudimentary shapes
are three untitled paintings (one now known as '*Abstract composition*'). Scattered black forms are painted over patches of white paint; mimicking collage,
they are separated from the canvas ground and thus seem to be remnants from
another work, torn out, discarded and then flung into limbo. Many of the black
forms are simple finger-like shapes, others more explicitly represent a phallus, and they evidently relate to Dalí's text 'The Liberation of the fingers' published in the final issue of *L'Amic de les Arts*, accompanied with photographs
of digits.[58]

Although Dalí was fascinated by the possibilities of morphological transformations and analogical association, the results that he magnified on these
large canvases are curiously illegible. The anti-paintings are profoundly
ambiguous; however, there has been little attempt to annex them to any critical
reading of Surrealism or modern painting. Whereas the interpretative struggle
between Breton and Bataille over Dalí's *Lugubrious Game* in 1929 has become
one of the key moments in contemporary critical historiography, the anti-
paintings have been ignored.[59] However, I would suggest that they could be
considered in relation to Miró's work of 1929–30, which is commonly related
to his own claim to 'murder painting'. A group of the most extreme of Miró's
paintings of 1929–30, which include the large *Painting* with three coloured
blots, aggressively graffiti-like canvases and the harsh black sand-paper collages were reproduced in Bataille's review, *Documents*, in 1930. In all probability they had been sparked by Dalí's anti-paintings. The fascination in these
works by Miró lies in the manner of their negation. What was once thought
as violence and aggression, or disequilibrium and dissonance, can become a
source of enjoyment. If one were to characterise modern painting, not by an

---

[57] 'Nous limits', trans. *Oui*, 36.

[58] See note 52 above.

[59] Bataille, denied permission by Dalí to reproduce *Le Jeu lugubre* in *Documents*,
resorted to a schematic drawing pointing out its obsessional iconography of castration; this
was an explicit challenge to Breton's catalogue preface to Dalí's Goemans exhibition of
October 1929 (where the picture was exhibited), which praised the painter's freedom of
imagination. The stark difference in their interpretations, with Bataille praising the
ugliness and violence of the painting and Breton its access to a dream world, characterises
a conflict within Surrealism that has dominated critical attitudes to the movement over the
last quarter century. Briony Fer, in *On Abstract Art* (New Haven and London: Yale
University Press, 1997), discusses Bataille's treatment of *Le jeu lugubre* in the context of
his discussion of Miró's paintings of 1929–30.

ordered disappearance of the subject in favour of geometrical abstraction nor by the pursuit of its own special means (surface, colour, line), but by decomposition and obliteration, Dalí's anti-paintings, like Miró's, are exemplary. The reaction of Georges Bataille to Miró could equally apply to Dalí:

> The few paintings by Miró reproduced here represent the most recent stage in the singularly interesting evolution of this painter. Joan Miró started from the representation of objects that was so minute that it turned reality, in a sense, into dust, into a sort of sun-shot dust . . . In the end, as Miró himself admitted that he wanted to 'kill painting', decomposition was pushed to such a point that only a few formless spots remained on the cover (or the tombstone) of the box of tricks. Then the little coloured and alienated elements went on to a new eruption, and disappear again today in these paintings, leaving the traces of one knows not what disaster.[60]

Immediately preceding this short text on Miró, Bataille placed his review of G.H. Luquet's book *L'Art primitif*. The two combined seem deliberately to undermine an earlier essay on Miró in *Documents* by Carl Einstein, which spoke approvingly of the paring down of Miró's recent work. For Einstein his work now rivals the 'simpler ignorance' of children's art and prehistoric painting.[61] Bataille proposed a much darker analysis of the impulse to scribble, to make marks. The example of children's drawings, such as those of Abyssinian children who reserved their graffiti for the doors and columns of churches, show the same tendency firstly to sully the support and then to deform the initial lines into another, different object: horse, head, man, which in the course of repetition become something else again. 'Art, for art it incontestably is, proceeds in this way by successive destructions. And insofar as it liberates *libidinal* instincts, these instincts are sadistic.'[62]

The contest between a conception of art that located its origin in a destructive and sadistic impulse and that which valued its imaginative freedom held Dalí at this moment in its sights. Each of these ideas involved 'liberation' but for Bataille this unleashed a sadistic instinct while for the surrealists it promised a sexual and social utopia. At this moment in 1928 Dalí's uncertainty, his prolonged questioning of the tensions between limits and liberation, accurately reflected the crossroads Surrealism had reached.

---

[60] Georges Bataille, 'Joan Miró, peintures récentes', *Documents*, no. 7, 2nd year (1930), 399.

[61] Carl Einstein, 'Joan Miró', *Documents*, no. 4, 2nd year (1930), 241. Einstein wrote a negative review of the 1929 exhibition *Abstrakte und Surrealistische Malerei und Plastik*. ('Enough empty cocktails of the absolute!'), where both Dalí and Miró exhibited.

[62] Georges Bataille, 'L'art primitif', *Documents*, no. 7, 2nd year (1930), 396.

Joan Miró, *The Tilled Field* (1923–24)

Salvador Dalí, *Soft Skulls and Cranial Harps* (1935)

Maruja Mallo, *Scarecrows* (1929)

Salvador Dalí, *Four Fishermen's Wives of Cadaqués* (1928)

Salvador Dalí, *The Great Masturbator* (1929)

Salvador Dalí, *Unsatisfied Desires* (1928)

Salvador Dalí, *The Lugubrious Game* (1929)

Salvador Dalí, *The Endless Enigma* (1938)

Salvador Dalí, *Impressions of Africa* (1938)

# 7

# Dalí's Small Stage of Paranoiac Ceremonial

## HAIM FINKELSTEIN

My point of departure lies at the very end of the period encompassed in this essay – in Dalí's *The Endless Enigma* (1938), one of the most complex works in the series comprising the 1938 multiple images. Related to a series of beach scenes created in 1938–9, these works exhibit a receding body of water that also evokes, generally in an ambiguous manner, an alternate image of a projecting spatial form constituting, upon different 'readings' of the image, parts of figures or objects. These might consist of a face and forehead, a fruit dish, or a dog's abdomen. *The Endless Enigma* is composed of six different images, several of which appear in the other works in the series. Thus we re-encounter the face and the fruit dish, the seated woman seen from the back, a dog, and a 'mythological Beast' having strangely rounded hindquarters – a shape dictated, in fact, by the additional images of a boat's prow and a mandolin. Presiding over these images is the figure of a 'reclining philosopher' formed by skyline and hills. The painting thus exhibits a number of 'systematic structures', which could be conceived of, at least in the terms proposed by Dalí in his theoretical writings, as having been formed by the tools of paranoiac-critical activity.

In *The Conquest of the Irrational* (1935), his definitive theoretical exposition of paranoia-criticism, Dalí defined paranoia as a 'delirium of interpretative association involving a systematic structure'. He set out literally to conquer the irrational by engaging in a paranoiac-critical activity in which different realities, irrationally explored, form a systematic structure that, in itself, is an interpretation of these elements. The stress is on the 'associations', 'relationships' or 'coherences', which, energized by the obsessive idea, inform the most diverse and apparently unrelated phenomena ('surrealist experimental material which is scattered and narcissistic').[1] The 1938 multiple images, while not Dalí's first venture into this domain of paranoiac systematization,

---

[1] *The Collected Writings of Salvador Dalí*, ed. and trans. Haim Finkelstein (Cambridge and New York: Cambridge University Press, 1998), 267. Hereafter referred to in the text as *CW*.

constitute one of his most sustained efforts in this respect. Dalí's ambition, which gained its most developed form in *The Endless Enigma*, was to refine his tools to such an extent that it would have been possible for him to draw a limitless number of 'systematic structures'. Unlike earlier examples of double images, in which the constituent images are contained within a single visual configuration, the six different images constituting *The Endless Enigma* encompass the whole visual field. The splintered forms, lending themselves to different readings – what André Breton eventually came to see as 'entertainments on the level of *crossword puzzles*'[2] – results in a vision of fragmentation and amorphousness on an all-embracing scale that also annuls the possibility of any ultimate reality lying behind all these simulacra of reality.

Such a reality, however, does exist in this painting, a reality incarnate in the form of a woman's head – the woman is Gala, Dalí's lifelong companion and wife – which is seen, partly cut off by the frame on the right, jutting into the painting at an angle. The head's peculiar position implies that she takes no part in what happens on canvas, although her eyes, a prominent feature of her face, satisfying Paul Éluard's evocation of a 'gaze that pierces walls', appear to probe beyond these surfaces of reality. My contention is that this 'apparition' of Gala's head suggests a few major concerns that have considerable bearing on Dalí's work in the late 1920s and throughout the 1930s – one has to do with the painting's spatial conception and Gala's emplacement in it and the other concerns the way Gala's gaze engages the beholder. The vista opening up for our perusal is ostensibly that of a panoramic beach scene; its spatial sense seems, however, quite ambiguously defined, with the various motifs establishing perceptions of scale that are quite different one from the other. Gala's head does not appear to be associated with any of the spatial orders implied by the different images. There is, however, one secure spatial anchor in the painting – what appears to be a tabletop placed at the foreground, jutting toward the beholder's space. That it is a tabletop we can easily ascertain in view of the pronounced edges, the falling tablecloth, and the red strip folding over its edge. This tabletop is the only thing in the painting that is spatially attuned to Gala's head. It also circumscribes space by forming a stage-like plateau, an arena to which the other motifs relate in some form or another. In the drawings of the six subjects of the painting made by Dalí to accompany the catalogue of his exhibition at Julien Levy's Gallery in New York in 1939, this tabletop is the spatial feature most prominently defined. It also establishes the position of the beholder with regard to Gala's gaze. These are then the two elements whose permutations I wish to trace in Dalí's art and writing up to the moment of *The Endless Enigma* – the tabletop or stage, largely defining the spatial conception of the painting, and Gala's engaging gaze, which addresses the beholder directly.

[2] André Breton, *Surrealism and Painting*, trans. Simon Watson Taylor (New York: Harper & Row 1972), 147.

The tabletop or stage jutting into space in *The Endless Enigma* casts us back to a similar rectangular plateau – a 'city-square', to designate its immediate model in the trapezoidal plateaus in de Chirico's works – in early paintings such as *Apparatus and Hand* (1927) or the 1928 *Inaugural Goose Flesh*. Questions concerning de Chirico's visual impact on Dalí's work would be more fruitfully pursued later with reference to Dalí's painted work in 1929 and later. What concerns me at this point is the shift from de Chirico's 'city square' to a tabletop, which might be surmised from considerations of scale in the paintings and is more directly spelled out in the writings. The small and curious organisms that began to fill up Dalí's canvases at the time – isolated limbs and fingers, flying breasts, thin wisps of vapor – make for an inconsistent scale that annuls any attempt to define actual sizes. Dalí's poetic texts of 1927–8 clearly reflect his predilection for the miniaturized worlds of small things in confined spaces, with the tabletop as a preferred setting. A tabletop is marked without any preamble as the primary setting of the poetic narratives 'Fish Pursued by a Bunch of Grapes' and '. . . Have I Disowned, Perhaps? . . . ' (1928). The latter text largely constitutes a frenzied description of things found on top of a strange table placed on the beach ('On this same table, an endless number of bread crumbs, each with its small minute hand, glistened in the sun like mica'). With the water rising around the table, '[t]he tablecloth formed by the surface made of the bunch of carnations is by now just a distant afternoon cloud. The winged ants, fleeing the sea which has already reached my knees, climb with difficulty on my naked body . . . ' (*CW*, 31)

Such transformations reflect Dalí's predilection for moving freely between the micro and the macro, especially in the evocation of things within things, in which the sense of containment of vision within a smaller frame is most pronounced, or in the magnification of small things through a lens, enlarging them so as to fill up the whole field of vision. This mode of seeing attained its most prominent exposition primarily in the essays on film and photography that Dalí wrote at that time. Dalí extolled the capacity of these mediums to procure a change of scale; such a change of scale, enthused Dalí, would enable us to see a lump of sugar on the screen as being 'larger than the interminable perspective of gigantic buildings' ('Art film, Antiartistic Film', *CW*, 55). It is in the light of such observations that one can apprehend Dalí's contention that in 'brutally reducing the field of our preferences, we gain in intensity what we have lost in huge and tasteless panoramas that are hybrid creations of a totally worthless superficial perfection' ('Reality and Surreality', 99). And it is in this reduced field that Dalí found the locale most propitious for studying the dialectics informing his concept of surreality. Dalí's texts in the last months of 1928 reflect a theoretical pursuit that is increasingly directed toward the exploration of a theory of reality that accounts for the osmosis between reality and surreality on the basis of patterns of meaning that synchronize the most diverse phenomena in a coherent conceptual system.

It is in the 'documentary of minutiae' that one finds 'proof once more for the constant osmosis established between reality and surreality' ('Review of Antiartistic Tendencies', 103–4). The preferred setting for gathering the pieces of information comprising the documentary is a radically circumscribed space, whether in the Jardin du Luxembourg where Dalí records the things 'intercepted during a five-minute interval within a square area twenty centimeters in size traced with a stick in the damp soil' ('Documentary', 116), or in a café, where he observes and records things on top of a table or just around it:

> 'There are' eighteen buttons, the one closest to me has a hair (perhaps an eyelash or a tiger's hair) coming out of one of its holes. Three centimeters to the right of this button there is a cookie crumb. There are still five more biscuit crumbs. . . . Beyond the crumbs and continuing to the right there is a dark abyss two hand-spans in width. On the other side of the abyss 'there is' a table hanging on a thin and long wisp of smoke.    ('Documentary', 115)

This manner of observing and recording things – which became, in fact, a guiding principle in his later elaboration of the theory of paranoia-criticism – constitutes an 'instantaneous possession of reality at the moment in which our mind considers the whole to which we have alluded apart from the stereotyped and anti-real image that the intellect has formed artificially' ('Joan Miró', 94). Such possession of reality, contended Dalí, is contrary to the perception of the real generally imposed by men of letters and intellectuals, which consists of a

> fabrication of a wholly conventional and arbitrary world . . . This world, in which everything is explainable and *politely* consistent, has already been totally shattered today by the research of modern psychology . . . However, alongside this made-to-order reality that fits the imbecility and the needed certainties, there are *facts*, simple *facts*, that are independent of convention . . . '    ('Un Chien andalou', 135)

Dalí's main objective in the essay cited above, published in conjunction with the showing of the film *Un Chien andalou* in Barcelona, was to refute any attempt to interpret the film, because he considered such attempts as reflecting the 'imbecile' notion that real facts are necessarily endowed with clear significance and coherent sense. These facts, even when examined by psychoanalysts, argued Dalí, do not become thereby any less irrational or mysterious. It is, however, quite conceivable – bearing in mind his formal and stylistic development at the time – that Dalí could not have remained oblivious to a possible correspondence between the falseness, as he saw it, of a world fabricated in such a process of accommodation – 'a wholly conventional and arbitrary world . . . in which everything is explainable and *politely* consistent' – and the methods and conventions underlying the systematic, legible, rationalized space of Renaissance perspectival vision.

To summarize Dalí's evolving spatial conception, it might be pointed out that, as a student in a painting academy, the young Dalí probably had a firm grounding in the Renaissance linear perspective commonly derived from Alberti's treatise. A concrete application of it – with the perspectival lines carefully drawn to converge in one vanishing point – is demonstrated in a study for his painting *Girl Sewing* (1926). It is interesting to note, however, that the study as well as the painting exhibit some distortion, especially close to their lower edge, in the considerable foreshortening of the chair and other pieces of furniture, and, to some extent, in the seated figure – a stretched-out effect not seen in normal vision. While this probably is due to the quite common error of bringing the station point – the observer's viewpoint – too close to the picture plane, it is quite telling that Dalí felt no qualm about applying this scheme in the completed painting, even though this was at the height of his work in the vein of Vermeer's realism. Quite possibly, this was one way of rendering more modern a work done in this manner, and Dalí would have had a ready model for this in his own forays into Metaphysical Art in 1924–5, when he had emulated the still-lifes of Carlo Carrà and Giorgio Morandi. The tilted plane marking the tabletop in *Still-Life* (1924, now at the Federico García Lorca Foundation in Madrid), with its well-defined trapezoidal form, comes up again in *Apparatus and Hand* (1927), and later in many of the works of 1929 and the following years.

To summarize later developments up to 1929, Dalí's work in the course of 1928 came close to a form of abstraction, especially in works based on Arp's open-ended morphology. It was the work on the film *Un Chien andalou* – mostly at the script-writing stage, but also the exposure, however slight, to the actual filming – which helped break the impasse to which the Arp-like abstract or semi-abstract works led.[3] The film revealed to him the rich vein of possibilities inherent in the combination of human action and symbolic representation, which entailed a return to the formal conception underlying the 1927 *Apparatus and Hand*. This corresponded to a more consistent spatial definition, with the earlier 'city square' now encompassing the whole visual field as a flat and quite featureless plane on which are situated objects and human figures spreading up to what appears to be a horizon line.

Dalí is often considered to be an authentic representative of the surrealist 'dream painting', an artist employing photographic illusionism, Renaissance perspective – 'the rational, culturally normative spatial structure of Renaissance painting'[4] – and other old-master techniques of representation. The terms employed refer to a 'vista stretching away and out of sight to the

---

[3] See Haim Finkelstein, *Salvador Dalí's Art and Writing 1927–1942: The Metamorphoses of Narcissus* (Cambridge and New York: Cambridge University Press, 1996), 95. Hereafter referred to in the text as *Art and Writing*.

[4] Nicholas J. Capasso, 'Salvador Dalí and the Barren Plain: A Phenomenological Analysis of a Surrealist Landscape Environment', *Arts Magazine*, 60 (June 1986), 76.

horizon',[5] or to a 'flat, uninterrupted, unbounded horizon which Dalí used to achieve a sense of vastness [which] also suggests infinity'.[6] While these observations might apply – somewhat tenuously – to paintings done around the mid-1930s, they appear quite incompatible with many of his paintings of 1929–30. There the spatial definition, while conveying a sensation of deep space, lacks coherence, with devices for locating a vanishing point functioning quite inconsistently. In this Dalí followed de Chirico, fully aware of the peculiarities of de Chirico's conception of linear perspective. Already at the beginning of 1928, in the first part of 'The New Limits of Painting', Dalí noted de Chirico's 'hallucinating distribution of his volumetric relations and his bloodied perspectives' (CW, 84). Referring, no doubt, to the vertiginous effect of de Chirico's works caused by the existence of different perspective points within the space of one painting, Dalí marked it as a 'new symptom' in painting. In his 1929–30 works, Dalí made this 'new symptom' into a reigning paradigm of his own spatial conception. De Chirico's linear perspective in his Metaphysical period, as noted by William Rubin, 'remains a purely schematic scaffolding that does not force a picture into a condition of spatial illusionism'.[7] To follow Rubin's argument, perspective orthogonals can be understood as a schematic indication of three-dimensional space or they can be seen as a pattern of lines on a flat surface. The latter possibility is exemplified by the receding plane of the plaza in Gare Montparnasse, which is tilted so vertically that it might be seen as being parallel to the picture plane. Dalí aimed at a comparable effect either by eliminating the horizon – at times by raising the ground plane in extreme perspectival distortion (for instance, in The Font [1930]) – or by an excessive foreshortening of structures depicted within the suggested pictorial space, which similarly annuls depth and enhances the surface pattern (as in the 1930 works Vertigo and Bleeding Roses). The extreme diagonal recession into space and the playing off of surface and depth have an obvious baroque character.

Perspectival distortions of this type as practiced by Dalí exhibit a marked kinship with the nature of distortion often found in mannerist painting. As observed by James Elkins, 'Mannerist paintings often give us what we would see if we had bad seats [in the theater]. Either we are too low, so that the proscenium steps tower overhead and the stage is lost to sight, or too far to one side, so that the measured recessions become at once precipitous (on the nearer side) and sluggish (on the other side).'[8] He notes, however, that 'it can be shown that the mannerists disassembled, sheared, and disjointed perspective

   [5] Dawn Ades, Dalí and Surrealism (New York: Harper & Row, 1982), 75.
   [6] Capasso, 76.
   [7] William Rubin, 'De Chirico and Modernism', in William Rubin (ed.), De Chirico (New York: The Museum of Modern Art, 1982), 61.
   [8] James Elkins, The Poetics of Perspective (Ithaca and London: Cornell University Press, 1994), 154.

without abandoning the theatrical perspective box they inherited from the earlier Renaissance'. This 'theatrical perspective box' accounts for the fact that, for all its perspectival distortions, Dalí's creation of pictorial space appears superficially to follow the spatial conception of Renaissance painting; all the more so, as the subversion of the Renaissance conception is accomplished more craftily, by the evocation of what appears to be an horizon line but on which practically no vanishing point might be located. In quite a few of his 1929–30 works, and later too for that matter, figures and objects, placed on a flat and featureless plane, appear to lie too close to the horizon line (their shadows at times cut off by it), with the result that the horizon – or rather the edge of this plane – is brought unnaturally close to the foreground, an effect enhanced by the total absence of atmospheric perspective. In many paintings, indeed, there is a suggestion of a sheer drop from the edge of the plane and into an unseen chasm lying beyond it (this is most obvious in the 1929 works *The Great Masturbator* and *Illuminated Pleasures*). The comparison with de Chirico is, in this respect, very telling, since we find in his paintings a similar spatial conception.[9] If Dalí's paintings still convey an impression of 'unbounded horizon' and 'sense of vastness', in most cases this is at best an illusory impression, often accomplished by the extreme scaling down of forms and the exaggerated or abrupt convergence of the lines of walls, platforms or other structures – an effect not unlike that of looking through a glass ball or a magnifying lens held at some distance from the eye (with the proviso that no spherical distortion is involved), when a whole landscape is scaled down to be contained within a small field of vision. Dalí was well aware of this effect of diminution of scale when he wrote: 'In a large and clear cow's eye we see, spherically deformed, an extremely white minuscule post-machinist landscape, detailed enough to delineate a sky in which float diminutive and luminous clouds' ('Photography: Pure Creation of the Spirit', *CW*, 47).

Perspectival distortions and the circumscription of space, that is, of the arena on which Dalí's motifs are distributed, as effected by the edge-of-the-plane conception (or edge-of-the-table, to go by the indeterminate scale in many of the works) – these seem to be Dalí's main procedures regarding spatial representation in the early years, until, say, 1933–4. I shall turn first to

---

[9] In de Chirico's painting *The Disquieting Muses* (1917), to take one outstanding example, which also sheds additional light on Dalí's conception, there is no horizon line in evidence since the plane is blocked off by buildings (this is true for most of his works). Normally, the great distance to these structures would have implied that the horizon is situated very close to the line separating the plane from the buildings. The painting, however, conveys a different sensation altogether, partially owing to the fact that the buildings and the plane seem to belong to two separate perspective schemes. Indeed, it seems as though the plane ends at a point that is closer to the figures in the foreground, and that it is not as vast as it would at first seem to be. This perception is further enhanced by the abrupt manner in which the plane is cut off on the left, revealing buildings situated behind, and somewhat underneath it.

what I consider to be the implication of the uses of perspective, and, primarily, perspectival distortions, in his paintings – mainly in the light of the theory underlying the paranoiac-critical activity.

A few of Dalí's early texts, specifically those written in 1931, reveal a marked preoccupation with questions concerning the emotional significance of perspective or perspectival distortions. The staging of a masturbatory fantasy that Dalí meticulously reproduced in a 1931 text entitled 'Daydream' (*Rêverie*) is associated with reflections concerning the control of affect through arrangement, which Dalí discerned in the works of painters as diverse as Vermeer, Böcklin, and de Chirico. Dalí does not present his ideas in full, and, as he himself is the first to acknowledge, they suffer from 'analytical shortcoming' (*CW*, 152). Thus he admits to having been thoughtless in believing that there is a lack of 'spatial perturbation' in Böcklin's paintings, in particular his *Island of the Dead*, and acknowledges that his mistake has been caused by his 'crudely reducing the idea of spatial perturbation to merely one of perspective'. I will return later to considering the full implication of what Dalí may have meant by 'spatial perturbation' as a notion distinct from perspective.

In the poem 'Love and Memory', written in the same year as 'Daydream', Dalí further probed the relationship between perspective and feeling: 'I would begin / the history of feelings / and nostalgia / at the moment / in cultural history when / the invention of perspective / combined with that of illumination / made the notions of time and space / perceptible for the first time' and when 'confusions of measurements' and the 'interception modifying measurements/ in the sense of lines extending to infinity / make up the principle / and the future / of representations of feeling' (*CW*, 167). Illumination, one would imagine, is associated in Dalí's mind with the concept of visual rays that underlies the theories of perspective since the Renaissance. If by 'confusions of measurements' and 'interception modifying measurements' Dalí meant 'perturbation of perspective' – as he refers to it in 'Daydream' – which, in this capacity, is a vehicle of feeling, then Gala subsists for Dalí in the poem as a vision of total liberation lying beyond memory and change, beyond affect. Free from any methods of affective representation, she is being envisioned as existing in a sterile (in the positive sense) mathematical time and space; beyond subjective time, on which all 'sentimental representations' depend, as well as beyond feeling, since 'feelings imply the absence of love'. The whole thrust of Dalí's ideas, so it seems, points to a correlation between linear perspective – in its ideal mathematical form as a geometric system of central projection – and the lack of feeling, whereas 'perturbation of perspective' – in other words, spatial distortion of some sort (a point to which I'll return later) – implies 'sentimental representation'.

Gala, as embodiment of the ideal of sterility of mathematical space and time, and, by extension, of linear perspective – in the essay 'L'Amour' (Love), included in the volume *La Femme visible* (1930), Dalí addresses her as 'femme violente et stérilisée' (violent and sterilized woman) – became associated in his mind at that time with the mathematical exactitude of paranoia-criticism. In 'The Sanitary Goat', another essay included in this volume, Dalí introduced some key notions that seem to have dominated his evolving theory. Dalí posited two contradictory kinds of thought. 'Poetic thought' is impressionistic and dependent upon 'simple psychological reactions of sensations', or, what Dalí terms 'biological apriorism'. Paranoiac-critical thought, on the other hand, is a form of 'knowing with mathematical exactitude' that is determined by the 'gratuitous', defined as constituting 'something like a geometric point', sheltered from 'any psycho-sensory influence; it is, in other words, isolated from any carnal or affective intercourse, and it lies outside physiology' (*CW*, 226–9). This 'new geometry of thought', extolled by Dalí in 'The Sanitary Goat', became, a few years later, a necessary condition for the element of systematic interpretation inherent in the paranoiac process. The latter aspect of the paranoiac phenomenon had grown in significance, together with Dalí's increasing awareness of the new role to be fulfilled by paranoia-criticism *vis-à-vis* the surrealist concepts of dream and automatism.

Notwithstanding Dalí's condemnation in this essay of anything that has to do with 'simple psychological reactions of sensations' or 'psycho-sensory influence', this type of thought remained an undivided part of the basic dichotomy informing his theory of paranoia-criticism. His elaboration of the theory, beginning with 'The Rotting Donkey' (1930, *L'âne pourri*), is marked by an ongoing effort to project his own obsessions and scatological pre-occupations on the world at large and thus endow them with a measure of universality. This allowed him to acknowledge his paintings' basis in libidinal urges and, more significantly, to avow their function as a form of vicarious self-gratification, while hinting, at the same time, that their images, actively solicited by him out of his unconscious, were not uniquely his own. Rather, they were drawn out of a substratum in the unconscious that is common to all men and thus they were universally applicable. This scheme is particular discernible in his most extensive feat of paranoiac-critical interpretation, documented in his book *Le Mythe tragique de l'Angélus de Millet* (written in part in the 1930s and published in 1963), in which he set out to prove that Millet's painting *L'Angélus* constitutes a sublimated expression of repressed sexual anxieties, unconsciously introduced into it by the painter but possessing a universal dimension.[10] One should not, however, lose sight of the fact that Dalí's concern is with a method of irrational knowledge based on systematization of delirious phenomena. The greater part of Dalí's interpretation partakes of the individual rather than the universal. It is himself that Dalí situates at the center, with his childhood recollections, his infantile sexual theories, the sexual terrors of his adolescence, his relationship with Gala. Furthermore, many of the associative links are forged within the framework

---

[10] Extensive excerpts from the book are included in *CW*, 282–97. See *Art and Writing*, Chap. 15, for a commentary on the text.

of chance encounters or coincidences. All these things belong to the individual sphere, but Dalí would like us to accept that there is a continuous association of the personal and the universal in his scheme, because of his uncanny ability to delve into the sources of universal symbols by gaining insights from his own personal situation – all this with the aid of the 'precise apparatus of paranoiac-critical activity' (*CW*, 263). Paranoia-criticism thus consists of the creation of a structure of interpretation that virtually exists independently of the interpreter, and yet it is he – Dalí himself, participating in this activity as 'actor and spectator simultaneously', as Breton aptly phrased it[11] – who brings it into existence through the power of his paranoiac faculty. This structure involves an association of elements that would have been downright arbitrary were it not for the obsessive idea that relates them to each other.

It is with this basic dichotomy in Dalí's theory in mind that we can return to the paintings themselves which subsume, as I will argue, this dichotomy of the universal and personal in their perspectival system and conception of pictorial space. The personal is subsumed in the inscription in the paintings of desire and perversion in thematic and stylistic form. This is accomplished in the framework of an aesthetic of libidinal gratification that assumes a willed regression to primary processes and the adoption of the forms of infantile sexuality, with its unlimited freedom of infant satisfaction, as associated with a polymorphous-perverse sexuality. From the late 1920s on, infant sexuality was introduced into Dalí's writing and art mostly in the form of scatological provocation. Scatology was largely supplanted, or rather complemented, in the early 1930s by the elaboration of food (and eating) as an embodiment of an 'overwhelming materialist prosaism of the immediate and urgent needs on which rest ideal desires', to cite a phrase from his most sustained exposition of these concerns in his 1933 essay 'Concerning the Terrifying and Edible Beauty of Art Nouveau Architecture' (*CW*, 197–8). Such 'ideal desires', however, cannot be dissociated from the anxieties arising from the oral and anal fantasies of destruction, sadism, incorporation or cannibalism of the anal and oral organizations. These concerns had their earliest formal expression in Dalí's art in forms bearing upon art nouveau ornamentation, and were manifested, after 1931, in terms of what he later referred to as the 'morphological aesthetics of the soft and hard'.[12] These involve a confounding of expectation of the hard and soft; the softening of hard objects and the hardening or, at times, fossilization or petrifaction of soft ones. These mechanisms were exemplified most prominently in the deformation of the human body, mostly the skull and bones, with a special emphasis on monstrously developed heads and all kinds of protrusions sprouting from the body, in which the borders

[11] Breton, 133.
[12] Salvador Dalí, *The Secret Life of Salvador Dalí*, trans. Haakon M. Chevalier (London: Vision Press, 1973), 304.

separating the animate from the inanimate are obliterated.[13] Dalí unquestion-
ably meant this universal eroticization of the objects of external reality to
extend to the whole of space. In his essay 'Aerodynamic Apparitions of
"Beings-Objects" ' (1934), he developed an extended conceit concerning the
extraction of comedones, or blackheads, out from the pores of the nose, equat-
ing what he considered to be the viscous consistency of the physical and conceptual space of modern thought with the flesh of the nose.

It would be something of a truism to point to the objects populating Dalí's
canvases, with their whole array of libidinal concerns, as projections of Dalí's
own body image (whatever the psychoanalytical meaning one may assign to
this term), or, rather, of Dalí's desiring self. A case could be made, however,
for a consideration of the visual order of the painting as a whole (the illu-
sionist space evoked in it as well as its surface patterning) as a projection of
Dalí's self – Dalí hints as much in his writings – and, furthermore, one may
regard his vision of fragmented anatomies and decomposition as an expression of a fragmented sense of the self or the loss of self. The implication of
this will be further insisted upon and amplified later on; for now I wish to
point to a possible correlation between the eroticization of space in Dalí's
paintings and their perspectival system, which also involves the consideration
of the position of the viewing subject in relation to the painting's perspective
and the way the painting addresses him.

Theoretical insights proposed in the last two decades could prove useful –
for instance, those developed by Norman Bryson and Martin Jay – although
not necessarily with respect to their overall theoretical import. Bryson discerns
in the Albertian conception of Renaissance perspective a 'persistence of the
body as the privileged term in its visual economy'.[14] This follows the Albertian
conception, which implies that 'both painter and viewer looked through the
same viewfinder on to a world unified spatially around the centric ray, the line
running from viewpoint to vanishing point' (104), and therefore the viewer is
assumed to be a physical, indeed corporeal presence. Following Bryson,
Martin Jay distinguishes between competing 'visual subcultures' in Western
art. 'Cartesian perspectivalism' (a term employed by Jay to denote the Renaissance perspective in the visual art in tandem with the Cartesian idea of subjective rationality),[15] implies, argues Jay, a 'withdrawal of the painter's
emotional entanglement with the objects depicted in geometricalized space';
the gap between spectator and spectacle widens, and the bodies of the painter
and viewer are 'forgotten in the name of an allegedly disincarnated, absolute

[13] See Chap. 11 of *Art and Writing*, 140–61, for a more complete exposition of these
developments.
[14] Norman Bryson, *Vision and Painting: The Logic of the Gaze* (New Haven: Yale
University Press, 1983), 107.
[15] Martin Jay, 'Scopic Regimes of Modernity', in Hal Foster (ed.), *Vision and Visuality*
(Seattle: Bay Press, 1988), 4.

eye' (8). As a result of the distance created between the disincarnated eye and the depicted scene, the painting 'lacks the immediacy associated with desire' (27); this is contrary to the baroque scopic regime, argues Jay, through which desire courses 'in its erotic as well as metaphysical forms' (18). The body returns, and with it the re-eroticizing of the visual order, once the Renaissance coherent essence opens up to accommodate a multiplicity of visual spaces as in the baroque. For Jay, the baroque holds up a mirror to nature that is 'anamor-phosistic'—one that distorts the visual image because of its 'dependence on the materiality of the medium of reflection' (17).

I suspect that Dalí had been thinking along similar lines when considering the notion of space in relation to the delirious phenomena associated with paranoia-criticism. In his essay 'Non-Euclidean Psychology of a Photograph' (1935) he focuses on a small 'threadless spool' found at the lower edge of a photograph – described as 'completely naked' and 'non-Euclidean' (*CW*, 302). The 'imperceptible existence' and 'invisible nature' of this threadless spool 'lend themselves to the sudden irruption peculiar to "paranoiac apparitions"' (303). Dalí's conclusion – this without describing in detail his whole involved argument – points to the representation of this spool in terms other than those of the metaphysical absolutes of Kant's time and space. Nor does he fully concur at this time with the metaphysical implications of de Chirico's method of 'spatial localization' – de Chirico is viewed by him as 'one of the last, and perhaps one of the most glorious consequences of the philosophy of Kant' (304). This spool, 'abandoned at the corner of the street of psychology',

> no longer accepts the antipersonal and antianthropomorphic immobility of the metaphysical absolute; it is there, and of such insignificance as the ones whose solicitations we Surrealists have, first and foremost, learned to listen to, solicitations revealed to us by dreams as characterizing our age, our life, with the utmost violence.   (306)

'Psychology is nothing other than human behavior *vis-à-vis* this physics,' the obvious physical reality of this spool, concludes Dalí. He probably did not know much about the mathematics concerned with non-Euclidean geometry, but he sensed that the view that Euclid's geometry constituted a metaphysical absolute should be rejected.[16] The solicitations of dreams and paranoia-criticism, Dalí appears to argue, lie in a non-Euclidean space, although this space itself is largely coincident with the Cartesian space. Whereas Dalí, a few years before, blamed himself, as we have seen, for 'crudely reducing the idea of spatial per-turbation to merely one of perspective', he may have come to the conclusion at this point in 1935 that it is the incarnated gaze, the body as the vehicle of the solicitations of dreams or, rather, of the 'new dream' of paranoia-criticism, that

---

[16] I am indebted to Jack Spector for providing many of the insights underlying these formulations.

accounts for this perturbation, one that finds its plastic expression in the sub-version of Cartesian or Albertian space, while retaining its basic parameters.

Dalí's spatial conception, with the dichotomy underlying it, has its corollary in Jay's perception of a basic dichotomy in the subject position in Cartesian perspectivalism, when he suggests that the 'monocular eye at the apex of beholder's pyramid could be construed as transcendental – that is, exactly the same for any human viewer occupying the same point in time and space – or contingent and solely dependent on the particular, individual vision of distinct beholders, with their own concrete relations to the scene in front of them' (11). Dalí's space certainly is not the Albertian one, and yet the conspicuous per-spective orthogonals – especially those defining platforms, pedestals and other structures – convey a pronounced sense of the existence of a vanishing point, even though this turns out to be merely a deception, the more so since behind these perspective orthogonals there lurks the anamorphotic rebus materialized in the distended skulls and other distorted forms.[17]

This is amply illustrated in a line engraving entitled *Soft Skulls and Cranial Harps* (1935), which contains some examples of the 'cranial harp', a variation of the soft skull motif. The skulls depicted in this engraving exhibit distensions that are obviously of anamorphotic origin and are quite reminiscent of the efforts of Mannerist practitioners of this diversion. The most curious element in the engraving is the figure of a man plucking the strings of a harp, the strings forming a net of lines (similar to lines drawn in a perspective drawing) meeting at some vanishing point in the eye socket of a small skull. This arrangement resembles Dürer's device for perspective drawing comprising a frame with strings passing through it toward different points on the object to be depicted. Such a device was also used to attain correct anamorphotic images. Alongside this 'harp' is depicted an elongated box or platform – of the kind populating Dalí's canvases – whose lines form part of the perspectival network suggested by the harp. Even the most meticulous perspectival arrangement, Dalí seems to suggest, ends up in a vanishing point which is the empty eye socket of an anamorphotic skull, whose implications far surpass the obvious phallicism of these distensions.[18] *Soft Skulls and Cranial Harps* thus epitomizes the dichotomy

---

[17]   The anamorphosis was a play of perspective popular in Mannerist art, a picture puzzle whose frontal view shows a jumble of lines, usually drawn laterally across the picture and depicting broad vistas. Yet viewed sideways, at a certain angle, the picture reveals distinct shapes, human figures, or portraits. For a full account of these devices, see Jurgis Baltrusaitis, *Anamorphoses ou magie artificielle des effets merveilleux* (Paris, 1969), 105; 39–60; the new edition of the book was published in 1984 under the title *Anamorphoses ou Thaumaturgus Opticus*.

[18]   Jacques Lacan relates those deformations or elongations to the effect of an erection – as if the original image hidden in the anamorphotic rebus has been traced on the sexual organ in a state of repose. Discerning in the anamorphosis something symbolic of the function of Lack (*manque*), the apparition of the phallic phantom, he relates the anamorphic image of the skull in Holbein's painting *The Ambassadors* to Dalí's soft watches and anamorphoses; both appear to him phallic self-representations implying threat of castration.

130 HAIM FINKELSTEIN

in Dalí's paintings between the universal, disembodied vision and the bodied eroticisation of vision; in other words, on one hand, the largely deceptive adoption of Renaissance perspective, and, on the other, its subversion by means of the anamorphotic vision of perspectival distortion. This dichotomy reflects, as I have contended before, the coexistence of the universal and personal in Dalí's paranoiac-critical activity, with Dalí appearing to insist on the universality of his vision as long as this vision is fully impressed with his own (Dalí's) stamp of libidinal concerns. That is to say, Dalí wishes the paintings to convince the beholder of their universal application while drawing him from his disembodied placement at the apex of the pyramid of vision into Dalí's own individual eroticized vision concealed behind the anamorphotic distortion.

These considerations of the position of the viewing subject relative to the painting's perspective and the way the painting addresses him are inextricably related to those concerning the second representational device to which I have referred earlier – the containment of vision and circumscription of space. As noted, this is accomplished by means of the edge-of-the-plane situation in tandem with perspectival distortion, ambiguous scale, and a continuous dialectics of monumentality and minuteness. There is an additional device for effecting such a circumscription of space, or, rather, of the arena on which are placed the figures and objects. These are the platforms or large pedestals whose ubiquitous presence in Dalí's work of these years attests to their conceptual importance. The platform – heir to the earlier 'city-square' area jutting into space, or to the tabletop in Dalí's writing – may comprise the whole extent of the plateau (as in the edge-of-the-plane situation noted above). It is often depicted as a low pyramidal arrangement whose steps extend all the way to the edge of the plateau, which, as noted before, may serve as an artificial horizon (*The First Days of Spring*, 1929; *The Hand*, 1930; *Premature Ossification of a Railway Station*, 1930). In several works, such an arrangement of platforms on different levels, placed within a broader vista, serves as the main setting for Dalí's motifs (*Surrealist Object, Gauge of Instantaneous Memory*, 1932).

All these devices – spatial constructions and perspectival conceptions alike – serve to accommodate two major conceptual schemes that inform quite a few of Dalí's works in these years. The two largely construct the beholder's mode of viewing of the work and consequently also affect the way the work addresses him. One has to do with the 'gallery' effect as imparted by the paintings, the other with the theater stage quality of Dalí's pictorial space. The 'gallery' effect and the utilization of framing devices comprise the conceptual basis of the poem 'The Great Masturbator' (1930), whose central part constitutes a description of

It should be noted that Lacan does not mention the fact that Dalí himself was well aware of the significance of Holbein's painting for his work, and included a small reproduction of it in the documentation for his *Minotaure* essay 'Aerodynamic Apparitions of "Beings-Objects"' (1934). See *The Four Fundamental Concepts of Psycho-Analysis*, trans. Alan Sheridan (New York: W W. Norton, 1981), 85–9.

large frames and sculpted images arranged in long alleys in what appears to be a vast museum. Dalí frequently alludes in the poem to the objects exhibited by evoking their character of 'mimetic confounding' (*l'erreur par mimétisme*) and by playing with notions concerning the false or counterfeit and the real. This conception is paralleled in the paintings primarily by the artificial or man-made quality of the objects represented. Such are the representations of living forms or objects, which appear to be calcified, frozen in time, and whose spatial positioning ensures the best viewing conditions. Contributing to this effect are the pedestals on which the figures are often placed, or the framing devices that are frontally oriented toward the viewer, like the frames found in *Illuminated Pleasures* and *First Days of Spring*, and the medals or reliefs found, for example, in *William Tell* (1930) and *Memory of the Child-Woman* (1931). It is readily apparent that most other elements in the paintings, besides the frames, conform to the 'gallery' conception. Figures, singly or in groups, in many paintings, are arranged separately, as if totally unrelated one to the other, each oriented toward the viewer by itself, very often in full frontal view, or in other postures that enhance the artificiality of the arrangement.

Much of what corresponds to the 'gallery' conception is also conducive to the conception of theater stage; the two, indeed, seem to complement one another in Dalí's mind. Dalí's predilection for theater stage is readily apparent in his constructions of boxes with painted glass panels, such as in *Babaouo* (1932) and *The Little Theater* (1934), or, a few years later, in the enclosed boxlike, or rather stagelike, conceptions of pictorial space in 1937 works such as *Queen Salomé and Herodias*, or even in the works on the theme of Palladio's Corridor (1937) that allude to Andrea Palladio's Teatro Olimpico in Vicenza. The latter, notwithstanding their obvious baroque character, also indicate that theater was associated in Dalí's mind at the time with the heightened effect of foreshortening – a designed perspectival distortion – that characterizes the corridors opening out of Palladio's proscenium arch, which rise and taper gradually in a way that enhances the perception of recession and depth. Dalí, it would appear, had been thinking all along in terms of the theater stage, as could readily be seen, in his earlier 1929 works, in the enhancement of stage-like effects – accomplished mostly, as noted before, by means of perspectival distortion – such as the excessive tilting up of the 'stage' behind the foreground figures in a pronounced diagonal perspective (somewhat in the manner of Serlio's stage), and, at times, in the lack of spatial continuity between foreground elements and the background, which seems at times like a backdrop.[19] Similarly, there is a pronounced stage-like quality to several

---

[19] To these one might add the lines extending into space found in many works, that are not unlike the boards of a stage. While they readily allude to similar motifs in de Chirico's painting, it seems likely that Dalí was also fully aware of their stage-like character, the more so since the theatrical dimension of de Chirico's work was a current notion at the time, and Dalí would also have been acquainted with de Chirico's forays into the theater

1931 paintings – *The Old Age of William Tell* (1931) foremost – in which a drapery hung like a curtain between two tall pedestals serves to hide what seems to be an obscene sexual activity taking place behind it.

Hints concerning what may have stood behind these all-pervading and largely coextensive conceptions of the 'gallery' and the theater stage – or the perspectival distortion underlying their plastic manifestation – are found in several of Dalí's texts. Such is a passage in the poem 'The Great Masturbator', which evokes the 'mental crisis' brought about by the visual configuration of the 'two faces of Great Masturbators, the huge frame and the sculptures of William Tell' (*CW*, 182). Similarly – Dalí appears to be hinting – the distribution of the elements within a painting and the 'rapports' between them are a plastic correlative for a certain state of mind that may not be defined in any other way. Such states of mind, suggests Dalí, would be communicated to the beholder in a process of 'successive contemplation' of these elements (186).

Control of affect and mastery over his materials seem to be Dalí's overriding concerns in 'Rêverie'. Dalí acts as a *metteur en scène* of his own masturbatory daydream, staging it with scrupulous attention to detail, maneuvering and shifting various features of the setting in conformity with every aspect of the fantasy, and making it as concrete in his mind as possible. It is as if he is trying to visualize a full-fledged scenario, in which every detail of the setting and placement of characters has the utmost importance to the overall effect:

> The garden pond has become twenty times bigger. I am none too satisfied with its real site in the garden, surrounded by huge oaks that conceal the sky. I have now transported the pond back of the house, so that it might be seen from the dining room, at the same time as the skies with Böcklian clouds and storms, that I recall having seen from this site that is overlooking a vast and unobstructed horizon. The placement of the pond has also been changed, because I had been accustomed to seeing it always lengthwise in perspective, and, in my fantasy it appears to me situated transversely. I see myself from the back in the dining room, finishing my snack . . .   (*CW*, 153)

He similarly fantasizes the fire burning the 'thick jumble of shrubs and trees', thus allowing him a clearer view of the fountain (157); also, since the fountain is still hidden by a section of a wall, he also devises an additional solution: 'I envision the scene of Dulita's initiation to be reflected in the large mirror in Dulita's room which is adjacent to the dining room' (158).

The staging of this fantasy is associated, as noted before, with Dalí's reflections concerning the control of affect through arrangement, which he discerns in the works of painters as diverse as Vermeer, Böcklin, and de Chirico (152).

itself. See Marianne W. Martin, 'On de Chirico's Theater', in William Rubin (ed.), *De Chirico* (New York: The Museum of Modern Art, 1982), 81–100.

The implication of the containment of vision within a stage-like circum-scribed space in his paintings goes further than that. To sum up briefly some of the points raised before, this circumscribed space serves as the locus of the unfolding structures of interpretation formed in the paranoiac process, with the visual order of the painting as a whole perceived as a projection of Dalí's own desiring self. In addition, the circumscribed space could be viewed as a manifestation of Dalí's overriding desire for mastery over his small stage of the libido, and, furthermore, over his body image. This desire for mastery also entails structuring the beholder's mode of viewing of the painting, with this primarily being a corollary of the painting's own mode of addressing the viewer. It could readily be seen that the 'gallery' and 'theater stage', in their coextensive role as the two dominant formal metaphors in most of Dalí's works of the period under consideration, point to the paintings' function as presentation rather than representation.

It would be useful to apply to Dalí some of the notions developed by Claude Gandelman in a very suggestive essay, in which he advances a classification of various forms of the rhetorical 'gesture of demonstration' in Italian quattro-cento painting. Gandelman argues that this gesture of demonstration 'not only appeals to us to focus our attention on a particular object or detail inside the painting. It also, by virtue of its merely being there as an important element in the painting, proclaims the whole picture to be an appeal structure and not an illusion of reality.'[20] Gandelman uses as a model the classification of speech acts as developed by J.L. Austin,[21] and suggests that the gesture of demonstra-tion can be classified analogously to the various classes of utterances. His interest – as is ours with regard to Dalí – is with the performatives – utterances that do something or cause someone to do something, with these divided fur-ther into subclasses:

> A painting which proclaims that it is showing something (and not creating the illusionistic appearance of the thing) thus is performing an illocutionary speech act, while a painting which tells us to look at a specific point within itself is performing a perlocutionary act.   (*Reading Pictures*, 9)

A few of the illocutionary and perlocutionary functions listed by Gandelman could well apply to Dalí's paintings, especially in the light of the suggestion that the figure of the demonstrator may have come from the late medieval the-atrical genre of *tableaux vivants*, with its silent and frozen actors on stage to which the demonstrator points and on which he comments. One illocutionary function is the Brechtian distancing: 'the demonstrator, or designator, in the

---

[20] Claude Gandelman, 'The Gesture of Demonstration', in *Reading Pictures, Viewing Texts* (Bloomington: Indiana University Press, 1991), 14.

[21] See J.L. Austin, *How to Do Things with Words* (London, Oxford, New York: Oxford University Press, 1962).

picture is telling the spectator, "I am showing you an enunciation", "I am showing you that I am showing you" '(21). In the context of the quattrocento painting, the painting declares that it is presenting a religious reality and is not a
representation of it. Dalí's paintings – especially in their 'theater stage' capacity – perform a similar function, even without an overt gesture of demonstration. Objects and figures often appear to position themselves specifically
for the beholder's perusal, arranged frontally, as if addressing him (or, to
extend the theater stage concept, as figures in a *tableau vivant*). Where this
arrangement is less conspicuous, the 'gallery' effect, and, often, the presence
of small figures in the role of observers or witnesses – at times an adult and a
child with the adult pointing to the 'objects' on display – accomplish the same
purpose of presentation or demonstration. Furthermore, even when the action
depicted seems more dramatic than the 'gallery' effect would allow for, as, for
instance, in *William Tell* (1930), the gestures of pointing or indicating by the
two figures, William Tell and his 'son', appear more directed at the viewer than
intended for the benefit of one another.

An illocutionary indexing function could similarly be applied to Dalí's
paintings (at least until the late 1930s), with the contention that they should be
viewed as indices or marks of the paranoiac-critical activity rather than a representation that mirrors reality. It is in this capacity that Dalí's double and multiple images should be viewed, as well as his anthropomorphic landscapes –
paintings that may be read as landscapes strewn with human figures and, alter-
nately, as a human face or, at times, a partial or full human figure.[22] More
ambiguous in this respect are the Morphological Echoes, with the perception
they offer of formal analogies between separate images or objects.[23] The
schematic arrangements of formal analogies may be perceived in a painting
such as *A couple with Heads Full of Clouds* (1936) as the conceptualized representation of paranoiac-critical elaboration of a 'systematic structure' rather
than as a mark of it. Such paintings, in any event, form a demonstration, and
as such they fit well in the general scheme proposed here. This is fully in line
with the whole tenor of Dalí's ambition with regard to his theories, which
bespeaks demonstration, indication and persuasion as the means of discredit-
ing one's perception of reality through the obsessive power of another mind.
In 'The Rotting Donkey', his first elaboration of paranoia-criticism, Dalí
argued that 'Paranoia makes use of the external world in order to set off its
obsessive idea, with the disturbing characteristic of *verifying the reality of this
idea for others*' [my emphasis] (*CW*, 223). Verifying the reality of an obsessive idea for others is a matter of showing or demonstrating; when the process

[22] For example, 1936 works such as *Le Grand paranoïaque*, or *Head of a Woman
Having the Form of a Battle*.

[23] Such is the painting *Nostalgic Echo* (1935), for instance, where an entrance cut in a
wall repeats the shape of a church tower, and a girl with a skipping rope is echoed by the
shape of the bell with the curve of the arch seen above it on top of the church tower.

has to do with the formation of mulitple images, 'the various forms assumed by the object in question will be controllable and recognizable by all, as soon as the paranoiac will simply *indicate* them' [my emphasis] (224).

A perlocutionary function, to which Gandelman refers as 'gaze directing' (25), is equally a valid proposition for Dalí's works. It constitutes the gesture of a hand, capturing the gaze of the observer and directing it toward a point in the picture, or it is the gaze of the demonstrator himself, which establishes a contact with an external observer. Figures in Dalí's paintings appear at times to be looking directly at the viewer, as if aware of being 'photographed' (which often is the case, as, for instance, in *Average Fine and Invisible Harp* (1932), for which Dalí in fact used a photograph), often in the act of show-ing.[24] Such direct representations of looking are, however, not always essen-tial for Dalí's purpose. The visual order of Dalí's paintings, with its circumscribed space and the theater stage quality, and especially the sense of a *tableau vivant* with the figures and objects facing the beholder, enhances our consciousness of a seeing presence within the painting. To paraphrase what Hal Foster says regarding Dutch still-life painting, and which seems to be fully applicable to Dalí – disposed for our gaze, figures and objects in Dalí's works threaten to 'dispossess us of our sight', as our gaze 'looks back from things, and threatens us'.[25] Several contemporary critics, following Sartre and Lacan, have considered the implications of this dialectic of seeing/being seen.[26] There is no need to account for the entire range of ramifications of the concept of the gaze in Lacan's theory in order to perceive in Dalí's paintings the presence of the unconscious Other – an Other subsumed in the reversal of subject and object, suggested by Dalí's engraving *Soft Skulls and Cranium Harps*, and epitomized by the anamorphotic skull located in the eye of the beholder, Dalí's own eye, for that matter. This Other, as I have hinted before, the non-Euclidean 'threadless spool' of his 1935 essay which, contrary to Kant's allegation that it is an 'object outside ourselves' (*CW*, 305), is for Dalí his own seeing presence within the painting.

This seeing presence, an alienated self, may pose a threat, reciprocating Dalí's vision of all-encompassing incorporation by vision. The relationship

---

[24] Other instances of displaying some object for the benefit of the beholder are found in works such as *Cardinal, Cardinal!* (1934), in which Gala is seen holding for the viewer's perusal an elongated, eel-like object. In *Suburbs of a Paranoiac-Critical Town: Afternoon on the Outskirts of European History* (1936), Gala holds up a bunch of grapes, as a demonstration of the concept underlying the 'morphological Echoes', that is, the formal analogies between the images occupying the space of the painting.

[25] Hal Foster, 'The Art of Fetishism: Notes on Dutch Still Life', in Emily Apter and William Pietz (eds.), *Fetishism as Cultural Discourse* (Ithaca and London: Cornell University Press, 1993), 265.

[26] An influential essay is Norman Bryson's 'The Gaze in the Expanded Field', in Hal Foster (ed.), *Vision and Visuality*, Dia Art Foundation Discussions in Contemporary Culture no. 2 (Seattle: Bay Press, 1988), 87–108.

between incorporation and desire comes up in his essay 'The Object as Revealed in Surrealist Experiment' (1932), in which Dalí evokes Surrealism's new 'fears' as that which replaces 'our former habitual phantoms', locating them at 'the limit of the emerging cultivation of desire' (*CW*, 239). There we can perceive, suggests Dalí, the existence of another body outside of ourselves that is akin to Feuerbach's 'second self'. The German philosopher Ludwig Andreas Feuerbach conceived of the object as being originally the concept of second self, and Dalí quotes Feuerbach to the effect that the 'concept of the object is usually produced with the help of the *you* which is the "objective self"'. Dalí appears to make use in this essay of Feuerbach's conception of religion as the means by which man projects an image of himself into some form of objectivity, and then makes himself an object to this projected image of himself. But while religion is the objectification of man's essence in ideal terms, Dalí sees that objective 'other' as a terrifying 'new dream' in which man's desire and perversions are vested. The perception by man of the objective 'other' depends on an alienation from himself.[27]

A dialectic of alienation and identification is also at the basis of Lacan's concept of the mirror stage.[28] What is of interest in the light of what I am proposing here is Lacan's contention that the infant seeing its own image in a mirror experiences a bewildering contrast between the size and the inverted symmetry of the specular image and the 'turbulent movements that the subject feels are animating him'. The form discovered by the infant in the mirror is thus a *gestalt* that situates the ego in a 'fictional direction', and 'prefigures its alienating destination'.[29] This results in the 'assumption of the armour of an alienating identity, which will mark with its rigid structure the subject's entire mental development' (*Ecrits*, 4).

It might be conjectured that both Feuerbach and Lacan were on Dalí's mind when he painted one of the most compelling stares in his oeuvre, the one associated with his self-portrait in *Impressions of Africa* (1938),[30] a painting usually seen as reflecting the visionary essence of Dalí's act of painting. Amid various double images of figures that are partially confluent with landscape elements, it is a one-eyed gaze that confronts the viewer (the other eye is hidden behind the easel), the staring eye located between the thumb and the

[27] As Dalí makes clear in his essay 'Aerodynamic Apparitions of "Beings-Objects"', this is a two-way action in which one can objectify one's essence by making oneself into an object – an 'other'.

[28] Closely associated with Lacan in the early 1930s, Dalí may have been exposed to this notion, probably in its embryonic form.

[29] Jacques Lacan, *Ecrits: A Selection*, trans. Alan Sheridan (New York: Norton, 1977), 2.

[30] The title refers to a novel by the idiosyncratic author Raymond Roussel, to whom Dalí acknowledged a great debt. In a short note on another book by Roussel, *Nouvelles Impressions d'Afrique* (*Le surréalisme au service de la Révolution*, no. 6 [May 1933]), Dalí identified the associative mechanisms utilized by Roussel in his writing with his own notion of the paranoiac phenomenon.

index finger of Dalí's hand, which is extended directly forward, in extreme foreshortening. The hand directed at the viewer and the fingers, which seem to encircle the eye as if to further focus its vision, assertively enforce 'gaze directing' toward a point outside the painting. The single staring eye could be construed as referring to the monocular vision in the Albertian perspective in its idealized form, with this implying a specific viewpoint for correct perspectival viewing of the painting. Here the tip of the inverted cone of vision is the beholder's eye or Dalí's own eye in the process of drawing his self-portrait. Dalí's eye in the painting is surrounded by a whole array of phantasmagoric images, which appear to be projected on a kind of backdrop or a screen behind him. To go by Dalí's own suggestions, the very explicit 'gaze directing' in the painting enhances the perception of the presence of the objective Other or Dalí's own alienated self. The Other consists of an alien staring eye (unseen but perceived by us) which is the target of the 'gaze directing', an eye that sees and subsumes the whole array of images surrounding Dalí's own eye in the painting. What is also quite noticeable is the ambivalence of Dalí's gesture: the fingers not only frame an eye, they also appear to repel, drive back, this observing Other. This ambivalence might be explained by the presence of another gaze in this painting, which is Gala's, whose head is seen above Dalí's, her dark orbs conjoined with the arched doorways of a low building placed behind her. The contrast between Dalí's staring single eye and Gala's unseeing eyes is too conspicuous to have been unintentionally conceived, especially when one has in mind Gala's open-eyed stare in *The Endless Enigma*, to which I return now. Painted around the same time as *Impressions of Africa*, it could well be considered its companion piece and dialectical opposite.

Dalí painted *Impressions of Africa* and *The Endless Enigma* about a year after coming out with his painting *The Metamorphosis of Narcissus* and the poem accompanying it. Dalí must have had the earlier painting in mind while working on *Impressions of Africa*, as attested by the kneeling figure with an egg-shaped head (to the right of Dalí's easel) that appears to reiterate the figure of Narcissus. It is my contention, however, that both paintings reflect some aspects of Dalí's version of the Narcissus myth as expanded in the poem. The process of metamorphosis is underlined by desire combined with self-annihilation, with Narcissus losing his being 'in the cosmic vertigo / in the deepest depths of which / is singing / the cold and dionysiac siren of his own image' (*CW*, 327). In the course of the metamorphosis of Narcissus, 'there remains of him only the hallucinatingly white oval of his head', with the metamorphosis reaching its apogee when this head splits and bursts open to reveal the 'flower, the new Narcissus, Gala – my narcissus' (329). In the terms proposed by Dalí before (in 'Love and Memory'), he has no feelings for Gala, because 'feelings imply the absence of love' (167), and thus Dalí's only way of loving Gala without feelings is to be unified with her – to merge into her.

The poem hints at several other levels of meaning that further deepen the implications of the metamorphosis of Dalí into a 'new Narcissus', embodied in his beloved Gala. These encompass a larger overview of Dalí's life and art, and I can only hint briefly at a few of them. We find echoes in it of Freud's theories concerning Narcissism and the instincts, as well as hints concerning the concept of regression, which had been uppermost in Dalí's mind since the early 1930s. Thus, the 'metamorphosis' of Narcissus might, in its first part, convey a sense of regression for the purpose of attaining the infant instinctual satisfaction associated with primary narcissism, along the lines proposed by Freud in *Beyond the Pleasure Principle* (1920).[31] The imagery associated with this process ('savagely mineral torrent', etc.) conveys a sense of loss of form, loss of boundaries or fragmentation. This regressive inertia is broken off in the course of the metamorphosis, to be replaced by a miraculous reversal of this process. The union of Dalí–Narcissus and Gala–Narcissus implies a regaining by Dalí of his experience of wholeness and ego-identity through his narcissistic identification with Gala in a process that reverses the Freudian regression. This involves a movement from fragmentation to unity or wholeness; this, in the terms of Dalí's paintings, might be associated with the conception underlying his double and multiple images. The experience of these images on the viewer's part implies a continuous pendulum movement between two perceptual forms, the fragments of diverse forms of objects and beings, and their clustering into a unified whole. On the analogical plane – and this fits in with Dalí's evolving thought and aesthetics in the latter half of the 1930s – it is a movement between the fragmentation and lack of restriction of the unconscious and the primary process, and the integration associated with consciousness.

This general movement is reiterated in the two paintings, *Impressions of Africa* and *The Endless Enigma*. Both exhibit spatially the small stage of paranoiac phenomena. *Impressions of Africa* employs the tilted plane of the paintings of the early 1930s. Dalí's figure is placed on this plane, but there is some spatial discontinuity between it and what appears to be, as I have suggested, a projection screen or a backdrop that encloses this 'stage'. This backdrop constitutes a frieze of double images in which parts of the human figure are – as illustrated by Gala's head – conflated with landscape elements. The painting represents one phase of the metamorphosis, in which Dalí, conjuring up a whole phantasmagoric array of paranoiac images, is losing his self to the beckoning 'dionysiac siren of his own image', in an alienating maze of mirrored identities. The sense of ineluctability is augmented by the horizon-less circumscribed space of the painting. With her 'unseeing' eyes, Gala is free of

---

[31] See *Art and Writing*, Chap. 16, for a detailed reading of the poem in the light of Freud's theories concerning narcissism as well as of Lacan's formulations in his 'Mirror Stage' article regarding the infant's perception of totality in viewing itself in the mirror as contrasted with the sense of a fragmented body image (*corps morcelé*).

this maze of seeing. Or, in terms of the Lacanian concept of the gaze, she represents the internality of the gaze as something that is independent of the organ of sight. Dalí's observing wide-open eye will be placed within her in the metamorphosis leading to the formation of the unified being Dalí–Gala. Gala's open-eyed gaze in *The Endless Enigma* – combining seeing and insight – represents this unified being. That she is also free of the maze of seeing is substantiated by her spatial placement in the painting. As I have noted earlier, Gala's head does not appear to be anchored to any of the spatial coordinates implied by the different motifs. Indeed, it floats in what seems to be a dimensionless void, as if it has slipped directly from Dalí's drawing board into the painting.[32] Gala also seems to be peeping in, or, rather, taking a parting look at the chaotic scene arranged around another small stage – the table-top around which nucleate the various paranoiac images. In this painting she is literally the *femme visible* – to refer to the title of Dalí's 1930 book whose title page is adorned with a photograph of her wide-open eyes. It should be emphasized that Gala's open-eyed stare is unlike Dalí's in *Impressions of Africa* – it doesn't involve the kind of 'gaze directing' found there. The beholder's viewpoint is inferred by a vanishing point that is partially defined by the table top and that refers to the vision of fragmentation surrounding it. The reversal of subject and object in this case affixes an 'other' that is wholly congruent with the amorphousness reigning over this vision. Gala's head, however, appears completely detached from it. Thus in her open-eyed stare and shifting eyes, and with her tangible reality, she seems to be leading the beholder – Dalí by extension – out of this world of fragments.

The poem 'The Metamorphosis of Narcissus' and the two paintings thus illustrated an ongoing situation in which Gala constantly guards Dalí from excessively giving in to his regressive tendencies or helps him to harness them. They also heralded profound changes in Dalí's thought and, eventually, his art, which were gradually taking place in the following years. Much of what I am saying here requires, of course, further elaboration, and I can only hint at these future developments. For Dalí these changes meant a reversal of his conscious assumption of regression as an aesthetic, theoretical and philosophical stance, and a perception that the unlimited freedom of infant satisfaction also implies a loss of self that is tantamount to the loss of form. This, consequently, constituted a return to a more restrictive formal and aesthetic orientation. Dalí's decision 'to become classic' meant abiding by a new set of

---

[32] This is no mere metaphorizing; two pencil drawings of Gala's head (one is in the collection of the Santa Barbara Museum of Art, the other at the Fundación Gala-Salvador Dalí at Figueres), appear to have served as direct models (they are both dated to 1939, but it seems reasonable to suppose that they were done around the time Dalí worked on *The Endless Enigma*). In both drawings and painting, Gala's head is adorned with a turban; her eyes shifted in their orbs look out of the painting or drawing toward the beholder's space. In fact, it seems as if Dalí simply tilted the drawing while copying it onto the canvas directly and with hardly any modification.

aesthetic attitudes that would altogether reverse the earlier ones; references to classical and Renaissance art abound in his writing and art beginning in the late 1930s. These changes were accompanied by a subtle, yet quite crucial, change in Dalí's vision of paranoia-criticism. It constituted a shift from a conception based on the uncertainty of the paranoiac vision, in which the fragments of reality nucleate in a variety of patterns and constructions on Dali's small stage of paranoiac ceremonial, to the assertion of an absolute vision of reality, tinged by an obvious metaphysical sense, and pivoting around the mythologized figure of the doubled being Gala-Salvador-Dalí.

# 8

# Rafael Alberti: Mind, Matter, Blood

## ROBERT HAVARD

The poetry of Rafael Alberti (1902–1999) is remarkable not only for its intrinsic quality but also because it charts the main currents of surrealist thought as this evolved from the late 1920s. Other figures may be identifiably more surrealist at any given point in their work, but Alberti, alone among his compatriots, it seems to me, offers a virtual gamut of the surrealist experience. That he does so with a distinctive Spanish imprint makes his work all the more illuminating.[1]

His most acclaimed volume, *Sobre los ángeles* [*Concerning the Angels*] of 1927–8, is his first committed foray into surrealist practice. Based on the poet's then desperate state of mind, this cathartic work has a therapeutic, Freudian ethos, while its mode of delivery – at first halting and brittle, later charged with oracular rhythms – reflects the dynamics of the unconscious and approximates to psychic dictation: 'I began to write blindly at any hour of the night,' Alberti recalls, 'with a kind of inadvert automatism.'[2] At the other end of the spectrum stand Alberti's political works, notably *El poeta en la calle* [*The Poet in the Street*] of 1931–5 and *De un momento a otro* [*Any Minute Now*] of 1934–8, in which his Marxism is defined against the upheavals of the Second Republic and the Spanish Civil War. Here a materialist bias, together with the poet's sensitivity to the issue of writing for or on behalf of the proletariat, recall the challenges Breton's circle faced in Paris when they sought to make Surrealism impact more directly on society.

Between these two extremes of psychoanalytical subjectivity and materialistic objectivity lies the point of intersection that Breton, via reference to Hegel, championed in his *Second Surrealist Manifesto* of 1929.[3] It found

---

[1] I develop this point in *The Crucified Mind: Rafael Alberti and the Surrealist Ethos in Spain* (London: Tamesis, 2001).

[2] Rafael Alberti, *The Lost Grove*, trans. Gabriel Burns (Berkeley: University of California Press, 1959), 262. For the original Spanish 'un automatismo no buscado' in *La arboleda perdida* (Buenos Aires, 1959; Madrid: Alianza, 1998), I have preferred the adjective *inadvert* (or else *unintentional, unsought*) to Burns' *undesirable* automatism.

[3] See André Breton, *Manifestoes of Surrealism*, trans. Richard Seaver and Helen R. Lane (Ann Arbor: University of Michigan Press, 1972). The *Second Manifesto* originally

expression in the so-called 'surrealist object' that sought, most typically in Dalí, to exteriorize purely mental phenomena. It is this point of confluence between mind and matter, between Freud and Marx, that I wish to investigate, with reference to the motif of *blood* in *Sermones y moradas* [*Sermons and Dwelling Places*] of 1929–30. Before doing so, however, it is necessary to locate the parameters of mind and matter with a little more precision.

*Sobre los ángeles* was Alberti's fifth collection in as many years and it links with his first, *Marinero en tierra* [*Sailor on Shore*] of 1924, in that it reflects upon his boyhood in El Puerto de Santa María, Cádiz. But whereas the first, written in a light traditional vein, is nostalgic for the Atlantic shoreline that Alberti reluctantly left in 1917 when his father's job as a wine salesman took the family to Madrid, the reminiscences in *Sobre los ángeles* are much less fond. Here, in a state of despair that borders on mental breakdown, the poet traces the events of his youth that have made him, by his mid-twenties, a dysfunctional insomniac, a traumatized paranoiac:

> ¿Quién sacude en mi almohada
> reinados de yel y sangre,
> cielos de azufre,
> mares de vinagre?
>
> ¿Qué voz difunta los manda?
> Contra mí, mundos enteros,
> contra mí, dormido,
> maniatado,
> indefenso.    (392)[4]

> Who scatters on my pillow / kingdoms of bile and blood,
> skies of sulphur, / seas of vinegar?
> What dead voice commands them?
> Against me, entire worlds, / against me, asleep,
> handcuffed, / defenceless.

The many causes of this turmoil – including his poverty, doubts about his poetry, jealousy of other poets, family tensions, a friend's suicide and betrayal in love – are itemized in his autobiography, *La arboleda perdida* [*The Lost Grove*].[5] They appear as leitmotifs in the poems too; but we come to realize, by its sheer persistence in his linguistic register, that the most deep-rooted factor is religion, that is to say, the severe repression he suffered as a child at the hands of his family and, more especially, the militaristic regime at the Jesuit

appeared as an article in *La Révolution surréaliste* (15 Dec. 1929), before it was published separately in definitive form in 1930.

    [4] Numbers in parenthesis indicate the page of reference in Rafael Alberti, *Obra completa, I, Poesía 1920–1938* (Madrid: Aguilar, 1988).
    [5] *The Lost Grove*, 262.

school of San Luis Gonzaga in El Puerto from which he was expelled at the
age of sixteen. Alberti's schooling is detailed in the first volume of his autobiography, while it is treated allusively in *Sobre los ángeles* in poems such as
'El ángel de los números' [The Angel of Numbers] and 'Los ángeles cole-
giales' [The Schoolboy Angels]. More significant, however, is the religious
patterning that permeates this work, for it derives in large part from the Jesuit
emphasis on Hell and damnation that sowed seeds of anxiety in the young
Alberti just as it did in Luis Buñuel at the Colegio del Salvador, Zaragoza, and
James Joyce at Belvedere School, Dublin.[6] Along with terror, it has to be said,
the Jesuits instilled the positive corollary of a transcendental disposition. This
was nurtured by the Loyolan practice of 'viendo el lugar' [seeing the place],
outlined in the Jesuit founder's *Spiritual Exercises*.[7] The practice centres on
imagining, via the senses, all the concrete, material features in a given subject
of contemplation: notably, the sulphuric fires of Hell with its clanking chains,
screams and stench of rotting flesh, but also the timber, nails, thorns, vinegar
and such like of Christ's Passion. The salient point is that these two prongs of
Jesuit teaching – suffering and transcendence – bear directly on surrealist
practice and on Alberti's disposition as a poet. Patently, the terrors of Hell sig-
nify as well as induce the psychical torment that is the *sine qua non* at the
Freudian core of Surrealism; but, no less clearly, the focus on material objects
as a means of promoting transcendent experience bears closely on the *sur*real,
or superreal, which the movement was increasingly wont to explore.

The religious register of *Sobre los ángeles* is announced in the volume's
title, while the *angels* that appear in virtually every poem constitute a variety
of psychical and moral values, as the individual poem titles indicate: 'El ángel
avaro' [The Angel of Avarice], 'El ángel de la ira' [The Angel of Wrath], 'El
ángel mentiroso' [The Lying Angel], 'Los ángeles crueles' [The Cruel
Angels]. This acute, even medieval sense of sin generates a pronounced
emphasis on suffering that is again evident in titles, 'El alma en pena' [The
Soul in Torment], 'Muerte y juicio' [Death and Judgement], 'Castigos' [Pun-
ishments], many of which reflect the Jesuit predilection for 'The Four Last
Things'. The process is confessional or, in Freud's terms, abreactive, while the
poem 'Desahucio' [Eviction] recalls the biblical parallel of exorcising
demons:

> Ángeles malos o buenos,
> que no sé,
> te arrojaron en mi alma . . .

---

[6] See Luis Buñuel, *My Last Breath*, trans. Abigail Israel (London: Jonathan Cape,
1984), 27–30 and James Joyce, *Portrait of the artist as a Young Man* (London: Jonathan
Cape, 1964).
[7] See Saint Ignatius of Loyola, *Personal Writings*, trans. with introductions and notes
by Joseph A. Munitiz and Philip Endean (Harmondsworth: Penguin, 1996), 298–9.

Humedad. Cadenas. Gritos.
Ráfagas.

Te pregunto:
¿Cuándo abandonas la casa,
dime,
que ángeles, malos, crueles,
quieren de nuevo alquilarla?

Dímelo.   (389)

Good or bad angels, / I know not, / threw you in my soul . . .
Dampness. Chains. Screams. / Blasts of wind.
I ask you: / When will you quit this house, / tell me,
so that bad and cruel angels will want to rent it again?
Tell me.

The motif of eviction, itself a paradigm for catharsis, is complicated here by
the echo of Luke (11: 24–26) in which a warning is given that banishing an
'unclean spirit' from the body/house may lead to its occupation by seven spirits that are even more evil. This point is explained – for me at least – in Roland
Barthes' critique of Loyola, which has broad application to brainwashing
techniques. Barthes argues that St Ignatius' method consists in making the
trainee Jesuit 'neurotic' by stripping him of his individuality and then occupying 'the totality of the mental territory'. Barthes concludes: 'Ignatius is then
a psychotherapist attempting at all costs to inject images into the dull dry and
empty spirit of the exercitant, to introduce into him this culture of fantasy.'[8]

There is evidence in *Sobre los ángeles* of such a systematic emptying out
or destruction of personality, notably in the poem 'El cuerpo deshabitado'
[The Uninhabited Body]:

Llevaba una ciudad dentro.
La perdió.
Le perdieron.

Solo, en el filo del mundo,
clavado ya, de yeso.
No es un hombre, es un boquete
de humedad negro,
por el que no se ve nada.   (394)

He carried a city within him. / He lost it. / They lost him.
Alone, on the edge of the world, / stuck with gypsum.
He is not a man, he's a hole / of black dampness,
through which nothing is seen.

---

[8] Roland Barthes, *Sade, Fourier, Loyola*, trans. R. Miller (London: Jonathan Cape,
1977), 69 and *passim*.

The same idea appears in 'El ángel mentiroso' [The Lying Angel], with its strong sense of indoctrination:

> Y fui derrotada
> yo, sin violencia,
> con miel y palabras.   (400)

And I was destroyed, / without violence, / with honey and words.

One destructive aspect of the procedure is seen in 'Can de llamas' [Dog of Flames] with its polarizing of the body and spirit, a dichotomy the Jesuits seem to have nurtured. Another is depicted in the poem entitled '5', which refers to the five senses on which St Ignatius based his meditative technique. For Alberti, these 'cinco vías' [five channels] and 'cinco navegables ríos' [five navigable rivers] are all closed down:

> Y no viste.
> Era su luz la que cayó primero.
> Mírala, seca, en el suelo.
>
> Y no oíste.
> Era su voz la que alargada hirieron.
> Óyela muda, en el eco . . .
>
> Y no tocaste.
> El desaparecido era su cuerpo.
> Tócalo en la nada, yelo.   (408–9)

And you saw not. / It was his light that fell first.
Look at it, withered, on the floor.
And you heard not. / It was his extenuated voice they wounded.
Hear it, mute, in the echo . . .
And you touched not. / What had disappeared was his body.
Touch it in the void, ice.

Treating the five senses successively, Alberti mimics the Jesuit practice of meditation that leads to the celebrated *composition of place*, but he gives this an entirely negative construction as we experience the systematic annihilation of the poet as a young boy.[9]

To return to Barthes' analysis of Loyolan practice, we recall that the trainee Jesuit's mind was emptied in order to make it ripe for 'fantasy manipulation'. This is effectively what happens in *Sobre los ángeles* when, in its later stages, the poet adopts a distinctly messianic voice. Precisely when he passes through

---

[9] The damage that religious teaching orders had inflicted on Spanish youth was an issue of sufficient importance to be raised in the Cortes on 13 October 1931 by the future premier, Manuel Azaña, who had experienced a Jesuit education. See *Diario de las Sesiones de las Cortes Constituyentes de la República Española (1931)*, 1671.

the crucible of suffering, as detailed in 'El alma en pena' [The Soul in Torment], the poet takes on a striking Christ-like identity. It surfaces in 'Los ángeles mudos' [The Dumb Angels], which follows the poem 'Ascensión' [Ascension], when Alberti describes his brief return to El Puerto and the way people look upon him in astonishment as if he were the Risen Christ: '– ¿Cómo tú por aquí y en otra parte?' (418) ['How can you be here and elsewhere?']. It gathers pace and conviction in the volume's third and final section when the poet's tone becomes omniscient, prophetic and didactic:

> Para ir al infierno no hace falta cambiar de sitio ni postura.   (434)
>
> To go to Hell you don't have to move a muscle or budge an inch.
>
> Pero yo os digo:
> una rosa es más rosa habitada por las orugas
> que sobre la nieve marchita de esta luna de quince años.   (443)
>
> But I tell you plainly:
> a rose is more of a rose when it is inhabited by caterpillars
> than on the withered snow of this fifteen-year-old moon.

The line of verse has now lengthened considerably to accommodate an oracular mode. Speaking in riddles, the poet addresses us collectively in the sermonic 'vosotros' [*you* plural] form of the verb, often with admonishing imperatives:

> La cal viva es el fondo que mueve la proyección de los muertos.
> Os he dicho que no acerquéis.
> Os he pedido un poco de distancia.   (441)
>
> Quick-lime is the foundation that stirs the projection of the dead.
> I have told you not to come close. / I have asked you for a little
> space.
>
> Oídme . . . Oídme aún . . . Oídme, oídme por último   (438–9)
>
> Listen to me . . . Listen to me further . . . Listen to me, listen to this
> last point

This onslaught culminates in 'Los ángeles muertos' [The Dead Angels] where messianic fantasy reaches paranoiac levels of delusion. At the same time, we sense a strange truth in what the poet has to say about matter or the objects around us:

> Buscadlos, buscadlos:
> en el insomnio de las cañerías olvidadas,
> en los cauces interrumpidos por el silencio de las basuras.
> No lejos de los charcos incapaces de guardar una nube,

unos ojos perdidos,
una sortija rota
o una estrella pisoteada.
Porque yo los he visto:
en esos escombros momentáneos que aparecen en las neblinas.
Porque yo los he tocado:
en el destierro de un ladrillo difunto,
venido a la nada desde una torre o un carro.   (442)

Look hard, look hard for them: / in the insomnia of forgotten drains,
in channels blocked by the silence of rubbish.
Not far from puddles that cannot hold a cloud, / lost eyes,
a broken ring / or a trampled star.
Because I have seen them: / in that momentary debris that appears
in mists.
Because I have touched them: / in the banishment of a deceased
brick, reduced to nothing from a tower or cart.

Mad, deluded, prone to absurd fantasies (that drains suffer insomnia, that bricks die or are banished), the poet casts himself as a witness whose urgency, conviction and insight ensure his words will not fall on deaf ears. But what is the substance of his message? At its simplest, it is perhaps no more than an affirmation of the pre-eminence of matter, and, one step farther, that we humans are inextricably bound to the objects that surround us. Alberti takes this still another step by suggesting that if we wish to (re-)discover our past or true selves – our 'ángeles muertos' [dead angels] – we should look in the discarded objects that were once part and parcel of our lives. Such objects, he implies, have affective value: in the above, for instance, it is not difficult to imagine what *a broken ring* represents, while the discarded bricks very likely relate to Alberti's sadness at finding his favourite uncle Vicente's house reduced to rubble – 'a complete ruin . . . a single wall with its windows open to the sky' – when he visited El Puerto after a three-year absence in 1919.[10] The potential for affectiveness in objects is very clear in the long inventory at the poem's conclusion. Here the images appear to have been taken at random from a rubbish-dump that is itself a perfect example of incongruously juxtaposed objects, a paradigm of both chance and the *dépaysement* that surrealists cherished:

gota de cera que sepulta la palabra de un libro . . .
firma de uno de esos rincones de carta . . .
casco perdido de una botella . . .
suela extraviada en la nieve . . .
navaja de afeitar abandonada al borde de un precipicio.   (442)

[10]  *The Lost Grove*, 32.

> drop of wax that entombs the words of a book . . .
> signature in the corner of one of those letters . . .
> broken shell of a bottle . . . /. . . shoe sole lost in snow . . .
> razor left on the edge of a precipice.

However, in the context of Alberti's life these objects allude specifically and respectively, I suggest, to poetry, love (letters), alcoholism (rife in his male relatives in El Puerto), poverty and suicide. Once we accept the principle that objects have affective value in relation to human life, it is a small step to assign sentience to them, for this merely involves a further attribution or projection of one's own feeling. Such bizarre statements as the following now begin to make more sense:

> Oíd la lentitud de una piedra que se dobla hacia la muerte   (439)
> Listen to a stone's slowness as it bends towards death . . .

> esas ausencias hundidas que sufren los muebles desvencijados   (442)
> those sunken absences that rickety pieces of furniture suffer.

It need hardly be said that the level of absurdity defines the speaker as surrealist, in the delusional or paranoiac sense that Dalí championed. In this connection let us also note the true value of the zany identification with Christ: namely, that it is through suffering, the neurosis-inducing suffering of the mind, that the creative artist finds his salvation. For Alberti, as for Dalí, madness equals transcendence; and suffering, ironically at the hands of religion, is the cross on which his greatest work is generated. Much in the spirit of Dalí too is the structuring and simulation, as Alberti parodies the Jesuit attachment to material objects for subversive ends. Indeed, he turns their message on its head by advocating that it is the self, not the devil or a divinity, that is to be found in the contemplation of objects, his search in drains and rubbish-dumps being a deliberate counter to otherworldliness.

\* \* \* \* \*

Turning briefly to see what became of Alberti's materialist momentum in the mid-1930s, we have to say, firstly, that he took some time to find his feet as a political poet, for the propaganda imperative often got the better of him in *El poeta en la calle* [*The Poet in the Street*]. These were fraught times and, after visiting Moscow on a government grant in 1933, an idealistic Alberti was bitterly frustrated to return home only to find that little had changed politically or amongst the intelligentsia:

> volví aquí en el instante en que unas pobres tierras cambiaban de
> dueño . . .
> y vi cadáveres sentados,

cobardes en las mesas del café y del dinero . . .
y os escupo    (524–5)

I came back just when a few scraps of land were changing
hands . . .
and I saw corpses sat in chairs, / cowards at business and coffee
tables . . .
and I spit on you.

The lines are indicative of the feeling that led Alberti in 1933 to found
*Octubre*, a political organ that he and his wife María Teresa León printed and
sold 'a gritos' [shouting it out] on Madrid's streets.[11] *Octubre* predated its
Parisian counterpart *Commune*, which was edited by Alberti's brother in arms,
Luis Aragon. Both journals were stridently Marxist, though, at a personal
level, Alberti was perhaps more successful than Aragon in balancing political
commitment with the demands of art, at least by the time of *De un momento
a otro* [*Any Minute Now*], 1934–8.

In this volume's opening section Alberti reflects once more on his childhood, but now with a view to tracing what had made him turn red. Over and
above his family's airs and graces, the decisive factor was again his schooling
at San Luis Gonzaga. The young Rafael had been allowed to attend this pres-
tigious institution – and rub shoulders with the sons of the richest Andalusian
landowners – as a day pupil, without paying fees. This concession was granted
the Alberti family, who had fallen on hard times, in reward for the protection
they gave the Jesuits during the First Republic forty years earlier when their
teaching order was banned. Jesuit generosity came at a price, however, as the
poet notes in 'Colegio (S.J.)' [School (S.J)], for day-boys were not allowed to
wear school uniform or enjoy the privileges of boarders. Alberti was thus
introduced to an invidious class system at an early age, and he associated it
with religion:

> Éramos los externos,
> los colegiales de familias burguesas ya en declive.
> La caridad cristiana nos daba sin dinero su cultura,
> la piedad nos abría los libros y las puertas de las clases.
> Ya éramos de esas gentes que algún día se las entierra de balde.
>
> (614)

> We were the day-boys,
> schoolboys of middle-class families who had known better days.
> Christian charity offered us its culture for free,
> pity opened books and classroom doors to us.
> We were the sort who'd one day get a burial plot for nothing.

---

[11] See María Teresa León, *Memoria de la melancolía* (Buenos Aires: Losada,
1970), 79.

Not surprisingly, Rafael, with a handful of fellow rebels, took to the nearby
dunes where he made his first gesture of defiance:

> tanta ira,
> tanto odio contenidos sin llanto,
> nos llevaban al mar que nunca se preocupaba de las raíces
> cuadradas
> . . . a las dunas calientes,
> donde nos orinábamos en fila mirando hacia el colegio.
> Éramos los externos.   (614–15)

> So much anger, / so much choked, tearless hatred,
> led us to the sea that had no notion of square roots,
> . . . to the hot dunes, / where we stood in a line facing the school
> and pissed.
> We were the day-boys.

After this inauspicious start, Alberti suffered the ignominy of expulsion
from school and exile to Madrid where his life as an impoverished artist soon
gave rise to health problems. During his convalescence from a tubercular illness he discovered poetry, which led him to meet the group at the Residencia
de Estudiantes [Student Residence] – including Lorca, Buñuel and Dalí – who
were mostly from privileged, provincial backgrounds. In the mid-1920s,
along with the important artist Maruja Mallo, his lover, Alberti also associated with the Vallecas school led by the incipient communists Benjamín
Palencia and Alberto Sánchez whose art had an earthy, materialist thrust.
When events took on a momentum of their own, with the fall of Primo de
Rivera's dictatorship, the abdication of King Alfonso XIII and the coming of
the Second Republic, Alberti committed himself to the proletarian cause. He
visited the Soviet Union twice, witnessing en route the burning of the Reich-
stag in Berlin, and he travelled to New York, the Caribbean and Spanish
America in 1934 in an effort to raise funds for the Asturian miners, excursions
that provided material for the centre part of *De un momento a otro*. Several of
his diary-like poems are outstanding, including 'New-York', which is built
around the motif of petroleum, a 'primary material' that in Alberti's Marxist
analysis underpins US imperialism. As he approaches the metropolis at dawn
aboard the *Bremen*, its famous skyline is invisible beneath the pall of fumes;
but if Wall Street's crimes lie hidden, the poet knows what evil radiates from
its capitalist centre to subjugate an entire continent: 'araña de tentáculos que
hilan / fríamente la muerte de otros pueblos' (641) [spider's tentacles that
coldly spin / other nations' deaths]. US policy is exploitative, based on 'la
extracción triste de metales . . . de cañas dulces . . . de café y de tabaco' [the
sad extraction of metals . . . of sugar cane . . . coffee and tobacco], which is
made possible by the petrodollar. Alberti fittingly concludes that Spanish
America's 'agónicas naciones' [dying nations] will one day rejoice at seeing

the stars and stripes burn 'en una justa, / libertadora llama de petróleo' [in a just / and liberating flame of petrol]. The sentiments in this organic poem are developed when Alberti takes us on a journey through Spanish America, listing sundry issues – racism in Cuba, revolution in Nicaragua, police in Costa Rica – but all to the unifying refrain of land ownership, peasant rights and the need to fight the *gringo*'s unjust system.

The volume culminates in its fourth and last part, 'Capital de la gloria' [Glorious Capital], which traces the Spanish Civil War, from the perspective of Madrid, up to the end of 1938 when, after the withdrawal of the International Brigades, defeat stared the Republic in the face. This section is not without propaganda, which can be jauntily rhythmic to uplift the spirits of men on the front:

> ¡A galopar,
> a galopar,
> hasta enterralos en el mar!   (689)
>
> Gallop on, / gallop on, / until we bury them in the sea!

– or crude as graffiti, as in 'Balada de los cuatro cerdos de la paz' [Ballad of the Four Pigs of Peace] which mocks those who signed the infamous Treaty of Non-Intervention. With Dada-like insouciance, Alberti coins and conjugates the verb 'cerdear', from 'cerdo' [pig]:

> Ya van a hozar reunidos los cuatro cerdos.
> – Para salvar a esta paloma cerdearé.
>           – ¿Cerdear?
>                     – Cerdeemos.
>
> Cerdeo,
> cerdeas,
> cerdea.
> Cerdeamos,
> cerdeáis,
> cerdean.   694–5)
>
> The four pigs are going to put their snouts in the same trough.
> 'To save that dove I'll pig.' / 'Will you pig?' / 'Let's all pig.'
> I pig, / you pig, / he pigs. / We pig, / you all pig, / they pig.

Overwhelmingly, however, this section consists of crafted poems that capture the tragedy of war in its political and human dimensions. As we see in the fine opening poem, 'Madrid-Otoño' [Madrid-Autumn], Alberti also addresses the thorny issue of being a poet whose duty it is to speak for the masses:

> Ciudad de los más turbios siniestros provocados,
> de la angustia nocturna que ordena hundirse al miedo

en los sótanos lívidos con ojos desvelados,
yo quisiera furiosa, pero impasiblemente
arrancarme de cuajo la voz, pero no puedo,
para pisarte toda tan silenciosamente,
que la sangre tirada
mordiera, sin protesta, mi llanto y mi pisada.   (671)

City of the most darkly conceived atrocities,
whose nightly suffering makes fear bury itself
open-eyed in livid cellars, / furiously yet impassively would I
tear out my voice by its roots, were it possible,
that I might walk upon you so silently / the spilt blood
would bite my grief and footstep without protest.

As Nationalist bombs rain on Madrid, driving its citizens into the bowels of the
city, Alberti seeks to lose his individuality, or distinctive poetic voice, in order
to merge with the communal spirit of resistance. This reflects a communist
ethic that, against the grain of poetry, demands the subordination of subjective
to collective content. Alberti goes a long way towards achieving this ideal,
described in 'Aniversario' [Anniversary] as 'haciendo de mi voz pulmón de
todo un pueblo' (689) [making my voice the lungs of a whole people]. Among
the devices he employs, we note: collective personification, as in his addressing the city of Madrid above, and the identifying of groups of people, be they
International Brigaders, the crack communist Fifth Regiment, or simply
volunteers from the land, 'Los campesinos' [The Peasants]. Noteworthy too is
the way the latter are described via the material circumstance and implements
of their rustic life: they are 'duros, color de la corteza' (681) [hard, bark-
coloured], dark 'como los padernales' [like flintstones], while they smell of wet
lambs or 'estiércoles y fangales' [manure and bogs]. In a repeated image, the
men's sacrifice is poignantly linked to the land:

van los hombres del campo como inmensas simientes
a sembrarse en los hondos surcos de las tricheras   (681)

country men like immense seeds / are sown in the trenches'
   deep furrows

The poet's attentiveness to nature and its seasonal rhythms strengthens the
sense of collective endeavour. Sometimes, as in 'Monte de El Pardo' [El
Pardo Mountain], the beauty of a scene provides an incongruous backdrop
to the horror of war. Elsewhere, as in 'Abril 1938' [April 1938], the coming
of spring, the season of hope, is at odds with the Republic's desperate situation. But even when an autumn gloom conveys an appropriately fatalistic
mood, there radiates a sense of elemental man and his perennial link with the
land:

El otoño, otra vez, Luego, el invierno. Sea.
Caiga el traje del árbol, el sol no nos recuerde.
Pero como los troncos, el hombre en la pelea,
seco, amarillo, frío, mas por debajo, verde.   (696)

Autumn, once again. Then, winter. So be it.
Let the tree's suit fall, and the sun not remind us.
Yet just like their trunks, the man in battle,
withered, yellow, cold, but underneath, green.

These classic alexandrines, complete with rhyme and caesuras, are far removed from the mode of expression in *Sobre los ángeles* and seem not at all surrealist. Yet we recognize that the form, as in 'Madrid-Otoño', is a poetic tribute to the common men who stood against fascism in defence of the democratically elected Republic. We also recognize that Alberti, in his materialist philosophy, has remained faithful to the evolving surrealist ethos by channelling his art to the service of the people.

\* \* \* \* \*

We turn back now to consider the point of intersection in the critical years of the late 1920s when Freudian input to Surrealism was enriched by metaphysical concepts, notably a concern for transcendence via subject–object integration. Alberti had ventured down this path in the closing stages of *Sobre los ángeles* when he posited, none too rationally, that our true selves are to be found in junk objects and rubbish dumps. In his next volume, the neglected *Sermones y moradas (1929–1930)* [*Sermons and Dwelling Places*], he develops the idea in different and challenging ways. Identification with Christ reaches new levels of (what has clearly become) simulated paranoia, as we see in the opening 'Sermón de las cuatro verdades' [Sermon on the Four Truths], perhaps his greatest single poem. This long piece is structured like a sermon, complete with exordium, admonishments, exhortations and a step-by-step – i.e. apparently logical – outlining of key principles or *four truths* in an echo of 'The Four Last Things'. Attention to number is in the spirit of Jesuit discourse, which, as Barthes observed, is a most literal form of *articulation*: 'everything is immediately divided, subdivided, classified, numbered off in annotations, weeks, points, exercises, mysteries, etc'.[12] Alberti's itemizing procedure – 'La primera verdad es ésta . . . / La segunda verdad es ésta' (451–2) [The first truth is this . . . / The second truth is this] – parodies Loyolan practice in the supposed separating out of points. In fact, he does not offer four discrete points as such but repeats the same ones over and over again in a variety of images that serve as exempla, his principal aim being to stress that all life is finite and the sooner we grasp this nettle the healthier our minds will be.

12 Barthes, 52.

The common denominator in his images is the material substance of life, which includes what is known as the soul:

> – Mi alma está picada por el cangrejo de pinzas y compases candentes, mordida por las ratas y vigilada día y noche por el cuervo.   (452)

> My soul is pierced by crab's pincers and burning compasses, gnawed at by rats and watched over day and night by the crow.

Behind this tormented sermoniser stands the supreme witness who is presented unequivocally as a Christ figure – 'He aquí el hombre' [Behold the man] (cf. John 19: 5) – and cited as a revered prophet: 'Escuchadle. Ésta es su voz' (453) [Listen to him. This is his voice]. His utterances are shaman-like, full of materio-mystical import:

> – Mi alma es sólo un cuerpo que fallece por fundirse y rozarse con los objetos vivos y difuntos.

> My soul is only a body that is dying to merge with and rub itself against living and dead objects.

His ascetic message of merging the self with matter is pointedly antithetical to the Christian one of salvation through the soul and rejection of the body as the site of sin. Only the soul's 'inutilidad en el mundo' (453) [uselessness in the world] is recognized here and the speaker argues that salvation lies in coarse matter:

> . . . yo os prevengo que cuando el alma de mi enemigo hecha bala de cañón perfore la Tierra y su cuerpo ignorante renazca en la torpeza del topo o en el hálito acre y amarillo que desprende la saliva seca del mulo, comenzará la perfección de los cielos.   (454–5)

> . . . I warn you that when my enemy's soul made into a cannonball perforates the Earth and his ignorant body is reborn in a mole's dimness or the acrid yellow breath that issues from a mule's dry saliva, heaven's perfection will be at hand.

Besides confirming the speaker's irrationality, this piling up of objects in ever-lengthening sentences conveys a sense of the prolific material substance of the world. At the same time, the reader/listener is sorely challenged by the violence done to syntax and by the overloading of information in sentences that extend to eight lines and seventy or so words. The rant is again parodic, no doubt in retaliation for the terrifying sermons the young Rafael had to endure and which Joyce captures so well in *Portrait of the Artist as a*

*Young Man.*[13] Linguistically too, it is designed to engender puzzlement, not simply because Alberti felt puzzled as a boy, but because this enhances the thematic confusion of the subjective and objective realms. As ever, confusion derives from the attribution of sentience to matter: 'Cuando los escabeles son mordidos por las sombras . . . / el polvo se desilusiona sin huellas' (455) [When footstools are bitten by shadows . . . / dust without footprints grows disillusioned]. Another pattern is found in the type of objects selected, which are, by and large, indices of death – 'esqueletos de las algas' [seaweed skel- etons], 'las espaldas de los muertos padecen de insomnio' [corpses' shoulders suffer from insomnia], 'burbujas agonizantes' [dying bubbles] – and as such edifying:

> Porque no existe nada más saludable para la arcilla que madura la muerte como la postrera contemplación de un círculo en ruina.   (454)

> Since there is nothing more healthy for clay in which death matures than the final contemplation of a circle in ruin.

The objects are mainly discarded ones that, in the manner of waste, rubbish and detritus, tend to lie strewn upon the ground. The penultimate stanza, with its wine-cellar setting, provides a good example:

> Bien poco importa a la acidez de los mostos descompuestos que mi alegría se consuma a lo largo de las maderas en las fermentaciones más tristes que tan sólo causan la muerte al hormigón anónimo que trafica con su grano de orujo.   (456)

> It makes no difference to the acidity of decomposing musts that my joy is consumed along timbers in the saddest fermentations that merely bring about the death of the anonymous ant that traffics with its grain of bagasse.

Though not one of the poem's longer sentences, it is typical of Alberti's inter- twining of the human – 'mi alegría' [my joy] – with the material – 'maderas' [timbers], 'grano de orujo' [grain of bagasse] – while somewhere between stand the low life of insects and must. Alberti's point is that his own life, or death, is of no consequence to the low life, nor should it be, for he is simply part of the materialist cycle to which no sentimentality attaches. Naturally, his downward, earth-bound focus is a deliberate counter to the heavenward tra- jectory of sermons and the like.

Downwardness is a trait Alberti learnt from the Vallecas school, as its spokesman Alberto Sánchez explains:

> Queríamos llegar a la sobriedad y a la sencillez que nos transmitían las tier- ras de Castilla . . . Tomamos la cosa con verdadero fanatismo. Nos dimos

13 Joyce, 123ff.

a coleccionar piedras, palos, arenas y todo objeto que tiuviera calidades
plásticas. Hasta el extremo de que una vez encontramos en un barbecho de
Vallecas un zapato viejo de mujer . . . [14]

We wanted to capture the sobriety and simplicity that we found in the
Castilian earth . . . We were truly fanatical about it. We began to collect
stones, sticks, sand, any object that had plastic quality. One day we even
found a woman's old shoe in an empty Vallecas field . . .

This orientation was also influential on Alberti's lover at the time, the free-
spirited Maruja Mallo, who painted a series of pictures with such titles as
*Tierra y excremento* [*Earth and Excrement*], *Basuras* [*Rubbish*], *La Huella*
[*The Footprint*], *Grajo y excrementos* [*Rook and Excrement*], *Cardos y
esqueletos* [*Thistles and Skeletons*], *Cloaca* [*Sewer*].[15] Maruja exhibited sixteen paintings under the collective title 'Cloacas y campanarios' [Sewers and
Belfries] at the Galerie *Pierre*, Paris, in May 1932. She spoke eloquently of
her fascination with objects found 'on the outskirts':

Over the cracked earth an aureole of débris rises. In these desolate panoramas the presence of man appears in footprints, clothing, skeletons and
corpses. This human presence, real but phantasmal, rising in the midst of
this vortex of refuse, is added to scattered stones, ash-strewn wastes, silt-
covered surfaces, in which the coarsest plants grow and the fiercest animals
roam . . . [16]

The virtual absence of colour in these paintings reminds one of Goya's *Black
Paintings*, like *Witches' Sabbath, Pilgrimage of Saint Isidore, Promenade of
the Holy Office*, which were also set in the outskirts of Madrid. Alberti, who
used to visit Maruja at Cercedilla, north of Madrid, recalls the strange landscape they discovered, 'De la mano de Maruja recorrí tantas veces aquellas
galerías subterráneas' [Hand in hand with Maruja I frequently visited those
subterranean galleries], and he freely admits to the influence of her work at
this time: '*Los ángeles muertos* . . . podría ser una transcripción de algún
cuadro suyo'[17] [*The Dead Angels* could easily be a transcription of one of her
paintings]. The same might be said of 'Elegías' [Elegies] which simply lists
seven clusters of earth-bound objects, for instance:

[14]   See Raúl Chavarri, *Mito y realidad en la escuela de Vallecas* (Madrid: Ibérico Europea,
1975), 40, 43.
[15]   The first-mentioned painting can be seen in the Reina Sofía Museum in Madrid,
while the best text for viewing the artist's work is still *Maruja Mallo: 59 grabados en
negro y 9 láminas en color (1928–1942)*, estudio preliminar por Ramón Gómez de la Serna
(Buenos Aires: Losada, 1942).
[16]   *Maruja Mallo*, 45.
[17]   See *La arboleda perdida, Libros III y IV* (Barcelona: Seix Barral, 1987), 29.

1. La pena de los jarros sin agua caídos en el destierro de los objetos difuntos.
3. La botella que no se rompió al caer y vive con el gollete clavado en los oasis de las basuras.
7. La caja vacía de cerillas junto al excremento de los caballos.   (471)

1. The suffering of waterless pitchers fallen into the banished land of deceased objects.
3. The bottle that didn't break on falling and lives with its neck stuck in the oasis of a rubbish-dump.
7. The empty box of matches alongside horse dung.

The seven exempla of matter are redolent with phantasmal human presence, as Maruja put it. Offered as objects worthy of contemplation, they are the leftovers, or epiplasm, that complete life's cycle and mirror man's destiny.

The rubbish-dump, an elegy to human life and necropolis of *last things*, recalls Jorge Manrique's sea to which all rivers flow; but in its desolation and utter plasticity, it is clearly an inversion of heaven. The same holds for another image, the barren scene depicted in 'Espantapájaros' [Scarecrow(s)], which is the title of an Alberti poem and likewise of a painting by Maruja Mallo. Maruja writes:

> On those lands encircled by limestone mountains and coal pits, stand the scarecrows: anatomies of nails and sticks that display chamber pots and brooms for heads. Their pitiful limbs of funereal aspect hold up cast-off civilian clothing, empty clerical gowns, rags billowing out and torn by the winds.[18]

Her haunting painting – purchased significantly by André Breton in Paris – depicts scarecrows standing with wooden arms outstretched over a Golgotha-like landscape. In his poem, Alberti takes the parallel with the Passion further, his speaking voice being unmistakably that of the Saviour who has assumed the cares of the world:

> Ya en mi alma pesaban de tal modo los muertos futuros que no
>      podía andar ni
> un solo paso sin que las piedras revelaran sus entrañas.
> ¿Qué gritan y defienden esos trajes retorcidos por las exhalaciones?
> . . . ¿Adónde ir con las ansias de los que han de morirse?
> . . . Mi alma no puede ya con tanto cargamento sin destino.
> . . . ¿Qué espero rodeado de muertos al filo de una madrugada inde-
> cisa?   (460)

> In my soul future deaths now weigh so heavily I cannot take a
>      single step

---

18 *Maruja Mallo*, 41.

without stones revealing their insides to me.
What do these clothes twisted by exhalations shout against and
   defend?
. . . Where shall I go with the anxieties of those who are doomed
   to die?
. . . My soul can no longer bear such a purposeless burden.
. . . What do I hope for surrounded by the dead on the verge of an
   unclear dawn?

The principal sorrow from which the speaker has sought to unburden humanity is death, his sacrifice bringing the prospect of eternal life in the eyes of the
faithful. Here, however, he is a bereft, disillusioned and literally empty figure
on a makeshift cross, unable to sustain the pretence any longer. His skeleton
of random objects draws attention, by contrast, to the material world, which
is the point Alberti confirms in his tribute poem, 'La primera ascensión
de Maruja Mallo al subsuelo' [The First Ascension of Maruja Mallo to the
Subsoil]:

Tú,
tú que bajas a las cloacas donde las flores más flores son ya unos
   tristes salivazos sin sueños
y mueres por las alcantarillas que desenbocan a las verbenas
   desiertas para resuscitar al filo de una piedra mordida por un
   hongo estancado . . .
Desde los pantanos
¿quién no te ve ascender sobre un fijo oleaje de escorias,
contra un viso de tablones pelados y boñigas de toros,
hacia un sueño fecal de golondrina?[19]

You, / you who delve into sewers where the most flowerly of
   flowers are but sad goblets of disillusioned spittle
and who expire in drains that flow into empty festivals only to be
   reborn on the edge of a stone bitten by a stagnant mushroom . . .
Who cannot see you ascend / from the marshes on a steady wave of
   slag against a sheen of smooth planks and bull dung / towards a
   swallow's faecal dream?

Religious motifs continue in the form of *rebirth* and *ascension*; but these
events occur under the auspices of base matter and the focus is decidedly
downwards, 'bajas a las cloacas' [you who delve into sewers]. This contradiction, as the title indicates, is central to the poem's message. It is also,

[19] This poem, originally published in *La Gaceta Literaria*, appears in Geoffrey Connell,
'The End of a Quest: Alberti's *Sermones y moradas* and Three Uncollected Poems', *Bulletin
of Hispanic Studies*, 33 (1965), 290–309. It was probably out of deference to his wife, María
Teresa León, that Alberti did not include it in *Obras completas*.

remarkably, the paradox at the heart of Jesuit practice, which Roland Barthes described in a telling phrase: 'Cette remontée vers la matière' [This upward movement towards matter].[20] For Barthes, the thrust of Jesuit practice lies in 'the very materiality of the objects whose representation Ignatius calls for'; 'Ignatius always follows this flow, which attempts to found meaning on matter and not on concept'.[21] Materiality, then, is the goal, and Alberti's *ascension towards matter* adheres to the most fundamental of Jesuit principles.

If the scarecrow is a random collage of junk objects that make up a human form, its corollary is the human being who consists of various types of matter, which is to say, every one of us. Alberti makes this simple but surprising point in 'Sermón de la sangre' [Sermon on Blood], a prose poem in which the verb subject is not disclosed in the opening stanzas:

> Me llama, me grita, me advierte, me despeña y me alza, hace de mi cabeza un yunque en medio de las olas, un despiadado yunque contra quien deshacerse zumbando.   (461)

> It calls me, shouts at me, warns me, casts me down and lifts me up, it makes my head an anvil in the midst of waves, a cruel anvil against whom [*sic*] one beats oneself into a pulp.

Not until the two-word, sixth and last stanza is it confirmed that the subject is 'Mi sangre' [My blood], though this might be surmised from the title. By contrast, the numerous object pronouns in the first stanza and elsewhere refer to the speaker. Thus the poem functions on the principle of a grammatical inversion: material substance (blood) = subject; while human entity (speaker) = object, which is to say, object becomes subject and vice-versa. The vicissitudes of emotion are experienced by and through the material element of blood, which determines how the speaker feels, thinks, reacts and desires: 'Hay que tomar el tren, le urge' [You have to take the train, it urges him], where the railway station hints at an anecdotal context; 'Sé que estoy en la edad de obedecerla' [I know I'm at an age where I should obey it], which suggests the dictates of instinct and youthful passion. At the poem's conclusion, we sense that the speaker is ruled by the uncontrollable pounding of blood in his bodily organs:

> Mientras me humilla, me levanta, me inunda, me desquicia, me seca, me abandona, me hace correr de nuevo, y yo no sé llamarla de otro modo:

> Mi sangre.

> While it humiliates me, lifts me up, floods me, drives me mad, dries me out, makes me run [*or vulgarly*, come] again, and I don't know what else to call it: My blood.

---

[20] Barthes (French version), 68; also English version, 63.
[21] Barthes (English version), 61–2.

A reversal of values applies in that human subjectivity is seen as subordinate to a material substance: blood. On this level, the poem's bias anticipates Alberti's Marxist phase. Yet blood, a curiously impersonal element that transfusion can drain from or insert in the body at will, is also an element that permeates the body and drives its most personal parts, from brain cells to sexual organs. On this level, the notion that an individual is prey to physiological impulses, mood swings and the like connects with psychoanalysis, at least insofar as it views the psyche as an entity that may be out of control and even at war with itself. The point comes across in another poem on the same motif, 'Adiós a la sangre' [Goodbye to Blood], where we sense an almost schizophrenic division in the speaker:

> Yo me decía adiós llorando en los andenes.
> Sujetadme,
> sujetad a mi sangre,
> paredes,
> muros que la veláis y que la separáis de otras sangres que duermen.
> ¿Yo me decía adiós porque iba hacia la muerte?    (464-5)

> I bid myself farewell crying on platforms.
> Hold me fast, / hold down my blood, / [inner] walls,
> [outer] walls that watch over it and separate it from other sleeping
>    blood.
> Did I bid myself farewell because I was travelling towards death?

The railway station motif appears again. Possibly it refers to Alberti's journeys by train to Cercedilla and his break-up with Maruja Mallo. Or it may recall his first departure at the age of fifteen from El Puerto, which would make sense of him saying goodbye to himself, or to his youth.[22] But the anecdotal or biographical source is of lesser importance. What matters is the trauma such a departure caused and the physiological reaction within him, in his blood. We are taken inside the speaker, into his arteries and veins, where the inner and outer cellular walls appear to isolate volatile, pumping blood from the same substance in other less responsive areas, perhaps capillaries. In this first stanza the speaker suggests that, in a highly charged emotional state, he depends for his survival on the thickness of tissue in the tubular vessels through which his blood pumps. His reference to death in the last line could be metaphorical or, given the materialist theme, a simple acknowledgement of life's finite principle. The remainder of the poem is, if anything, more puzzling:

> Ahora,
> cuando yo diga *ahora*,
> haced que el fuego y los astros que iban a caer se hielen.
> Que yo no diga nunca esa palabra en los trenes.

---

22 Alberti's departure from his native town is recounted in *The Lost Grove*, 93–4.

> Porque,
> escuchad:
> ¿Es vuestra sangre la que grita al hundirse en el agua con los
>     puentes?   (465)

> Now, / when I say 'now',
> make the fire and stars that were about to fall freeze.
> Let me never say that word on trains.
> Because, / listen:
> Is it your blood that screams on sinking with bridges into water?

The first imperative, 'haced' [make], contains a paradox: the speaker, at a moment of his choosing – 'ahora' [now] – wishes to see burning stars frozen, presumably in time, and presumably so that they might escape the inexorable fate of death and decay. The final image of collapsing bridges complements this entropic vision, while it also connects with the railway motif and its sense of unstoppable momentum. It is difficult to know who or what the imperatives address, though grammatically it should be the 'muros' and 'paredes' [outer and inner *walls*] of the previous stanza. If this is the case, the poet is speaking to his arterial or corpuscular self and asking if the blood they contain is what cries out in agony. This amounts to an acknowledgement that he does not know where the boundaries of personality, self and body lie. Indeed, as opposed to the body–spirit dichotomy beloved of the Jesuits, we have something approaching an osmosis or interpenetration of the subjective and objective constituents of selfhood.

At this point the poem reaches impenetrable levels on the cusp of the psychical and bodily elements in human composition. Alberti had in fact planned an entire volume to be called *Vida de mi sangre* [Life of My Blood],[23] which seems an extraordinarily ambitious project and one that, perhaps unsurprisingly, he did not bring to fruition. Blood remains a revealing and important motif, however, for reasons that bear on his standing as a surrealist. Essentially, the motif serves as an index of irrationality and impulsiveness that connects with the early Freudian phase; but at the same time it presupposes a materialist argument on which his political work would be based. In addition, Alberti's endoscopic analysis is a supreme example of his search for meaning in matter, a feature he learnt from the Jesuits. What is remarkable in Alberti is the way his Jesuit formation continued to play such an important role in his work as a poet. In *Sobre los ángeles* it is the principal cause of the neurosis that is his source material, while in *De un momento a otro* it is a decisive factor in shaping the vitriol of his class consciousness. Everywhere it imbues him with an urgent and even transcendental quest for meaning in matter.

---

[23]  See Rafael Alberti, *Correspondencia a José María Cossío*, ed. R. Gómez de Tudanca and E. Mateos Miera (Madrid: Editorial Ayuso, 1973), 42, 48.

# 9

## García Lorca's *Poemas en prosa* and *Poeta en Nueva York:* Dalí, Gasch, Surrealism, and the Avant-Garde

### ANDREW A. ANDERSON

In Spain in the latter half of the 1920s, the French surrealist movement was commonly seen as another iteration of the avant-garde impulse among a throng of other 'isms', and one that had arrived rather late on the scene (cf. Bergamín, 1929 and Masoliver, 1930). Furthermore, although it undoubtedly offered certain exciting innovations and paths to be explored, there was no vacuum that Surrealism in particular served to fill, for there had been a continuous tradition of avant-garde writing in Spain from 1919 onwards (earlier in Catalonia), embodied first in the Ultra movement (1919–24) and later (1925–8) in a number of largely independent authors.[1]

Conventional literary history situates the ten poets most commonly thought of as belonging to the so-called 'Generation of 1927' at the centre of poetic production in Spain in the 1920s and 1930s, and over the decades there has been a marked tendency to single out four of them – Alberti, Aleixandre, Cernuda and García Lorca – as the paragons of 'Spanish Surrealism'. And of course, since Lorca is the best-known of all, it is his collection *Poeta en Nueva York* [*Poet in New York*] that has sometimes been held up as the 'pinnacle of Spanish Surrealism' (Marco, 1).[2] This categorization is what I wish to test and question in what follows. The whole issue of the relationship of Lorca's poetical works with Surrealism needs to be addressed anew, stripped of the many accumulated layers of hasty labelling, received wisdom and unthinking repetition. Such a

---

[1] Among them Luís Amado Blanco, César M. Arconada, Rogelio Buendía, Pedro Garfias, Juan Gutiérrez Gili, José María Hinojosa, Juan Larrea, Fernando María de Milícua and Juan Vidal Martínez. Information on all these figures can be found in Juan Manuel Bonet's *Diccionario de las vanguardias en España (1907–1936)* (Madrid: Alianza, 1995).

[2] Titles of Lorca's works, once translated, will subsequently be given only in Spanish. Quotations from ancillary texts will be given exclusively in English translation; quotations from primary texts will be given in Spanish with English translation.

project can be approached in two possible ways, from the historical and biographical angle, and from an ahistorical and intrinsic perspective, and I propose to utilize both – that is, the contextual and the textual – in what I hope will be a complementary fashion.

Lorca would likely have browsed the articles about Surrealism and translations of surrealist works appearing in such Spanish magazines as *Revista de Occidente*, *Alfar*, *Litoral* and *La Gaceta Literaria*, and it was no doubt a topic that arose from time to time in the café *tertulias* that he attended.[3] However, biographical evidence suggests that he would have learnt most about the movement and discussed it most intensely within the framework of his friendships and correspondence with Salvador Dalí and the Catalan art critic Sebastià Gasch.

Lorca met Dalí at the beginning of 1923, and their relationship evolved and deepened over the subsequent years. The period of interest here is 1927–8, when Dalí was gradually moving closer to Surrealism, and when Lorca spent an extended period of time in Catalonia over spring–summer 1927. The two never saw entirely eye-to-eye, but Lorca took very much to heart Dalí's commentaries and criticisms of his poetry,[4] and he was motivated to explore a more avant-garde aesthetic by Dalí's encouragement and by his example in both paintings and diverse writings. Their discussions are transparently reflected in a little-known, undated dialogue fragment that Lorca entitled 'Corazón bleu y coeur azul' [Blue Heart and Blue Heart] (*PP*, 91–2). Here 'I' (i.e. Lorca) still defends metaphor and the image: 'I see the fragile thread that could connect everything with each thing', whereas 'My Friend' (Dalí) favours quite simply 'things alone and in themselves' that produce 'true poetry' (*PP*, 91). The significant impact of Dalí's ideas and artistic practice can be gauged above all in Lorca's two 1928 lectures, 'Imaginación, inspiración, evasión' and 'Sketch de la pintura moderna' [An Outline of Modern Painting], and in his prose poems of 1927–8 (*Poemas en prosa*), to be discussed below.[5]

---

[3] An early and representative example: in November 1925 he wrote to his brother Francisco, then in Bordeaux, and asked his impression of 'the surrealist kids' (*EC*, 308).

Parenthetical references in this essay will use the following abbreviations: *EC* for *Epistolario completo*, 'IIE' for 'Imaginación, inspiración, evasión' [Imagination, Inspiration, Escape], *PNY* for *Poeta en Nueva York*, and *PP* for *Poemas en prosa* [*Prose Poems*], followed by page number(s).

[4] Compare Dalí's lukewarm response to *Canciones* [*Songs*] (1927), in his letter XXV (*Salvador Dalí escribe a Federico García Lorca (1925–1936)*, ed. Rafael Santos Torroella, special double number of *Poesía*, nos. 27–28 (Winter–Spring 1987), 58–9), with his dismantling of *Romancero gitano* [*Gypsy Ballad Book*] (1928), in letter XXXVI (88–94).

[5] I study Dalí's influence on Lorca in more detail in my article 'Lorca at the Crossroads', *Anales de la Literatura Española Contemporánea*, XVI (1991), 149–73, and see Mario Hernández, 'García Lorca y Salvador Dalí', in *L''imposible/posible' di Federico García Lorca*, ed. Laura Dolfi (Naples: Scientifiche Italiane, 1989), 267–319. The two lectures appear in vol. 2 of Lorca's *Conferencias*, ed. Christopher Maurer (Madrid: Alianza, 1984), 9–31 and 33–49.

Lorca met Gasch in the course of the same 1927 stay in Catalonia, and they corresponded at some length over the remainder of that and the following year. Although Lorca mentions his new writing projects in these letters, perhaps the primary topic of discussion are the drawings that he was producing, many of which he sent to Gasch. Among the numerous articles that Gasch published over this period were a review of Lorca's exhibition of drawings at the famous Dalmau gallery in Barcelona (held in late June 1927), and a subsequent piece entitled 'Lorca dibujante' [Lorca the Draftsman]. Gasch was a fervent but not indiscriminate apologist of modern art. Firmly believing that modern artists needed to combine inspiration in subject matter with a degree of formal or compositional care, he lambasted those painters who tended to either pole and provided only one of these two essential elements. The latter stages of synthetic Cubism and total abstraction were for him two egregious examples of empty formalism, while on the other hand Surrealism was the worst offender in purveying nothing but the outpourings of uncontrolled instinct or inspiration. Exempted from this condemnation were, among others, Picasso and Miró, who, despite their connection with Surrealism, nonetheless achieved in Gasch's opinion the fusion or equilibrium that he sought.[6]

During these same years Lorca found himself at an important but difficult juncture in his own writing. In autumn 1927 he was finishing up the last of the poems for *Romancero gitano* (*EC*, 521), which was published the following summer, in December he repeated his lecture 'La imagen poética de don Luis de Góngora' [The Poetic Image of don Luis de Góngora] at the Residencia de Estudiantes, and later that same month he recited poems from the *Romancero* in Seville. By early spring 1928, though, he had embarked in earnest on his planned book of *Odas* [*Odes*] (*EC*, 550, 576, 579, 582, 587), a project that he described as being the 'opposite pole to the *Ballad Book* and I believe with greater lyrical keenness' (*EC*, 590).[7]

Despite the fresh direction marked by the *Odas*, the time was plainly ripe for a more radical break. Since the summer of 1926, Dalí had been elaborating a personal aesthetic based on the iconographic representation of the martyrdom of Saint Sebastian, a figure who embodied for the painter what he called 'Holy Objectivity'.[8] This culminated in his Catalan text 'Sant Sebastià'

---

[6] I summarize here a considerably more detailed account of Gasch's ideas on modern art that can be found in my article 'Sebastià Gasch y Federico García Lorca', in *Federico García Lorca i Catalunya*, ed. Antonio Monegal and José María Micó (Barcelona: Universitat Pompeu Fabra-Institut Universitari de Cultura / Diputació de Barcelona-Area de Cultura, 2000), 93–110.

[7] As was the case with several other projects, the *Odas* were never published, despite a report in 1934 that the book was ready for the press. A partial reconstruction is possible based on extant manuscripts.

[8] Dalí, 1987, 42; see also 44, 46, 48, 59. For a detailed commentary on the concept, see Hernández 1989 and Antonio Monegal, 'Las palabras y las cosas, según Salvador Dalí', in

[Saint Sebastian], a unique cross between an aesthetic manifesto and a prose poem, that appeared in print at the end of July 1927, dedicated to Lorca, just a few days after he had left Catalonia. Saint Sebastian would, therefore, have doubtless been one of their topics of discussion, and upon receiving the issue of *L'Amic de les Arts* in Granada Lorca responded effusively in letters to Dalí, his sister Ana María and Gasch, calling it 'a new prose piece full of unsuspected relations and the most subtle *points of view*' and 'one of the most intense poems that can be read' (*EC*, 511–12; 506; 508).

But this was not all. On 25 August 1927 Lorca informed Gasch that:

> In prose what I am working on now is an essay in which I am most interested. I set for myself two literary themes, I develop them and then I analyze them. And the result is a poem. I try to combine my instinct with the virtuosity that I may possess.                           (*EC*, 513–14)[9]

Almost certainly what he is describing here is 'Santa Lucía y San Lázaro' [Saint Lucy and Saint Lazarus], the first of the *Poemas en prosa* and the only one written in 1927. As McMullan has demonstrated, the piece includes a multitude of details that testify to an intimate acquaintance with the geography of Barcelona. But above all the indebtedness to Dalí is manifold: the text is a hybrid, a narrative cum prose poem cum aesthetic meditation, and each of the two aesthetic positions delineated is centred on the figure of a saint. And when 'Santa Lucía' appeared in the *Revista de Occidente* in November, dedicated to Gasch, he reported to Lorca Dalí's generally warm and positive response (Gibson, I, 527).

There is no evidence to suggest that Lorca returned to the prose poem genre until August 1928. But during the intervening eleven months Dalí was busy sending him a series of writings, and publishing some of them, which again would serve as a model and catalyst for Lorca's later compositions. Conflating poetic prose, prose poems and free verse, we can hypothetically reconstruct this corpus as follows: 'a strange prose writing, with great successes, but *outrageous*'; 'Poem of the Little Things'; 'almost a whole book of *poems* by me'; 'my "poem" with photographs for *gallo*'; 'Poem [Hairs Beneath the Arm]'; 'Fish Pursued by a Grape'; 'your latest things [. . .] your poems'; 'Two Proses: "My Girlfriend and the Beach". "Christmas in Brussels (An Ancient Tale)" '; 'some poetic essays that are a delight'; and 'Poem [To Lydia of Cadaqués]', of which six texts are extant and several more are presumed lost.[10]

---

*El aeroplano y la estrella*, ed. Joan Ramon Resina (Amsterdam / Atlanta: Rodopi, 1997), 151–76.

[9] 'Instinct' and 'virtuosity' correspond, of course, to the two basic elements required by Gasch.

[10] References for the complete list are, respectively: (1) September 1927: *EC*, 521, unidentified/lost; (2) October 1927: Dalí, 1987, 68, later published in Catalan as 'Poema de les cosetes' (August 1928); (3) October/November 1927: Dalí, 1987, 71, unidentified; (4)

Meanwhile, as already noted, from early February till late September 1928 Lorca was working primarily on his *Odas*. But in the course of this latter month he started to mention a shift of emphasis: 'I am working [. . .] on several things in very different genres. I am writing poems of all kinds. [. . .] My poetry now is launching out on another flight that is keener still. It seems to me a personal flight' (*EC*, 585). The new initiative referred to here is precisely that of the *Poemas en prosa*, and as the *Odas* were brought to a close, their period of composition overlapped briefly with what lay ahead: 'After constructing my *Odes*, in which I have such high hopes, I am closing this cycle of poetry in order to do something else' (*EC*, 587).[11]

Besides the sense of the cycle of odes coming to a close, another reason for striking out in a new direction was surely Lorca's extended meditation on that onslaught of intensely avant-garde texts sent to him by Dalí over the immediately preceding months.[12] Lorca's first response seems to be evidenced in the composition of 'Degollación del Bautista' [Beheading (Throat-slitting) of John the Baptist] in August 1928, the date that appeared at the foot of the text upon its publication in 1930. And then, very soon afterwards, Lorca received one of the last letters of substance written to him by Dalí, which spelt out his withering critique of *Romancero gitano* and proposed a very different aesthetic, one already well down the road that led from 'Sant Sebastià' and 'Holy Objectivity' to Surrealism. The letter in question likely arrived in Granada at the very beginning of September.[13] The precise dates are significant because the first draft of another prose poem, 'Nadadora sumergida' [Submerged Woman Swimmer], is dated 4 September, and was therefore probably composed in the immediate aftermath of its receipt.[14] Furthermore, like 'Santa

November 1927: Dalí, 1987, 74, lost; (5) c. November 1927: Dalí, 1987, 75, text preserved, letter lost; (6) c. November 1927: Dalí, 1987, 76–9, text preserved, letter lost, later published in Catalan as 'Peix perseguit per un raïm' (September 1928); (7) November 1927: *EC*, 532–3, among them 'Pez perseguido por una uva'; (8) published in Catalan (November 1927); (9) January 1928: *EC*, 543, unidentified; (10) published February 1928.

[11] 'Santa Lucía y San Lázaro', stylistically somewhat different from the rest of the *Poemas en prosa*, constitutes the exception to this chronological rule. Similarly, Lorca would take up again the fourth and last part of 'Oda al Santísimo Sacramento del Altar' [Ode to the Most Blessed Sacrament of the Altar] in September 1929, when he was in New York.

[12] Obviously, they also continued to correspond, and there are nine surviving letters from Dalí (XXVII–XXXV), which date from the intervening eleven months (September 1927–July 1928): Dalí, 1987, 64–84.

[13] Letter XXXVI: Dalí, 1987, 88–94. Santos Torroella dates its composition to the beginning of September, but it was most probably sent at the end of August (*EC*, 584–5, n502). The content overlaps considerably with Dalí's article 'Realidad y sobrerrealidad' [Reality and Superreality], published 15 October 1928.

[14] A more detailed account of the chronology appears in my 'Lorca at the Crossroads', 150–1. On the heels of the appearance of the news item in the Spanish press (30 August), on 1 September 1928 Lorca had also composed the 'Meditaciones a la muerte de la madre

Lucía', 'Nadadora' can be read, in part, as an aesthetic statement, and certain passages in the text assert the need for a radical break with the past.

The other three published prose poems followed in short order.[15] 'Suicidio en Alejandría' [Suicide in Alexandria] must have been written either immediately before or after 'Nadadora', as Lorca sent the pair to Gasch for publication in *L'Amic de les Arts*, where they appeared in the number dated 31 [*sic*] September 1928.[16] That autumn he must also have composed 'Amantes asesinados por una perdiz' [Lovers Murdered by a Partridge], as it, along with 'Degollación del Bautista', were sent to Juan Guerrero Ruiz for the issue of *Verso y Prosa* slated to appear in December 1928/January 1929 but which, in the event, was never published (*EC*, 599–600). Likewise, 'Degollación de los Inocentes' [Massacre (Throat-slitting) of the Innocents] was set down before the end of the year, as it came out in *La Gaceta Literaria* in January 1929. With the exception of 'Santa Lucía', then, the *Poemas en prosa* fall into a narrow temporal band with dates of composition between August and, at latest, December 1928. It is entirely plausible that Lorca would have considered himself well on the way towards producing a whole sequence of prose poems, a genre much in vogue in the 1920s, but the only direct reference we have to such a collection comes years later: in 1936 when asked by an interviewer what books he had ready to be published, Lorca replied, with some hyperbole: 'five [. . .] *Earth and Moon, Diván of the Tamarit, Odes, Prose Poems* and *Suites*'.[17]

As regards *Poeta en Nueva York*, the details regarding its textual history are well documented and need only be briefly rehearsed. There was a gap of at least seven months between the composition of the last of the *Poemas en prosa* and the first of the poems included in *Poeta en Nueva York*, during which time Lorca, uncharacteristically, wrote virtually nothing. All, or almost all, of the poems belonging to this collection were set down between August 1929 and June 1930; thereafter the book and its texts underwent a complex process of repeated revisions over the subsequent six years. Lorca dropped off a semi-finished typescript at the *Cruz y Raya* offices of José Bergamín in late

---

de Charlot' (*PP*, 93–100) [Meditations on the Death of Charlie Chaplin's Mother], a prose piece with many connections to the prose poems.

[15] Two further compositions were never finished: a nearly complete text entitled 'Coeur azul. Corazón bleu' [Blue Heart. Blue Heart] (not to be confused with the Lorca–Dalí dialogue), and a brief fragment 'Mi amor en el baño' [My Love in the Bath] (*PP*, 89–90; 103).

[16] In an August 1928 letter to Gasch, Lorca announced 'some drawings and an unpublished poem' that he was going to send to the magazine (*EC*, 579), which could have been 'Suicidio'. Lorca then sent two drawings, followed later by their 'corresponding poems', i.e. 'Nadadora' and 'Suicidio' (*EC*, 585, 588); all four works appeared on the same page in *L'Amic*.

[17] This is the source of the title for the putative collection. The interview was published posthumously: Antonio Otero Seco, 'Una conversación inédita con Federico García Lorca', *Mundo Gráfico* (24 February 1937).

June 1936, clearly with the intent to bring out the volume with that magazine's publishing house (Ediciones del Árbol) the following autumn. In the event, of course, *Poeta en Nueva York* appeared in New York and Mexico City, in two different 'first editions', in the spring of 1940.[18]

\* \* \*

Before considering *Poemas en prosa* and *Poeta en Nueva York*, we need to familiarize ourselves with the specific critical vocabulary that Lorca used during this period. In particular, he articulated the radical break mentioned above around a shift from a poetry based on 'imagination', which uses 'human logic' to construct 'metaphors' with elements drawn from 'reality', to one now based on 'inspiration', which deploys a 'poetic logic' to create '*hechos poéticos*' [poetic facts / events] that in turn enable the poem to rise to a 'different reality' existing on a 'plane of purity and simplicity' ('IIE', *passim*). This parallels a development in modern painting where, in a reaction against Purism and Constructivism, there had arisen a 'spiritualist mode in which the images are no longer given by the intelligence, but rather by the unconscious, by pure, direct inspiration' ('Sketch de la moderna pintura', *Conferencias*, II, 38). Here Lorca was following Dalí at every turn: in rejecting the decipherable, riddle-like metaphor, in setting inspiration against imagination, in calling the building blocks of the new poetry '*hechos poéticos*', and in referring to a spiritualist mode.[19] However, in championing the concept of the mysterious and irreducible '*hecho poético*' Lorca stopped short of Dalí's emphasis on the literalness of things in and of themselves (the distinction that was nicely made in 'Corazón bleu y coeur azul').

From 'Corazón bleu' (1927?) to 'Imaginación, inspiración, evasión' (1928–30), to his commentary-recitals of *Poeta en Nueva York* (1932–5) and *Romancero gitano* (1935–6), Lorca unwaveringly reiterated his adhesion to

---

[18] After many years of uncertainty and controversy, the whereabouts of this typescript (which also included a few printed clippings and some autographs), once thought lost or destroyed, have now been ascertained. While at the time of writing this 'original' is still in private hands and unpublished, the edition of *Poeta en Nueva York* from which I cite (ed. Christopher Maurer, New York: The Noonday Press, 1998), has been revised in the light of a photocopy of said document.

[19] On the riddle, see letter XXX, Dalí, 1987, 71, and 'Realidad y sobrerrealidad'. On imagination versus what Dalí calls Lorca's 'aphrodisiac instinct', see Dalí, 'Federico García Lorca: exposició de dibuixos colorits' [FGL: Exhibition of Coloured Drawings], and for imagination versus 'pure inspiration', see Dalí, 'Les arts. Joan Miró' [The Arts. Joan Miró]. References to 'spiritualist theory', 'spiritualist painting', etc. abound in Dalí's article on Lorca's exhibition. As for the '*hecho poético*', Dalí writes of 'Sant Sebastià' that 'free and clear of symbolisms, he was a *fact* in his sole and simple presence', he places a quotation from Le Corbusier concerning the 'fait poétique' as an epigraph to an article published March 1928, and the Catalan phrase 'fet poètic' appears in two articles that he published in September and October 1927.

the '*hecho poético*', but it is not a concept easily defined, as he usually described it with language that was itself poetic. Basically, the '*hecho poético*' seems to be a kind of image that affects or moves us without recourse to a metaphorical link to reality, and which therefore is resistant to traditional forms of interpretation and requires a certain kind of receptiveness on the part of the reader. All these characteristics suggest a close similarity with T.S. Eliot's notion of the 'objective correlative'.

Finally, Lorca called the act of breaking free from reason and the plane of reality and entering into this new and mysterious world an '*evasión*' [escape]. He saw at least two ways of achieving this, via the paths of dream and the sub-conscious offered by Surrealism, and via the path of the '*hecho poético*' ('IIE', *Conferencias*, II, 18, 20–1, 25–6). He himself favoured the latter alternative, for while giving dream and the subconscious their due, he characterized them as 'very pure' but 'far from diaphanous', and although they might catch on in Northern Europe, he felt that in Spain they would not, as 'we Latins want pro-files and visible mystery. Form and sensualit*es*' (*Conferencias*, II, 21).

Yet again Lorca had borrowed this concept of 'escape' and its relationship to Surrealism from Dalí. While the term starts off in the latter's letters mean-ing little more than an avant-garde rejection of convention, it evolves into a radical shift of *gestalt*, enabling the viewer to see the world anew, free of all received ideas and prejudices:

> Precisely I am convinced that any effort nowadays in poetry only makes sense in the escape from the ideas that our intelligence has artificially forged over time, until we can endow these [ideas] with their exact real sense.                                             (XXXVI, 1987, 89)[20]

As of August 1928, then, Dalí went on to define his current position in this way:

> Surrealism is *one* of the means of escape.
> It is *that* escape that is important.
> I continue to have my own ways on the fringes of Surrealism, but it is something truly alive.   (XXXVI, 1987, 94)

Just as Dalí prioritizes the escape, points to Surrealism as one of the means, and defines his own position alongside, but not inside, Surrealism, so Lorca does exactly the same, and declares his allegiance to the '*hecho poético*' over dream/the unconscious. But where Dalí would soon advance to a full espousal

---

[20] The prior references can be found in letters XXVIII and XXXII (Dalí, 1987, 67, 74). In letter XXXVI (late August 1928), Dalí exemplifies the *gestalt* shift with how we might perceive a rider on horseback, and in his article on Joan Miró (June 1928), with a similar example involving a canopied cart pulled by a horse; both are repeated in 'Realidad y sobrerrealidad'.

of Surrealism,[21] Lorca went no further, for he shared with Gasch (and perhaps influenced by him) certain nagging doubts and suspicions.

All this enables us to appreciate exactly Lorca's statements as to what he was aiming at in the *Poemas en prosa*. In the month before he delivered the 'Imaginación, inspiración, evasión' lecture, he wrote to Jorge Zalamea:

> Now I am writing a poetry of *opening one's veins*, a poetry that has made good its *escape* from reality with an emotion where all my love for things and my kidding-around with things is reflected.   (*EC*, 587)

and shortly afterwards the oft-quoted passage to Gasch:

> Attached I am sending you the two poems. [. . .] They correspond to my new *spiritualist* manner, raw pure emotion, released from logical control, but, careful!, careful!, with a tremendous *poetic logic*. It is not Surrealism, careful!, the clearest *consciousness* illuminates them.
>
> They are the first ones that I have written. Naturally, they are in prose because verse is a restriction that they will not bear. But in them you will indeed notice, of course, the tenderness of my heart as it now is.   (*EC*, 588–9)

These poems, then, have been composed without 'logical control' (i.e. the 'human logic' of imagination) and rather with the 'poetic logic' of inspiration, and have hence managed to 'escape from reality' and correspond to his new 'spiritualist manner'. Whether rightly or wrongly, in 1928 Lorca, together with Gasch, still closely associated Surrealism with psychic automatism, and so, while Lorca thought he was doing something quite similar or analogous, it was *not* in his opinion Surrealism, as he remained conscious, while the surrealists immersed themselves in dreams or the unconscious. The difference between North and South Europe, between the hazy and the limpid, is, *mutatis mutandis*, the same contrast made here between Surrealism (i.e. automatism) and consciousness combined with poetic logic. However, even though it was relatively easy for Lorca to draw the theoretical distinction, unsuspecting readers might have been forgiven for mistaking the texts as examples of Surrealism, given the proximity of the styles and the results.

* * *

All of Lorca's early books of poetry (from *Libro de poemas* [*Book of Poems*] through to *Romancero gitano*) clearly operate under the aegis of what might broadly be called a symbolist / postsymbolist / modernist aesthetic, and the first true exploration of the spirit of the avant-garde occurred with the

---

[21]  By October, in 'Realidad y sobrerrealidad', Dalí was praising on equal terms 'all direct art, produced under an intense pressure of the unknown and the instincts' (i.e. Surrealism) and 'all anti-art'.

innovative and genre-bending *Diálogos* [*Dialogues*] of 1925. His second
incursion came with the *Poemas en prosa*, not coincidentally another hybrid
form, and upon reading these pieces, one is most immediately and forcefully
struck by their radically illogical quality, both on a micro and macro scale:
everywhere there are lexical mismatches, narrative *non sequiturs*, disconcerting juxtapositions, unmotivated actions and so forth.

But before exploring further the implications of this style of writing, three
other shared characteristics should be noted: (1) pastiche, which here involves
the incorporation or more indirect suggestion of various set styles, evoked and
combined with a parodic or other subversive intent; (2) a kind of allegory,
where the 'surface' texture of what masquerades as narrative covers and at the
same time gestures to a very different kind of content, not story-telling at all
but rather an aesthetic meditation; and (3) a dead-pan tone of recounting
extraordinary, incoherent and often horrific events.

Thus 'Santa Lucía' offers a disconcerting mixture of travelogue, hagiography
and biblical tale; 'Nadadora' a combination of love story, society column,
newspaper *fait divers* and police report; 'Suicidio' another overwrought love
story; 'Amantes' love story again, together with mystery novel and autobiographical confession; while 'Degollación del Bautista' and 'Degollación de los
Inocentes' transform the biblical accounts they are based on, the first again
adding elements of hagiography and sports page.

As regards the second characteristic, definitive statements are more difficult, as it is not always easy to gauge to what extent the text in question is
itself *enacting* the kind of aesthetic upon which it also appears to offer a veiled
meditation. The subterfuge is most obvious in 'Santa Lucía', with its debts to
Dalí's 'Sant Sebastià' and that text's barely hidden programmatic nature. Lucy
is associated with eyes and sight, surfaces and exteriors, and hence comes to
embody an aesthetic stance very similar to Dalí's 'Holy Objectivity'. Lazarus,
on the other hand, is connected with ears and hearing, as well as with death
and resurrection, and so comes to represent the opposite to Lucy, interiors,
depths, and their subjective exploration. There is no clear expression of preference for one over the other, nor is it clear if the text is propounding a fusion
of the two or some kind of equipoise; certainly the style of the writing suggests an intermediate position. Just as in the 'manifest' story-line, the subtext
of 'Nadadora' involves a farewell, not to lovers or friends, but rather to an old
world and to outmoded cultural values and artistic approaches: the speaker
asserts that after his last embrace with the countess, 'dejé la literatura vieja
que yo había cultivado con gran éxito. / Es preciso romperlo todo para que los
dogmas se purifiquen y las normas tengan nuevo temblor' (*PP*, 68) [I abandoned the old literature that I had cultivated with great success. / It is necessary to break it all so that the dogmas may be purified and the norms may have
a new frisson].

With respect to the seemingly emotionless tone, in that letter from late
August 1928, Dalí had also written:

Ugly – pretty? Words that have ceased to have any meaning. Horror, that is
something else again, that is what affords us, distant from any *aesthetic*, the
knowledge of reality, since lyricism is only possible within the more or less
approximative notions that our intelligence can perceive of reality.

(XXXVI, 1987, 91–2)

and in a slightly earlier missive, the following:

No animal better qualified for *cruelty* and disagreeability than the little
dove.

No animal on the other hand better qualified for tenderness than the *hip-
popotamus*. (XXXIV, 1987, 83)

Combining both sets of ideas, in his lecture 'Imaginación, inspiración,
evasión' Lorca insisted that:

The poem that has escaped from imaginative reality avoids the dictates
of ugly and beautiful as they are now understood and enters into an astonishing poetic reality, sometimes full of tenderness and sometimes full of the
most piercing cruelty. (*Conferencias*, II, 18)

and in a speech as late as May 1929 he still referred to:

the duel to the death that I am engaged in [. . .] with poetry, in order to construct, in spite of it and which defends itself like a virgin, the true and wide-
awake poem where beauty and horror and the ineffable and the repugnant may
live and collide in the midst of white-hot joy. (*Obras completas*, III, 414–15)

The *Poemas en prosa* are the first compositions in which Lorca strives to make
good that escape, and in them he also seeks to transcend the traditional categories of aesthetics, eliminate sentimentalism, adopt objectivity, and reach
that 'astonishing poetic reality' where tenderness and cruelty coexist and
where such apparent extreme opposites might even interact or combine.
Reflecting on Dalí's important painting *La miel es más dulce que la sangre*
(1927) [*Honey is Sweeter than Blood*], Lorca had asserted that 'the chopped-
up woman is the most beautiful poem that can be made of blood' (*EC*, 499),
and now he proceeded to put these opinions into practice.

'Santa Lucía' lingers over Lucy's martyrdom, in 'Nadadora' the speaker has
a scalpel stuck through his throat, and the Countess of X is found with a fork
impaled in the nape of her neck, 'Suicidio' opens with a severed head and ends
with honeymooners' double suicide, 'Amantes' similarly suggests lovers'
double suicide, despite the alternative cause of death implied by the title,
while the gore ramps up, predictably enough, in the two 'Degollaciones' (*PP*,
58–9, 67, 68, 70, 71, 73, 75). A howling, blood-thirsty crowd attends the

ceremony of the beheading of John, and the narrator exclaims: 'Hay que lev-
antar fábricas de cuchillos. Para que el horror mueva su bosque intravenoso'
(*PP*, 79) [Knife factories must be built. So that the horror can move its intra-
venous forest]. The enthusiastic witness of the second text treats the slaugh-
ter of the children as pure poetry, calling it an '¡Alegrísima degollación!'
[Most joyous throat-slitting!] and concluding that 'Si meditamos y somos
llenos de piedad verdadera daremos la degollación como una de las grandes
obras de misericordia' (*PP*, 82) [If we meditate and are filled with true mercy
we shall perform throat-slitting as one of the great works of compassion].

   Lorca's conception of that 'astonishing poetic reality' is certainly reminiscent of the sur-reality of Surrealism, but is it the same? Riffaterre writes that:

> Because logical discourse, teleological narrative, normal temporality, and
> descriptive conformity to an accepted idea of reality are rationalized by the
> reader as proof of the author's conscious control over his text, departures
> from these are therefore interpreted as the elimination of this control by sub-
> conscious impulses. This is precisely what creates the appearance of
> automatism (regardless of whether this appearance is obtained naturally or
> by artifice). I shall call it the *automatism effect.*   (223–4)

In his analysis of two passages from André Breton's *Poisson soluble* (1924),
he demonstrates how each of the two prose poem-like sections chosen follows
a model ('typical folktale', 'common sexual fantasy', 224), and the 'pre-
dictability' produced by the prior familiarity of the reader with the model 'can
only underscore the discrepancies that create the automatism effect' (224).
Although Riffaterre does not refer explicitly to pastiche, what he describes is
surely similar to one of the primary effects of the *Poemas en prosa*, which
likewise offer tantalizing glimpses of comfortingly recognizable genres in the
interstices between the wholesale 'departure from logic, temporality, and ref-
erentiality' (223). While the laws of syntax are rigorously maintained, incompatibilities or nonsense occur, again as Riffaterre indicates, on both the macro
and micro levels: sometimes sentences, logical in themselves, do not 'follow'
one from the other, sometimes the lexical components within a sentence do
not 'fit', and often the combination of both. Thus: 'Era preferible no haber
hablado con él. En las islas Azores. Casi no puedo llorar. Yo puse dos tele-
gramas' [It was preferable not to have talked with him. In the Azores islands.
I almost cannot weep. I sent two telegrams], or '¿Será posible que del pico de
esa paloma cruelísima que tiene corazón de elefante salga la palidez lunar de
aquel transatlántico que se aleja?' [Will it be possible for the lunar pallor of
that ocean liner that is moving away to emerge from the beak of that most
cruel dove which has the heart of an elephant?] (*PP*, 76, 73).

   On the other hand, Lorca has not been able to banish completely all traces
of his powerful image-creating ability, and hence it is on occasions possible
to make perfect sense of what at first sight looks arbitrary. One instance will

have to suffice. In 'Nadadora' the speaker observes that 'la orquesta lejana luchaba de manera dramática con las hormigas volantes' (*PP*, 67) [the distant orchestra was fighting in dramatic fashion with the flying ants]. A disturbingly strange and unnatural combat is given a very different twist if we conceive of the flying ants as an extravagant metaphor of the semiquavers on the musicians' scores, that, given the speed of the music, the orchestra was struggling to play.

Beguiled but not one hundred percent won over by Dalí, with the *Poemas en prosa* Lorca sought to achieve a new departure in his poetic writing, one that paralleled the compositional technique that he was using for his drawings from the same period. But Lorca was also heavily influenced by Gasch, for whom, as for the great majority of Spaniards in the 1920s, Surrealism was virtually synonymous with automatic writing, and so he worked out the theory of the '*hecho poético*', which achieved much that was distinctly fresh and challenging without falling into the potential traps of dream or the subconscious. But whether the *practice* of the '*hecho poético*' produced perceptibly different works is a lot less clear. Riffaterre's opinion, of course, is that the question is irrelevant, for the 'automatism effect' is purely text-based:

> Thus it really does not matter whether automatic texts are genuine or not; their literariness does not reside in their recording of subconscious thought. Their literariness stems from their function as a mimesis of that subconscious.
> (238)

Notwithstanding, a few of Lorca's contemporaries and friends did offer their judgements on the matter. Unfortunately, we only have Dalí's reaction to 'Santa Lucía' and not the other prose poems from 1928. He wrote to Gasch:

> I suppose that you will have read the marvellous piece of writing by Lorca [. . .]
> Lorca seems to be coinciding with me – oh paradox! – on many points, that piece of writing is very eloquent [. . .]
> Lorca, however, is passing through an intellectual moment, that I believe will not last long (although given its appearance the philistines will believe that it's a case of surrealist writing) . . .                    (Gibson, I, 527)

In a letter to Juan Guerrero, Vicente Aleixandre predicted that commentators would link his *Pasión de la tierra* with Surrealism, but he asserted that his prose poems 'that seem to be at liberty, follow an implacable rigour, that of poetic logic, which is not the external [rigour] of apparent reality. I believe that there is a firm thread that grabs on to words and meshes them together' (Morelli, 21).[22] Aleixandre continued that: 'In Spain this kind of prose is

---

[22] While the first phrase seems to refer to Futurism's 'words in freedom', his appeal to '*lógica poética*' is identical to Lorca's in his 1928 lecture.

unknown. Or rather a month ago I saw a thing by Lorca in *La Gaceta [Literaria]* that comes from Surrealism: "The Massacre of the Innocents". We are going along different paths' (Morelli, 21).

Luis Buñuel's response to the same text, in a letter to José Bello, is quite different:

> You will understand the distance that separates you, Dalí and me from all our poet friends. They are two conflicting worlds, the [north] pole of the Earth and the south of Mars, and that all of them without exception are in the crater of the most foul-smelling putrefaction. Federico *wants* to write surrealist things but [they are] false, made with the intelligence, THAT IS INCAPABLE OF FINDING WHAT INSTINCT FINDS. An example of his wickedness is the last fragment published in the *Gaceta [Literaria]*. It is as artistic as his 'Ode to the Most Blessed Sacrament', a fetid ode [. . .] In spite of everything, within the sphere of the irremediably traditional, Federico is among the best, if not the very best, that there is.  (Sánchez Vidal, *Buñuel, Lorca, Dalí, 198*)

It is surely not coincidental that two of Spain's most thorough-going surrealists – Dalí and Buñuel (cf. Masoliver and Hernández, 312) – should concur in finding Lorca's avant-garde writing essentially cerebral ('intellectual', 'intelligence'), and hence in contravention of the fundamental principle of Surrealism. In 'The Intentional Fallacy' Wimsatt argued that 'the design or intention of the author is neither available nor desirable as a standard for judging the success of a work of literary art', and so Riffaterre is arguably doubly right in insisting on an 'automatism effect' that exists in the textual realm and, hence, in excluding *a priori* any inquiries – whose results would, of course, be quite impossible to verify – regarding the actual process of composition.[23] Nonetheless, it is tempting to trust the acute sensibilities of such accomplished practitioners as Dalí and Buñuel; like the expert antiquarian who intuitively senses the difference between a skillful reproduction and the real thing, perhaps they too could tell that Lorca's heart was not quite in it, that the automatic-seeming writing was indeed predominantly cerebral in nature.

\* \* \*

*Poemas en prosa* as a collection was left unfinished and unpublished. In early editions of the Aguilar *Obras completas [Complete Works]*, the texts were grouped together under the erroneous label of 'Narraciones' [Narratives] and not even recognized as prose poems. Their first publication as a separate edition in book form occurred in 2000. *Poeta en Nueva York*, although posthumous, followed a very different course. The second English translation, made

---

[23] Such considerations lead us to the question of whether Surrealism is to be viewed as a literary style or an ethics and/or metaphysics. If the latter, then by definition only those espousing Surrealism could possibly write truly surrealist works.

by Ben Belitt and published by Grove Press in 1955, was 'discovered' by a whole new generation of writers and critics, most of them non-Spanish speaking, a literary phenomenon that then gradually seeped back into Spain and contributed significantly to the emerging against-the-grain reading of Lorca as a modernist and antifolkloric writer: it was *Poeta en Nueva York* versus *Romancero gitano*, with the former increasingly triumphant.

But as the *Poemas en prosa* were essentially invisible, they were not recognized or acknowledged as the most profoundly avant-garde and most nearly surrealist poetry that Lorca produced, nor could readers realize that *Poeta en Nueva York* was a step back from the most audacious innovations, and a further stage in the ongoing process of poetic evolution that would lead in the 1930s to *Diván del Tamarit* and *Llanto por Ignacio Sánchez Mejías* [*Lament for Ignacio Sánchez Mejías*] (Martínez Nadal, 106; García-Posada, 1997, 171). At the same time, it is hard to escape the impression of the *Poemas en prosa* as exercises, as attempts on Lorca's part deliberately to write his way into the new aesthetic, and, because of the imperative of cool objectivity, it is very clear that the writer behind the texts is not emotionally engaged in their content.

Things are very different in *Poeta en Nueva York*. Where the *Poemas en prosa* foregrounded dislocation, indifference, cruelty and irony, in the next collection we find Lorca's visceral reaction to the city and the reappearance of certain enduring personal preoccupations that lie squarely within the Romantic–Expressionist–Existential tradition. Stylistically, he stays generally faithful to his concept of the '*hecho poético*', and in the 1932 commentary-recital he warned his audience that:

> this kind of poems that I am going to read [. . .], because they are full of poetic events exclusively within a lyrical logic and closely woven upon human feeling and the architecture of the poem, are not suitable for rapid comprehension . . .     (*Obras completas*, III, 348)

However, Lorca is not now aiming to transcend the ugly/beautiful dichotomy and not interested in horror for its own sake, and the metaphor-spinning and often highly symbolic poet, that he had tried to suppress in the *Poemas en prosa*, is allowed to return to the scene (García-Posada, 1981, 89).

In point of fact, the poetic discourse in *Poeta en Nueva York* is very varied and mixed, and few critics, other than Derek Harris, have attempted to analyze, categorize and generalize about it, preferring rather to concentrate on thematic material or explicate individual poems (Harris, 1978, 15; Harris 1994 & 1995, *passim*). For the purposes of my analysis, I shall establish four working categories of discourse that can be found in the collection: direct, non-imagistic language, which is actually relatively rare, and at least three levels of imagistic language, which I shall seek to differentiate both by its internal functioning and by the degree of difficulty involved in interpreting it. These latter may be described as: (1) straightforward, readily understandable metaphors and symbols, whose modes of operation are already familiar; (2) difficult but nevertheless ultimately decipherable images; and (3) enigmatic, hermetic images.[24]

By direct, non-imagistic language, I mean this kind of phrase: 'No es el vómito de los húsares sobre los pechos de la prostituta, / ni el vómito del gato que se tragó una rana por descuido' (*PNY*, 48) [It is not the vomit of the hussars on the breasts of the prostitute, / nor the vomit of the cat who unintentionally swallowed a frog]. Similarly, type (1) imagery can easily be demonstrated. In the lines 'No importa que cada minuto / un niño nuevo agite sus ramitos de venas' (*PNY*, 60) [It does not matter that each minute / a new(-born) child shakes his little branches of veins], the dendritic pattern of the newborn's circulatory system is likened to that of a tree (with the further reverberations of tree trunk – human torso [trunk] and of bloodline/family [genealogical] tree).

Type (2) takes several forms. One frequently occurring means of producing this kind of imagistic writing is through radical ellipsis and the resulting compression (Harris 1977; 1998, 89). Thus the line 'el árbol de muñones que no canta' (*PNY*, 4) [the tree of stumps that does not sing] will produce on first reading a disconcerting and troubling impact, but on further reflection it can be 'unpacked' and understood quite logically. The 'stumps' are not those of felled trees, but rather of amputated limbs, and so here we have a tree that has been severely pollarded; furthermore, if it has no branches (limbs), no birds can perch in it, and hence no singing will emanate from it (Harris, 1978, 26). The image works in two ways: emotively, as immediately suggestive of nature mutilated and unjoyous, and intellectually, as we 'unpack' and comprehend its precise terms.[25]

Another way of producing type (2) imagery is through the linkage of dramatically distinct symbolic elements that may have an imprecise but emotional impact on the literal level and which can also be 'worked out' intellectually on the symbolic level (but note that in this case there is no ellipsis). Thus 'mariposa ahogada en el tintero' (*PNY*, 4) [butterfly drowned in the inkwell] immediately elicits feelings of sorrow and distress and of something gone terribly wrong. As we venture further into the image we tease out the various connotations of butterfly: small, delicate, fragile, beautiful, colourful, elusive, and so on, as well as a possible allusion to Psyche, the personification of the soul. Likewise, the inkwell seems to suggest the writer and his craft, in addition to

[24] I offer more extended analyses of all these types in my article '*Et in Arcadia Ego*: Thematic Divergence and Convergence in Lorca's "Poema doble del lago Edén" ', *Bulletin of Hispanic Studies* (Glasgow), LXXIV (1997), 409–29.

[25] As with 'type (1)' imagery, this technique is again not greatly different from that which Lorca used earlier in his career. Compare two lines from *Canciones* (1927): 'Ojos de toro te miraban. / Tu rosario llovía' [Bull's eyes were looking at you. / Your rosary was raining] (from 'La soltera en misa' [The Spinster at Mass]). Here the ellipsis involves first a church painting of St Lucy with her eyes on a tray, and then the metaphor of beads like raindrops.

the idea of a miniature wellshaft containing a staining black liquid. When these two symbolic elements are linked by the notion of drowning, various complementary interpretations are generated: in the city the natural is destroyed, the poet can no longer write of the beautiful, colourful, fragile, etc., and perhaps the speaker also feels soulless.

*Trompe l'oeil* images (again to be found in the earliest of Lorca's writings) normally involve an embedded metaphor, and with a minor shift of perception one can grasp, for instance, that the strange scene of 'la nieve que ondula / blancos perros tendidos' (*PNY*, 70) [the snow that undulates / stretched-out white dogs] actually refers to shifting snowdrifts. One other rather different technique that also creates a certain sense of mystery is direct transliteration. Hence 'esos perros marinos se persiguen' (*PNY*, 78) [those marine dogs pursue each other] is not an obscure reference to a rare type of dog or fish, but rather to seasoned sailors – 'sea dogs'. Likewise 'las heladas montañas del oso' (*PNY*, 26) [the frozen mountains of the bear] may not be a recondite reference to the topography of the Arctic Circle but rather to Bear Mountain, situated north of New York City and on the way to Newburgh (where Lorca spent a few days).

Lastly, there is a good measure of truly perplexing, enigmatic or hermetic imagery (type (3)). Sometimes it is possible to assign a broadly negative or positive connotation to it, and sometimes it leaves the reader thoroughly disoriented (García-Posada, 1981, 330). Thus the opening of 'El rey de Harlem' [The King of Harlem], where the protagonist takes on crocodiles and monkeys with nothing but a spoon, has received extraordinarily divergent interpretations, and no 'definitive' reading seems possible. When Lorca writes: 'Era el momento de las cosas secas: de la espiga en el ojo y el gato laminado' (*PNY*, 40) [It was the moment of dry things: / of the ear of wheat in the eye and the laminated cat], the images in the second line are likely taken as negative, but in an unfocused way. The first has a vaguely biblical feel, perhaps combining the usually positive connotations of wheat with the mote in the eye. Animals are frequently under attack in these poems (crushed, flattened, etc.), but why, one wonders, specifically this rather technical verb here?

An important feature to notice is that all these images, whether type (1), (2) or (3), are always cast within grammatically correct sentence patterns. Consequently, when trying – most often in vain – to discover meaning in type (3) images, we encounter disparate and apparently nonsensical lexical elements presented in formally acceptable syntactic structures, and it is here that *Poeta en Nueva York* comes closest to Riffaterre's 'automatism effect'. An example: 'Un traje abandonado pesa tanto en los hombros / que muchas veces el cielo los agrupa en ásperas manadas' (*PNY*, 66) [An abandoned suit weighs so heavily on the shoulders / that many times the sky gathers them together in harsh herds].

Furthermore, sometimes it appears that the incongruous concatenation of words has been determined by a process of acoustic generation (alliteration, etc.) (Harris, 1994; 1995); for instance: 'las puertas de pedernal donde se pudren nublos y postres' (*PNY*, 48) [the doors of flint where clouds and desserts rot]. However, the greatest number of these cases is actually found in discarded manuscript variants, and here, if the links are initially created by some kind of free association, then the results, and the different iterations of the line as it is progressively revised, do seem subsequently to be judged by a conscious, artistic, guiding mind, and then rejected, accepted or modified as the poet moves on (Harris, 1994, 312, 314; 1995, 34).[26]

If we agree with Marshall McLuhan that the medium *is* the message, then two rather different arguments could be made. The radical disjunction that the poet-persona feels in these urban surroundings, the overwhelming swirl of negative sensations and the tenuous grasp on a sense of self are *rendered* in the discourse itself, as he clings to the architecture of grammar as the only support or structure in a disconcerting, incongruous, dissolving and hostile world, an experience that the reader then relives at second hand as he or she tries to make sense of the text – in other words, this is again Expressionism rather than Surrealism (Harris, 1998, 85–7). Conversely, it is interesting to note that chaotic enumeration is not prevalent here, nor do we find the actual breakdown of syntax, equally or even more extreme poetic techniques, which might suggest that the poet-persona had actually succumbed, falling over the precipice into the abyss.

To sum up, I would argue that all type (2) and (3) imagery falls within the scope of Lorca's '*hecho poético*'. These are not hard-and-fast categories, as one always reads this poetry waiting, as it were, for the kind of minor epiphany that will illuminate what had up to that moment been an utterly hermetic phrase.[27] Emotively, a great deal of both type (2) and (3) imagery functions in exactly the same way as Eliot described the 'objective correlative' (Harris, 1978, 12), but unlike the true 'objective correlative' some of it can also be teased out intellectually and assigned a fairly clear and unambiguous meaning or value (Harris, 1998, 86). In part, this is because there is such a strong symbolic current underpinning all the writing in *Poeta en Nueva York*, with elements deriving from mythology, Christianity, Nature, as well as Lorca's own personal 'imaginative world'. These symbolic elements, though often polyvalent, are not arbitrary or indeterminate. Finally, because all of these kinds of poetic discourse are mixed together in different measures and patterns throughout the poems, an individual text can seem to go in and out of focus (sometimes repeatedly) as the reader progresses

---

[26] Many of the autograph first drafts of poems from *Poeta en Nueva York* are reproduced in facsimile in *Manuscritos neoyorquinos*. We should remember also that discarded manuscript variants were never intended for public consumption.

[27] See, for instance, José Luis Rodríguez Herrera's interpretation of some perplexing lines previously commented on by Harris in 'La coherencia de la imaginería surrealista en *Poeta en Nueva York*', *Philologica Canariensia*, no. 1 (1995), 363–80.

through its lines and stanzas, which can appear by turns transparent and
opaque. Likewise, some poems are considerably more approachable than
others.

The collection covers a number of themes, both philosophical and social in
nature. The uniting thread, if there be one, is that of pain and suffering (Havard,
112). The adult human is shut off from the innocence of childhood, he or she
struggles unsuccessfully to achieve authenticity or any kind of satisfying
human relationship, and is subject to the twin constants of passing time and
mortality. The city is a place of inhuman buildings, relentless commerce, runaway consumption and polluting industry, of avarice, superficiality, rootless-
ness, alienation and (hypocritical) organized religion; poverty and exploitation
are all around. On occasions Lorca adopts an apocalyptic tone in looking forward, though in vague terms, to a day when all this will somehow be swept
away and replaced by a natural, integrated new order.

These are not themes or attitudes that we most characteristically associate
with French Surrealism; Lorca is primarily concerned with the real world,
with the here and now and the human condition. There is no interest in the
state of *surréalité* described in the First and Second Manifestoes nor in setting words free and celebrating this new radical freedom (Harris, 1998, 114).
There is no truly metaphysical exploration here, as the philosophical dimension points directly to Existential concerns, nor did Lorca warm to Dalí's
'paranoia-critical method', the gestation phase of which he was able to
observe first-hand. Where one does discover a possible overlap with Surrealism is in the desire to cast off bourgeois prejudices and inhibitions; Lorca, like
Cernuda, must have imagined a world in which it would be easier to live
openly as a homosexual (though the surrealists themselves were hardly very
liberal on this particular issue), and a world with greater social justice, though
it should again be remembered that one did not have to be a surrealist to think
like this.

Ironically, by the time he reached Cuba and then on his return from the New
World (1930) Lorca started asserting with regard to *Poeta en Nueva York* what
he had vehemently denied concerning the *Poemas en prosa*, namely that the
compositions were indeed surrealist. We have at least two testimonies to this
effect:

> When I arrived in Havana I went to look for him at his hotel [. . .] I found
> him [. . .] in the middle of twelve or fourteen youths who were listening to
> him, dumbfounded.
> 'What is this, Federico? What the devil are you reciting?'
> 'They are my poems of New York and they are surrealist.'   (Salazar, 30)

> The oral memory of his companions of the same generation recounted
> that when Lorca returned to Spain he would read the manuscript of *Poet in
> New York* to his friends and that he – himself highly enthusiastic – would
> ask from time to time: 'It **is** surrealist, isn't it?'   (Blanco Aguinaga, 115)

I believe that we need to take Lorca's judgement with a grain of salt, and that he was influenced by extra-literary factors. In the 'Imaginación, inspiración, evasión' lecture, fearing that he was lagging behind the latest trends, he had tried to present difficult but eminently 'solvable' metaphors from *Romancero gitano* as if they were true '*hechos poéticos*', and he would stick to this view in the late commentary-recital of that collection (1935–6: *Obras completas*, III, 343) (cf. García-Posada, 1997, *passim*). These reported comments on *Poeta en Nueva York* are very much, I believe, in the same vein. With one stroke – the publication of *Sobre los ángeles* in June 1929 – Alberti had positioned himself at the very forefront of Spanish poetic production, and contemporary critics were calling *Sobre los ángeles* surrealist, nowadays a debatable judgement. In the summer of 1929, upon his arrival in New York, Lorca was not slow to rise to the challenge of regaining his position on the cutting edge (García-Posada, 1997, 172).

The poems of *Poeta en Nueva York* certainly share some surface similarities with surrealist works, but the modern critic needs to go beyond Lorca's wishful thinking. If the imagery in the collection is predominantly of the types analyzed above, and if similarly the major themes are as they have been described, then we must entertain very severe reservations regarding the stretching of the surrealist label to cover a literary work so many of whose facets do not fall squarely within the purview of Surrealism proper (Monegal, 1991, 57–8). There is a clear need in criticism of Spanish poetry of the 1920s and 1930s to distinguish between modernist writing (broadly continuing a symbolist line) and avant-garde writing, and again between avant-garde writing and specifically surrealist writing. As a case in point, *Poeta en Nueva York* can be found to be solidly avant-garde but very little surrealist, in intent, theme or poetic discourse.

# 10

# Lorca's Trip Back To a Future Surrealist Theatre and Cinema Departing Gómez de la Serna Via Buñuel and the French Connection: *Teatro de almas* (1917) to *El sueño de la vida* (1936)

## PATRICIA McDERMOTT

Nietzsche had spoken of the shadow of God on the wall of the human cave as the shade that had to be exorcized in order to say yes to the will to live, the law of desire. Surrealism's utopian vision was the liberation of the human spirit in its material body beyond the good and evil of the old Judeo-Christian morality, the Freudian social superego as censor and represser, source of neurosis and madness. The old centre no longer held and a terrible beauty was born. After attending the first night of Jarry's *Ubu roi* (1896), that degree zero in modern vanguard theatre, the symbolist Yeats proclaimed: 'After us the savage God.'[1] Jarry's technique was one of surprise to provoke a double-take on reality including the relationship of individual and collective conscience on the part of the audience in its relationship with the stage. It was the principle behind the Dada provocation-spectacles and the surrealist theatre that emerged out of them: a shock therapy treatment (in which carnivalesque humour and mockery played an important part) to liberate a new consciousness via the revelation of the unconscious, by making the invisible visible on stage. The double vision of Surrealism engaged in the theatre combined 3-D and X-ray vision, only fully realized in the fourth dimension of the spectator's (all too often the reader's) mind. This was the battleground in a war of world-views, the old and the new. The difference in strategy, if not always in tactics, between Expressionism and Surrealism in the theatre of war was grounded on a difference in focus: if the expressionist aimed to provoke a social revolution in order to change the mindset, the surrealist aimed to change the mindset in order to effect the social revolution – that was the original battle order of the 'surrealist revolution', amended later in 'Surrealism at the service of the revolution'.

---

[1] See C. Innes, *Holy Theatre Ritual and the Avant Garde* (Cambridge: Cambridge University Press, 1981), 22.

A shock tactic common to both was the profane parody of Christian iconography, sacred ritual, morality plays and mysteries. Mystery was a key word in surrealist theatre, signalling divergence from the significance of the Christian model and a return to origins in the pagan mysteries of Antiquity as a way forward. The classic dramas of Catholic Imperial Spain, Calderón's *La vida es sueño* [*Life's a Dream*] and *El gran teatro del mundo* [*The Great Theatre of the World*], were ghostly paradigms in much European vanguard theatre and its Spanish counterpart. The Counter-Reformation theological theatre became the modern Freudian theatre of the mind, a split mind to be restored to wholeness, an inverse holiness to that of Christian orthodoxy, in the cathartic experience of theatre as the ritual space of a new morality. Any attempt to produce an anti-sacramental act on the homeground of the *auto sacramental* was a provocation, particularly in the 1930s in the context of a constitutional polemic on Spanish national identity – Catholic or secular? – when the ideological war of words and images would be converted into the reality of bloodshed in civil war.

Ramón Gómez de la Serna was an advance guard and guru of the 1920s' vanguard. In the prologue of his *Drama del palacio deshabitado* [*The Uninhabited Palace*] (1909), Ramón issued a vanguard prospectus that proclaimed its genealogy: the mixed parentage of evolutionary philosopher and *poète maudit* and the dramatic inspiration of Goethe's *Faust*. It was a Nietzschean life-transforming rallying call: 'un *Viva a la Vida*' [*Long Live Life*].[2] The single act, bearing an enigmatic epigraph from Nietzsche, 'All that is profound loves the mask', is introduced by a piece of meta-theatrical play: the appearance of a masked-everyman whose authorized function is to present the absurd spectacle of life and death and to mediate its viewing for an audience who are to act as mediumistic participants in theatre as spiritualist séance. In the *huis clos* of the abandoned palace, including centre-stage a processional Cross (the collective Christian mentality), the ghost sonata of the shades who haunt the shuttered space, because of unfulfilled or guilty sexual desire in life, discuss the possibility of a way out of their spectral condition in the future spiritual evolution of humanity in the phenomenology of matter. Don Dámaso and his ghostly paramour Leticia gain their release and transmogrify in the sunlight of the garden of delights outside when Leticia conjures up, by the incantation of a folksong, a living healthy peasant girl Rosa and her suitor Juan, whom the phantom pair subliminally excite to embrace in a kiss. The description of Rosa in her entry stage direction as 'garrida' [buxom] confirms a cross-reference to the Arcipreste de Hita's *Libro de buen amor* [*Book of Good Love*] and the modern transvaluation of the medieval values of *buen amor / loco amor* [*good love / mad love*]. The textual triptych is completed by an epilogue in which the author recounts a trip to the morgue to face the

---

² R. Gómez de la Serna, *Drama del palacio deshabitado* (Madrid: Editorial América, 1926), 11.

physical fact of death in the clinical scrutiny of a corpse: having projected himself into the object of his meditation, Ramón experiences an epiphany of resurrection as he rises from the marble slab and takes his first steps in a new life, free from the fear of death. This transcendence-cum-immanence of self in the corpse is a precursor of the paradoxical significance of Dalí's putrefying donkey, the revelation in nature that out of death and decay come rebirth and renewal, indeed, the work of art itself as product of that inverse mysticism, which Robert Havard has so pertinently named 'materio-mysticism'.[3]

*Drama del palacio deshabitado* signposts major themes in surrealist theatre: the mingling of different states of being and perception; the synchronicity of being in time in different dimensions in relation to eternity; the subversion of repressive socio-moral codes and the proclamation of free love as *open sesame* to the meaning of life and the universe; folk poetry as the innocent word that works the magic transformation. Coming out of symbolist theatre, it also employs techniques that become the stock of surrealist (and expressionist) theatre: the mixing of individually and generically named types and symbolic figures; individual and group choreography, with specific instructions for anti-naturalistic movement, gesture and voice; the adaptation of the meta-theatrical device of the dramatic introduction to create a self-conscious audience response to the representation and its relationship to the real world outside. Ramón was under no illusion, however, that at the time of writing his play could be performed in Spain and had to be content with its first publication in his magazine *Prometeo* [*Prometheus*] (no. 12, 1909). Given the seminal importance of the *greguería*, a forerunner of zany surrealist humour, it is notable that there was as yet no revolution in language in the text of *Drama del palacio deshabitado*. It would be left to Lorca twenty years later to realize the surrealist revolution in dramatic poetry in his own 'impossible' theatre.

Whether Lorca read Ramón's play is not known, but his juvenile attempts at play-writing bear a striking resemblance to it, particularly his 'dialogue of shades', entitled *Sombras* [*Shades*], the germ of his surrealist mystery cycle in 1929–30. A first fragment entitled *Teatro de almas* [*Theatre of Souls*] (1917) is Lorca's debut attempt at a secular morality with its cast of Dreams, Lust, Love, Good, Evil, a Man, a Star, the Shade of Christ, Death; a note on the title-page reverse indicates that the 'Dream of Love' stands out and takes on various forms. Extant is the presentation by an Actor who instructs the audience on the play's reception in collective empathy, with a nostalgic 'twilight of the gods' memory of pre-rational innocence, a vision in white of childhood devotion to Christ and the Virgin Mary: 'pero todo evoluciona, comprendemos nuestras tragedias y queremos buscar el asilo espiritual de una igualdad de Amor en todo' [but everything evolves, we understand our tragedy

---

[3] R. Havard, *The Crucified Mind: Rafael Albert and the Surrealist Ethos in Spain* (London: Tamesis, 2001), 30.

and want to find spiritual refuge in an equality of love in everything].[4] In the manuscript of *Sombras*, the date of composition 1920 has been superimposed over 1910, the significant date of Lorca's pubescent crisis of faith and sexuality. A possible source for the Lorcan shade of Christ, desperately seeking the Father in *Sombras*, has been traced to the most famous 'Dream' of Richter transmitted through the French of Madame de Staël;[5] but the major source of inspiration may be nearer home.

Surrealism: a recurrent dream mode in Spanish tradition or contemporary novelty imported from France? It is not necessarily a case of *either / or*, but the Hegelian synthesis of *both / and*, the surrealist ideal. The titles of two of Lorca's dramatic prose poems in 1927–8, 'Coeur azul. Corazón bleu' [Blue Heart. Blue Heart] and 'Corazón bleu y coeur azul', which introduce motifs to be exploited in his European-oriented theatre, say it all.[6] The bilingual play in an aesthetic dialogue with Dalí points to the dialogical relationship between Spanish and French culture dating back to the Enlightenment and the Romantic Revolution: the head / intellect (Voltaire)–heart / intuition (Rousseau) dialectic. Blue, the colour that lights the most surreal moments in Lorca's theatre, symbolic colour of the infinite and of art as the quest for an absolute, had been read in French (Mallarmé) and assimilated into Spanish by Hispanic poets (Darío) to become the colour-stamp of a shared symbolist point of departure. Lorca's linguistic fusion plays with the sound / semantic systems of French and Spanish to image the process of exchange in a culturally hybrid mindset; three-way traffic between Paris, Barcelona and Madrid had eliminated the Spanish cultural time-lag. Breton, in Barcelona for the opening of a Picabia exhibition in November 1922, quoted the Uruguayan Ducasse/Lautréamont as the source of a new concept of beauty and imagery based on surprise, on unexpected and arbitrary juxtapositions: '[. . .] beautiful as the chance meeting, on a dissecting table, of a sewing-machine and an umbrella'.[7] To revolutionize language through free association was to be the source of the word's power to act on the world in an as yet unnamed Surrealism. In April 1925, three days after *La Révolution surréaliste* had recorded the end of the Christian era on its front-cover, Aragon presented himself in the Residencia de Estudiantes as an *agent provocateur* of Surrealism, declaring open a new era of metamorphosis and inciting spiritual terrorism in the name of Artaud as its dictator.[8] The soon-to-be-celebrated trio of 'residents', Lorca, Buñuel and Dalí, may not have attended Aragon's lecture, but his message was heard and understood. By the end of the decade Lorca was verbally assaulting the

---

[4] F. García Lorca, *Teatro inédito de juventud*, ed. A. Soria Olmedo (Madrid: Cátedra, 1996), 91–3.

[5] E. Martín, 'Sombras', *Quimera*, no. 36 (March 1984), 51–5.

[6] *Poemas en prosa*, ed. A. Anderson (Granada: Editorial Comares, 1999), 89–91.

[7] C.B. Morris, *Surrealism and Spain 1920–1936* (Cambridge: Cambridge University Press, 1972), 222.

[8] Morris, 228–31.

skyscrapers in his New York poetry and Buñuel and Dalí had hi-jacked the surrealist movement in Paris as a vehicle for the creation of its most enduring icons in painting and the cinema.

Before his collaboration with Dalí on *Un Chien andalou* (1929), Buñuel had collaborated with another *residente*, José Bello, on a dramatic *divertissement* entitled *Hamlet*, which Sánchez Vidal considers to be the first Spanish piece of surrealist theatre.[9] It is the germ of his films from first to last and a contestant for Lorca in his major experiments in surrealist drama. The Buñuel–Bello travesty was performed by an all-male group of friends who included Francisco García Lorca in the summer of 1927 in a Montparnasse café. It was a skittish exercise, in the cabaret/music hall tradition, out of Jarry by Valle-Inclán with more than a nod in the direction of Apollinaire's gender-bending *Les mamelles de Tirésias* [*The Tits of Tiresias*] (1917). *Hamlet* is in the modern Strindbergian tradition of the 'dream play', a psychodrama in which all the characters, male and female, are facets of a divided self in an alogical dream-world in which tricks are played with time and space. After Freud, it focuses on death anxiety, sexual desire / sublimation and the Oedipus complex in relation to the mother, fixating on the breasts and womb. Hamlet is modern man in search of identity / soul, the goal of whose quest is union with the heavenly Leticia. Her name indicates the link with Gómez de la Serna, and its declension in the *Dramatis Personae* links Leticia to the declension by a mad boy of *musa, musae*, i.e. she is the feminine muse. Hamlet is the lover of her 'upper part' and his rival Agrifonte the lover of her 'interesting spot';[10] Leticia in turn has a lower counterpart, Margarita (after Goethe and Dumas). Agrifonte introduces the puzzle of identity: 'who is my mother's son?' (66); Hamlet's reply, inverting gender, implies that the son *is* the mother, although the meaning of the riddle is postponed for later. A remarkable piece of theatre follows, involving a decomposing bishop, the Christian superego buried in the unconscious, rising up to harrass the conscious ego. Hamlet (ego) and Agrifonte (id) speak and act in unison in a play of shadows as hounds of God, chasing away the ghost of the past, the putrefaction of bourgeois morality.

Freed from its shadow, Hamlet is now able to accept Margarita's invitation to love her lower parts. The euphemism 'build' is playfully substituted for 'fornicate', as the two set about building a brick wall, an unfinished business as, in one of the dream-time tricks, Margarita has not turned up for their date. Buñuel attributed his conversion to film-making to the impression made on him by the scene of Death building a cemetery wall in Fritz Lang's *Weary*

---

[9] A. Sánchez Vidal, *Buñuel, Lorca, Dalí: El enigma sin fin* (Barcelona: Planeta, 1988), 352.

[10] G. White, *Hamlet* in *An Unspeakable Betrayal: Selected Writings of Luis Buñuel* (Berkeley: University of California Press, 2000), 65–76 (at 65). Subsequent references bracketed in text.

*Death* (1921). Thus the wall on stage is a *memento mori* of the womb as tomb in sexual procreation, as Hamlet's soliloquy in the cemetery on the ages of woman confirms. A red bicycle, symbol of the bloody reproductive cycle, cuts through the sky of the set, and Hamlet preaches a gnomic lesson that harks back to Agrifonte's initial statement that all lives and deaths are the same, the only lives that are different being those susceptible to proof as in a theorem: 'What good is the wrinkled skin of your drum? Girl or maiden, woman or old lady, that is your dilemma: thus Boy = Girl; then I say to you that Man is what we wanted to prove' (74). Is *Man* the 'Universal Man', Adam Kadmon, who according to Cirlot 'symbolises the whole pattern of the world of manifestation, that is the complete range of possibilities open to mankind',[11] or the hermaphroditic *coincidentia oppositorum*, which in relation to the psyche signifies the union of the masculine and the feminine in the whole human being, and in relation to salvation in art, the artist as androgyne?

In the final scene on board a ship as floating coffin, Hamlet experiences union with the object of his love-quest, Leticia. The denouement is narrated in stage directions: the two bodies become one in an embrace that lasts for centuries, until suddenly Hamlet lets out 'a terrible incestuous *ay*!' (76) and falls back on the deck. The solution to the mystery that leaves the audience/reader meditating on the mystery of the solution is given in the final direction: '(Leticia [. . .] is none other than Hamlet himself – he, the very Hamlet brought into the world by his mother.)' The fall is the moment of illumination, the self-recognition of the ground of being in the unconscious, the Great Mother, the cycle of life and death, destruction and creation. Hamlet, the masculine idealist, in the embrace of his feminine ideal, Leticia, has embraced the eternal feminine in himself, the imago of the mother; the alchemical marriage that produces the great work (art) is not the incestuous union of brother and sister, but rather that of mother and son. The mystery is a terrible one but the cathartic 'ay!' of the horror is dissolved by the humour of the parody with its anti-Lorcan, anti-Andalusian folkloric note.

Presumably Lorca knew of this play in performance through the involvement of his brother. The short playscript *El paseo de Buster Keaton* [*Buster Keaton's Trip*], published in April 1928 in his little magazine *Gallo* [*Cock*], would appear to be a reply, but for the very deliberate dating of its composition: July 1925. Part of a shared surrealist cult of Buster Keaton, Lorca's playlet establishes his primacy in the exploration of a surrealist theatre.[12] This is Lorca's first engagement with contemporary international popular culture in the attempt, as with traditional folksong, to see the world anew through the

---

[11] J.E. Cirlot, *A Dictionary of Symbols*, trans. J. Sage (London: Routledge & Kegan Paul, 1962), 198.

[12] V. García de la Concha, *El surrealismo español* (Madrid: Taurus Ediciones, 1982), 15, identifies the first recorded use of the Spanish adaptation *surrealista* by Lorca in a letter (1925) to his brother in France requesting news of the 'surrealist guys'.

innocent eye, that of the silent film comedian. He represented the innocent abroad, alienated in modern industrial society, facing the perils of the promised land of the New Frontier, enacting the final loss of Western innocence, deflected defensively in comic vein. In the same spirit of ironic humour employed in the *Romancero gitano* [*Gypsy Balladbook*], Lorca parodies the salvation drama that begins with the temptation in the Garden, transposing the garden of delights to a modern mythical America in *El paseo de Buster Keaton*. The eyes have it: '(Sus ojos, infinitos y tristes, como los de una bestia recién nacida, sueñan lirios, ángeles y cinturones de seda. [. . .] A lo lejos se ve Filadelfia' [His infinitely sad eyes, like those of a newborn animal, dream of lilies, angels and silken belts. [. . .] In the distance can be seen Philadelphia].[13]

Keaton came out of the circus–vaudeville tradition, and his impassive face and soulful eyes cast him as the white-faced Pierrot; David George quotes the significance of the French development of the figure: 'both the frivolous dilettante and the Christ-like prophet-victim', he is Hamlet dressed as a clown.[14] An association with sexual impotence made the Pierrot a cult-figure for those *fin de siècle* artists who cultivated art as a liberation from the will to live, pessimistically seen after Schopenhauer as a blind force going nowhere, an option for voluntary sterility, which paradoxically expresses itself in artistic creativity. It is therefore easy to detect behind the objective mask of Buster Keaton the subjective psyche of a Lorca who continually drew himself as a clown-with-shadow and to interpret his *paseo* as a dream-trip dramatic correlative of his sexual conflict at a time when he was under family pressure to make a career and marry. Keaton's entry on stage is a violent one, a savage yet tender father, who kills his four sons (the number of the Evangelists) with a wooden dagger: 'Pobres hijitos míos' [My poor little children] (893). This is a dramatic example of the poetic (f)act, which Lorca would describe in a 1928 lecture, freed from the control of logic but not from that of a poetry beyond the conventions of beauty and ugliness that mingles tenderness and cruelty.[15]

The mock massacre of the innocents is heralded and rounded off by the sound of a cock crowing. The latent symbolism of the sound in the dream-work is both denial of the Christian resurrection of the body and a proclamation of homo-eroticism, which opts out of the procreation of sons-in-the-flesh and sublimates paternity in the creation of art. In some traditions of story-telling, the cock's crow signals the end of the story and the transition to day-time reality; here it signals the beginning of the transition to an alternative

[13] *Obras completas*, ed. A. Del Hoyo (Madrid: Aguilar, 1967), 894. Bracketed references to Lorcan texts, unless otherwise stated, are to this edition.
[14] D. George, *The History of the Commedia dell'Arte in Modern Hispanic Literature with Special Attention to the Work of García Lorca* (Lewiston/Queenston/Lampeter: Edwin Mellen Press, 1995),12–13 and 33.
[15] 'Imaginación, inspiración, evasión', *OC*, 88–9.

poetic surreality that still retains the basic morphology of the fairy-tale. Lorca in *El paseo de Buster Keaton* takes his alter ego back to Genesis, developing a double series of running gags (mechanical and natural) in relation to sexual orientation and behaviour, which call into question the orthodox concept of original (sexual) sin and guilt. The machine which is introduced into the garden is the bicycle (peddling, as with the choruses of girls plying Singer sewing-machines or playing pianos, being associated with auto-eroticism). The stage direction is explicit and enigmatic: 'Es una bicicleta como todas, pero la única empapada de inocencia. Adán y Eva correrían asustados si vieran un vaso lleno de agua, y acariciarían, en cambio, la bicicleta de KEATON' [It's a bicycle like any other, but the only one imbued with innocence. Adam and Eve would run away frightened if they saw a glass full of water, but would fondle Keaton's bike] (894). Given the use of 'correr' [come] and 'acariciar' [stroke], the sense seems to be that the masturbatory emission of semen is natural, its retention unnatural; this would also illuminate the mysterious claim that the inhabitants of the city named brotherly love cannot tell the subtle poetic difference between a cup of hot tea (heterosexual passion) and cold tea (masturbation). The parallel introduction of birds, the significance of '*pájaro*' [bird] = penis and the pun '*paja*' [straw] = masturbation (in relation to a black minstrel eating his hat), associates onanism and music (Schopenhauer's pure manifestation of the will). Significantly, apart from the mute parrot, a parody of the Holy Spirit, the songs of the owl, the nightingale and the swan are songs of the night, of the violation of love and of death, the dark sounds of the daemon *duende*.

When Buster Keaton falls off his bike with the lament (in parody of *deep song*), 'Ay, amor, amor' [oh, love, love!], the bicycle has a will of its own and chases two grey butterflies: 'Va como loca a medio milímetro del suelo' [It careers madly half a millimetre from the ground] – 'del sueño' [dream] in the original, indicating as in all the spatial/temporal references, that this is a measurement of the dream perspective. 'Mariposa' [butterfly], symbol of the psyche and of rebirth, like 'loca' [mad woman], is a slang term for homosexual; grey, the colour of ashes, symbolizes the death of the body and the immortality of the spirit. When he picks himself up, Buster declines to speak (= come out?) and a voice off pronounces him a fool, leaving him to face heterosexual temptation in the garden. The American girl on a bicycle in the Cocteau–Satie–Picasso *Parade* for the Ballets Russes (1917) is split into two Bosch-like personae: an American Girl wearing crocodile shoes as predatory female (prostitute) and a Young Girl with a nightingale's head riding a bicycle, the spirit of romantic love (virgin). The former's leading questions regarding Buster's heterosexual (a sword wreathed in myrtle leaves) or homosexual (a ring with a poisoned stone) identity are responded to with expressive mime, which begs the to-be-or-not-to-be question of sexual indecision: shrugging the shoulders and lifting the right (righteous) leg / closing the eyes and lifting the left (criminal) leg. When left alone, Keaton expresses a desire to transcend the limitations of self and sexuality in the impossible wish to become a swan, the bird sacred to both Venus and Apollo, hermaphroditic in relation to its long neck (masculine) and round body (feminine): 'In sum, then, the swan always points to the complete satisfaction of a desire, the swan-song being a particular allusion to desire which brings about its own death.'[16]

The young bird-woman rides to his rescue, but faints on hearing his name and falls off her bike. The original stage direction indicated the musical finale of romantic love to be relayed by a thousand gramophones whose mechanical voice has replaced birdsong: 'En América no hay ruiseñores' [There are no nightingales in America] (896). But the final piece of stage play has a panicking Buster Keaton, in his attempt to revive the girl (her name Eleonora, a variant of Elena [Helen], the eternal feminine cultural ideal), speaking ever more softly and bending ever more closely until he finally kisses her. Will the prince arouse the sleeping princess (heterosexuality) with the kiss? The final visual image is that of a shining blow-up of the star-badge of the Philadelphia cops projected on the backcloth-horizon, external symbol of the authority of a social order that anathematized homosexuality, internalized as the policeman of the superego. There is, however, no third and final cock-crow of betrayal / triumph / closure: the open ending leaves the author behind the mask of Buster Keaton time to come out of the closet in a future dream-work of which this is a short trailer.

Rupert Allen interpreted *El paseo de Buster Keaton* as a piece of film criticism, cast in the form of a film scenario,[17] but the stage directions are very literary and, while more easily realized in the medium of film, the difference can be seen in a comparison with the film-script Lorca wrote entitled *Viaje a la luna* [*Trip to the Moon*].[18] When he came to write it in New York (1929–30), in response to the challenge of *Un Chien andalou* and the stimulus of the film theory of Buñuel and Dalí (after Jean Epstein) published in *La Gaceta Literaria* (1927–8), Lorca had absorbed their lesson, which would be put into practice in the film-script and adapted in the playtexts being written at the same time. In an article translated for *La Gaceta Literaria* (no. 24, 15 Dec. 1927), 'Time and nature of the drama', Epstein speaks of the particular capacity of film, speeding up / slowing down, flashing back / flashing forward, to convey the emotional force of qualitative as opposed to quantitative time, the flux or *durée*. Buñuel, in a key article on '*Découpage*' [Cutting] in a 'seventh art' special issue (no. 43, 1 Oct. 1928), highlighted the crucial scripting of sequences prior to shooting the miraculous flow of images with the command to think in and feel with images.

[16]  Cirlot, 322.

[17]  R. Allen, 'A Commentary on Lorca's *El paseo de Buster Keaton*', *Hispanófila*, no. 48 (May 1973), 23–5.

[18]  Edited by M. Laffranque (Loubressac: Braad Editions, 1980) and A. Monegal (Valencia: Pre-Textos, 1994). Laffranque's numbering followed.

   In the scenario of *Viaje a la luna*, the burgeoning film-writer Lorca is thinking and feeling in visual moving images and the novice shows his potential
mastery of the Eisensteinian technique of metaphoric montage. In 71 numbered shots, his mental camera eye runs the whole gamut of possible angles:
close-ups / long shots, double / triple exposures and fades-in / out, travelling
shots that move backwards and forwards, up and down, the time and motion
of sex and violence: 'Doble exposición de la rana vista enorme sobre un fondo
de orquídeas agitadas con furia. Se van las orquídeas y aparece una cabeza
enorme dibujada de mujer que vomita que cambia de negativo a positivo y de
positivo a negativo rápidamente' [Double exposure of the frog blown-up over
orchids shaken with fury. The orchids disappear and a drawing appears of an
enormous vomiting head of a woman in a fast-change negative–positive positive–negative] (32). As Boschian filmed images disappear, Lorca mixes media
inserting his own drawings, and even has one or two tricks in the projected
use of a meta-cinematic subjective camera – the camera as womb's eye view
/ the camera swallowed by a phallic fish – far in advance of *Un Chien
andalou*. Exploiting the dynamic of film to convey psychic processes through
symbolic images as in a dream, *Viaje a la luna* creates the visual sensation
of a vertiginous journey from womb to tomb, life as sexual conflict from birth
to death. Woman is the moon as mother, lover and destroyer; the infant–
adolescent–grown man is the living–agonising–dying fish. A major motif in
the black and white, negative / positive images is that of blood, which flows
out of various orifices, nose, mouth and womb. The extant drawing *Muerte de
Santa Rodegunda* [*Death of Saint Rodegund*] (36) has red blood haemorrha-
ging out of the womb on the delivery table, or is it out of the anus of the son
delineated within? Blood is spewing out of the mouth of the son, designated
with the half-moon eyebrows of the artist himself. This is the new poetry of
'opening up the veins', fruit of the obsession with death and the mockery of
death in art.[19]
   The drawing of the circulation system on the skin of naked male bodies,
first revealed in the image of a boy divested of the harlequin costume of dual-
ity / ambivalent heterosexuality (41), has its expressionist origin in the
sketches (nerves and tendons painted on skin) Kokoschka made for his play
inspired by fear of the feminine principle, *Murder Hope of Women* (1909).
There is also a debt to Cocteau's *Orpheus* (and a wink at Duchamp) in the
final appearance of the heterosexual reproductive couple as death and her clinical assistant, *sans* harlequin costume in a white lab-coat and rubber gloves,
who paint a moustache on a dead man's head and laughingly kiss on a grave
(68/69). There is a remarkable coincidence, which anticipates the idea behind
the first part of *The Immaculate Conception* (1930), a joint composition of
Breton and Éluard, now like the Spanish writers consciously simulating the
conditions of dream and madness, and which may owe something to the shared

[19] Letter to Jorge Zalamea, *OC*, 1664.

influence of Dalí and his intra-uterine memory. Stimulated in part by Otto Rank's development of Freudian theory, attributing neurosis to the initial trauma of birth, 'Man' follows the sequence: conception, intra-uterine life, birth, life and death. Similarly, *Viaje a la luna* is a sexual parody of a nativity play followed by a passion play. The vestiges of the sacred plot are mystified temporally and spatially by disjunction, repetition and protean change, but the violent and bloody images powerfully suggest the origin of the fear of the female genitals, castration complex, sadism and death anxiety in the birth trauma. The anti-Pauline perils begin with the conception (*not* a virgin birth) of a game in bed of the heterosexual number 2, the initial journey down the birth canal and expulsion into the world; the primal shriek is projected in a parodic title as a triple cry for help (5) and the first wailing a response to having the bottom smacked by a woman (12).

The child-beating image appears to be a reminiscence of Max Ernst's 'The Virgin thrashing the Child Jesus in front of three witnesses (A.B., P.E. and the painter)', reproduced in *La Révolution surréaliste* (no. 8, 1 Dec. 1926), a parody of Freud's 'A child is being beaten' (1919). Is this also a source of the three men (counterparts of the male trios of friends in *El Público* [*The Audience*] and *Así que pasen cinco años* [*When Five Years have Come to Pass*]) who contemplate the moon, which fades into a sex organ, which fades into a shrieking mouth in (44)? Their place is taken by 'the veined man', adult version of the boy in (41), who strikes a crucified pose (46), which links him with the Red Nude in *El Público*. He fades into a metaphoric montage of a triple exposure of express trains, symbolic of sexual activity and a visual pun on the Stations of the Cross, made explicitly in *El Público* in relation to the crucified homosexual. Here the trains dissolve into a double exposure of piano keyboards and fingers playing (48), with the libidinous association of auto-eroticism and the release of *angst* in the making of music. The flayed man is last seen as a corpse, dumped among discarded newspapers and dead herrings (66), after having passionately kissed a plaster-cast of the girl, identified in the fourfold echolalia of the title in (64) as Elena, a restoration to order of the disjointed variants of the name in (32): the voracious disordered womb transformed into the ideal feminine represented in the mask of art. Unlike the Red Nude, the flayed man has betrayed his naked homosexual truth in the Judas kiss of heterosexuality, an act of spiritual and artistic suicide. The final ironizing close-up of the romantic screen kiss of the heterosexual couple / death on top of the grave (70) and fast-forward pan of the moon and swaying trees (71) provoke a double-vision of an artistic representation of the truth of the human condition in denial and the future possibility of free exposure through the symbolic images of art.

If this script had been filmed, Lorca would have been in the vanguard of European cinema; equally, if the playscript of *El público* had been performed, he would have been in the vanguard of European theatre. A first version was completed in Cuba in 1930, part of a project, conceived in New York, to create a homosexual theatre that would outdo Wilde.[20] He recognized that it was unperformable, not because of technical difficulties, but because of its subject matter: the apologia for homosexuality on the public stage. Breton in Barcelona (1922) had quoted Nietzsche: 'Everything is allowed'; but in their researches on sexuality, the French surrealists (like Buñuel followed by Dalí) proved themselves to be homophobic. Their liberating 'blind love' (amour fou) was based on finding the woman; Lorca liberated loco amor to embrace whatever object of desire, in a theatre whose protagonist is the fairy philtre from a Midsummer Night's Dream: 'una flor venenosa' [a poisonous flower].[21] The transvaluation of values in linguistic signs is signalled by the reverse sound play of words: 'Gui-guiller-guillermi-guillermina. Na-nami-namiller-namillergui' (111), sings the discarded ballerina's costume of the closet-homosexual Director, avatar of William Shakespeare, author of the 'Dark Sonnets'; '¡Abominable!/Blenamiboa' (37), chorus the Horses, dispelling the Biblical anathema against homosexuality.

Paul Smith in his exegesis of El público quotes Foucault on the language of homosexuality as a 'reverse discourse';[22] thus the undisguised homosexual First Man's assertion (75) that the anus is man's punishment, failure, shame and death should be understood as the reverse. The linguistic solvent in the alchemical poetic transmutation is piss and spit, slime and shit: inside is out, impure pure and vile sacred. The breaking of linguistic taboos on stage turns orthodox cosmology, bourgeois morality and decorum upside down: '¡Oh amor, amor, que necesitas pasar tu luz por los calores oscuros! ¡Oh mar apoyado en la penumbra y flor en el culo del muerto! [Love that needs pass your light through dark heat! Sea upheld in shadows and flower in the dead man's arse!] (101), marvels the Black Horse with a graphic reference to Bosch's The Garden of Delights. Scatology is indeed an eschatology and out of putrefaction a thing of sublimated beauty (art) is born.

Meaning and interpretation are undermined and relativized, because the revealed authority of Sacred Scripture is denied: 'Ya sabéis lo bien que degüello palomas. Cuando se dice roca yo entiendo aire. Cuando se dice aire yo entiendo vacío. Cuando se dice vacío yo entiendo paloma degollada' [You know how well I behead doves. When they say rock (Peter) I understand air. When they say air I understand void. When they say void I understand beheaded dove (Holy Spirit)] (97). The speaker is the Black Horse, Thanatos, in the sepulchre scene of an elliptical reworking of Romeo and Juliet, against an unstable wall made of the sands of time which he associates with the sleep

[20] Ian Gibson, Federico García Lorca 2. De Nueva York a Fuente Grande 1929–1936 (Barcelona: Grijalbo, 1987), 104.

[21] El público y Comedia sin título, eds R. Martínez Nadal and M. Laffranque (Barcelona / Caracas / Mexico: Seix Barral, 1978), 41. References bracketed in text.

[22] P.J. Smith, The Body Hispanic. Gender and Sexuality in Spanish and Spanish-American Literature (Oxford: Oxford University Press, 1989), 129.

of death. His claim is matched by that of the first of the White Horses, Eros, boasting that they have demolished the mangers and the windows of the stable (Bethlehem) with their cocks. In chorus they command the *loca* Juliet, the boy dressed as a girl with celluloid breasts, to strip and expose her rump to the whiplash of their tails: '¡Queremos resucitar! [We want to resurrect!] (99). The apple of heterosexual temptation turns to ash in the reproductive cycle; the phallus can rise again in an artistic (circular) form, defined by the Black Horse: 'Ansia de la sangre y hastío de la rueda' [Yearning of the blood and weariness with the cycle] (95). He defines the visionary truth of art as intimation of mortality in a triad of traces of pain and suffering seen through a glass darkly: 'Cuando se haya quitado el último traje de sangre, la verdad será una ortiga, un cangrejo devorado, o un trozo de cuero detrás de los cristales' [When the last bloody costume has been taken off, truth will be a nettle, a devoured crab, or a scrap of skin behind the glass] (103). This is the elusive goal of the true theatre, the 'theatre under the sand', which the Horses, repeating the Men (41), claim to be inaugurating: 'Para que se sepa la verdad de las sepulturas' [So that the truth of the grave be known] (103). It is expressed in a surrealist chain of concrete images, which associate to compose a mentally imaged still-life of death. The transformation of figures and objects to create a new spiritual reality / invisible identity by substitution through the magnetic attraction of love / death – 'Romeo puede ser un ave y Julieta puede ser una piedra' [Romeo can be a bird and Juliet a stone] (129) – is detected by the Students in repetition of the Men (39), and confirmed by the Director after his conversion from the inauthentic 'open air theatre'. The Conjurer, master of illusion, claims to be able to turn a sailor into a sewing-needle, and the Director replies that this is what happens in the theatre: 'Por eso yo me atreví a realizar un dificilísimo juego poético en espera de que el amor rompiera con ímpetu y diera nueva forma a los trajes' [That is why I dared put in effect a very difficult poetic game in the hope that love would burst through and give new shape to the costumes] (157). This is the dynamic of Lorca's revolution in dramatic poetry in *El público*; the surrealist revolution begins with language and the first victim of the terrorist bomb reported in the theatre-within-the-theatre is a professor of rhetoric, husband of the heterosexual myth Elena.

Theatre, like cinema, exploits non-verbal signs, and in *El público* Lorca tranfers to the stage *découpage* techniques in the fragmentation of scenic action in the five extant acts. This is seen at its most dramatic in the fifth, which simultaneously enacts and cuts between the back-stage passion play of the death agony of the Red Nude / First Man and the irruption from the theatre off-stage, under siege from counter-revolutionary forces, of reactionary bourgeois lady and revolutionary student members of the audience trying to escape. They discuss audience reaction to the reenactment of *Romeo and Juliet* played by homosexual lovers, which has led to the murder of the actors and pursuit of the Director and has triggered the revolution. The theatre–cinema link is indicated in the lighting direction at the moment of transposition of the Red Nude / First

Man: a silvery screen tint, which washes the backcloth in a grainy blue, the phantasmagoric light of surreality, the liminal zone of dream / reality, life / death. Blue, the colour of equilibrium, of truth (death) and art, is the colour of the set in the first and last scenes in the Director's office. Its X-ray film windows indicate the revelation of the unseen, the process of unmasking behind the screen that will take place in the hallucination of the dying mind: the triple agony of Christianity, sexual identity and commercial 'open air theatre', labour pains of the birth of the 'theatre under the sand'. The giant hand impressed on the wall is not the hand of God, but that of the artist-creator, the great masturbator whose onanism, sterile in terms of sexual reproduction, is transformed into the play of an art with dangerous consequences. In the finale, onto the set whose focal points are a large horse-head stage-left and a great eye (anus) with trees and clouds (nature) stage-right, the Conjurer with a wave of his fan brings down a slow-motion fall of white gloves which, with another wave, turn into snow-flakes, emblematic of death for Lorca.[23] The echo by a voice-off of the repetition in the first scene of the Servant's announcement of the arrival of the audience and the Director's instruction to let it in is the threefold signal that the performance is about to begin: it is the command to audience participation in the recognition of collective destiny in the eternal return of the Big Sleep.

Michel Leiris, in a glossary of the oracular virtues of key surrealist words in *La Révolution surréaliste* (no. 3, 15 April 1925), defined metamorphosis as the metaphysical disease of the dead. In *El público*, from the perspective of death the great leveller and anal art, horses metamorphose into men and men into circus and ballet costumes and classical figures, the masks of shifting sexual identities in a synthesis of the European tradition of representation. Scene 2, set in a Roman ruin, is a balletic leap back into an *après-midi d'un faune* world-view of pagan Antiquity in which the quest for Pan (the All-in-One) in the ever-changing Proteus (the Many) of the Orphic nature mysteries is figured in the dance and duet of the Figure with Vine Leaves and the Figure with Bells, watched by their alter egos, the First Man–Gonzalo and the Director–Enrique (the name of Goethe's Faust). In the chameleon changes of the descent from spirit into matter in their verbal duel, 'nube / ojo' [cloud / eye] > 'caca / mosca' [shit / fly], and the reversals of active–passive / dominant–submissive in their warring / loving embrace, the two-in-one embody the *coincidentia oppositorum*, Adam, the original androgyne before the separation and limitation of gender, Lorca's homosexual ideal. The arrival of the Emperor, beheader of boys who refuse to affirm: 'Uno es uno y nada más que uno' [One is one and only one] (69), suggests a parody of the Christian Trinity in the complex relationship on stage of the three types of homosexual according to Gide: the pederast, the sodomite and the invert. The enigma of unity revealing itself as a triad, in the microcosm of each individual as in the

---

[23] M.C. Millán (ed.), *El público* (Madrid: Cátedra, 1991), 81–92, itemizes the debt to Cocteau.

macrocosm of universal nature, is celebrated in the mystifying canticle of the Horses on the parallel wrestling match between the Director and the First Man: 'Amor, amor, amor. / Amor del uno con el dos / y amor del tres que se ahoga / por ser uno entre los dos' [Love, love, love. / Love of one with two / and love of three choking / to be one among two] (107).

Lorca was obsessed with the crucifixion of Christ and possessed by His image as messianic martyr of sacrificial love, shockingly here, of homosexual love. Blasphemous parody is consummated in *El público* in the depiction of the agony of the Red Nude, the alchemical Christ in the (red) stage of sublimation. His death scene is punctuated by the Pirandellian meta-theatrical debate on a theatre of gay liberation and its consequences for those involved in the theatre, a debate in turn punctuated by the First Man's cries of agony. Crowned with blue thorns, he is on a perpendicular bed centre-stage 'as if painted by a primitive' (121). The central motif is taken from the base of the Apocalypse side-panel of *The Garden of Delights* in which a red nude is pinned to a gaming-table by a blue wheel-of-fortune, surrounded by the emblems of his downfall, dice and cards (including the ace of hearts), inspiration for the Conjurer and the Card-Players of *Así que pasen cinco años*, figures of fate. The medieval board becomes a modern hospital bed; the patient is being prepared for his death in a parody of the Passion in an operating-theatre that is being prepared for the Consecration in a parody of the Mass, Lorca's paradigm of sacred spectacle.[24] If humour is a distinguishing mark of Surrealism, the dominant note here is sick: DESNUDO [NUDE] 'Padre: en tus manos encomiendo mi espíritu' [Father: into thy hands I commend my spirit]. / ENFERMERO [NURSE] 'Te has adelantado dos minutos' [You're two minutes early] (137). As the bed swings round to reveal – *Ecce Homo* – the outstretched First Man in his frock-coat, the Nurse and two Thieves exit in a burlesque dance; black comedy gives way to the tragedy of man alone in his moment of truth: 'Soledad de los edificios, de las esquinas, de las playas, donde tú no aparecerás ya nunca' [Solitude of buildings, street-corners, shores, where you will never again appear] (145).

A carnivalesque change of mood and mode in this transgeneric theatre marks the transition to the Director's final confession of the theatre's justification in the trangression of moral law (159). This is the mock pastoral solo of the Foolish Shepherd, dancing to the sound of his hurdy-gurdy and riddling in music and rhyme: 'La musiquilla, la musiqueta / de las púas heridas y la limeta' [Music, music, music / of wounded spikes and bald head / bottle] (149). The

---

[24] See A. Anderson, '*El público, Así que pasen cinco años* y *El sueño de la vida*: Tres dramas expresionistas de García Lorca', in *El teatro en España: Entre la tradición y la vanguardia 1918–1939*', eds D. Dougherty and M.F. Vilches de Frutos (Consejo Superior de Investigaciones Científicas, 1992), 215–26. See also J. Huélamo Kosma, 'Lorca y los límites del teatro surrealista español', in Dougherty and Vilches de Frutos, 207–14, and *El teatro imposible de García Lorca: estudio sobre 'El público'* (Granada: Universidad de Granada, 1996).

image conjures up not only the Christ-head crowned with thorns, but also the musical-phallus retort on top of the inverted platter of the Baptist-head, which contemplates the backside of its broken-shell body / theatre in Bosch's Apocalypse panel. The Foolish Pastor's traditional name is John and he is wearing the animal skins of the Baptist and the bizarre headgear of a funnel (alchemy) filled with feathers (homosexuality). He is a comic parody of the prophetic voice crying in the wilderness, his song a demonic reversal, turned by the death-mask of God, of the revelation of John the Divine. The *poète maudit* is the eagle whose auto-erotic word eclipses that of the Holy Spirit, the carnivorous buzzard: 'Las águilas usan la puñeta / y se llenan de fango bajo el cometa. / Y el cometa devora la gipaeta / que rayaba el pecho del poeta' [Eagles wank / and get covered in mire under the comet. / And the comet devours the buzzard / which scored the breast of the poet] (149). But like Prometheus, those who proclaim their *non serviam* to the gods are punished; the students, who embrace the 'gay science' with hallelujahs, comment on the violent reaction outside the theatre of an audience who may have been moved to compassion within but are brandishing knives and cudgels in defence of dogma without.

Reed Anderson has suggested that *Así que pasen cinco años*, which Lorca was working on in New York–Cuba and completed in the Huerta de San Vicente on 19 August 1931, may well be the authentic 'theatre under the sand'.[25] On the contrary, it may well be a confession of the postponement of such a theatre, a hedging of bets in the writing of a play that is the half-way house to the artistic 'bad faith' of the heterosexual 'open air' theatre of the folk tragedies. The play is an intratextual dialogue within Lorca's own *corpus*, past and future, and an intertextual dialogue with Buñuel's *Hamlet* and French Surrealism, possibly inspired by Ernst's depiction of three dream-selves in 'Night Revolution', which had illustrated Aragon's Residencia lecture in *La Révolution surréaliste*.[26] The set is lit in varying intensities of blue light, which signals the juxtaposition on stage of different dimensions of reality and art in the dream space-time. The tenses employed in this 'Legend of Time' create a Bergsonian mystification of time and memory in which future is past and happening now, ever-fluid, ever-changing. The 'now' of modern consciousness, however, is set in a 'here', which is measured by the clock and bounded by the foreknowledge of a self-ending in time. 'Aquí' [Here] is the last word echoed in the protagonist's dying fall as the clock strikes twelve. Is this an echo-effect of the clock striking six at the beginning and end of the first act or the full chimes at midnight? Has the dream-action taken place in the split-second between the strike and its echo, or has it taken place in mid-strike of the chiming of the midnight-hour? The repetition of the cocktail-hour

[25] R. Anderson, *Federico García Lorca* (London: Macmillan Press, 1984), 142.
[26] No. 4 (15 July 1925), 13; a mannequin (on the staircase of the Paris Opera?) was on the front cover and a Picasso harlequin inside.

would sound the note of frozen progression;[27] the full chime of the witching-hour would signal the mystery threshold of time / eternity, the absolute midnight of Baudelaire and Mallarmé. Either way, the final tableau is a dramatic illustration of that convulsive beauty captured by Breton in the expiration of movement.

Lorca later referred to *Así que pasen cinco años* as a 'mystery of time', and it is another self-conscious salvation drama of the psyche and its representation within a theatrical tradition. The scene is set in the first act, and in the final scene of the last, in the library of the Young Man's house, symbolizing both higher consciousness and the cultural archive. The first scene of the final act is set in a dark wood (shades of Breton's eternal surrealists Dante and Shakespeare), which contains, centre-stage and accessed by a staircase, a baroque theatre, which is subsequently revealed to contain the library-set in miniature. In this theatrical *mise-en-abîme* there is no upper divine stage; the theatre of the world is contained within the human mind contemplating itself through the ages. The instinctual wood is the domain of circus costumes and carnival masks: Harlequin, in the chequered colours green / black of life / death, and his sinister playmate, the spangled Clown with the white death-head face, who play tantalizing truth-and-lies games with those who enter the wood, mediating access to the inner set and giving confusing directions on the way out. Ultimately, there is only one way out (death) and only one salvation (the art of music): ARLEQUIN [HARLEQUIN] 'La mortaja del aire' [The shroud of the air]. / PAYASO [CLOWN] 'Y la música de tu violín' [And the music of your violin] (1129). The music of Harlequin's violin is heard in counterpoint to the distant sounds of hunting horns in the wood, an audio equivalent of the police badge and persecution.

Like Buñuel's Hamlet, 'a virginal insomniac', the Young Man protagonist is an idealist, the procrastinator who postpones the existential choices of love, life and art; all the other characters and masks, male and female, are aspects of the divided self in the past/future of the imagination/dream.[28] The First Friend is a realist who covers up his homosexual tendency with the mask of heterosexual Don Juan, the Second Friend an infantile Peter Pan who wants to regress to the unconsciousness of the womb. The Old Man as guru is an ambivalent guide: he asks the Young Man the key question regarding his love for the Fiancée whose return is imminent: '¿No se atreve usted a huir?, ¿a volar?, ¿a ensanchar su amor por todo el cielo? [Don't you dare flee, fly, expand your love throughout the sky?] (1049); yet he interrupts the wrestling match *à la* Figures of Vine Leaves and Bells of the Young Man and the First

[27] See S. Wright, *The Trickster-Function in the Theatre of García Lorca* (London: Tamesis, 2000), 63.
[28] See R. Allen, 'The Psychological Perspective *As Soon as Five Years Pass*', in *The Symbolic World of Federico García Lorca* (Albuquerque: University of New Mexico Press, 1972), 61–157.

Friend. The Dead Child who is to be buried in his white First Communion suit is, *pace* the prologue of *Teatro de almas*, dead innocence and loss of belief in Christian resurrection. The animal-spirit who accompanies the Dead Child into the dark night of sexually undifferentiated eternity is the blue Cat, stoned to death by children, who claims she is a 'gata' [she-cat] not a 'gato' [tomcat], although she has no 'cuca' [pussy] and the Child believes he has. The Cat's gender-change recalls the legend of the Madonna's cat that at the birth of Christ gave birth in the same stable and confirms the negation of the Annunciation of the Incarnation on the lips of the Child: 'y una paloma muerta por la arena / con las alas tronchadas y en el pico una flor' [and a dead dove on the sand / with its wings cut off and in its beak a flower] (1086). The hand that unceremoniously pushes them off-stage is an absurd parody of the hand of God. Buñuel had translated Maldoror's dogs, baying with an insatiable thirst for the infinite, into the grotesque shadow-play of the death of God in *Hamlet*; Lorca translates the associated sequence of similes in the *Songs* – a hungry child, a wounded cat, a pregnant woman, a man dying of plague, a young woman singing a sublime air – into a suite of lyrical songs by figures who are not exempt from the grotesque.

The Fiancée is the romantic ideal of heterosexual marriage who on the drawing-board of the mind is converted into a hag's head in a fairground mirror; her romantic ideal is the macho Rugby-player (>*Bodas de sangre* [*Blood Wedding*]). In a process of artistic detachment that makes the emotion more poignant, the frustration of the bride-and-mother-never-to-be is projected onto the 'convulsive beauty' of the dehumanized Mannequin (>*Yerma*) and the mourning of the bereaved mother onto the stylized yellow Mask, double of the unseen concièrge / mother of the dead child. The Mannequin's maternal frustration is mirrored in the Young Man's paternal desire and the changing versions of the Mask's relationship with the Italian count and his son in Paris parallel the Typist's complex relationship with the Young Man. The Typist, mirror image of the Fiancée, is the first female figure to enter and the last to leave. She crosses the stage weeping as the clock strikes six and the Young Man echoes the Old Man's maxim (a definition of art in time): 'Sí, hay que recordar hacia mañana' [Yes, you have to remember back to the future] (1047); her last words in the theatre in the wood are that she will be waiting for him, and his last words as he exits the wood express his wish to return. She produces the clean copy of his letters, and her love is based on a childhood memory of seeing him bleed after a fall: 'Todavía tengo aquella sangre viva como una sierpe roja, temblando entre mis pechos' [I still bear that living blood like a red serpent, trembling between my breasts] (1055). She could thus be considered the blood-letting muse whom the Young Man would love if the Old Man did not advise caution, pronouncing her a dangerous woman. When they meet in the wood after the flight of the Fiancée, the Young Man is free to recognize her as the love of his life whom he now wishes to possess and carry off naked to where white (blank?) sheets await. She, however, requests the distance of

contemplative height and up in the theatre, it is the Typist who takes control.
When the Dead Child crosses the stage and the Yellow Mask appears lament-
ing her son, it is the Typist who makes the connection between writing, the
child the Young Man requests her to help set free from his heart, and herself:
'No es tu hijo, soy yo' [It's not your child, it's me] (1125). Affirming passionate love, she reiterates her need for contemplative detachment; the muse
of the love that knows no bounds, and an art that knows no European fron-
tiers, voluntarily distances herself from the Young Man: he is not ready *now*
to see her naked, their mystical union will have to wait five years. The Old
Man in anguish points the way out of the theatre, back to the library where
the Young Man will lose his heart in the game of chance with fate. The final
tableau is one of death and potential renewal. The Servant, whose name is
John, who had covered the sleeping Typist with a white cloak in the theatre
in the wood, now responds to the mocking echo of the Young Man's death-
bed summons and final question: is there no man there? No longer entering
incongruously as a ballet dancer on points, the Servant's lighted candelabra is
a beacon over the void of a future pregnant with possibility. The 'theatre under
the sand' may have descended into limbo, but the date of its resurrection has
been set in the suspense of fairy-tale – five years hence.

   Five years later *Así que pasen cinco años* was in rehearsal with the feminist
amateur theatre group Anfistora, and Lorca was revising the final version of *El
público* and returning to the dramatic formula of the 'unperformable' play in a
surviving fragment identified as the untitled social drama mentioned by Lorca
in interviews, hence the title *Comedia sin título* [*Untitled Play*],[29] also referred
to as *El sueño de la vida* [*The Dream of Life*]. In the finale of *El público* the
Director had proclaimed the need to destroy the theatre or to live in it; in *Comedia sin título* the walls come tumbling down with sets crashing under bom-
bardment on a front-stage drama in a rehearsal play of *A Midsummer Night's
Dream*. In a meta-theatrical Pirandellian first act that demolishes the footlights-
boundary between stage and audience, the Director has now become the
Author, who explicates the significance of Shakespeare's play and the reason
why it is no longer theatrically valid in the present social context. In the historical *now*, individual concerns regarding the accidental nature of love must
be sacrificed to an altruistic collective imperative: liberty, equality, fraternity.
The evolution in Lorca's ideal theatre had followed the evolution within main-
line French Surrealism to put itself at the service of social revolution. The
Author is explicit in his opening 'sermon' to the audience about his didactic
voice, albeit crying in the wilderness. In disputation with its bourgeois members, he preaches salvation in the reversal of illusion and reality by replacing
the lies of the theatre with the incredible truth of the street – mothers and children dying of hunger. Ironically, it is the Servant, who brings the Author his
coffee, who unmasks the cruelty of carnival as bourgeois entertainment in a

---

[29] See M. Laffranque's introduction, *El Público y Comedia sin título*, 275–316.

graphic image out of Bosch that fuses crucified man (*El público*) and cat (*Así que pasen cinco años*) in a self-parodic acknowledgement of the irrelevance of Lorca's own subjective theatre: 'El año pasado vino un borracho tocando el violín. Todavía me río de recordarlo. ¿Sabe usted lo que era el violín? Era un gato crucificado boca arriba sobre una tabla de lavar, el arco era un gran manojo de zarzas y al pasarlas sobre el animalito éste daba grandes maullidos que servían de música para el baile de dos mujeres muy bien vestidas, eso sí ¡de raso!, una de Pierrot y otra de Columbina' [Last year a drunk came playing the violin. The memory still makes me laugh. D'you know what the violin was made of? It was a cat crucified face up on a washboard, the bow was a big handful of brambles. As they were passed over the little animal it gave out great miaows that served as music for the dance of two women, very well dressed indeed, in satin!, one as Pierrot and the other as Colombine] (333). Socio-economic justice must now prevail equally over the box-office and sexual liberation and the Author commands that the doors of the theatre, whose scene-shifter is nick-named Bakunin, be opened to the revolution outside. The fragment ends with the plebs breaking down the doors and the Author, whose name is Lorenzo (martyrdom by fire), going off-stage to meet them, inciting the revolutionary destruction of the *ancien régime* in the theatre itself; his last words as he exits and the theatre is lit up in red are the incendiary: '¡Y el fuego! [And fire!] (363). Laffranque has pieced together an outline of the subsequent development of the action (including a scene in the morgue) in which the author, who had declared that this would be his last day in the theatre, goes out into the street and is killed.

With hindsight, the piece is prophetic of the role of its location, the Teatro Español, in the urgent task of Republican wartime propaganda in which surrealist experiment was inevitably foresaken or subsumed; more poignantly, it is prophetic of the real author's end. The fragments in which Lorca realized himself as a dramatist, a work in truncated progress, remained underground for years after his death. *El público*, undoubtedly his greatest achievement in play-writing, had to wait until the fiftieth anniversary (1986) before it found a producer and an audience in the national theatre, and was still revolutionary fifty years on. Read together, *El público* and *Comedia sin título* provide a pioneering blueprint in the 1930s of what a future theatre might be, like the project of the Théâtre Alfred Jarry of the surrealist heretics Vitrac and Artaud, which existed more on the page of text and theory than in practice on the stage. Lorca's lesser-known 'Theatre under the Sand' rivals Vitrac's 'Incendiary Theatre' and Artaud's 'Theatre of Cruelty' or 'Alchemical Theatre'. These projects would be taken up by the dramatists and directors in exile in Paris in the 1950s and 1960s who, after the Holocaust, created the Theatre of the Absurd. Lorca's last published words in his interview (10 June 1936) with the caricaturist Bagaría, his testament as man and artist, concluded with the commandment to bid all wild things resist, particularly the flowers (the symbol of his art): 'Porque les pondrán esposas y las harán vivir sobre los vientos corrumpidos de los muertos' [Because they will put handcuffs on them and make them live on top of the putrid winds of the dead] (1819). Fernando Arrabal, on release from jail in Franco's Spain on charges of blasphemy and sedition, would salute his forerunner in the title of a play written on his return to Paris: *Et ils passèrent des menottes aux fleurs* [*And They Put Handcuffs on the Flowers*].

# 11

# Surrealism and Romanticism in Luis Cernuda's *Un río, un amor*

## JAMES VALENDER

While it is now generally agreed that the work of the French surrealists made an important impact on several Spanish poets of the 1920s, it is no easy matter to determine the exact nature and extent of this influence. Surrealism itself is a complex, even contradictory, phenomenon and the aims of surrealists in France underwent radical changes in a very short period of time. Their work as poets did not always coincide with their literary programmes (automatic writing is a salient example of the frequent contradictions to be observed between theory and practice). At all events, their main goal was not a literary one: it was to change the way we live, not simply to introduce a new poetic style, though of course for them the two issues were not entirely separate. Liberating language was one way they hoped they could help liberate mankind.

These complexities, in turn, go towards explaining some of the problems a literary historian faces when setting out to trace the possible effects of this movement beyond the border of France (in this case, in Spain). What should be the guiding criteria to determine whether a given Spanish writer can properly be termed a surrealist – the writer's ideological stance or the presence of certain linguistic qualities in the texts that they create? If we decide on the former, we run the risk of labelling virtually any revolutionary writer of the period as surrealist. Evidently, in addition to being a person convinced of the need to change the world, the writer must also share an interest in questioning conventional literary language as a means of achieving this end. But just how orthodox should this person be in making use of automatic writing? Should the writer follow step by step the recommendations set out by André Breton in his *First Manifesto*, even though other leading figures such as Paul Éluard and Louis Aragon soon played down the importance of automatism in their own work? Or should the Spanish poet be allowed (as Breton and his colleagues allowed themselves) to take inspiration rather from the famous precursors of the French movement (from Rimbaud, Lautréamont and Nerval, for example), and thus leave automatism, in the

strict sense of the word, to one side? Furthermore, how do we go about prov-
ing that such and such a text is indeed an authentic example of automatism
at work? Critics have found this a much more difficult point to prove than
it sounds. Even if such authenticity could be proved, the application of this
criterion would lead to accepting as surrealist only those texts that show a
total submission to a set of preconceived norms, a practice that, paradoxically, would be completely at odds with the creative and rebellious ideals
that Surrealism set itself. Yet the alternative line of action hardly seems any
more helpful. For if one abandons the criterion of automatic writing, one
appears to be left without any yardstick by which to judge the surrealist
quality of any given work.

In view of this complicated panorama, it is perhaps only natural that the
studies published on the question of Surrealism in Spain have taken varied
and, at times, contradictory paths. In addition, it is worth noting that the poets
usually identified with the movement likewise reacted, at the time, in very
different ways to this interpretation: Alberti and Lorca, for example, always
tended to deny any significant influence of Surrealism in their work, as did
Aleixandre (despite the fact that of all the Spanish poets of the group, he was
the one whose work came closest to Breton's ideal of automatic writing);
Prados and Cernuda, on the contrary, recognized the key role Surrealism
played in a certain moment of their careers, while Hinojosa, executed in the
first weeks of the Civil War, never left any explicit testimony other than his
poetry. In recent years research has put together the story of several failed
attempts, by Prados, Cernuda and Hinojosa, to launch a Spanish 'branch' of
the surrealist movement between 1930 and 1931.[1] However, discussion still
continues. Questions are occasionally asked as to the degree to which each of
these poets identified with the ideological goals that the movement defended.
The seriousness of Hinojosa's surrealist fervour, for example, is held in doubt
by many, who express surprise at the fact that in 1931, as a result of a personal crisis in his life, he suddenly decided to abandon writing altogether,
return to the prosperous bosom of his bourgeois family and become a
campaigner for a right-wing political party. The brevity of Prados' identification with Surrealism is attributed, on the contrary, to the rapid radicalization
of his political ideas, which soon led him (as it did Éluard and Aragon) to
leave Surrealism behind and join the Communist Party. This leaves Cernuda,

---

[1] See, for example, Alfonso Sánchez Rodríguez, '1930: Salvador Dalí en Torremolinos.
Cómo se frustra – y por qué – la aparición de una revista del surrealismo español en
Málaga', in Gabriele Morelli (ed.), *Treinta años de vanguardia española* (Seville:
Ediciones El Carro de la Nieve, 1991), 193–204; James Valender, 'Emilio Prados y el
surrealismo', in Francisco Chica (ed.), *Emilio Prados. Un hombre, un universo* (Málaga:
Centro Cultural de la Generación del 27, 2000), 301–15; and Francisco Chica, 'Luis
Cernuda y la tentación surrealista', in James Valender (ed.), *Entre la realidad y el deseo.
Luis Cernuda (1902–1963)* (Madrid: Residencia de Estudiantes / Sociedad Estatal de
Conmemoraciones Culturales, 2002), 211–33.

who, despite a brief flirtation with communism in the 1930s, was perhaps the only poet of the group to have understood and assimilated the full *moral* purpose of the surrealist movement, as Octavio Paz once suggested.[2] It was a purpose to which he would remain faithful throughout his life, even if his interest in automatic writing would prove to be short-lived.

As to the literary debts each of these writers owed to the French movement, here too there has been much discussion. Opinion has varied regarding, for example, whether to see the Surrealism of the Spanish poets as something inherited directly from the French or to interpret it as an entirely new modality that develops parallel to the movement in France in response to promptings and aspirations that are entirely Spanish. The latter approach was taken by Paul Ilie in *The Surrealist Mode in Spanish Literature*,[3] which, as the title suggests, defended the idea of the development in Spain of a movement parallel to the one in France, but rooted in the Spanish cultural tradition (Machado, Valle-Inclán, Solana, Goya). The identification of Surrealism with the grotesque is an interesting one, but the limitations of this approach are apparent in the logical (if paradoxical) decision to exclude all consideration of poets such as Cernuda and Hinojosa who, in Ilie's opinion, turned their back on the Spanish surrealist 'mode' in order to embrace the French one.[4] The opposite approach was exemplified by Brian Morris in a book that took Ilie to task for his apparent contempt for literary history.[5] For Morris the only surrealist mode was the one created by the surrealist group in France and

---

[2] Paz writes that 'para Cernuda el surrealismo fue algo más que una lección de estilo, más que una poética o una escuela de asociaciones e imágenes verbales: fue una tentativa de encarnación de la poesía en la vida, una subversión que abarcaba tanto al lenguaje como a las instituciones. Una moral y una pasión. Cernuda fue el primero, y casi el único, que comprendió e hizo suya la verdadera significación del surrealismo como movimiento de liberación – no del verso sino de la conciencia.' See Octavio Paz, 'La palabra edificante', in Derek Harris (ed.), *Luis Cernuda* (Madrid: Taurus, El escritor y la crítica, 1977), 143. For an excellent account of Cernuda's life-long allegiance to the surrealist ethic, see Jordi Doce, 'Pervivencias surrealistas en la poesía de Luis Cernuda', *Ínsula* (Madrid), no. 669 (September 2002), 9–12.

[3] Paul Ilie, *The Surrealist Mode in Spanish Literature* (Ann Arbor: University of Michigan Press, 1968).

[4] Following criticism of this kind, Ilie finally decided to include an appendix on Cernuda and Hinojosa when the book was translated into Spanish. See Ilie, 'La órbita francesa (Cernuda, Hinojosa)', *Los surrealistas españoles* (Madrid: Taurus, 1972), 293–302. Ilie was not the first to publish a monograph on the subject. Almost twenty years earlier Manuel Durán wrote a study that seems to have passed almost unnoticed: *El superrealismo en la poesía española contemporánea* (México D.F.: Universidad Nacional Autónoma de México, 1950). Another book of historical importance was Vittorio Bodini's anthology *I Poeta Surrealisti Spagnoli* (Turin: Giulio Einaudi, 1963), a work that awoke considerable interest in Spain when the introductory study was published in a Spanish translation under the title *Los poetas surrealistas españoles* (Barcelona: Tusquets, 1971).

[5] C.B. Morris, *Surrealism and Spain 1920–1936* (Cambridge: Cambridge University Press, 1972).

therefore he felt that his primary task as a literary historian was to establish
the textual evidence of the literary influence wielded by this group in certain
Spanish writers. This same aim has inspired the more recent work of Derek
Harris who takes the discussion beyond the registering of lexical borrowings
to embrace the question of the linguistic strategies that Spanish poets borrowed from their French contemporaries in their attempt to create 'a reality
that has been radically altered in defiance of the laws of logic and physics'.[6] If
Harris's book offers a more convincing approach to the subject of Surrealism
in Spanish poets, it is not only because he has managed to come to grips with
many of the formal traits that characterize the language of Surrealism, but also
because, in the process, he recognizes that surrealist language is not the only
literary influence at work in the so-called surrealist poetry of the four poets
that he analyses; that even as Spaniards discovered new forms of expression
in the work of Breton, Éluard and Aragon, they were also exploring (as
the surrealists themselves had done) the work of the major poets of the
Romantic–Symbolist tradition in which Surrealism is deeply rooted. This
dialogue between Romanticism and Surrealism expresses itself in ways that
Harris has pointed to, but which, in my opinion, have yet to be fully explored.
In what follows I will examine the specific case of Luis Cernuda, who seems
to me to exemplify many of the more interesting aspects of this twin process
of assimilation. Although Cernuda wrote two collections that are normally
considered to be surrealist-inspired, *Un río, un amor* [*A River, A Love*] (1929)
and *Los placeres prohibidos* [*The Forbidden Pleasures*] (1931), for reasons of
space my comments will be limited to the first of the two.

## Surrealism and Romanticism

While Cernuda was reading the work of the surrealists with great interest
from at least as early as 1926,[7] he did not attempt to write anything in a similar vein until the spring of 1929, when he was working as *lector* in the École
Normale in Toulouse. Taking advantage of the relative freedom that this
brief experience of living abroad gave him, he took the plunge and wrote
the first three poems of what would be his first surrealist collection, *Un río,
un amor*.

---

   [6] Derek Harris, *Metal Butterflies and Poisonous Lights: The Language of Surrealism in
Lorca, Alberti, Cernuda and Aleixandre* (Anstruther: La Sirena, 1998), 76. Harris is also
the author of an important critical edition of Cernuda's two surrealist collections: *Un río,
un amor / Los placeres prohibidos* (Madrid: Cátedra, 1999). All quotations from Cernuda's
poetry will be taken from this edition and identified by bracketed page numbers.
   [7] For a description of, and commentary on, Cernuda's readings during his early years
in Seville, as these were reflected in the orders he sent to the Madrid bookseller León
Sánchez Cuesta, see James Valender, 'Luis Cernuda y el surrealismo: primeras lecturas
(1925–1928)', in Renata Londero (ed.), *I mondi di Luis Cernuda* (Udine: Forum / Editrice
Universitaria Udinese, 2002), 31–41.

According to a statement Cernuda made in 1958 in his autobiographical essay 'Historial de un libro' [Story of a Book], the first three poems of the book (and also, one assumes, those that followed) were 'dictados por un impulso similar al que animaba a los superrealistas' [dictated by an impulse similar to that which inspired the surrealists].[8] It is interesting to note that this quickness to associate himself with the surrealist movement was not something that Cernuda seems to have demonstrated at the time he was writing these poems. The first three were published in May 1929, in the Málaga magazine *Litoral*, and were followed almost immediately by a series of translations of poems from Éluard's most recent book, *L'amour, la poésie* [*Love, Poetry*]. In the note written to accompany these translations, which were similarly published in *Litoral*, Cernuda made a brief statement as to the reasons why he admired the work of Éluard, but contrary to all that one might expect in the circumstances, he never once mentioned the surrealist movement. On the contrary, he did all he could to convince us that Éluard, like all true poets, is in fact a Romantic. That is to say, he is a poet who finds it impossible to explain the mysterious origins of the force that inspires him: 'resulta ahora ocioso, por no decir imposible, intervenir en tan misterioso dominio donde solamente nos es dado suponer pero nunca comprobar' [it is now pointless, if not impossible, to intervene in such a mysterious domain in which we are only allowed to make assumptions but never to verify them]. His life is entirely given over to trying to give expression to this hidden force, despite being aware all along of the pointlessness of such an endeavour: 'porque en definitiva nada hay que no sea fracaso, incluso, en primer lugar, la poesía [since clearly nothing exists that isn't a failure, including, and above all else, poetry]. His only solace consists in the knowledge that he has no option but to assume this destiny of a life devoted to an impossible ideal: 'Ella [la poesía], pues, es el destino de esos alguien que dicen: "tú me escogiste para ti, yo ¿qué había de hacer sino seguirte?"' [Poetry then is the destiny of those somebodies who say: 'since you chose me for yourself, what could I do but follow you?']. All of which supposes, as Cernuda himself concludes, an entirely Romantic concept both of poetry itself and of the poet's fidelity to his art: 'el resultado o residuo poético, tentativa de alguien que creyó en la poesía, es fatalmente romántico' [the poetic end-result or residue, being the effort of someone who believed in poetry, is inevitably Romantic]. Just as there is no mention of the surrealist movement, so there is no discussion either of automatic writing. Cernuda makes it clear that his own personal concern as a poet consists not so much in giving free rein to subconscious impulses but in reducing his means of expression to the barest essentials, stripping language of its material body so as to expose it in all its spiritual nudity: 'el espíritu es lo que importa' [the spirit is what matters]. He goes on to suggest that the Spanish poetic

---

[8] Luis Cernuda, 'Historial de un libro', *Obra completa II, Prosa I*, ed. Derek Harris and Luis Maristany (Madrid: Siruela, 1994), 634.

tradition is too full of empty rhetoric for it to be able to assume the full thrust of this Romantic yearning for spiritual purity. In Spain, he argues, 'Amamos o, mejor, se ama demasiado la palabra para ser románticos; sólo interesan las palabras, no la poesía'[9] [We love, or more precisely, people love words too much to be Romantic; all that matters are the words, not the poetry]. But however impervious he may think the Spanish poetic tradition is to the true Romantic spirit, Cernuda nonetheless clearly identifies his own values, and those he attributes to Éluard, with the European Romantic movement, rather than with Surrealism.

This note on Éluard was published, together with the translations, in the June 1929 issue of *Litoral*. Two months later, having just returned to Madrid from Toulouse, Cernuda published a second note, which must have seemed to many even further removed from the spirit of Surrealism than the one inspired by Éluard. The subject of this second text, which appeared in the *Revista de Occidente*, was the work of Cernuda's former teacher and mentor in Seville, Pedro Salinas, a poet, like Jiménez and Guillén, clearly aligned with the *purista* school of poetry that Cernuda had himself defended when writing the poems of *Perfil del aire* [*The Slender Air*] (1924–6) and *Egloga, elegía, oda* [*Eclogue, Elegy, Ode*] (1927–8) and from which he had subsequently distanced himself when writing *Un río, un amor*. In the light of this evolution in his own aesthetic, and particularly in view of the notable differences that separate Salinas's poetry from Éluard's, it is surprising to find Cernuda not only writing an enthusiastic review of Salinas's work, but also, in doing so, bringing the same poetic principles into discussion. Once again, what Cernuda is anxious to defend is a poetry that is as free as possible from rhetoric: 'lo esencial en esta cuestión no es la forma más o menos externa, sino el espíritu' [the essential point here is not the more or less external form but rather the spirit within]. Hence the terms in which he formulates his praise for Salinas, who is presented as an excellent example of spiritual asceticism; that is to say, as a poet able to express himself 'sin más artificio literario que el indispensable para manifestarse poéticamente' [without any more literary artifice than the minimum necessary to express himself poetically]. In this same note Cernuda develops another question touched upon in his text on Éluard: the identification of the poetic impulse with love: 'Salinas, repito, es uno de aquellos poetas para quienes el nuevo libro representa, cada vez con más nitidez y precisión, una misma aspiración poética, un unánime deseo. Han encontrado para siempre la forma perfecta de su amor. Ninguna efímera hermosura vendrá a turbar esa correspondencia apasionada, hecha de entrega total, entre el poeta y su ideal poético, entre el amante y el objeto de su amor' [Salinas, I repeat, is one of those poets for whom each new book represents, with increasing clarity and precision, the expression of a single poetic aspiration, a unanimous desire.

---

[9] Luis Cernuda, 'Paul Éluard', *Obra completa III. Prosa II*, ed. Derek Harris and Luis Maristany (Madrid: Siruela, 1994), 15–17.

Such poets have found once and for all the perfect form of their love. No ephemeral beauty can come to interrupt the passionate dialogue, reflecting total devotion, between the poet and his poetic ideal, between the lover and the object of his love].[10] Between Cernuda's tormented vision of love and the more cheerful and playful experience that characterizes Salinas's poetry there was, of course, a whole world of difference, but this was evidently not a difference that Cernuda was on this occasion interested in pointing out. In the present note he was satisfied with simply insisting, as he had done in his text on Éluard, that the genuine poet is the one who remains faithful, come what may, to the stirrings and demands of this loving impulse. Once again, the values defended by Cernuda are quite clearly Romantic ones. Surrealism has little or nothing to say.

The profoundly Romantic nature of Cernuda's poetic thought is summed up, finally, in a third note, published in the *Revista de Occidente* in October 1929, shortly after the poet had completed the last of the poems of *Un río, un amor*. The subject of Cernuda's deliberations was Jacques Vaché, a figure who had exerted a strong moral influence on Breton during the Dada years, as Breton himself had explained in 'La confession dédaigneuse' [The disdainful confession], one of the essays included in *Les Pas perdus* [*The Lost Steps*]. While Vaché never formed part of the surrealist movement himself (he died in rather mysterious circumstances in 1919), he was certainly one of the few contemporaries that the members of the French group respected and admired unreservedly. Cernuda himself was likewise in no doubt: 'El suprarrealismo, único movimiento literario de la época actual, por ser el único que sin detenerse en lo externo penetró hasta el espíritu con una inteligencia y sensibilidad propias y diferentes, fue, en parte, desencadenado por Jacques Vaché' [Surrealism, the only literary movement of worth at the present moment, since it is the only one to have gone beyond external reality to penetrate the spiritual world and to have done so in a different way, with an intelligence and sensibility all of its own, was partly sparked off by Jacques Vaché]. This opening sentence is important, not only for the defence it makes of Vaché, but also because it includes the first explicit confirmation of Cernuda's interest in Surrealism. What immediately becomes apparent, however, is that Cernuda again identifies the supposed object of his analysis (in this case, the surrealist movement) with his own Romantic vision of a spiritual reality lying beneath the material surface of verbal expression. To ensure that no one jumps to any false conclusions about the nature of this other 'spiritual' reality, he gives us the following definition:

> Esa situación espiritual, ese desorden en el orden es lo que constituye en esencia la obra suprarrealista. Conviene quizá recordar esto ahora aquí, cuando algunos menores de treinta años – aún otra frase de moda – cometen

---

[10] Luis Cernuda, 'Pedro Salinas y su poesía', *Prosa II*, 18–21.

su pequeño suprarrealismo, en realidad su eterno supraverbalismo, porque
una raza de escritores tan odiosamente verbalista – ese sentido vulgar de la
lengua, Vaché dice implícitamente y repetidamente que le falta – corrompe
cualquier posible espiritualidad con su vulgar locuacidad sin contenido
alguno posible. ¡Ah, Hamlet, príncipe mío!

[That spiritual situation, that disorder in the heart of order, is what constitutes
the essence of the surrealist work. It may be as well to bear that in mind here
in Spain, where several people under thirty – yet another phrase that is very
much in fashion – are busy perpetrating their petty Surrealism, in fact their
never-ending superverbalism; for a race of repellently verbalist writers – Vaché
implicitly and repeatedly insists that he is quite lacking in such a vulgar sense
of language – corrupts any possible spirituality with its vulgar loquacity devoid
of any possible content whatsoever. Oh, Hamlet, my prince!]

Leaving aside the allusion to Hamlet's famous soliloquy ('Words, words,
words . . . '), these lines make it clear that the spirituality Cernuda is interested in salvaging has nothing whatsoever to do with traditional religious
values. On the contrary, it is an essentially disruptive and destructive force,
bent on opposing and demolishing all existing norms: 'ese desorden en el
orden es lo que constituye en esencia la obra suprarrealista' [that disorder in
the heart of order is what constitutes the essence of the surrealist work]. The
definition could well be inspired by Cernuda's reading of Breton's *Manifesto*,
but it could also derive from Rimbaud's famous recommendation that the poet
give himself over to 'un long, immense et raisonné *dérèglement de tous les
sens*' [a long, immense and reasoned *disordering of all the senses*].[11] But in
the course of his note on Vaché it emerges, yet again, that the real source of
Cernuda's poetics goes back much further in time, to the origins of the
Romantic movement, and more specifically to Goethe. For in developing his
notion of 'ese desorden en el orden' [that disorder in the heart of order] which
inspires the surrealists, Cernuda explicitly equates it with 'una fuerza diabólica, corrosiva, tan admirable en su trágica violencia' [a diabolical, corrosive force, admirable in its tragic violence]: a mysterious, rebellious force that
looks forward to the notion of the 'poder daimónico' [daimonic power]
invoked in the poet's 'Palabras antes de una lectura' [Words before a Read-
ing], an important theoretical statement drawn up in 1935.[12]

*White Shadows*

The three brief pieces just commented on offer a surprising back-drop
against which to read the poems of *Un río, un amor* that Cernuda was writing

[11] Arthur Rimbaud, letter to Paul Demeny dated 15 May 1871, in Rimbaud,
*Oeuvre–Vie*, ed. Alain Borer (Paris: Arléa, 1991), 188.
[12] Luis Cernuda, 'Jacques Vaché', *Prosa II*, 22–4.

at the time, inviting us to interpret the surrealist features of these poems within a Romantic frame of reference. But the notes are also revealing for a different reason. In their attempts to define the nature of the poetic quest that Cernuda is embarked on, they anticipate, or echo, certain motifs that are of central importance in the poetry. As a way into the poems, let us therefore start by drawing attention to the motif which, to my mind, governs many of the principal tensions present in them: the contrast between darkness and light. In a definition of poetry included in his note on Éluard, Cernuda writes: 'Me complace, es verdad, considerar así el poema como algo cuya causa, a manera de fugacísima luz entre tinieblas eternas o sombra súbita entre la luz agobiadora, permanece escondida; ya es bastante difícil la huella incierta, falsa a veces, no importa, para buscar además el cuerpo invisible negado eternamente' [I like to think of the poem, it is true, as something whose cause, rather like the briefest ray of light penetrating the eternal darkness or like a sudden shadow emerging in the midst of an unbearable light, remains hidden from sight; its uncertain, occasionally misleading trace is in itself sufficiently difficult to detect, although that doesn't matter, for anyone to think of also trying to track down its invisible body eternally denied].[13] As the reader can observe, it is not so much a case of light substituting darkness, but rather of an impossible combination of the two realities, light suffusing the darkness or, alternatively, darkness shining through the light. This ultimate reality is unattainable because it is built on a patent contradiction that normal logic cannot conceive of and that language is even less able to express. However, this blending and reconciliation of opposed poles of experience, as symbolized by the merging of darkness and light, is the ultimate goal of the poet's search.

It is interesting to observe that in his note on Éluard Cernuda resumes the matrix of opposing ideas and experiences in a single image: 'una sombra blanca más o menos corpórea' [a more or less corporeal white shadow]. The shadow is corporeal because all verbal language must have material substance to it. Yet, what is important to the poet is the spirit that shines through the darkness, the white light that the shadow, paradoxically, allows us to glimpse. It is important to take note of this image, because it reappears in the poems of *Un río, un amor*: briefly in 'Habitación de al lado' [Room next-door] and more conspicuously in 'Sombras blancas' [White Shadows]. In his autobiographical essay 'Historial de un libro [Story of a Book], Cernuda later explained that 'Sombras blancas' was inspired by a film he saw in Paris on his visit there in the spring of 1929: *White Shadows in the South Seas*. The film apparently offers images of an ideal natural existence of the sort celebrated by Gauguin, and this probably inspired the poet to create a much more luminous vision of life than that which the majority of the poems depict. However, 'Sombras blancas' would seem to reflect not so much the scenery or the action of the film itself as the magic that the poet discovers in the words that form

---

[13] Cernuda, 'Paul Éluard', 15.

the title, words in which he appears to have found an image perfectly suited
to his contradictory vision of the world. The luminous shadow is at once the
object of the poet's sexual desire and the goal of his thirst for a poetic
absolute:

> Sombras frágiles, blancas, dormidas en la playa,
> Dormidas en su amor, en su flor de universo,
> El ardiente color de la vida ignorando
> Sobre un lecho de arena y de azar abolido.
>
> Libremente los besos desde sus labios caen
> En el mar indomable como perlas inútiles;
> Perlas grises o acaso cenicientas estrellas
> Ascendiendo hacia el cielo con luz desvanecida.    (51)
>
> [White, fragile shadows, asleep on the beach,
> Asleep in their love, in their universe flower,
> Remaining unaware of the ardent colour of life
> On a bed of sand and abolished chance.
>
> From their lips kisses freely fall
> Into the indomitable sea like useless pearls;
> Grey pearls or perhaps ashen stars
> Ascending to heaven with vanished light.]

While in other poems this ideal is evoked as something remote or unattainable, in the very first line of 'Sombras blancas' it is presented in all its dazzling
immediacy. Nevertheless, it is clear that the vision of love (or poetic harmony
and perfection) has no sooner emerged than it rapidly disappears from sight: the
*white shadow*, like everything else that exists in Cernuda's world, is carried
away by time. The *pearls* are finally *grey*, and the *stars* prove to be *ashen*. The
light, it would seem, only exists inasmuch as its emergence coincides with its
fading into the darkness. Light is simply energy wasting itself away.

Even where no mention is made of the *white shadow*, the reconciliation of
opposing elements is an essential element of the poetic vision expressed in
many other poems of the book. It is particularly evident, for example, in the
second poem, 'Quiero estar solo en el sur' [I Want to be Alone in the South],
in which we find:

> El sur es un desierto que llora mientras canta,
> Y esa voz no se extingue como pájaro muerto;
> Hacia el mar encamina sus deseos amargos
> Abriendo un eco débil que vive lentamente.
>
> En el sur tan distante quiero estar confundido.
> La lluvia allí no es más que una rosa entreabierta:
> Su niebla misma ríe, risa blanca en el viento.
> Su oscuridad, su luz son bellezas iguales.    (50)

> [The South is a desert that weeps as it sings,
> And its voice is not silenced like a dead bird:
> It heads its bitter desires in the direction of the sea
> Setting off a slight echo that lives on slowly.
>
> In the faraway South I want to lose myself.
> There the rain is just a half-opened rose:
> Its very mist laughs, white laughter in the wind.
> Its darkness, its light are equal forms of beauty.]

The poet's yearnings are projected on to a mythical South that many years later Cernuda insisted had nothing whatsoever to do with his native Andalusia. Evidently we would be wrong to try and give a strictly biographical reading, not only to these lines but to any of the poems of *Un río, un amor*. What characterizes the poet's vision is not a particular geographical location but rather a complex perception of human existence in which suffering and laughter go hand in hand, as do desire and its extinction, life and death, lightness and dark. No single form can exist without its opposite expression to complement it. The vision is a complex and contradictory one, and the striking thing is that here, as in several of the other early poems of the collection – including 'Sombras blancas' – the means used to express it are surprisingly traditional ones. As critics are quick to point out, the language relies quite heavily on conventional symbols – *a half-opened rose*; *heads its bitter desires in the direction of the sea* – while the rhythm is couched in regular alexandrine lines. There are one or two vivid examples of personification – *The South is a desert that weeps as it sings* – but there is, as yet, little sign of Cernuda's declared interest in Surrealism.

In many of the poems of *Un río, un amor* the play between darkness and light is reflected in the obsessive recurrence of nocturnal imagery, which establishes a sort of emotional back-drop against which more luminous images are projected. Several of the titles include references to darkness and the night: 'Remordimiento en traje de noche' [Remorse Dressed in Night], 'Decidme anoche' [Tell me last night], 'Oscuridad completa' [Complete Darkness] and 'Nocturno entre las musarañas' [Nocturne among the Day-Dreams]. In other poems the setting is established in the opening line: 'Como el viento a lo largo de la noche' [Like the wind throughout the night] (57); 'Aquella noche la mar no tuvo sueño' [That night the sea wasn't sleepy] (68); 'Albergue oscuro con mendigos de noche' [Dark hostel with night-time beggars] (70); and 'La noche por ser triste carece de fronteras' [The night being sad lacks frontiers] (72). However, as is evident in another first verse, 'A través de una noche en pleno día' [Through a night in the plain light of day] (61), what the poet is interested in capturing is not the substitution of darkness for light, but rather the confusion of the two. What seizes his vision is not the light nor the dark, but rather their coexistence: 'la noche deslumbrante' [the dazzling night] evoked in 'Razón de las lágrimas' [Cause for Tears] (72).

It is also interesing to note that, either because of the traditional connotations they themselves carry or because of the more original values with which the poet endows them, nearly all the light-related images that Cernuda introduces in his poems function simultaneously as symbols of the transient character of the experience evoked. This is the case, for example, in the *flowers*, *waves* or *smiles* which, like the *lamp* and *stars*, tend to be linked semantically to the light: 'Flores de luz tranquila' [Flowers of tranquil light] in the poem 'Cuerpo en pena' [Body in Torment] (53); 'las olas [que] / Abrazan a tanta luz aún viva' [the waves / That embrace so much light still living] (66); 'Sonrisas, oh miradas alegres de los labios; / Miradas, oh sonrisas de la luz triunfante' [Smiles, oh happy gazes of lips; / Gazes, oh happy smiles of triumphant light] (53). These images of light all have a marked temporal aspect that allows the poet to underpin the fleeting or inconstant nature of the world he envisions, as in the following lines from 'Linterna roja' [Red Lantern]:

> Los cuerpos palidecen como olas,
> La luz es un pretexto de la sombra,
> La risa va muriendo lentamente,
> Y mi vida también se va con ella.   (70)

> [Bodies turn pale like waves,
> Light is a pretext for shadow,
> Laughter slowly dies away,
> And my life dies away with it.]

Needless to say, if this elegiac note were the only one present, the poems would be slightly more traditional in style than they are. For the fact is that, when the poet's perception is kept at its highest intensity, the simultaneous presence of light and dark, of life and death, makes it impossible for him to distinguish between before and after, between time past and time still to come. Time destroys, but, as it destroys, it recreates . . . a repetition of what has just gone. Darkness puts an end to the day, but it also heralds the coming of dawn. Or, as Heraclitus put it: the way up and the way down are one and the same. This being so, it is impossible to make any progress in time. One is destined simply to return to one's point of departure, anguished at being constantly devoured by time, but unable to make any further sense of the universe in which one finds oneself living . . . and dying. The decay and destruction of all things are not only foreseeable and foreseen, they have already occurred; the future exists in the past, just as the past is about to be relived in the future. Hence such a disconcerting title as 'Decidme anoche' [Tell me last night], which contemplates the possibility of taking action in the present whose effects will be felt in the past, or lines such as these from 'No sé qué nombre darle en mis sueños' [I don't know what name to give it in my dreams], in which the simultaneity of different temporal perspectives produces a similarly hallucinatory effect:

El día ya cansado secaba tristemente
Las futuras auroras, remendadas
Como harapos del rey.   (74)

[The already tired day sadly hung out
The future dawns to dry, all patched
Like rags belonging to the king.]

For the poet, all future dawns are as worn out as all the past ones: they are, in fact, all one and the same occurrence. Indeed, according to this vision of life, all human endeavour, and especially all human attempts at love, are doomed to futility. All that exists is the initial illusion of transcendence; but it is an illusion that is soon spent, in a moment not of knowledge but of self-effacement or oblivion, from which the subject emerges only to find himself in exactly the same impossible existential situation as before. This process is particularly well summed up in the second stanza of 'La canción del oeste' [The Song of the Far West], in verses that Lorca, interestingly enough, chose to put at the head of the first section of his *Poeta en Nueva York* [Poet in New York]:

Noches como una sola estrella,
Sangre extraviada por las venas un día,
Furia color de amor,
Amor color de olvido,
Aptos ya solamente para triste buhardilla.   (80)[14]

[Nights like a single star,
Blood gone astray in the veins one day,
Fury the colour of love,
Love the colour of oblivion,
No longer fit for anything but a sad attic.]

Just as desire induces the poet to create an ideal pretext for his yearnings (that is to say, an idealized object of love), so this pretext makes it impossible for him to apprehend the real world. Desire intensifies its yearnings, but all it can provide, at best, is momentary oblivion. This pessimistic vision of love, and of human existence generally, finds expression elsewhere in images that insist on the circularity of the experience undergone. In 'Vieja ribera' [Shore of Ages], for example:

Unos dicen que sí, otros dicen que no;
Más sí y no son dos alas pequeñas,
Equilibrio de un cielo dentro de otro cielo,

---

[14] For a reading of these lines in the context of Lorca's poetry, see James Valender, 'Lorca y Cernuda: el zumo amargo', in Laura Dolfi (ed.), *Federico García Lorca e il suo tempo* (Rome: Bulzoni Editore, 1999), 123–35.

> Como un amor está dentro de otro,
> Como el olvido está dentro del olvido.    (79)

> [Some say yes, others say no;
> But yes and no are two small wings,
> The balance of one sky inside another sky,
> Just as one love is inside another,
> Just as one oblivion is inside another oblivion.]

No sense of progress or of achievement is possible. One can only strive vainly after an unattainable ideal, compounding one impossible love on top of another, experiencing one brief moment of oblivion that immediately melts into all the other identical moments already lived or about to be undergone.

## The Ownerless Heaven

When the first three poems of this book were published in *Litoral*, in May 1929, they appeared under the joint title of 'Cielo sin dueño' [Ownerless Heaven]. In Cernuda's correspondence the same title is used to identify the collection as a whole for several months after it had been completed. However, in March 1930 a new title emerged, when two further poems were published in a Madrid magazine under the English heading 'A Little River, a Little Love', a title which in its Spanish equivalent, 'Un río, un amor', would prove to be the definitive label under which the book would appear when it was finally published in the first edition of *La realidad y el deseo* [*Reality and Desire*] in April 1936. As I have suggested on a previous occasion, the first title, 'Cielo sin dueño', reflects a metaphysical concern that, in those first months, the poet was evidently anxious to underline: that of a world without God.[15] As a way into this theme, it may be helpful to return to the poem 'Sombras blancas' and recognize that the final stanza introduces a contradiction that is somewhat disconcerting, inasmuch as it seems to posit the existence of something that goes beyond the immediate realm of light and dark, life and death, in which the poet's world tends to move:

> Bajo la noche el mundo silencioso naufraga;
> Bajo la noche rostros fijos, muertos, se pierden.
> Sólo esas sombras blancas, oh blancas, sí, tan blancas.
> La luz también da sombras, pero sombras azules.    (51)

> [Beneath the night the silent world runs aground;
> Beneath the night expressionless, dead faces lose themselves.

---

[15] See James Valender, '*Los placeres prohibidos*: A Study of the Prose-Poems', in Salvador Jiménez-Fajardo (ed.), *The Word and the Mirror. Critical Essays on the Poetry of Luis Cernuda* (Cranberry, N.J.: Associated University Presses, 1989), 80–96.

> Just those white shadows, so white, so very very white.
> The light also throws shadows, but ones that are blue.]

The disconcerting image is that of 'sombras azules' [blue shadows]. How should we interpret them? It could well be that Cernuda is here simply playing with an image that was highly popular in the period, in Picasso's painting as well as the 'blues' of jazz musicians. Yet, irrespective of the colour chosen and its possible cultural connotations, it seems that the poet is here drawing a distinction of some importance that has to do with the ontological nature of the ideal he pursues. To all intents and purposes, he would seem to be totally absorbed (both fascinated and harrowed) by the workings of time, by the magical and lethal transformations it makes, by the constant deaths and resurrections. But is this the ultimate reality? Could it not be that beyond the creations and destructions of time there is a transcendental realm, free from the passage of time, in which all contradictions are resolved? That beyond the *white shadows* there is one that is blue?

The poet's reply to this all-important question would seem to coincide with that formulated by an important French Romantic poet that Cernuda was translating at this time: Gérard de Nerval. One of the works by Nerval that Cernuda was particularly taken by was his famous sonnet cycle 'Le Christ aux Oliviers' [Christ in the Mount of Olives], in which the French poet's anguished doubts about the existence or non-existence of God were projected on to Christ's tribulations on assuming the final sacrifice of crucifixion (Mathew 26: 36–46). Significantly, the series of sonnets in headed by a quotation from Jean-Paul Richter, the German Romantic whose *Dream* had first proclaimed the death or non-existence of God: 'Dieu est mort! le ciel est vide . . . Pleurez! enfants, vous n'avez plus de père' [God is dead! Heaven is empty . . . Weep! children, you no longer have a father]. In the first of Nerval's sonnets Christ vainly raises his arms up to heaven, 'comme font les poètes' [as poets do]. Turning to his sleeping disciples, he cries out: 'Frères, je vous trompais: abîme! abîme! abîme! Le dieu manque à l'autel où je suis la victime . . . Dieu n'est pas! Dieu n'est plus' [Brethren, I was deceiving you; abyss! abyss! abyss! God is not to be found at the altar where I am the victim . . . God does not exist! God is no longer alive].[16] For Cernuda too it would seem to be a case not only of living in a bleak meaningless universe but, more importantly, of having lost a faith previously held in the existence of God. God may or may not be alive, but what has become evident to the poet

---

[16] Gérard de Nerval, *Oeuvres*, I, ed. Albert Béguin and Jean Richer (Paris: Gallimard, 1960), 6–7. This sonnet is included in the selection of poems by Nerval that Cernuda was evidently working on in 1929–30. The other poems were 'Avril', 'Myrtho', 'Antéros', 'Delfica', 'Fantaisie', 'Epitaphe' and 'Dans les bois'. In 1933, at the front of an anthology of his poems (*La invitación a la poesía*), Cernuda set the following inscription, taken from Nerval's *Petits Châteaux de Bohème*: 'J'ai fait les premiers vers par enthousiasme de jeunesse, les seconds par amour, les derniers par désespoir'.

is that there is no one in charge of the Universe. Heaven is derelict: it is *without an owner*. In 'Destierro' [Exile], Cernuda writes:

> Ante las puertas bien cerradas,
> Sobre un río de olvido, va la canción antigua.
> Una luz lejos piensa
> Como a través de un cielo.
> Todos acaso duermen,
> Mientras él lleva su destino a solas.   (55)

> [In front of well-locked doors, carried along
> On a river of oblivion, the age-old song goes on.
> Far off a light meditates
> As if from the other side of a sky.
> They are all perhaps sleeping,
> While he bears his destiny alone.]

Man's position in the universe is presented here in terms very similar to those used by Nerval. On the one hand, he is unable to communicate with the Creator: the gates of Heaven are *well-locked*. On the other, he is unable to communicate with his fellow men: as in the case of Christ's disciples, the latter are *perhaps sleeping*. That is to say, Man finds himself irremediably alone, faced with the terrible fact of his own mortality. This much said, it must be admitted that in 'Destierro' Cernuda's attitude is less extreme than that of Nerval: God would seem to exist (*Far off a light meditates*), but is somehow cut off from the world He has created. The same idea comes across in the poem 'El caso del pájaro asesinado' [The Case of the Murdered Bird], where Cernuda speaks of 'alguien quizá triste en las piedras, / En los muros del cielo' [Someone perhaps sad in the stones, / In the walls of Heaven] (63). But whether God has ceased to exist or is simply cut off from His creation, the consequences for mankind are equally disturbing.

The loss of faith is evidently an important issue for Cernuda, for the change in consciousness that this has brought him is evoked on several occasions. Most characteristically, it is projected as an existential *fall* into the world: a fall that has occurred at an imprecise mythical moment outside of time, but which, paradoxically, has had the effect of immersing him in the mortal currents of temporal existence, since when life has never been, nor will ever be, the same. In 'Daytona', for example, the poet sadly recalls, 'Hubo un día en que el día no engañaba' (65) [There was once a time when time didn't deceive]; while the opening lines of 'Desdicha' [Misfortune] emphasize the terrible frustration he suffers as a result of acquiring this new awareness: 'Un día comprendió cómo sus brazos eran / Solamente de nubes; / Imposible con nubes estrechar hasta el fondo / Un cuerpo' (67) [One day he came to understand that his arms / Were just clouds; / With clouds it is impossible to embrace deep down / A body]. In keeping with both Romantic and surrealist doctrines, Cernuda identifies paradise lost with childhood, a world that is tenderly evoked in the opening lines of 'Vieja ribera' [Shore of Ages]: 'Tanto ha llovido desde entonces, / Entonces, cuando los dientes no eran carne, sino días / Pequeños como un río ignorante / A sus padres llamando porque siente sueño' (69) [It has rained so much since then, / Since the time his teeth were not flesh, but days / As small as an unwitting river / That calls out to its parents because it feels sleepy]. Evidently, the only possible way out of the existential impasse is to return to the intemporal form of existence the poet enjoyed before the fall, a solution he puts forward, with intense yearning, in 'No sé qué nombre darle en mis sueños' [I don't know what name to give it in my dreams]:

> Si mis ojos se cierran es para hallarte en sueños,
> Detrás de la cabeza,
> Detrás del mundo esclavizado,
> En ese país perdido
> Que un día abandonamos sin saberlo.   (74)

> [If my eyes close it is to find you in my dreams,
> Behind my head, / Behind the enslaved world,
> In that lost country / We one day leave behind us without realizing it.]

Of course, the yearning is quite impossible. Hence the embittered, angry and even destructive tone that pervades so many of the poems. Like Vaché and so many rebellious spirits before him, Cernuda is unwilling to sit back and dutifully accept the fallen condition he has inexplicably had thrust upon him. 'Nunca la palabra *caído* podrá aplicarse tan justamente' [Never could the word *fallen* be applied more appropriately], Cernuda wrote in his note on Vaché, referring not only to Vaché himself but also to Rimbaud and Lautréamont. 'No se adivine, sin embargo, nada angélico en ellos [. . .]. Al contrario, una fuerza diabólica, corrosiva, tan admirable en su trágica violencia, les animaba. Caídos, sí, mas no de cielo extranjero alguno, sino de su misma divina juventud'.[17] [Don't imagine, however, there was anything angelical about them [. . .] On the contrary, they were inspired by a diabolical, corrosive force, admirable in its tragic violence. They had certainly fallen, though not from any foreign sky, but rather from their own divine youth]. Like the three surrealist forerunners – Vaché, Rimbaud, Lautréamont – but also like Romantics such as Goethe, Blake or Nerval, Cernuda too sees himself as a fallen spirit.

At some point in 1930 Cernuda seems to have decided to do away with the title 'Cielo sin dueño' and replace it with the definitive one of 'Un río, un amor'. Why he made this change, one can only speculate. It may have been that he came to dislike the playful cleverness of the original conceit 'cielo sin

---

[17] Cernuda, 'Jacques Vaché', 22.

dueño'. It may also have been that he feared the possible misunderstanding
that might arise from the theological context suggested by this title. In any
event, it was the immanent world of epistemological confusion and erotic
frustration that Cernuda was above all interested in evoking and not the harmony of paradise lost. As he was quick to insist in his note on Éluard: 'ya es
bastante difícil la huella incierta, falsa a veces, no importa, [de la poesía en
este mundo] para buscar además el cuerpo invisible negado eternamente. Mi
subjetividad y el Creador es demasiado para un cerebro – decía Lautréamont'
[poetry's uncertain, occasionally misleading trace is in itself sufficiently difficult to detect, unimportant as that may be, for anyone to think of also trying
to track down its ever denied, invisible body. My subjectivity and the Creator
is too much for one brain – as Lautréamont put it]. In comparison with *Cielo
sin dueño*, the new title, *Un río, un amor*, is more simple and direct in its formulation, while it also places us much nearer to the existential conflict to
which the poems give expression. Its ambiguous juxtapositon of opposing
poles tells us that love can be swept away by the river of time; but it also
reminds us that love, in the form of desire, is itself a temporal reality, perhaps
the only reality that the poet is capable of experiencing. In short, *Un río, un
amor* is only one step away from the general title that in 1936 Cernuda was
to bestow on all his poetic work, *La realidad y el deseo*.

## That Disorder in the Heart of Order

Our discussion so far has centred on the Romantic vision to which the poems
of *Un río, un amor* give expression. Attention must now be given to the surrealist aspects of the poet's work. Several critics (Morris and Harris among them)
have identified numerous borrowings that demonstrate the extent of Cernuda's
familiarity with the literature produced by French surrealists, notably his readings of the important books produced by Éluard and Aragon in the 1920s.
However, rather than insist on this question of lexical appropriation, interesting though it is, I should like to examine more general aspects of Cernuda's
use of language, for I believe that it is above all in matters of rhythm and tone
that his allegiance to Surrealism can best be appreciated.

In *Metal Butterflies and Poisonous Lights* Derek Harris has convincingly
demonstrated that, while personification, symbol and allegory are systematically used to establish a fairly coherent semantic order, the poems are at the
same time studded with incongruent images that have a disorienting effect on
the reader, sowing, as it were, 'that disorder in the heart of order' that Cernuda identified with Surrealism. These incongruencies may take the form of
juxtaposing semantically incompatible lexemes, as for example in the title
'Decidme anoche' [Tell me last night] already mentioned. Alternatively, they
may be evident in the poet's decision to introduce a series of images that are
generated not by semantic analogies but simply by phonetic echoes (alliteration or assonance). While they establish sound patterns that are rhythmically

interesting, they also create oneiric worlds that are often profoundly disturbing inasmuch as they defy our usual suppositions about the natural world and,
indeed, all normal reason or logic. One particularly striking example is to be
found in the first stanza of the poem 'Nocturno entre las musarañas' [Nocturne
among the Day-Dreams], which, were it not made up almost entirely of a traditional combination of verses of seven and eleven syllables, would read very
much like a piece of automatic writing:

> Cuerpo de piedra, cuerpo triste
> Entre lanas con muros de universo,
> Idéntico a las razas cuando cumplen años,
> A los más inocentes edificios,
> A las más pudorosas cataratas,
> Blancas como la noche, en tanto la montaña
> Despedaza formas enloquecidas,
> Despedaza dolores como dedos,
> Alegrías como uñas.   (83)

> [Body of stone, sad body,
> Among woollen clothes with universe walls,
> Just like races when they have their birthdays,
> Like the most innocent of buildings,
> Like the most modest of waterfalls,
> White like the night, while the mountain
> Shatters maddened forms,
> Shatters pains like fingers,
> Joys like fingernails.]

One of the first things to disconcert the reader, as he or she enters the thicket
of these verses, is the syntax. A subject is announced right from the beginning, but we are never provided with a main verb, only a long series of
phrases in apposition, followed by a protracted adverbial clause, 'en tanto la
montaña . . . ' [while the mountain . . . ]. Even more unsettling is that the
subject itself is far from easy to apprehend. What is the 'cuerpo de piedra'
[body of stone] and why is it 'triste' [sad]? How should we interpret the
'lanas' [wool or woollens] and the 'muros de universo' [universe walls] that
supposedly define its physical situation? What are we to make of the 'razas'
[races] supposedly – but absurdly – celebrating their birthdays? Rather than
in any esoteric or mythical interpretation, the logic of these opening verses
would seem to lie, as Harris suggests, in phonetic recurrence: in the assonant
rhyme in *a–a* between 'lanas' and 'razas', for example, or in the *e–o* rhyme
between 'cuerpo', 'idéntico' and 'universo'. The initial image ('Cuerpo de
piedra') may or may not have been entirely gratuitous, but it would seem
clear that the poet makes use of sound patterns to establish his opening
theme, which at this stage is almost entirely rhythmical. The first line of the

poem offers us the somewhat unusual *tempo* of a nine-syllable line, but the versification very rapidly gravitates towards the more familiar beat of the seven and eleven syllable verses. The sixth verse, though presented as a single line of 13 syllables, is in fact split rhythmically in two by a hemistich and a comma, which invite us to read the words as two separate seven-syllable lines, a metre that is picked up again in the ninth verse. It is also interesting to note that in much the same way, though not with exactly the same immediacy, the link between images gradually ceases to be purely phonetic and comes to rely increasingly on semantic considerations. For example, in the series of anaphora dependent on the adjectival phrase 'idéntico a' [just like] – a construction reminiscent of the surrealists' predilection for 'beau comme' – the first term of comparison would seem to be suggested entirely by questions of sound ('lanas', 'razas'), but not the two that follow. On the contrary, 'edificios' [buildings] recall, semantically, the world of construction suggested by 'muros' [walls] and 'piedra' [stone]. 'Cataratas' might be another case of a rhyme in *a–a*, but the adjective 'pudorosas' [modest] undoubtedly belongs to the same semantic pool as the adjective 'inocentes' [innocent] used to define the 'edificios' in the previous line. That is to say, semantic considerations gradually affect and determine the rhythm as much as the phonetic associations do.

The image of the 'pudorosas cataratas' [modest waterfalls] in line 5 marks a turning point in this respect, awaking as it does semantic analogies with a group of ideas (water, waves, light . . . ), which, as we have seen, are absolutely central to the poet's vision of the world. In this way, in line 6 the poet suddenly gives expression to an image, which, despite its contradictory nature, sums up this vision very vividly: 'Blancas como la noche' [White like the night]. But what is this white, luminous night? On the one hand, the poem gradually develops the idea of something soft, innocent and sad – 'cuerpo triste / Entre lanas' [sad body / Among woollen clothes] – that is trying to affirm itself in vain, while at the same time it suggests the presence of something hard, impenetrable and destructive ('muros de universo') [universe walls], that is frustrating these efforts. But the curious thing is that both contrasting elements would seem to emerge from the single image with which the poem begins, 'Cuerpo de piedra, cuerpo triste' [Body of stone, sad body]. That is to say, the creative forces are seen to be one with the forces of destruction: they are all equally 'blancas como la noche' [white like the night]. Hence the ambiguity of the final lines, in which the violence of the mountain which 'Despedaza formas enloquecidas' [Shatters maddened forms] is felt to be an independent force, foreign to love, and yet at the same time to be the loving impulse itself, which, in its frustration, likewise seeks to destroy the very object of its passion: 'en tanto la montaña / Despedaza formas enloquecidas, / Despedaza dolores como dedos, Alegrías como uñas [while the mountain / Shatters maddened forms, / Shatters pains like fingers, / Joys like fingernails]. The recourse to alliteration is again very evident here, but these verses are far less vulnerable to the sort of 'semantic drift' created by similar phonetic devices in the opening lines. The stanza has gradually evolved away from the apparently gratuitous imagery with which it began, to make the reader more aware of the implications of the contradictory experience summed up in the initial image of the 'Cuerpo de piedra' [Body of stone]. Love and hate, tenderness and violence, form as inseparable a continuum as darkness and light.

Another important poetic device that Cernuda took from the surrealists was the use of *collage*. In 'Historial de un libro' he was to recall that several of the poems of *Un río, un amor* were set in motion by chance encounters with certain words, which may have formed the title of a song from the period, or the title of a film.[18] His brief visit to Paris in the spring of 1929 seems to have been especially productive in this sense:

> Dado mi gusto por los aires de jazz, recorría catálogos de discos y, a veces, un título me sugería posibilidades poéticas, como este de *I want to be alone in the South*, del cual salió el poemita segundo de la susodicha colección, y que algunos, erróneamente, interpretaron como expresión nostálgica de Andalucía.[19]

> [As a result of my taste for jazz songs, I spent time looking through record catalogues and a title would occasionally suggest poetic possibilities to me, as in the case of *I Want to be Alone in the South*, which gave rise to the second short poem in the aforementioned collection and which some people mistakenly took to be an expression of nostalgia for Andalusia.]

Another case in point was the film *White Shadows in the South Seas*, whose title, as already mentioned, inspired the poem 'Sombras blancas'. In order to exemplify the way in which Cernuda made use of these 'objets trouvés', I should like to examine a third example he mentions in 'Historial de un libro':

> Uno de los letreros de cierta película muda que vi en Toulouse, me deparó esta frase para mí curiosa: 'en (no recuerdo el nombre de lugar que se mencionaba) los caminos de hierro tienen nombre de pájaro', y la usé, como en un *collage*, dentro del poemilla 'Nevada'.[20]

> [One of the advertisements for a certain silent film I saw in Toulouse provided me with a phrase that struck me as curious: 'in (I don't remember the name of the place that was mentioned) the railways are named after birds' and I used it, as if in a *collage*, in the short poem 'Nevada'.]

---

[18] On the possible influence of film in Cernuda's surrealist poetry, see C.B. Morris, *This Loving Darkness: The Cinema and Spanish Writers 1920–1936* (Oxford: Oxford University Press, 1980), 112–21.

[19] Cernuda, 'Historial de un libro', 635.

[20] Cernuda, 'Historial de un libro', 635.

After reading this brief explanation, it comes as no surprise to discover that
the rhythm of the poem 'Nevada' consists of a series of rapid variations on the
significance implicit in these two initial images: Nevada itself, which for
Cernuda has nothing whatsoever to do with the American state of that name,
and the railways. The first stanza begins with a statement of the two motifs,
fused together in a single sentence:

> En el Estado de Nevada
> Los caminos de hierro tienen nombres de pájaro,
> Son de nieve los campos
> Y de nieve las horas.

> [In the State of Nevada / The railways are named after birds,
> The fields are composed of snow / And snow too are the hours.]

The informed reader knows that the railway image was a detail that the poet
accidentally came across in an advertisement. But what special value does it
assume in the poem? Similarly, in what sense are the fields and the hours in
Nevada composed of snow? Is the poet simply playing with words, enjoying
the absurd (if aesthetically stimulating) idea that railways should have the
same names as birds, or the equally irrational notion that the State of Nevada,
for etymological reasons, is obliged to be buried in snow? No explanation is
given here to the reader, who must simply accept these images at their face
value, and not only in these opening lines. In the stanzas that immediately follow, the poet would likewise seem to be in no hurry whatsoever to reveal their
hidden significance to the reader, heading off as he does in an apparently different direction:

> Las noches transparentes
> Abren luces soñadas
> Sobre las aguas o tejados puros
> Constelados de fiesta.

> Las lágrimas sonríen,
> La tristeza es de alas,
> Y las alas, sabemos,
> Dan amor inconstante.

> [The transparent nights / Open up dream lights
> Over the waters or pure roof-tops
> Bespangled with festivity.

> Tears smile, / Sadness has wings,
> And wings, as we know, / Are fickle in love.]

Instead of developing the opening motifs, the poet here reworks the poetic vision
that characterizes most of the poems of the collection. Hence the evocation of

'noches transparentes' [transparent nights] that are seen to open 'luces soñadas' [dreamed lights], a notion that, of course, returns us to the central image of the 'sombra blanca' [white shadow]. The subsequent stanza restates the parallel idea of the reconciliation of opposites ('Las lágrimas sonríen,/ La tristeza es de alas' [Tears smile, / Sadness has wings], as well as underlining the poet's acutely pessimistic sense of temporality, 'Y las alas, sabemos, / Dan amor inconstante' [And wings, as we know, / Are fickle in love]. Neither of these two stanzas would seem to have anything to do with the motifs introduced at the beginning of the poem. However, as the poem draws to a close, Cernuda masterfully brings all the threads together, allowing the reader to understand just how the *objets trouvés* of the opening stanza are intimately tied in to his overall vision of the world:

> Los árboles abrazan árboles,
> Una canción besa otra canción;
> Por los caminos de hierro
> Pasa el dolor y la alegría.
>
> Siempre hay nieve dormida
> Sobre otra nieve, allá en Nevada.   (56)

[The trees embrace trees, / One song kisses another song; Along the railways / Pain and joy pass by. There is always snow asleep / On other snow, over there in Nevada.]

In these final lines, the reader suddenly becomes aware that what the poet intuited, both in the name Nevada and in the railways, was a certain image of love. The two parallel lines of the railway are made to symbolize the twin impulse of pain and joy that characterize his pursuit of the erotic ideal (desire, implicitly, would seem to be symbolized by the train that hurtles passionately into the dark), while the snow-covered landscape of Nevada creates a luminous effect that, in turn, helps to create the *transparent night* in which the erotic dream is to be realized. At the same time, the two central motifs are also made to convey the notion of eternal repetition, which, as we have seen, underscores Cernuda's experience of love. Love is but a transient moment of self-effacement that dissolves away as soon as it emerges: a notion perfectly encapsulated in the image of the train pressing on into the night, leaving the fields of snow behind it. Human existence is similarly destined to push blindly on, leaving behind it experiences that, in the realm of love, are never anything more than a simple repetition of the same self-effacement. One tree embraces another, one song kisses another. Oblivion melts into oblivion just as imperceptibly as snow falls on snow.

Both *collage* and the phonetic generation of text have to do with the pace or *tempo* of the poem, with the rhythm established by the dialogue between external form (the signifier) and internal meaning (the signified). In 'Nocturno entre las musarañas' [Nocturne among the Day-Dreams], by a process of sustained analogies that constantly move between the phonetic and the semantic spheres, meaning is gradually teased out of what seems to be quite arbitrary imagery. 'Nevada', on the contrary, develops by a process of apparent digressions, or semantic leaps, whose relevance is revealed at the end of the poem, where form and meaning come together. Each poem has its own music: despondent and embittered in the 'Nocturne'; song-like in 'Nevada'.

The other question I should like to mention is that of tone, which to a large degree is a matter of the poet's relationship to the experience he creates in his poems. One of the more interesting aspects of *Un río, un amor* consists precisely of the split vision, or *desdoblamiento*, that structures so many of the poems. There is the recreation and explanation of experience that the poet attempts to project in what he writes, while at the same time there is the presence of a critical mind at work that constantly questions and undermines all validity in the world that is in the process of being created. In this way, the reader is led in two opposite directions at the same time: towards identifying with the meaning that the poet is attempting to give to his experience, and, conversely, towards accepting the poet's final insistence that it is impossible to give verbal expression to the absurd incongruencies that he sees as characterizing human existence.[21]

The impossibilty of any sort of logical epistemology is a recurrent theme in the poems. Cernuda states, for example, at the beginning of 'El caso del pájaro asesinado' [The Case of the Murdered Bird]: 'Nunca sabremos, nunca,/ Por qué razón un día / Esas luces temblaron levemente' [We shall never ever know / Why one day / Those lights slightly trembled]. After a series of frustrated attempts to give sense to life's mystery – allegorized here in the case of the murdered bird – he is finally forced to return to the initial hypothesis of Man's total inability to understand the world he lives in:

> Mas de ello hoy nada se sabe.
> Sólo un temblor de luces levemente,
> Un color de miradas en las olas o en la brisa;
> También, acaso, un miedo.
> Todo, es verdad, inseguro.   (63)

> [But we know nothing about it today.
> Just lights trembling slightly,
> A colour of gazes in the waves or in the breeze;
> Also, perhaps, a fear.
> Everything, it is true, is uncertain.]

The adverb 'acaso' [perhaps] is one that recurrs with great frequency in *Un río, un amor*, along with its synonym 'quizá' [maybe]. In both cases the adverb

---

[21] For a slightly different reading of this phenomenon, see C.B. Morris, '*Un río, un amor* and the Evasive Subjectivity of Luis Cernuda', in Salvador Jiménez-Fajardo (ed.), *The Word and the Mirror*, 44–57.

serves to distance the poet from the world he is creating, to suggest his uncertainty regarding the validity of the explanation he is offering. Other examples include the following:

> Quizá mis lentos ojos no verán más el sur
> [Maybe my slow eyes will never see the South again]
> > 'Quisiera estar solo en el sur'    (50)
> > [I Want to be Alone in the South]

> Todos acaso duermen
> [They are all perhaps sleeping]
> > 'Destierro'    (55) [Exile]

> Con vida misteriosa quizá los hombres duermen
> [Possessed of a mysterious life, the men are maybe sleeping]
> > 'Decidme anoche'    (58) [Tell me last night]

> Un grito acaso pasa disfrazado con luces
> [A cry perhaps passes by disguised with bright lights]
> > 'Decidme anoche'    (59) [Tell me last night]

> Un grito acaso pueda ofrecer más encantos
> [A cry perhaps has more charms to offer]
> > 'Mares escarlata'    (71) [Scarlet Seas]

> Acaso los amantes acuchillan estrellas,
> Acaso la aventura apague una tristeza.
> [Perhaps the lovers stab stars,
> Perhaps the adventure extinguishes a sadness.]
> > 'Razón de las lágrimas'    (72) [Cause of Tears]

The repetition of these and other adverbs, qualifying as they do the poet's faith in the world he creates, produces a deliberately blurring effect. The image is no sooner formulated than it is being erased by the critical consciousness that accompanies the poet's creative mind.

In Cernuda's note on Vaché there was, as we saw earlier, a reference to Hamlet's famous monologue decrying the vanity of words. This same theme is developed in many poems of *Un río, un amor* where the poet laments not only the insufficiency of words but also the absurd obligation that he feels to use them to give expression to his experience. 'No sé por qué he de cantar / O verter de mis labios vagamente palabras, / Palabras de mis ojos, / Palabras de mis sueños perdidos en la nieve' [I don't know why I am bound to sing / Or vaguely pour forth words from my lips, / Words from my eyes, / Words from my dreams lost in the snow], he writes, for example, in 'Oscuridad completa' [Complete darkness] (60). This is a fairly straightforward – or literal – statement of the predicament in which he finds himself. In other moments he prefers to create an allegory that demonstrates – paradoxically, through its own inadequacy – the uselessness of verbal language.[22] This is true of the poem 'Linterna roja' [Red Lantern], which, as the opening stanza suggests, attempts to project the poet's own existential situation on to a group of beggars huddling from the cold in a dark, unfriendly doss-house:

> Albergue oscuro con mendigos de noche
> Abrazando jirones de frío,
> Mientras que los grupos inertes, iguales a una flor de lluvia,
> Contemplan cómo pasa una sombra.

> [Dark hostel with night-time beggars
> Huddling in shreds of cold,
> While the lifeless groups, like a rain flower,
> Watch how a shadow passes by.]

Later in the poem, having completed the presentation of these miserable bodies with their 'ojos sin luz o de arena caída' [lightless eyes or eyes of fallen sand], the poet goes on to give what seems an explicit and clear-cut explanation of the symbolic value they supposedly hold for him, as representatives of all those who have come up against, and been destroyed by, the impossibility of love:

> Esos mendigos son los reyes sin corona
> Que buscaron la dicha más allá de la vida,
> Que buscaron la flor jamás abierta,
> Que buscaron deseos terminados en nubes.

> [These beggars are the uncrowned kings
> Who pursued happiness beyond life,
> Who pursued the never opened flower,
> Who pursued desires that ended up in clouds.]

As Derek Harris has pointed out, in these lines, with their defiant inversion of values, there is another clear echo of Cernuda's reading of *Hamlet*: 'Then are our beggars bodies, and our monarchs and outstretched heroes the beggars' shadows.'[23] But what is particularly important to note is that in the verses that follow, instead of simply restating or developing this theme, the poet allows his allegory simply to collapse. Quite suddenly, in the final stanza, the symbolism of the beggars ceases to have all validity for him, and he deliberately brings the whole construction crumbling down:

> Mas las sombras no son mendigos o coronas,
> Son los años de hastío esta noche con vida;

---

[22] This device is the subject of a penetrating study by Juan Ferraté, 'Luis Cernuda y el poder de las palabras', in Harris (ed.), *Luis Cernuda*, 269–79.
[23] *Hamlet*, 2, 2, 269. See Harris, 70.

Y mi vida es ahora un hombre melancólico
Sin saber otra cosa que su llanto.

[But the shadows are not beggars or crowns,
They are the years of boredom being alive tonight;
And my life is now a melancholy man
Who knows nothing but his tears.]

In this way the reader's attention is quite abruptly made to move away from what the poem is saying to contemplate the act of creation itself: to fix on the absurd situation in which the poet finds himself, as he struggles to express himself, using a vehicle (words) that he knows to be totally ineffective. Yet, rather than the end result, what is important to observe, once again, is the ironic dialogue between the two spheres: between the story that is being told, on the one hand, and, on the other, the faith or interest that the poet has in the story that he is telling. It is here, in this question of attitude or tone, that Cernuda exercises the critical control over language that he, rightly or wrongly, identified with the basic aims of the surrealist movement. By using language to subvert language, he attempts to penetrate the surface reality of words and release the spiritual realm hidden beneath.

In his sceptical reflection on the words he is forced to use in his poetry Cernuda is also able to give vent to the profound disgust and loathing he feels for the world around him. This last point was evidently of no small importance to Cernuda when writing the poems of *Un río, un amor*, for as he was later to insist, it was principally the rebellious, defiant attitude of the surrealists that had attracted him to their movement: 'la protesta del mismo, su rebeldía contra la sociedad y contra las bases sobre las cuales se hallaba sustentada, hallaban mi asentimiento' [their critical attitude, their rejection of society and the bases on which it was built, won my approval].[24] The poet's uneasy relationship with society is not often the subject for explicit comment in *Un río, un amor*, but it comes across instead, as Cernuda suggests, through his questioning of language and normal logic, 'las bases sobre las cuales [la sociedad] se hallaba sustentada' [the bases on which society was built]. The sarcastic opening lines of '¿Son todos felices?' [Is Everybody Happy?] constitute, in this sense, something of an exception, with their violently explicit rejection of conventional social values and their subversive defence of nihilism as the only honest attitude to adopt:

El honor de vivir con honor gloriosamente,
El patriotismo hacia la patria sin nombre,
El sacrificio, el deber de labios amarillos,
No valen un hierro devorando
Poco a poco algún cuerpo triste a causa de ellos mismos.

---

[24] Cernuda, 'Historial de un libro', 636.

Abajo pues la virtud, el orden, la miseria;
Abajo todo, todo, excepto la derrota,
Derrota hasta los dientes, hasta ese espacio helado
De una cabeza abierta en dos a través de soledades,
Sabiendo nada más que vivir es estar a solas con la muerte.    (82)

[The honour of living gloriously with honour,
The patriotic defence of the nameless homeland,
The sacrifice, the duty of yellow lips,
Are not worth an iron gradually devouring
A body that is sad precisely because of them.

Down then with virtue, order, misery;
Down with everything, everything, except defeat,
Defeat up to the teeth, up to that frozen space
Of a head split in two across horizons of solitude,
Just managing to be alive is to be on one's own with death.]


## Coda

For reasons of space, comment has here been limited to the first of Cernuda's two surrealist collections. His second book, *Los placeres prohibidos* [The Forbidden Pleasures], written in the spring of 1931, far from representing a break with *Un río, un amor*, offers a logical development of the themes and forms of expression introduced in his earlier work. The idea of a fall from childhood is taken up again and elaborated. The twin consciousness, or the tension between poet as protagonist and poet as spectator or *raconteur*, is likewise made more explicit, leading to a more complex use of the split inner vision or *desdoblamiento*. In addition, the moral and critical aspects of the poet's vision are given a wider canvass on which to express themselves, the panorama now including a transparent defence of homosexuality, a topic only very briefly alluded to in *Un río, un amor* (specifically in '¿Son todos felices?'). All these aspects, and many more, call for careful, independent examination. However, I trust that some of the points raised in the present chapter may likewise be relevant to a reading of *Los placeres prohibidos*.

In recent years Cernuda's poetry as a whole has enjoyed a growing popularity both in Spain and Latin America, but it is fair to say that critical enthusiasm has tended to centre on his later work, especially on that written during the Civil War and in exile. The earlier collections, notably the two surrealist books, have come to be considered by many as aesthetically inferior. I think this is a mistaken view, however much one admires, say, *Las nubes* [*The Clouds*] (1938–40) or *Desolación de la Quimera* [*The Disconsolate Chimera*] (1956–62). I believe that both *Un río, un amor* and *Los placeres prohibidos* reveal not only an exceptional tenacity in facing up to experiences of extreme spiritual anguish and desolation, but also a remarkable talent for creating a stimulating aesthetic order out of these experiences. As I hope to have demonstrated, Cernuda was a poet willing to open himself up to the meaningless disorder that life can often prove to be when reduced to its barest essentials. He was also a poet who was anxious to channel this disorder towards the construction of a work that was emotionally moving and artistically satisfying. This may have made him, like his contemporaries Lorca, Aleixandre and Alberti, a very unorthodox surrealist, but it also made him an exceptionally fine poet. Doubtless it is this second point that should principally interest us when we sit down to read his poetry.[25]

---

[25] The translations included in this essay are my own; they only attempt to offer a more or less literal equivalent of the original. Readers interested in more creative translations of some of the poems mentioned can consult Anthony Edkins and Derek Harris (eds), *The Poetry of Luis Cernuda* (New York: New York University Press, 1971), and Luis Cernuda, *Selected Poems*, trans. Reginald Gibbons (Berkeley: University of California Press, 1977). I am grateful to Anthony Stanton for his comments on a first draft of this essay.

# 12

# Prophet, Medium, Babbler: Voice and Identity in Vicente Aleixandre's Surrealist Poetry

## DEREK HARRIS

Luis Cernuda, who should certainly know, once described Vicente Aleixandre as the great surrealist poet that France never produced.[1] Aleixandre's dedication to surrealist writing lasted longer than most of his Spanish contemporaries influenced by Surrealism, beginning in 1928 and continuing until the outbreak of the Spanish Civil War. After commencing his writing career with a slim volume of symbolist poems, *Ambito* [*Ambience*] (1924–7), he produced four books in the surrealist manner between 1928 and 1936. After 1936 he turned to a more direct social orientation in his work, which he characterised as poetry of communication, although the presence of Surrealism returns to the two collections of poems produced before his death in 1984, *Poemas de la consumación* [*Poems of Consummation*] (1968) and *Diálogos del conocimiento* [*Dialogues of Knowing*] (1974).

The first surrealist book is *Pasión de la tierra* [*Earth Passion*] (1928–9), a collection of pieces in prose, followed by three volumes of verse, *Espadas como labios* [*Swords like Lips*] (1930–1), *La destrucción o el amor* [*Destruction or Love*] (1932–3) and *Mundo a solas* [*World Alone*] (1934–6). Aleixandre claimed the initial collection of prose pieces was the product of his reading of Freud, although he had direct access to the books and magazines of the French surrealists and was an avid reader of them. At the time and for many years later he sought to deny that he was a surrealist poet in the years leading up to 1936, initially perhaps to distance himself from the Parisian surrealists and so emphasise his own originality. This attitude was maintained after the end of the Civil War in the oppressive cultural and political climate of Franco's Spain. Aleixandre had been prevented from going into exile by serious ill health, but he shared the fate of many others in Spain who suffered internal exile. It was

---

[1] 'El superrealismo francés obtiene con Aleixandre en España lo que no obtuvo en su tierra de origen: un gran poeta', Luis Cernuda, *Estudios sobre poesía española contemporánea* (Madrid: Guadarrama, 1957), 195.

not until 1971 that he felt free publicly to accept that the label *surrealist* was applicable to his work.[2]

Aleixandre's surrealist books do indeed have a very particular character that makes them unlike the surrealist writing of any of his Spanish contemporaries. This particular character will be the focus of this chapter and will be approached by listening to the voice that speaks these poems and by looking at the perspective from which that voice delivers its utterances. The varied and often cryptic, even Gnostic nature of the voice is one of the principal factors that give to Aleixandre's poetry the strangeness of another parallel world that is one of the hallmarks of surrealism. The constant presence of this voice also focuses the poetic process on the way language functions often mysteriously to open up that other surrealist world.

The opening poem of *La destrucción o el amor*, 'Selva y mar' [Forest and Sea], begins with a focus fixed on a very distant point:

> Allá por las remotas
> luces o aceros aún no usados,
> tigres del tamaño del odio,
> leones como un corazón hirsuto,
> sangre como la tristeza aplacada, se baten con la hiena amarilla que
>     toma la forma del poniente insaciable.
> Largas cadenas que surten de los lutos,
> de lo que nunca existe,
> atan el aire como una vena, como un grito, como un reloj que se para
> cuando se estrangula algún cuello descuidado.   (117)[3]

> [Over there among the remote
> lights or still unused steels,
> tigers the size of hatred,
> lions like a hirsute heart,
> blood like soothed sadness,
> fight the yellow hyena that takes the form of the insatiable sunset.
> Long chains springing from mourning,
> from what never exists,
> tie the breeze like a vein, like a shout, like a watch that stops
> when some careless neck is strangled.]

If we leave aside the strong presence of Lautréamont in the violent and unconventional similes in these lines, what is striking here is that this liminal text

---

[2] Vicente Aleixandre, *Poesía superrealista. Antología* (Barcelona: Barral Editores, 1971). Aleixandre's prologue to this anthology is the most extensive statement of how he saw his relationship to Surrealism.

[3] Vicente Aleixandre, *Espadas como labios. La destrucción o el amor*, edición de José Luis Cano (Madrid: Clásicos Castalia, 1972). All references to Aleixandre's poetry are to this edition, unless stated otherwise. Page references are given in brackets after quotations. This edition of *Espadas como labios* respects the almost complete lack of punctuation of the book's first edition in 1932.

opens onto a world that is both physically remote and also greatly distanced from the conceptual paradigms that might normally accompany a conventional land / sea binary conjunction signified by the poem's title. The horizon is not only very far away but the expectations of that horizon have been replaced by some strange and disquietening elements. The reader has entered an extremely idiosyncratic world. This is the far edge of reason, or perhaps even beyond it.

Similar circumstances occur throughout these poems. One more example will suffice. The poem simply entitled 'Mina' [Mine], again a text from *La destrucción o el amor*, is a companion piece to 'Selva y mar', employing much of the same image cluster as that poem. The fifth and sixth stanzas of 'Mina' deal with the action of a pickaxe breaking through rock:

> Dejadme entonces, comprendiendo que el hierro es la salud de vivir,
> Que el hierro es el resplandor que de sí mismo nace y que no espera
>     sino la única tierra blanda a que herir como muerte,
> dejadme que alce un pico y que hienda a la roca,
> a la inmutable faz que las aguas no tocan.
>
> Aquí a la orilla, mientras el azul profundo casi es negro,
> mientras pasan relámpagos o luto funeral, o ya espejos,
> dejadme que se quiebre la luz sobre el acero,
> ira que, amor o muerte, se hincará en la piedra,
> en esta boca o dientes que saltarán sin luna.    (133)

> [Let me then, understanding that iron is the health of living,
> that iron is the radiance born of itself and hopes for nothing but the
>     only soft earth to wound like death,
> let me raise a pick to split the rock,
> the immutable face the waters do not touch.
>
> Here at the shore, while the blue depth is almost black,
> while lightning or funereal mourning pass by, or even mirrors,
> let the light be broken on the steel,
> wrath that will be struck, love or death, into this rock,
> into this mouth or teeth that will be knocked out moonlessly.]

This might be seen as an explanation of the remote light and still unused steels at the beginning of 'Selva y mar' [Forest and Sea] as the sparks fly from the pick striking the rock. Leaving aside again the romantic substratum here, it may be noted that although the distant point observed in 'Selva y mar' may have been reached, the viewpoint of the poem is on the inside of something and is striving to break out. It may be noted too that what we have here could be read as a speech act, as opposed to the narration – or perhaps even composition of place – found in 'Selva y mar'. The narrator of that poem finds a voice in the subsequent poem.

Something of the nature of the voice to be listened to is set out by Aleixandre in his prologue to the second edition of *La destrucción o el amor* in 1944:

El poeta, esencialmente, es el vate, el profeta. Pero su 'vaticinio' no es
vaticinio de futuro; porque puede serlo de pretérito: es profecía sin
tiempo. Iluminador, asestador de luz, golpeador de los hombres, posee-
dor de un sésamo que es, en cierto modo, misteriosamente, *palabra de
su destino*.
El poeta es un hombre que fuese más que hombre: porque es además
poeta. El poeta está lleno de 'sabiduría', pero no puede envanecerse,
porque quizá no es suya: una fuerza incognoscible, *un espíritu habla por
su boca*. Con los dos pies hincados en la tierra, una corriente prodigiosa
se condensa, se agolpa bajo sus plantas para correr por su cuerpo y *alzarse
por su lengua*. Es entonces la tierra misma, la tierra profunda, la que
llamea por ese cuerpo arrebatado. Pero otras veces el poeta ha crecido,
ahora hacia lo alto, y con su frente incrustada en un cielo *habla con voz
estelar*, con cósmica resonancia, mientras está sintiendo en el pecho el
soplo mismo de los astros.
La diminuta hormiga, la brizna de hierba dulce sobre la que su mejilla otras
veces descansa, no son distintas de él mismo. *Y el puede entenderlas y
espiar su secreto sonido*, que delicadamente es perceptible entre el rumor
del trueno.[4] (Emphasis added)

[The poet is in essence the vate, the prophet. But his prophecy is not
prophecy of the future: because it can also be of the past: it is prophecy
without time, illuminating, a wound of light, striking out at men, the
possessor of an open sesame that is in some way, mysteriously, the *word of
his destiny*.
The poet is a man that could be more than a man: because he is in addition
a poet. The poet is full of 'wisdom', but he cannot take pride in this, because
it is perhaps not his: an unknowable force, *a spirit speaks through his
mouth*. With his two feet firmly planted on the earth, a prodigious force
gathers beneath his feet, condensing to run through his body and *rise up in
his mouth*. It is then the earth itself, the depths of the earth, that flame
through that ecstatic body. But on other occasions the poet has grown tall,
now towards the heights, and with his forehead inserted in a sky *he speaks
with a stellar voice*, with cosmic resonance, while he feels in his breast the
very breath of the stars.
The tiny ant, the sweet blade of grass on which his cheek at other times
rested are not different from him himself. *And he can understand them and
discover their secret sound*, which can be heard delicately against the rum-
ble of thunder.]

These declarations loudly proclaim their Romantic pedigree, but the phrases to
which emphasis has been added provide a very specific character to the concept
of the poet within the Romantic frame of reference. The image of the
poet–prophet is at the centre of English, French and German concepts of the poet
that dominate the nineteenth century: Coleridge, Hugo, Hölderlin, Whitman. But

---

[4] Vicente Aleixandre, *Obras completas* (Madrid: Aguilar, 1968), 1444–5.

Aleixandre's poet–prophet is not a visionary, a Rimbaldian 'seer', Aleixandre's poet is a 'sayer' of oracular revelations, a source of heuristic discovery to be communicated to others. His poet is Lord Byron's babbler in the quotation used as an epigraph to *Espadas como labios*: 'What is a poet? What is he worth? / What does he do? He is a babbler.' The poet is a medium through which telluric and cosmic forces communicate verbally. But in *Espadas como labios* the language is so radically aphasic that the speech acts remain primarily as acts failing to complete the process of communication with others. The poet speaks in tongues, evidence of other powers and another realm, but does not move beyond the position of delphic revelation. This is not a case of 'in the beginning was the Word' but of the 'word' as a potential beginning to something as yet uncomprehended.

Aleixandre's poems are often speech acts. The problem is to know who, or what is speaking. There are some very odd entities who give voice in the poems, as in 'Acaba' [Die] from *Espadas como labios*, which seems to be spoken by a wasp.

> ¿Te acuerdas? He vivido dos siglos dos minutos
> sobre un pecho latiente
> he visto golondrinas de plomo triste anidadas en ojos
> y una mejilla rota por la letra
> ............................................
> Escúchame Soy la avispa imprevista
> Soy esa elevación a lo alto
> que como un ojo herido
> se va a clavar en el azul indefenso    (75–6)

> [Do you remember? I have lived two centuries two minutes
> on a pulsing breast
> I have seen sad lead swallows nesting in eyes
> and a cheek broken by a letter of the alphabet
> .............................
> Listen to me I am the unexpected wasp
> I am that elevation to the heights
> which like a wounded eye
> will thrust itself into the unguarded azure]

An insect protagonist may not be totally unusual in itself, but one that talks like that is. Note that the vespine interlocutor addresses its remarks to a listener – the Spanish text makes it clear that it is a single listener. The injunction 'escúchame' [listen to me] is repeated throughout *Espadas como labios*, but what sort of entity the receptor of that command might be is never clarified or identified. The interlocutor and the receptor remain mysteries. Even the actual speech acts themselves are problematic. On occasions it is impossible to decide if a poem is spoken by one or two voices, neither of whom are listening to each other. This is the case with the opening poem of *Espadas como labios*, entitled, significantly, 'Mi voz' [My Voice]. This poem is a

continuous speech act, but the interlocutors are unidentified and their relationship unknown. Indeed, only one of them may appear to speak, vainly
seeking a response from the other.

> He nacido una noche de verano
> entre dos pausas Háblame te escucho
> He nacido Si vieras qué agonía
> representa la luna sin esfuerzo
> He nacido Tu nombre era la dicha
> Bajo un fulgor una esperanza un ave
> Llegar llegar El mar era un latido
> el hueco de una mano una medalla tibia    (45)

> [I have just been born one summer's night
> between two pauses Speak to me I am listening to you
> I have just been born If only you could see the death throes
> the moon so effortlessly performs
> I have just been born Your name was happiness
> Under a bright light a hope a bird
> Arrive arrive The sea was a pulse
> the hollow of a hand a warm medal]

This is clearly a birth / creation poem, for the conventional trope remains
evident despite the fragmentation of the trope's components by the paratactic
syntax and the anaphora that gives a sense of breathless urgency to the utterance. But even that conventional element still visible beneath the poem's
unusual diction is given a very particular mode by the sense of immediacy
established through the use of the perfect tense. The birth has just occurred
and the evidence of that birth is the speech act now taking place. Yet this
speech act is deeply problematic. It is bounded by silence, uttered between
two pauses. The appeal for dialogue is unanswered, met also by silence. The
first comment to move outside the frame of personal reference is to death on
a suprapersonal scale. The voice speaks but the summer's night provides
evidence of an overarching mortality made manifest in what may be assumed
to be a waning moon, and this despite the initial allusion in the poem to a
Shakespearian magical circumstance. The subjunctive past tense of the verb
'vieras' [you could see] places this manifestation of death perhaps in a period
prior to the birth just announced, while happiness and all the images associated with it are located at some time in the future, indicated by the idea of
arriving, and the concept of happiness itself was conceived in the past with
reference to the name of some other individual, a name that obviously should
be capable of being spoken.

These lines exhibit a thoroughly ambiguous chronology that confirms
Aleixandre's assertion of the possibility of prophesying the past and by so
doing superseding temporality. In addition the status of the speaker of these

lines is ambiguous. The entire speech continuum could be the act of one speaker seeking to communicate with an unidentified other who has either departed, not yet come, will not or cannot reply, or who perhaps does not exist. Or the speech continuum could possibly be a dialogue, with the utterance of each of the voices indicated by the use of capital letters. In other poems of *Espadas como labios* capitals indicate a new sentence and are at the beginning of a line. But in 'Mi voz' capitals occur in mid-line without punctuation. This could indicate the change between two voices. So the initial statement of birth is met by the expression of interest and willingness to dialogue. The response of the first voice is a laconic, severely truncated repetition of the statement of birth, shorn of any possible celebratory quality. The second voice then makes the declaration about the moon and death, which is both a riposte to the birth statement and a deviation from the previous expression of willingness to dialogue. The second voice is now making a statement that separates it from the first voice, emphasising the difference in their status, since the second voice pre-exists the first and has what seems to be a more formed experience of the world. The response of the first voice is to repeat the same basic truncated statement of birth, which now rings decidedly hollow in the context of the assertion of death's dominion. The second voice then continues with what might be termed the retro-prophecy of the promise that the first voice had represented in the past. The latter then responds with the telegrammatic, temporal disarticulation in the repeated infinitive 'llegar' [to arrive],[5] the voice now reduced from laconicism to a stammer. The second voice continues the retro-prophecy with a declaration of the symbiosis between the human and the natural worlds.

If this reading of the poem as a speech act for two voices is correct then the remaining lines of the poem are spoken entirely by the first voice, as if the recognition of the ideal Romantic unity of the natural world and the human presence causes the voice to find itself again and to restate the sense of future potential in an extensive hypotactic sequence of enumerative images.

> Entonces son posibles ya las luces las caricias la piel el horizonte
> ese decir palabras sin sentido
> que ruedan como oídos caracoles
> como un lóbulo abierto que amanece
> (escucha escucha) entre la luz pisada    (45)

> [Then are already possible the lights the caresses the skin the horizon
> that saying of senseless words
> that roll along like ears snails
> like an open lobe that dawns
> (listen listen) among the trodden light]

---

[5] The term 'llegar' [to arrive] is ambiguous since the Spanish infinitive can also be used as an imperative. The translation has opted for this second meaning.

242 DEREK HARRIS

The two temporal conjunctions in the first line of this statement are in fact part of a discourse of ratiocination, recognition of the continuing validity of the retro-prophesied happiness eminent in the unseparated listing of human and natural images. The possibilities also include speech acts, which may be lacking in communicable sense but which have the vitality of natural elements and which, furthermore, are so clearly perceptible that the first voice can direct the urgently repeated injunction to listen presumably at the second voice and also, by implication, at the reader.

However, the status of both possible readings of this poem as a continuous speech act by a single voice or as a dialogue between two voices is rendered even more problematical by the possibility that one or other or both of the voices do not emanate from human sources, at least directly. The voice of the poet–prophet, in Aleixandre's Romantic cosmography, is after all not his but that of the earth or of the firmament speaking through the poet. Although the final image of 'luz pisada' [*trodden* light] does indicate the possible presence of a human footfall, the voice and the foot may not belong to the same entity. The reader cannot know whose voice is indicated by the possessive adjective of the poem's title, but the reader can ascertain the characteristics of the voice and the attitudes, interests and preoccupations the voice conveys. The reader, in short, has to obey the injunction to listen.

The poem 'Memoria' [Memory], also from the first section of *Espadas como labios*, forms a close parallel with 'Mi voz'. It is another continuous speech act embracing again two entities, although here the object of the interlocution does appear to remain silent.

> Un bosque de veleros
> Te he preguntado si vivías
> El viaje si vieras qué lisura
> sobre el brazo lejísimos al frente
> Horizonte horizonte
>       Te he mentido
> porque hay curvas Muchas
> Escúchame Mi nombre es azucena
> No humedezco los dientes que pronuncian
> aunque un viento de luz cierre los ojos
> roce la delgadez que los defiende
> Escucha escucha Soy la luz perdida
> que lapidan las aguas en el fondo
> Soy tu memoria muerta por los trópicos
> donde peces de acero sólido te imitan   (52)

> [A forest of sailing boats
> I have asked you if you were living
> The journey if you had seen that smoothness
> on the arm very far away in front
> Horizon horizon

> I have lied to you
> because there are bends Many of them
> Listen to me My name is lily
> I do not moisten the teeth that speak
> even though a wind of light should close eyes
> brush against the slimness that protects them
> Listen Listen I am the lost light
> that the waters in the depths stone
> I am your dead memory in the tropics
> where solid steel fish imitate you]

The title here might indicate another retro-prophecy, with the seascape at the poem's beginning a reminiscence of Aleixandre's childhood in Malaga. The port of Malaga at the beginning of the twentieth century would be full of sailing ships, their forests of vertical masts – a clichéd image in this context – would be set against the horizontal line of the horizon. Such a strong visual, preverbal memory would remain imprinted on the mind. This obviously is a companion text to 'Mi voz'; the same exhortation to listen, the same use of the structure si vieras . . . ' [if you had seen] to indicate the superior experience of the speaker over that of the listener, the associative link of the repeated 'horizonte horizonte' [horizon horizon] with 'llegar llegar' [arrive arrive] in the previous poem. The question 'te he preguntado si vivías' [I have asked you if] is a response to the declaration 'he nacido' [I have just been born] made in 'Mi voz', but made now from the point of view of the listener to the declaration in that poem. It might be concluded that the speaking voice in 'Memoria' belongs to the other entity in the dialogue of the book's opening poem. This conjecture apart, the voice in 'Memoria' identifies itself. It has a name, a character and even a provenance from the past. 'Azucena' [Lily] would not be an impossible name for a woman, although in the context of the poem and of the book as a whole it should perhaps be read as referring to a natural presence. It also comes from the past and from the depths of the sea, from a past period of light now gone, which justifies the past tense of 'si vieras' [*if you had* seen] in line 3, while the idea of the light being stoned by the waters of the depths adds a note of great violence that indicates the painful ongoing mutilation of some paradise lost. The final retro-prophecy that the voice is the dead memory of the listener in this text suggests that the listener has also lost a past paradise, a distant, tropical paradise now denatured by biologically dysfunctional fish that might be seen as an obverse elaboration of André Breton's concept of soluble fish. These dysfunctional creatures have as their paradigm the listener who must therefore be assumed to suffer from the same serious disadvantages. Solid metal fish could only inhabit the bottom of the sea, unable to rise towards the light. The listener is disabled or disenabled, encased in silence and unresponse. The speaker is a voice from a distant past, an echo of a life displaced. This is not even a dialogue of the deaf, but a voice beset by a radical isolation, which, although referred to in terms of distance in time and place, does not exist within any recognisable temporal continuum. This is a voice

sounding in a metaphysical wilderness and sustained only by the faintest thread
of memory that prevents it disappearing into a surrounding void of silence.

One of the areas of experience that the voice or voices seek to express is
eroticism, although not with great success. The erotic impulse is repressed,
held in a hostile incarcerating environment like the metal fish at the bottom
of the sea. One of the poems of *Espadas como labios* was originally entitled
'En el fondo del pozo' [At the Bottom of the Well], a title later changed to 'El
enterrado' [The Buried Man], which makes the incarceration a watery grave,
the realm of death. The bottom of the well is a place of motionlessness and
silence where there is no breeze to move flowers, no scent of man, no presence of the sea, all dominated by permanent cold. A suggestion of an aspiration upwards is partly represented by a voice, although this is quickly stifled.

> Acaso una voz una mano ya suelta
> un impulso hacia arriba aspira a luna
> a calma a tibieza a ese veneno
> de una almohada en la boca que se ahoga     (62–3)
>
> [Perhaps a voice a hand already detached
> an impulse to rise up aspires to moon
> to calm to coolness to that poison
> of a pillow on the choking mouth]

The circumstance of repression is clearly evident here, a repression that
manifests itself as evasion in sleep and dreams suggested by the image of the
pillow. Certainly the following stanza of the poem begins with the exclam-
ation '¡Pero dormir es tan sereno siempre!' [But sleep is always so peaceful!]
followed by a list of elements on which to sleep that includes 'una palabra
yerta' [an inert word]. Two stanzas later the speaker records some fragmen-
tary memories: 'Recuerdo que el color blanco o las formas / recuerdo que los
labios sí hasta hablaban' [I remember that the white colour or the shapes /
I remember that the lips yes even talked].

These memories lead then to an evocation of a past that is presented as a time-
less paradise when love was a living and vital presence, 'Tiempo de los suspiros
o de adórame' [Time of sighs or of please love me]. Note that the sentimentality
here acquires an erotic dimension through the free indirect speech act of
'adórame' [love me]. This presumably is the speech act that the voice aspiring to
the moon seeks to make and the speech act that is repressed in this watery interment, enclosing the incipient vitality just as the poem is enclosed by its final
detached two lines, which are cross-referenced with the poem 'Memoria': 'Una
flor de metal que así impasible / chupa de tierra un silencio o memoria' [A metal
flower that impassively / sucks a silence or memory of earth].

The second poem of *Espadas como labios* has the title 'La palabra' [The
Word] and again centres on a very problematic speech act: 'Aquí al oído voy
a decir . . . Voy a decir . . . Voy a hablarte muy bajo' [Here in your ear I am

going to say . . . I am going to say . . . I am going to speak to you very quietly]. However, it is not clear if this whispering of sweet nothings is to be taken literally or as a metaphor for a problem of interpretation that is compounded, as always in these poems, by the difficulty in ascribing an identity to either the speaker or the object of the speech act. The object of the whisperings is separated from a distant paradisiac realm and is told that this is located 'adonde no llegarán nunca tus besos' [where your kisses will never reach]. What is more the speaker would seem to be resident in some form of grave – 'en este dulce hoyo no me duermo' [In this sweet hollow I do not sleep] – in another assertion of the interment motif clearly indicated in the poem 'En el fondo del pozo' [At the bottom of the well]. The speaker also appears to be beset by a sequence of images representing pain, violence and repression: 'Mi boca suelta humo . . . Metales sin saliva . . . estas cabecitas de niño que trituro' [Smoke comes from my mouth . . . Metals without saliva . . . these tiny children's heads that I crush]. The move between declaration and suppression characterises the whole poem, and indeed the book as a whole.

> Aquí en el fondo hecho un caracol pequeñisimo
> convertido en una sonrisa arrollada
> todavía soy capaz de pronunciar el nombre
> de dar sangre
> Y. . .
> Silencio   (46–7)

> [Here in the depths turned into a tiny snail
> changed into a rolled up smile
> I am still able to pronounce the name
> to give blood
> And . . .
> Silence]

   The word the speaker is still able to pronounce and which is here cloaked in silence may be revealed in other poems. In the ending of 'El vals' [The Waltz]:

> y ese beso que estaba (en el rincón) entre dos bocas
> se convertirá en una espina
> que dispensará la muerte diciendo:
> yo os amo   (61)

> [And that kiss that was (in the corner) between two mouths
> will turn into a thorn
> that will dispense death saying:
> I love you all]

Or the word may be that which occurs at the end of 'Acaba' [Die]:

Me transformo en la pura brisa de la hora
en ese rostro azul que no piensa
en la sonrisa de la piedra
en el agua que junta los brazos mudamente
En ese instante último en que todo lo uniforme pronuncia la palabra:
ACABA[6]   (76)

[I change myself into the hour's pure breeze
into that blue unthinking face
into the stone's smile
in the water that wordlessly links arms
in that last moment when all things identical say the word
DIE]

The conflation of Eros and Thanatos is a particular feature of Aleixandre's
surrealist poems, very obviously so in *La destrucción o el amor*, and also
clearly evident in *Espadas como labios*. The word is that created by the fusion
of Eros and Thanatos, an echo of Aleixandre's reading of Freud, but a concept for the poet that still awaits a clear designation. The erotic dimension of
the word is overtly declared in 'La palabra' [The Word], immediately following the silence that breaks the flow of the speech act: 'Esta música nace de tus
senos' [This music is born of your breasts]. This is however followed by a
request for the grave to be filled with earth and a statement of the separation
between the speaker and the object of the speech act:

que sepas que mi madera es carne
que mi voz no es la tuya
y que cuando solloces tu garganta
sepa distinguir todavía
mi beso de tu esfuerzo
por pronunciar los nombres con mi lengua   (47)

[Remember that my wood is flesh
that my voice is not yours
and that when you sob your throat
can still distinguish
my kiss from your attempt
to pronounce the names with my tongue]

The other who receives the speech act will now at some future time seek
also to articulate not just the word but the words, like Adam giving the names
to the flora, fauna and all the elements of Creation. The initial speaker of the
text will then speak through the other from beyond the grave, although the
final image of the poem, 'tú pisas caracoles / que aguardaban oyendo mis dos

---

6 'Acaba' literally means 'he / she / it ends' or is the command 'end' or 'finish off'. The
translation has extrapolated the command 'die' from this last meaning.

labios' [you are treading on snails / That were waiting as they listened to my two lips], brings a destroying presence into the world that had been awaiting the prophecy uttered by the initial speaker.

All of this talk can be clearly traced back to Romantic paradigms. The closing lines of 'Acaba' quoted above are deeply imbued with Romantic nature mysticism that celebrates the symbiosis between the human and the natural. The Eros–Thanatos conflation is also Romantic. So too is the image of Adam as the namer of the universe. The nominalist focus of these poems also links with the absolute nominalism of Surrealism as proposed by Louis Aragon.[7] But a text like 'La palabra' [The Word] is not simply a restatement or re-elaboration of an old Romantic trope, although that trope is a central ingredient in the poem's construction and function. The Romantic trope, the creation myth and all that is associated with it, acts as a metaphor by means of an ironic reversal of the trope's conventional function. In Aleixandre the trope is recontextualised in a circumstance of incommunication, of loss of meaning and loss of function. There is no Word, even if there was one at the Beginning. There are words and there are voices, perhaps disembodied, non-human voices, perhaps metaphorical voices, spirits of the earth speaking though unknown entities. But coherence does not emerge from these speech acts, so there is no communication, save the communication of incoherence. The poems are all locked into a vicious circle.

The restricted and repressed expression is exemplified in the poem 'Suicidio' [Suicide], which declares itself to be the expression of the true voice of the speaker. It begins with a composition of place and the now familiar plea for the object of the speech act to take heed of what is being said.

> Carne de cristal triste intangible a las masas
> Un farol que reluce como un seno mentido
> Aquí junto a la luna mi voz es verdadera
> Escúchame callando aunque el puñal te ahogue     (99)

> [Flesh of sad glass intangible to the masses
> A lantern shining like a deceitful breast
> Here beside the moon my voice is the true one
> Listen to me and keep quiet even though the dagger stifles you]

These lines seem to be a recomposition or collage of fragments of a sentimental circumstance in a nocturnal urban setting such as that to be found in a novelette, although the lone individual in a city street is a literary figure common in surrealist texts as well as any sentimental sub-genre of narrative. However, in a surrealist context the sentimentality would have been eschewed, yet here it remains. The isolated figure in the crowd is emotionally wounded flesh, perhaps reflected in a shop window, suffering from erotic

---

[7] Louis Aragon, *Une Vague de rêves* (Paris: Gallimard, 1924), 102.

deception in the moonlight, while the entity to whom this speech is directed
is also beset by painful and threatening elements, stifling and the knife that
is the Romantic cliché for the wound of love. But the compression and the
rearranged relationships of these lines make them as a whole into a metaphor
for illusory and deceptive experience. That 'seno mentido' [deceitful breast],
the erotic equivocation, could be either the globe of the street lamp or the
moon itself, just as the 'carne de cristal' [glass flesh] could be a reflection in
a window. These lines form a complex conceit where one thing is expressed
in terms of another, where attributes are interchanged between elements of
the image, where nothing is clear or fixed. All is deceptive and illusory, even
the sentimental basis on which the fragmented images are built and
rearranged. And this deceptiveness, this illusoriness is the 'true voice' of the
speaker.

The extreme equivocalness of the opening lines is followed by a change of
point of view in an enumerative evocation of the speaker's former self:

> Yo era aquel muchacho que un día
> saliendo del fondo de sus ojos
> buscó los peces verdaderos
> que no podía ver por sus manos    (99)

> [I was that boy who one day
> emerging from the depths of his eyes
> sought the true fish
> that he could not see through his hands]

The initial allusion to Goethe's 'Da ich ein Knabe war' [Then I was a lad]
might seem to give a fixed point of literary reference to the poem, a contextualisation in convention, but this too is illusory, as the enumeration in this
stanza and the two following ones becomes increasingly illogical. We have
here again the characteristic residence in watery depths and the attempt to rise
up from there in search of some hidden ideal, breaking through surrounding
repressive forces:

> Manos de ocho montañas
> confabulación de la piedra
> dolor de sangre en risco
> insensible a los dientes    (99)

> [Hands of eight mountains
> conspiracy of stone
> pain of couched blood
> insensitive to the teeth]

What emerges from this violently repressive circumstance is speech, or at
least vocal noise:

> Bajo las estrellas de punta
> Hay gritos que se avecinan
> Bajo mi corazón de resorte
> lenguas mudas estallan
>
> [Beneath the sharpened stars
> There are gathering screams
> Beneath my heart of spring coil
> mute tongues explode]

In the circumstance of tension indicated by the image of the heart as a coiled spring the release of the kinetic energy in the heart / spring seems to take the form of a violent release of silent or silenced tongues. But the whole image remains clouded in ambiguity. The plurality of the tongues could indicate that they do not belong to the speaker, raising the possibility that they are the voices of external entities using the speaker as a medium. It also remains unclear if the tongues have broken their previous silence or maintained it, since the verb 'estallan' [explode] could be read literally and not figuratively. Shattered tongues imply a definitive silence.

The presence of vocal noise is transposed in the following stanza into an appeal for bucal activity: 'un beso / unos labios que irritan / árboles despi-adados' [just one kiss / Some lips made to itch / By pitiless trees].[8] This revelation of the erotic character of the repression sparks off an enumeration of hallucinatory images that flows on to the end of the poem, and seems to be initially provoked by an underlying visual image of objects hanging in a tree like votive offerings hanging in a church. Voices continue to sound throughout this enumeration: the 'voz insólita' of a dying muscular cramp, hair seems to be in the process of learning to speak or at least learning to speak slowly. Vocal and bucal activity inform the violent climax to the poem.

> Sangre en los peñascales sangre por los espantos
> ramas que de los pulsos crecen hasta las voces
> cuerpo que pende al viento ya sin limitaciones
> herido por las lenguas que chupan sus hormigas    (100)
>
> [Blood on the crags blood where the terrors are
> branches that grow from the pulses up to the voices
> body that hangs in the wind now limitless
> wounded by the tongues that suck its ants]

In a recapitulation of the poem's focus on erotic repression these lines clearly refer back to the imagery of mountains and blood in the poem's third

---

[8] There is complete syntactical ambiguity here. *Lips* and *trees* could be both the subject and object of the verb, although the juxtaposition with *kiss* makes *lips* the more likely subject. However, in a surrealist text everything becomes possible.

stanza and to the legs hanging on trees in stanza 6. The images of violence are contained within a context of nature mysticism, the symbiosis of the human and natural dimensions in the image of the sap / blood rising through the branches / body and the image of the body swinging in the wind beyond all bounds. But ultimately these lines are again diffused into ambiguity. The adjectival complement 'ya sin limitaciones' [now limitless] could refer both to the wind and to the body, 'herido' [wounded] could also refer to either of these nouns, while the subject of 'chupan' [suck] could be both the tongues and the ants. Such ambiguity could be a reflection of the nature mysticism that equates and combines the human and the natural. But this easy response is overwhelmed by the addition to ambiguity of the wildly unrealistic and hallucinatory imagery of the final line. The imagery here cannot be reduced to any mimetic explanation in the case of either of the readings offered by the syntactic ambiguity. The lack of mimetic control and the lack of syntactic control create a superimposition of both imagistic possibilities, a montage that constantly changes focus between the two possible combinations of the images' elements. Any hermeneutic resolution is thus made even more difficult and unlikely. The words remain senseless, non-communicating.

The question why clearly presents itself here. An autobiographical answer is perhaps too easy to give. Aleixandre's reading of Freud, whom he records having discovered in the course of writing his previous book *Pasión de la Tierra* [*Earth Passion*], would have inevitably focussed his mind on the concept of the displacement of sexual repression into disguised forms of imagistic or verbal expression. A more precise focus would have been provided by Aleixandre's homosexuality. The problems with the inabilities and difficulties of verbal communication in *Espadas como labios* [*Swords like Lips*] can then be seen simply as the projection of sexual repression, the voice of the love that dare not speak its name. But this is too simple. The incommunication here is too radical and its contextualisation in large, amorphous mythical constructs like Creation and Paradise with a very clear and very extensive Romantic substratum take the verbal difficulties beyond personal, autobiographical realms. The poems examined here are enmeshed still in the post-Romantic symbolist problems of language. The unspoken point of reference is Mallarmé's 'vide papier que la blancheur défend' [blank paper protected by its whiteness] from his poem 'Brise marine' [Sea Breeze] and that poet's much-quoted endeavour: 'donner un sens plus pur aux mots de la tribu' [to give a purer meaning to the tribe's words] contained in the poem 'Le Tombeau d'Edgar Poe'. This attitude towards language is almost the complete obverse in certain respects to the surrealist attitude to language, which makes the speaker subservient to language. Surrealist language speaks through the writer, who is simply a medium for the message, that is a Blavatskian medium rather than a McLuhan one. Surrealist language overpowers the forces of repression. But the language of at least a part of *Espadas como labios* is in a stage that might be termed pre-surrealist, not yet set free from the tyranny of controlling forces.

One of these controlling forces is represented by the paradigm of the Byronic babbler in the rubric that initiates the entire text of *Espadas como labios*, fixed at the beginning like a compass needle set in the force lines the texts follow. The lode star and the force lines flowing from it and leading back to it is that powerful Romantic substratum evident in the concept of the poet as *vate*. These poems are in thrall to a Romantic cosmography that restrains them within a conventionality from which Surrealism sought to break free. In *Espadas como labios* the speaking voice is still in large measure a Romantic prophet, medium and babbler. This is because Surrealism derives from Romantic sources – the German Romantics after all 'discovered' the unconscious – but the freedom of language production that Surrealism promoted separates surrealist texts from this basis, introducing a space between the basis and the text that can be measured by the degree of alogicality in the language. The exploitation of syntactic flexibility and alliteration helps to produce a new surrealist level of incoherence that is mined from language itself, from words set free from the tyranny of mimesis. Aleixandre's contribution to Surrealism in *Espadas como labios* is to set beside the place of alogicality a space that is often occupied by incoherence, the disability to utter. The 'senseless words' are so because conceptualisation in linguistic form is fettered by repression. Expression is disenabled, communication is not taking place; no one is listening because the speaking voice cannot give effective linguistic formulation to concepts and experiences that are denied any clarity by repression. Here the modernist 'raid on the inarticulate' is transformed from the rescue of the inarticulate into a confirmation of incommunicability, a 'surrender to the inarticulate'. The Romantic release of repression in the voice of the prophet, medium and babbler is achieved by surrealist articulation, giving that amalgam of neoromantic and surrealist dimensions that is one of the major characteristics of much of surrealist writing in Spain.

# Coda

# Spanish American Surrealist Poetry

## JASON WILSON

In 1947, Jean-Paul Sartre called Surrealism eclectic and 'Protean', and he was right. He also acknowledged that it was the sole poetic movement of the first half of the century, leading to a freedom that was 'purely imaginary'.[1] Octavio Paz described the basic surrealist terms of love, freedom, poetry and revolution as rotating signs. Such methodological confusion over the label Surrealism is increased by distance from Paris, as in the case of Surrealism in Latin America. Geographical distance is also linguistic and cultural, with the vastness of Latin America and the lack of communication between the different urban centres very marked. Distance is also temporal and determines cultural life at the periphery so that Surrealism arrived at different times in different places, with varying degrees of orthodoxy and mimicry of the well-organised Parisian movement led by André Breton from the early 1920s to his death in 1966.

For example, the Argentine doctor and populariser of surrealist orthodoxy, Aldo Pellegrini (1903–1973), echoed Breton's Surrealism as early as 1928, with the first number of his magazine *Qué*, but only effectively launched a surrealist group under Peronism in Buenos Aires in the late 1940s and 1950s. The Chilean surrealist group, led by the poet Braulio Arenas (1913–1988), corresponded with Breton while he was in exile in New York during the war, when critics like Maurice Nadeau had decreed that Breton's movement was over. Octavio Paz (1914–1998) befriended André Breton in the late 1940s in Paris, when Breton's surrealist group was displaced by the existentialist debates about political 'engagement', yet returned to Mexico with polemical surrealist views in the 1950s. I shall be returning to these historical moments, in relation to the periphery and cultural distance.

So who was or was not a surrealist is a question of adhering, or not, to Breton's decisions. However, there is the language question. In 1961, Aldo Pellegrini published his *Antología de la poesía surrealista*, with Breton's approval. The only Latin American poet included in these translations from

---

[1] Jean-Paul Sartre, *Situations, II. Qu'est-ce que la Littérature?* (Paris: Gallimard, 1948), 318, 325, 324.

the French was the Peruvian César Moro (1906–1956), a pseudonym for César Quispes Asín, who changed languages to write in French, and thus participate in the surrealist adventure from 1925 to 1933 (when he returned to Peru). He was the sole Latin American poet to write in the surrealist magazine, *Le Surréalisme au Service de la Révolution*. Jean-Louis Bédouin followed Pellegrini, also with Breton's approval, with his anthology *La Poésie surréaliste* in 1964, and he too included Moro, and this time Octavio Paz, in French.[2] So, from the viewpoint of Bretonian orthodoxy, we have only two officially approved surrealist poets, Moro and Paz. This line was developed by Stefan Baciu with his *Antología de la poesía surrealista latinoamericana*, 1974. He discounted the inclusion of Pablo Neruda *because* André Breton had decreed him not to be a proper surrealist, without having read him in Spanish.[3] Baciu included a section on 'precursors' and confined himself to the three surrealist groups of Buenos Aires, Santiago de Chile and Lima, with Paz on his own in Mexico. In 1985, Angel Pariente's *Antología de la poesía surrealista* opened the net wide, dissented from Bretonian approval (Breton had died in 1966) and among the Spanish American poets included Pablo Neruda, and even the baroque-inspired Cuban poet José Lezama Lima.

Surrealism had a massive influence on Latin American culture. Equally, Latin America attracted European surrealists like Artaud, Péret, Michaux, Caillois, Varo, Carrington and Breton to travel there. Surrealism drew many Latin American poets, writers and painters to long and short stays in Paris, some joining Breton's inner circle, like Moro, Matta, Lam, Tamayo and Paz, and some at the fringe like Carpentier, Asturias and Sabato. As a theory of poetic licence (and much formless free-verse), as a proposal about love and change, as a theory about the primacy of the imaginary, Surrealism 'touched' many different writers, and led to countless reactions against its dominating influence. Much prose-writing has been deeply shaped by surrealist affinities, for Surrealism broke down genre expectations.

I intend to explore these issues by opening with the 'Paris journey' and then deal with Latin-American surrealist clusters, where some kind of group activity took place.

## The Paris Journey: Huidobro, Vallejo, Neruda, Girondo, Pizarnik, Paz, Moro

### Huidobro

A typical example of the pilgrimage to Paris was taken by the wealthy Chilean poet Vicente Huidobro (1898–1948). He arrived in Paris in 1916, having already read Apollinaire carefully and published avant-garde poems

2  Jean-Louis Bédouin, *La Poésie surréaliste* (Paris: Éditions Seghers, 1964).
3  André Breton, *Entretiens 1913–1952* (Paris: Nouvelle Revue Française, 1952), 285.

like *El espejo de agua*, 1916. He joined Pierre Reverdy's Cubist literary magazine *Nord-Sud*, and befriended those involved, dedicating poems to Max Jacob, Blaise Cendrars, Paul Dermée, Juan Gris, Pablo Picasso and others in a who's who of the avant-garde of the time. The crucial point was, however, that he switched languages, modified his name to Vincent, and wrote in French. In fact, he sounded so like Reverdy that a public quarrel arose as to who was first in the new 'Cubist' style. Reverdy was later cited approvingly by André Breton in the first surrealist manifesto of 1924.

Huidobro knew at first hand who counted in Paris. He wrote for Tzara's *Dada* in Zurich, and co-authored a 'novel' with Hans Arp; he introduced 'Creacionismo', his own brand of the avant-garde, to Latin America, and Spain in 1918, where it became 'Ultraísmo' (propagated by Juan Larrea and Gerardo Diego). He published his long punctuation-free poem *Ecuatorial*, 1918, dedicated to Picasso, in Madrid, defining himself as the new leader proclaiming 'QUE DE COSAS HE VISTO' [How many things have I seen] and juxtaposing aeroplanes, jazz, travel in trains, the Eiffel Tower, with himself as the only genuine cosmopolitan. In 1925, vying with Breton's 1924 *Manifeste du Surréalisme*, Huidobro published his *Manifestes*, in French. Here he attacked Breton's central tenet of automatic writing as impossible; he criticised the notion of making poetry available to all as debasing poetry into a hobby; he mocked the Freud adulation: 'I find that Surrealism today is but the cello of psychoanalysis.'[4]

However, as critics have noted, Huidobro incorporated aspects of Surrealism into his modern 'epic' *Altazor o el viaje en paracaídas*, 1931, published in Madrid, with his portrait by Picasso.[5] Huidobro claimed that he begun the poem in 1919, and certainly his prologue is jokey experimentalism, as opposed to the anguished free-fall and conversations between several selves of the following seven cantos. A section was published in French in 1925. Huidobro continued to view himself as the sole poet-'mage'. He took several basic surrealist concerns on board, from dreams – 'Dadme la llave de los sueños cerrados' [give me the key to closed dreams] – to breaking free from the prison of syntax, language and memory to attain freedom – 'La matanza continua de conceptos internos . . . Liberación de todo / De la propia memoria que nos posee' [The continual killing of internal concepts . . . freedom from everything / from memory itself which possesses us] – to love-passion (Breton's *L'amour fou*), to dismissing the traditional lyric poet, 'Manicura de la lengua es el poeta . . . Matemos al poeta que nos tiene saturados' [The poet is a manicure of languagee . . . let's kill off the poet with whom we're fed up], to attacking Christianity, to the notion of liberated words, 'Jugando

[4] Vicente Huidobro, *Obras completas*, 1 (Santiago de Chile: Zig-Zag, 1964), 661–6.

[5] E. Caracciolo Trejo, *La poesía de Vicente Huidobro y la vanguardia* (Madrid: Gredos, 1974), 79–97; René de Costa, *En pos de Huidobro* (Santiago de Chile: Editorial Universitaria, 1978), 60–9.

con magnéticas palabras' [Playing with magnetic words].[6] Despite the neologisms of the final canto and its untranslatable cry of anguish, *Altazor* is not an automatic text, but does mimic mind-flow.

Later, back in Chile in the 1930s, Huidobro became mentor to a local Chilean group, insulted the Peruvian surrealist César Moro, and continued his life-long rebelling against the system that links all the surrealist poets: 'Going against the current has always pleased me'.[7] He is best defined as a catalyst of the avant-garde in general, including Surrealism, as Saúl Yurkievich noted.[8]

## Vallejo

In 1923, after 112 days in prison in Trujillo, Peru, and having published his experimental *Trilce* to a critical vacuum a year before, César Vallejo (1892–1938) left for Paris, where he died, having never returned to Peru. He was one of many Latin American writers on the fringes of Parisian café avant-garde life. With Juan Larrea, he founded *Favorables-París-Poema* in 1926 (where he published Huidobro), and moved from the Dada-ish poems written in Peru in *Trilce*, to take a critical and politicised stance against Breton's Surrealism in the late 1920s in Paris, siding with Parisian writers expelled from Surrealism's inner circle. Although Juan Larrea and André Coyné have written on Vallejo's Surrealism, Vallejo's position defining himself against Breton is self-evident, while the great earlier poetry of *Trilce* is a blend of the European avant-garde, read from Lima in the 1920s.[9]

In 1927, Vallejo wrote his poem 'Un hombre pasa con un pan al hombro' [A man passes with a loaf of bread on his shoulder], in Paris, during the Pierre Naville crisis in Surrealism, when the kind of revolution needed was split into two camps, the surrealist and the Marxist. In this poem, Vallejo opposed, in a couplet, social injustice with self-indulgent Surrealism: 'Un cojo pasa dando el brazo a un niño / ¿Voy, después a leer a André Breton?' [A cripple passes with a boy in hand / Will I then read André Breton?], clearly siding with the cripple against Breton's Surrealism.[10] In 1930, Vallejo wrote his article 'Autopsy of Surrealism', from a Marxist perspective, accusing Surrealism of being a 'recipe' for churning out poems based on Apollinaire's earlier work, witty 'salon' games, a formula, a hoax, and anarchistic and nihilist as well. When Breton joined the Communist Party, Surrealism seemed 'worthy' of being the major movement of the times, but at heart the surrealists remained

---

  6  Huidobro, 375–6.
  7  Huidobro, 702.
  8  Saúl Yurkievich, *Fundadores de la nueva poesía latinoamericana* (Barcelona: Barral Editores, 1973), 56.
  9  Stephen M. Hart, *César Vallejo* (London: Tamesis, 2002), annotated items 110 and 161.
  10  See my article exploring these issues: 'César Vallejo and "El bruto libre": Notes on the Burden of European Culture', *Romance Quarterly*, 49, no. 3 (Summer 2002), 206–14.

'incurable anarchists'. Vallejo insulted Breton himself as a 'rebel in a lawyer's office', a 'hopeless bourgeois'.[11] In essence, Vallejo was recycling the surrealist dissidents in their 1930 pamphlet *Un cadavre* attacking Breton.[12]

## Neruda

Pablo Neruda (1903–1973, pseudonym for Ricardo Neftalí Reyes Basoalto) left Chile for Paris in September 1927, on his way to an obscure consular posting in Rangoon, Burma. He had given up studying to become a teacher of French, his second collection of poems, *Veinte poemas de amor y una canción desesperada*, 1924, had appeared to critical and popular acclaim, and he had moved into experimental writing with his neglected *Tentativa del hombre infinito*, 1925. This long poem without punctuation approaches surrealist orthodoxy. It is a search for inspiration and dramatises a poetic self in conflict with the 'night', the subconscious, the past. Neruda is 'embarcado en ese viaje nocturno' [embarked in this nocturnal journey]. The introspective journey is modulated by expressions of suffocation, of entrapment: 'allí tricé mi corazón como el espejo para andar a través de mi mismo' [There I smashed my heart like the mirror to walk through myself]. Surrealist dream poetics envelops the whole poem in obscurity: 'como el sonámbulo al borde de su sueño' [like the sleepwalker at the edge of his dream].[13] Emir Rodríguez Monegal noted this poem's surrealist echoes, and Gordon Brotherston found it close to Surrealism's uninhibited automatic writing.[14] It is clear that from Chile, Neruda had been closely reading Huidobro and was testing out his own version of the avant-garde, confusedly reaching him from Europe.

Neruda was aware of his poetic dependency on Europe, and longed to travel to Paris, but as poor and working class, he did not have the means to remain in a Paris populated by fellow Latin American artists (he met Vallejo there in 1927). However, before he left Chile, Neruda had begun to write the early poems of *Residencia en la tierra 1*, 1933. During his five years of exile in the Far East, he would adapt surrealist techniques like accumulations of metaphors or random lists of nouns and objects ('chaotic enumeration'), explore dreams and fierce sexual passion in poems written out of deep loneliness while in Burma, Indonesia and Ceylon, with scant contact with Chilean culture. Neruda's own description of these difficult, personal poems is that they repeat the rhythm of waves breaking on a shore. The poems are provocative, and daring as in 'Caballero solo', where the poet feels so isolated sexually, it is as if

[11] César Vallejo, *El arte y la revolución* (Lima: Mosca Azul, 1973), 72–9.

[12] Gérard Durozoi, *History of the Surrealist Movement* (Chicago & London: University of Chicago Press, 2002), 192.

[13] Pablo Neruda, *Obras completas I* (Barcelona: Galaxia Gutenberg, 1999), 203–13.

[14] Emir Rodríguez Monegal, *El viajero inmóvil. Introducción a Pablo Neruda* (Buenos Aires: Losada, 1966), 54; Gordon Brotherston, *Latin American Poetry. Origins and Presence* (Cambridge: Cambridge University Press, 1975), 114.

there is a 'collar de palpitantes ostras sexuales' [necklace of palpitating sexual oysters] around his neck. In 'Walking About' (the title originally in English), written while passing through Buenos Aires in 1934, he writes 'Sin embargo sería delicioso / asustar a un notario con un lirio cortado / o dar muerte a una monja con un golpe de oreja' [However, it would be delicious to scare a notary with a cut lily / or kill a nun with a blow with an ear], images that epitomise surrealist provocation. In 1926, Neruda boasted, in quasi-surrealist terms, that he was an 'enemy of laws, governments and established institutions. I feel repulsion for the bourgeois and I like the life of dissatisfied people, whether artists or criminals.'[15] In 1935, Neruda published *Residencia en la tierra i y ii*, in Madrid, where the civil war caught him and abruptly changed his poetry. Years later in 1962, Neruda acknowledged that Surrealism 'freed us from numbness'; that it was 'fertile', introduced him to Lautréamont's fury, and the idea of provocation ('stick a moustache on Mona Lisa').[16] Neruda viewed Surrealism in 1920s terms, and did not mention Freud, erotic love or revolution.

By the 1950s, a card-carrying member of the Chilean Communist Party, Neruda mocked the self-indulgent surrealists, and was in turn attacked by the Chilean surrealists, and dismissed by Breton as a Stalinist. Critics of his poetry divided into Cold War positions, and the myth of the two Nerudas grew, so that the later, politicised one, admitted that he found his earlier *Residencia* poetry depressing.[17] Juan Larrea declared that Neruda was the earliest surrealist in the New World.[18]

*Girondo*

The Argentine poet Oliverio Girondo (1891–1967) first visited Paris as a child in 1900. Like many land-owning Argentines, he was brought up admiring French culture. In 1922, in Paris, he published his first collection, *Veinte poemas para ser leídos en el tranvía*, illustrated by his own water-colours. These prose poems capture the speeding up of urban life, with provocative and black-humoured erotic imagery, directly associated with the avant-garde freedom of the time. In the brief 'Apunte callejero' [Street note], the poet observes a café, some passing breasts, noisy cars, and comments 'I think how will I keep the news stands, the street lights, the pedestrians that enter into me through my pupils. I feel so full that I'm scared of bursting.'[19] In 'Exvoto', the young girls of the 'barrio' of Flores 'squeeze their legs together, frightened that their sex will fall onto the pavement' (69), while men 'ejaculate' words in their ears, and their nipples light up like

[15] Neruda, 1999, 217.
[16] Neruda, *Obras completas II* (Buenos Aires: Editorial Losada, 1968), 1094.
[17] Pablo Neruda in conversation with Rita Guibert, *The Paris Review*, no. 51, 1967.
[18] See Juan Larrea, *El surrealismo entre viejo y nuevo mundo* (México: Ediciones Cuadernos Americanos, 1944), 86–91.
[19] Oliverio Girondo, *Obras completas*, introducción de Enrique Molina (Buenos Aires: Losada, 1968), 63.

fireflies. The tone is jokey, daring, and pleased Ramón Gómez de la Serna, who became a close friend. The young Jorge Luis Borges linked these two avant-gardists, calling Girondo a 'violent man' who stares long at things and 'suddenly knocks them over with a sweep of his hand'.[20] Girondo's prologue argued that daily life was absurd, that habit killed, that Spanish had to be revived by the Spanish Americans, and saw himself at war with 'frock coats'.

Girondo was the guiding presence behind the avant-garde magazine *Martín Fierro* in Buenos Aires, which ran from 1924 to 1927, ironically named after the gaucho protest poem as an Argentine or 'criollo' version of modern writing. He wrote the manifesto in number 4 of 1924, the same year as Breton's surrealist manifesto in Paris. Here he reiterated his attack on solemnity, insisting that art had to deal with everyday life in modernised language, and that Buenos Aires was as modern as Paris. The tone is a blend of European Dada, Futurism, and early 'heroic' Surrealism, with a 'criollo', anti-European slant.

Girondo's prose poems *Espantapájaros (al alcance de todos)* [Scarecrow. Within Reach of Everybody], with its surrealist allusion to poetry being available to everybody, appeared in 1932. By the 1930s, Girondo had shifted into a surrealist position, from mocking comments on urban life to prose explorations of his inner dreamscape, a 'strolling around my brain' (167); when he blows his nose, he finds a dead cockroach in his hanky. His poems dramatise a multi-self: 'I do not have a personality, I am a cocktail, a conglomeration, a demonstration of personalities.' Girondo promoted his book by touring the city with a huge scarecrow on a cart. By 1946, Girondo had married Norah Lange, the sole woman poet in the Argentine avant-garde. Both became mentors to younger local surrealist poets like Enrique Molina and Aldo Pellegrini (the later edited an anthology of Girondo's work in 1964),[21] and his house on calle Suipacha became a meeting-place in the 1950s for an Argentine surrealist cell. By now, Girondo had invented his own kind of automatic writing: 'It is not I who write these orphaned words,' leading in 1954 to the publication of his anguished fragmenting of Spanish syntax and language, *En la masmédula*. In 1959, he translated Rimbaud into Spanish with Molina, who edited Girondo's complete poetry in 1968. Guillermo Sucre summarised Girondo as constantly 'irritating' his public; Yurkievich as 'provocatively defying social consensus'.[22]

*Pizarnik*

Alejandra Pizarnik's (1936–1972) work in poetry and prose taps into the same dicey zones as Sylvia Plath's, for it is hard not to read her work

[20] Borges in Jorge Schwartz, *Homenaje a Girondo* (Buenos Aires: Corregidor, 1987), 330–1.

[21] Aldo Pellegrini, *Oliverio Girondo* (Buenos Aires: Ediciones Culturales Argentinas, 1964).

[22] Guillermo Sucre, *La máscara, la transparencia* (Caracas: Monte Avila, 1975), 277; Yurkievich, 144.

biographically in terms of her suicide, especially because she meditated obsessively on suicide within her texts. She moved to Paris in 1960 and lived there
for four years, befriending Octavio Paz and Julio Cortázar. Her fourth book,
*Árbol de Diana*, 1962, had a prologue by Paz; she wrote on André Breton's
*Nadja*, her favourite book, and, as César Aira noted, she turned herself into a
Nadja, identifying also with Cortázar's 'la maga'.[23] She translated surrealist
poets, and absorbed the surrealist subversive tradition of meditating on the
'unthinkable', along Georges Bataille's lines. Aira located her in the surrealist
'wake', where her Surrealism was based on reading, rather than automatic
writing tapping into the 'unconscious'. Her friend Ivonne Bordelois concurred,
finding Pizarnik's work far from unconscious outpourings for she weighed
every word, obsessively.[24] Cristina Piña, her biographer, put the same another
way; her relationship with Surrealism was obvious, but her writing was far
from it.[25] Pizarnik's themes are easy to list; she circles round Rimbaud's proposition 'Je est un autre', playing with conflicting selves in her inner theatre. Key
words like 'inocencia', 'viajera', 'lila', 'noche', 'silencio', 'canto', 'mudo',
'sonámbula' [innocence, traveller, lilac, night, silence, song, dumb, sleep-
walker] and so on create a reduced, reiterated private vocabulary for her explorations around her inner vacuum: 'sólo la sed / el silencio / ningún encuentro'
[Only thirst / silence / no meeting]. This severely introspective writing can be
related to the Argentine passion for psychoanalysis; in her diary Pizarnik saw
her poetry as therapy, as mending the 'fundamental wound'.[26]

Pizarnik's most complete surrealist book was *Extracción de la piedra de
locura*, 1968 [Extraction of the Stone of Madness], written in prose, and
based on a Hieronymus Bosch painting. The collection illustrated Bataille's
theory of extreme art and transgression, creating an intensity akin to mental imbalance (and Artaud) and led to the creation of her 'poète maudite'
reputation. There is no outside world; all is a silent inner music close to
death, that she cannot grasp in language; 'Death always by my side / I listen to what it says / I only hear myself'. Her writing tried to capture this
inner absence: 'La tenebrosa luminosidad de los sueños ahogados. Agua
dolorosa' [the gloomy luminosity of drowned dreams. Painful water] (285).
Pizarnik is hard to paraphrase, and her work tends to paradox. She had
become a cult figure by the 1990s, reconceiving Breton's Surrealism as
inner vertigo. As she said about a famous phrase of Breton's, 'no, words do
not make love, they make absence'.[27] A considerable posthumous work,
based on garrulous blasphemy and satire, only confirms her late take on Surrealism.

[23] César Aira, *Alejandra Pizarnik* (Rosario: Beatriz Viterbo, 1988), 36.
[24] Ivonne Bordelois, *Correspondencia Pizarnik* (Barcelona: Seix Barral, 1998), 18.
[25] Cristina Piña, *Alejandra Pizarnik* (Buenos Aires: Planeta, 1991), 164.
[26] Bordelois, 295–7.
[27] Bordelois, 304.

*Paz*

The Mexican poet and thinker Octavio Paz (1914–1996) arrived in Paris in 1945. From 1946, when Breton himself returned from the United States, to 1951, Paz acted as cultural attaché to the Mexican embassy, while joining the surrealist inner circle. He had spent the war years in the United States, rethinking his allegiances to 'revolution'. A poem written out of his isolation from Mexican and Marxist politics is aptly titled 'Soliloquio de medianoche' [Midnight soliloquy] and suggests that God, Heaven, Friendship, Revolution and Fatherland are 'elocuentes vejigas ya sin nada' [eloquent bladders now with nothing inside].²⁸ The wording underlines Paz's cerebral poetics, based on moral criticism. Paz began his career as a poet under Juan Ramón Jiménez's 'pure' poetry, was struck by reading T.S. Eliot in translation in the experimental literary magazine *Contemporáneos* in 1931. He also explored a Marxist revolutionary position as a way out of the Mexican Revolution's impasse, so that he was chosen by Rafael Alberti, passing through Mexico, to attend the cultural congresses held during the Spanish Civil War. By the Stalin–Hitler pact, and then Trotsky's murder in Mexico City, Paz felt betrayed by the Left. Over the ensuing years, he worked out an alternative revolutionary tradition, which he confirmed as a fringe member in Breton's post-war surrealist group, adopting Breton as mentor (Breton had visited Mexico in 1938, and Mexico figured largely in the 1929 surrealist map of the world).²⁹ In Paz's lucid obituary in 1967 on Breton, first written in French, he admitted that he wrote as if Breton read over his shoulder, approving and disapproving. He argued that Breton owed more to Rousseau than de Sade. His main insight suggested that Breton's Surrealism was ethical, and not technical.

Paz did dabble in automatic writing. The section 'Trabajos del poeta' from *¿Aguila o sol?* [*Eagle or Sun*], 1951, his most surrealist collection, written in prose, conveys a literal battle with resistant language, a search for inspiration from the table where the poet is sitting at night, writing. But Paz diverted his fascination with surrealist poetics from craft and technique to what he called 'intransigent affirmations of certain values'. These can be reduced to a dynamic intertwining of poetry, love and freedom. Paz himself, in his intellectual autobiography *Itinerario*, 1991, quoted his poem 'Un poeta' of 1951 to evoke this version of Surrealism as a matter of values.³⁰ The poem, in two parts, deals with two kinds of poet; the first, in italics, is the surrealist exploring his inner space where knowing is dreaming and dreaming doing, where the vision happens, and language is no longer alienated. The second kind of poet tries to be useful, reads Marx, the newspapers, does manual work, but his tongue is swollen with politics. These poets, tied to the Communist Party, obey Stalinist dictates, like Pablo Neruda and Paul Éluard.

²⁸ Octavio Paz, *Poemas (1935–1975)* (México: Editorial Seix Barral, 1979), 113.
²⁹ Reproduced by Patrick Waldberg in *Surrealism* (London: Thames & Hudson, 1965), 25.
³⁰ Octavio Paz, *Itinerary*, trans. Jason Wilson (London: Menard Books, 1999), 73.

As I have shown before, Paz did take part in local surrealist activities, from demonstrating at Cannes over Buñuel's film *Los olvidados*, to signing collective petitions and manifestos, to being translated for the surrealist magazines like *Almanach surréaliste* and *Le Surréalisme, même*, and figuring in Bédouin's 1964 anthology. He was close friends to other faithful surrealists like Benjamin Péret (who had lived eight years in Mexico, and translated Paz's long poem *Piedra de sol* [*Sun Stone*] into French).[31] The title, *Libertad bajo palabra*, collecting his work first in 1949, then again in 1960, refers to surrealist values of freedom.

More to the point was that Surrealism's wide-ranging, 'Protean' concerns stimulated Paz to reread the Mexican poetic tradition, culminating in his fundamental revisionist anthology *Poesía en movimiento. México 1915–1966*, 1966, and with numerous essays, establishing a new canon. More crucially, Surrealism prompted Paz to explore his Mexican roots and identity, from the exotic Aztec past to the lies of the Mexican Revolution, in essays, especially the massively influential *The Labyrinth of Solitude*, 1950, written in Paris, which overlaps with his prose poems. Breton told an interviewer that Mexico was the surrealist country *par excellence*, admiring its 'still active mythic past'.[32]

The prose poem 'Obsidian Butterfly', with its erudite footnote about ancient erotic goddesses, is narrated from within this Aztec muse, a retelling of the Conquest and her conversion into a Catholic saint; she instructs the poet about love, and pleads with him to revive her through his poems: 'From my body burst images: drink in these waters and recall what you forgot when you were born' (216). This rich, magical Mexican past lent Paz an exotic cultural prestige, compared to that of a post-war Parisian surrealist. In 'Dama Huasteca', it is evident that he is the privileged one: 'Few have seen her. I will tell you her secret: by day, she is a stone at the side of the road; by night, a river that flows by man's side' (222). Speaking from inside the Mexico that the surrealists called 'surreal' granted Paz a multi-layered, unexpected persona, explored in his marvellous 'The Blue Bouquet' (actually a nightmare). It asks who the natural surreal poet is, whether the learned, urban narrator, or the Mexican peasant who unexpectedly asks for a bouquet of blue eyes (178–80).[33]

Following from his Parisian surrealist leanings, Paz, as a critic and reader, has been sensitive to surrealist poetry written by his contemporaries around Spain and Latin America. He has penned prologues and commented on works by Alejandra Pizarnik, Blanca Varela, Enrique Molina and Alvaro Mutis, as well as resuscitating Luis Cernuda's surrealist phase. Even more telling, Paz

---

[31] See Jason Wilson, *Octavio Paz* (Boston: Twayne, 1986), 27–73.
[32] Cited in Ida Rodríguez Prampolini, *El surrealismo y el arte fantástico de México* (México: UNAM, 1969), 53.
[33] See Wilson, 1986, 57–68.

explored the nature of poetry itself in surrealist terms as a process of waking creativity up, in many poems (one of his main themes in *El arco y la lira*, 1956, being the writing of poems itself, a meta-poetry). In Breton's terms, poetry is equally a defence against the misery of the times. But the ideas that most reflect his surrealist ties are to do with love, and freedom. Paz's poem 'The Prisoner' attacks the surrealist devotion to the Marquis de Sade's selfish and destructive erotic philosophy, in terms of opening the imagination to the other: 'La imaginación es la espuela del deseo, / su reino es inagotable e infinito' [Imagination is desire's spur / its kingdom is inexhaustible and infinite] (122). However, he does accept that de Sade offered surrealists an example based on 'desmesuras: tu medida de hombre' [excess; your measure as a human being]. Paz's version of love is that it can save the world, as he writes in his long Mexican-sourced poem *Piedra de sol* [*Sun Stone*], 1957, 'amar es combatir, si dos se besan / el mundo cambia, encarnan los deseos, / el pensamiento encarna, brotan alas / en las espaldas del esclavo . . . ' [To love is to fight, if two people kiss / the world changes, desires embody / thoughts embody, wings sprout / on the shoulders of slaves] (269). Here Breton's call to fuse Rimbaud and Marx and change the world and the individual is achieved through love, in the mind. Love's ecstasy is a momentary plenitude that fuses all contradictions, outside clock time and societal identity: 'no hay tú ni yo, mañana, ayer ni nombres' [There is no you nor I, nor tomorrow, yesterday or names]. Paz's Surrealism asserts quasi-religious freedoms that are not only artistic and imaginary, but that can change the reader's consciousness. These concerns promise a new society: 'The poem prepares an amorous order' (229), where Paz's admiration for Breton's utopian debt to Fourier is evident.

The opening poem of his collection *Salamandra*, 1962, following a further two-year stint in Paris from 1959 to 1961, is called 'Noche en claro' [Sleepless Night] and is dedicated to the surrealists Breton and Péret. The title also suggests how Surrealism has clarified the darkness of his times, the world wars, history in general, thanks to love and these two surrealists. The poem places the three poets in the café de Inglaterra in Paris, talking; they split up and Paz confesses that 'llevo sus palabras como un tesoro ardiendo' [I take their words like a burning treasure] (352), that these words open a meaning – 'bebo cordura' [I drink sanity] – in the city, and he experiences 'presencia', real time. In 1993, Paz sketched out a history of love in his essay *La llama doble*, from Dante, through courtly love, to Breton's *L'amour fou*, a book he called '*electric*', fifty-seven years after having first read a chapter from it in the Argentine magazine *Sur* in April 1936.[34] Breton had been exemplary in proclaiming 'unique love', for that was Surrealism's superiority; 'not of aesthetic orders but spiritual ones' (140). Paz's version of Surrealism, separating

[34] Octavio Paz, *La llama doble. Amor y erotismo* (Barcelona: Seix Barral, 1993), 139. See *Sur*, no. 19 (April 1936), 71–99, and Breton's ascent to the Tenerife peak.

the techniques from its universal values, has been immensely influential, has diverted readers away from Breton's own insistence on automatic writing as a key defining item. Evodio Escalante called this 'universalizing of Surrealism', Paz's 'master stroke'.[35]

## Moro

César Moro, born in Lima in 1903, left for Paris in 1925, as a painter. He exhibited in collective shows in Paris and Brussels, and then discovered Surrealism in 1928, to become Spanish America's most orthodox surrealist.[36] For him, Surrealism was a dynamic, interlocking system, based on 'poetry, love and rebellion'.[37] Moro published his poem 'Renommée de l'amour' in number 10 of Breton's *Le Surréalisme au Service de la Révolution* in 1933, signed the collective homage to Violette Nozière, and organised a surrealist protest against the Peruvian government (*La Mobilisation contre la guerre n'est pas la paix*, 1933), though he could not sign it as a foreigner.[38] Crucially by 1933, Moro had changed language, and wrote in French. Coyné summarised his meagre, but passionate surrealist activity as 'always scandalous' and moral.[39]

However, Moro's published poetry and essays, kept in the public eye by André Coyné, were written on his return to Latin America, where he lived in Peru from 1934 until 1938, then in Mexico until 1948, when he returned to Peru, and died there. Moro did not publish his first book until 1943, *Le Château de Grisou*, followed by *Lettre d'amour* in 1944. In Lima in 1954, he published his third book, *Trafalgar Square*, also in French, and punning on 'algues' [seaweed]. He did, however, leave a manuscript with Éluard and Breton in 1932, which, according to a letter from Éluard, cited by Coyné, got lost.[40] The rest was posthumous: *Amour à mort*, 1957, and his first in Spanish, *La tortuga ecuestre*, 1957. Only by 1970 was Moro's position established as the opening poet of Mirko Lauer and Abelardo Oquendo's anthology of Peruvian surrealist poetry, *Vuelta a la otra margen* (the title taken from a poem by Westphalen), where the editors noted the impossibility of finding Moro's poems.[41]

[35] Evodio Escalante, 'La vanguardia requisada', *Fractal*, www.fractal.com.mex, 5 of 13.

[36] See Emilio Adolfo Westphalen, 'Pinturas y dibujos de César Moro', *Amaru*, no. 9 (March 1969), 53–9.

[37] André Coyné, 'César Moro entre Lima, París y México', in Julio Ortega (ed.), *Textos en el aire* (Barcelona: Tusquets, 1974), 215–27.

[38] Alvaro Mutis translated this poem as 'Renombre del amor' in Westphalen's magazine *Amaru*, no. 9 (March 1969), 51–2.

[39] André Coyné, 'Danger-Merveille', in César Moro, *Amour à mort* (Paris: Le Cheval Marin, 1957), 7–9.

[40] André Coyné, 'Estos poemas . . . de César Moro', *Diario 16. Culturas* (21 June, 1978), II.

[41] Mirko Lauer & Abelardo Oquendo, *Vuelta a la otra margen* (Lima: Casa de la Cultura, 1970).

Moro's poems themselves are automatic texts; there is nothing picturesque or anecdotally Peruvian or Mexican about them, and all deal with the inner-scape. Américo Ferrari stressed that his fascination with words was always erotic.[42] The poems are monologues, soul diaries. Moro's angry and aggressive poems aim to upset his readers. They are often based on lists and enumerations and much word play.[43] His main exploration is of passionate love, as epitom-ised by his titles, by aphorisms like 'It is not so much freedom that we need, but to be only chained by what one loves', and by poems like 'Carta de amor', translated by fellow Peruvian surrealist Emilio Adolfo Westphalen in his liter-ary magazine *Las Moradas*, no. 5, 1948. This poem offers liberating images for physical, erotic love. It opens: 'Pienso en las holoturias angustiosas que a menudo nos rodeaban al acercarse el alba / cuando tus pies más cálidos que nidos / ardían en la noche / con una luz azul y centelleante' [I think of the anguished sea slugs which often used to surround us as dawn approached / when your feet, warmer than nests / burnt in the night / with a blue, sparkling light] (117), where the lover's body is the sole reality, where the lover's face is an 'inmóvil brasa de donde parten la vía láctea' [motionless embers from which the milky way begins], with further cosmic analogies; life without this lover is a prison of loneliness 'en que este poema me abandone' [in which this poem abandons me](118). The poem ends on a plea for more 'storms' and 'fire' as Moro's version of Breton's surrealistic aim to 'repassioner la vie', for with-out passion, life is meaningless. In a 1945 letter to Coyné, Moro asked that this poem be read 'in one single breath' to feel its excessive intimacy.[44] The poem 'Amo el amor', written in Spanish, defines love as a 'dagger', as 'rage', as 'nakedness', as a 'burning kingdom', with the lovers released into their pas-sion as 'blind sleepers' who are able to navigate freely into the last line: 'la vida oscura empieza' [dark life begins].[45] Another poem in Spanish, 'Viaje hacia la noche', published in the magazine *Las Moradas* in May 1947, written from Lima 'la horrible', echoes this inner journey into darkness and the unknown. It ends on Moro's defence of poetry 'en el silencio piramidal / mortecino parpadeante esplendor / para decirme que aún vivo / respondiendo por cada poro de mi cuerpo / al poderío de tu nombre oh Poesía' [In pyramid-like silence / dim blinking splendour / to say to me that I still live / answering with each pore of my skin / to the power of your name, oh Poetry].[46] This inner dark-ness is what Moro meant by 'living under seaweed', the fluid dream world. In another poem, 'A vista perdida', this loss of control approaches 'madness' and

[42] Américo Ferrari, 'César Moro y la libertad de la palabra', *El Nacional* (Caracas) (2 February 1969), 2.

[43] Moro, *Amour à mort*, 31 (written in 1948).

[44] André Coyné, *Vida de poeta. Algunas cartas de César Moro escritas en la ciudad de México entre 1943 y 1948* (privately published, Lisboa, 1983), no page numbers.

[45] Mirko Lauer, 42–6.

[46] César Moro, 'Viaje hacia la noche', *Las Moradas*, 1, no. 1 (May 1947), 9.

'el lenguaje afásico y sus perspectivas embriagadoras' [aphasic language and its inebriating perspectives]. In 'Oh furor . . . ', Moro defined his surrealist credo: 'I belong to darkness and wrapped in darkness I lie on a bed of light.'

Moro was an internationalist. His inner world was not topographically or culturally Peruvian. As a surrealist, he attacked Peruvian 'indigenista' painters, mocking them with the actual misery of the Peruvian Indians. 'Indigenismo' is the 'touchstone' when analysing Peru, he wrote. The attempt to create a wall of China between Peru and Europe was made ridiculous by the absence of a critical tradition in a 'stagnant' Peruvian culture and language inherited from Spain. But Peru is just part of a 'stupid continent', with Buenos Aires leading, for all that can be found there that is original is tango, while real poetry is locked in insane asylums.[47] In an interview, Moro called Latin America a 'prodigious continent, inhabited by pygmies'.

In 1934, on his return to Lima, Moro had attacked Peruvian poetry as being 'facile, improvised, bucolic-lyrical and hurried', a 'refuge' for 'cowards' (but strangely, never mentioned Vallejo). Love too was defined as being reduced to marriage and virginity (6). In this context, surrealist poetry was a 'threat', an awakening of inner impulses like violation or rape, suppressed by social consensus in a Peru as sordid as an empty barrel. The 'deadly bomb' of Surrealism would jolt Peruvian readers of poetry to 'more and more despair'. Moro mocked the bourgeois Peruvian who had translated a reference in a Dalí painting's title from 'sodomise' to 'fertilise' (9). Anything, then, to provoke the public, the 'fascist beast, the Stalinist beast'. These terms, reaching beyond Peruvian parochialism, linked Moro directly to Breton, equally lucid about Stalin. Moro praised Breton's 'priceless moral and mental quality, his faultless honesty' (26–7), terms that could be applied to himself. Only later in 1944, did Moro distance himself from Breton (57–8). In 1969, Álvaro Mutis thought that Moro's critical prose was, with Octavio Paz's, the most lucid in Latin America.[48]

Julio Ortega noted that Moro was an acute reader of surrealist poetry, especially as a translator of Péret, Reverdy, Leonora Carrington, and Artaud. Translating for Moro was a compensation 'for the exile we live in this mortal prison of Peru'.[49] He edited an anthology of surrealist poetry in Mexico in 1943, later republished in Spain in 1974. In that way, Moro also spread the surrealist gospel abroad. For Ortega, Moro's poetry is a personal version of Surrealism, based on a 'seditious' marginalisation, at odds with Parisian group belonging. Ortega equated his importance within Peru to Vallejo's.[50]

---

[47] César Moro, *Los anteojos de azufre. Prosas reunidas y presentadas por André Coyné* (Lima: Editorial San Marcos, 1958), 92.

[48] Alvaro Mutis, 'Encuentro con César Moro', *Amaru*, no. 9 (March 1969), 52.

[49] Julio Ortega, 'Prológo' to César Moro, *Versiones del surrealismo* (Barcelona: Tusquets, 1974), 7.

[50] Julio Ortega, 'Notas sobre poesía peruana contemporánea', *Eco*, no. 136 (August 1971), 394.

Mario Vargas Llosa's effeminate French teacher Fontana in his novel *La ciudad y los perros*, 1962, was in fact Moro. For Vargas Llosa, in 1958, Moro was a 'pure', authentic poet because he never commercialised his art, nor falsified his feelings, nor wrote bookish poetry reeking of tomb and 'masturbation'.[51] Moro was an exemplary rebel, 'instransigent', an 'iconoclast' wrote Westphalen in 1969.[52] Durozoi decided that his was a truly surrealist activity.[53]

## Urban centres of surrealist activities: Lima, Santiago, Buenos Aires and México

### Lima

César Moro was very active on his return to Lima in 1934. He organised the first surrealist Exhibition, with 52 paintings, of which 38 were his. A year later, with poet Emilio Adolfo Westphalen and Manuel Moreno Jimeno they published five clandestine numbers of *Cadre*, in defence of Republican Spain. Moro's friendship with Westphalen became the nucleus for Surrealism in Lima. There were further peripheral admirers, like Carlos Oquendo de Amat, with his 'Poema surrealista del elefante y del canto', but his experimental *Cinco metros de poemas*, 1927, opened like a concertina, and played with typography. Xavier Abril was also linked with Surrealism, but turned his back on Moro.

One polemical incident summarises surrealist activity in Lima. In Peru's first surrealist art show's catalogue, Moro accused Vicente Huidobro's poem 'The Giraffe' of plagiarising 'The Tree' by Luis Buñuel. Moro called Huidobro the 'veteran of arrivisme', his poetry reflected his vineyard wealth, he was the 'mouse' of modern literature, a 'nauseating literary puppet'. Huidobro, furious, responded with a vicious attack on Moro in his magazine *Vital*, in June 1935 insulting Lima's 'Rimac school', especially 'Don César Quispez, Morito de calcomanía' [little transfer moor], a 'homosexual louse' fallen from the André Breton bird's feathers. Moro was a Parisian arriviste, a prostitute who chased like a dog after the surrealists, and plagiarised Max Ernst. He fawned to his 'master' Breton, was Surrealism's sad servant, absorbed modern French art 'through his bottom', and more homophobic insults.[54] The Chilean poet and anthologist Eduardo Anguita followed suit, with racist slurs on Moro as a 'presumptuous little Indian'. In February 1936, Moro retaliated with his 'Vicente Huidobro o el

---

[51] Mario Vargas Llosa, 'Nota sobre César Moro', *Literatura*, no. 1 (February 1958), 5–6.

[52] Westphalen, 'Pinturas y dibujos de César Moro', *Amaru*, no. 9 (March 1969), 54 and 59.

[53] Durozoi, 409.

[54] *Vital*, no. 3 (June 1935), director Vicente Huidobro, no page numbers. The subtitle is 'Contra los cadáveres, los reptiles, los chismosos etc etc'.

obispo embotellado' (*the bottled bishop*, an allusion to a Huidobro poem), addressing the 'famous cretin' whose work was just a 'brothel'.

Moro's younger surrealist ally was Emilio Adolfo Westphalen (1911–2001), who published *Las ínsulas extrañas*, in 1933 (after a line from San Juan de la Cruz), and *Abolición de la muerte*, in 1935, illustrated by Moro, and then remained silent until 1979. This silence was due to never writing at will, and that the times militated against poetry.[55] With Moro, they edited one number of a surrealist magazine, *El uso de la palabra*, in December 1939. The opening page in newspaper format has a poem by Moro in Spanish, 'Varios leones al crepúsculo lamen la corteza rugosa de la tortuga ecuestre', dedicated to the surrealist painters Alice Paalen (who had illustrated Moro) and Valentine Penrose. The poem is a list, ending with the poet 'spitting' on the Angelus. Next to it, Westphalen has an essay on 'Poetry and Critics', defending authentic poetry against the ignorant, 'anodyne, sloppy' Peruvian critics who 'define, classify, give prizes, condescend, encourage' but 'poetry is elsewhere'. Westphalen picks on Luis Alberto Sánchez's anthology of Peruvian poetry as dishonest intellectually, packed with 'putrefying rhymesters'. Not even Vallejo's poetry escaped the invective ('the usual defects linger'). Westphalen particularly attacked the critics for using surrealism as an exotic adjective when they did not understand something (7), to stun their friends. These critics are simply 'fatuous' and 'stupid'. Surrealism for Westphalen is not a new school, but a human attitude.

Later, in 1947, Westphalen started *Las Moradas*, on his own, as an open-minded review, with surrealist tendencies. Moro sent pieces from Mexico in all eight numbers. Westphalen continued to edit avant-garde magazines like *Amaru* (1967–71). Towards the end of his life he collected his writings on art and poetry, and his poems.[56] He first met Moro in 1934, and added a drawing from Moro to his second book, *Abolición de la muerte*, 1935. Through Moro, he became involved with psychoanalysis, Marxism and anthropology, and helped organise the 1935 surrealist exhibition, which 'scandalised' the public. In the catalogue, he published his last poems for nearly 45 years.[57]

*Santiago de Chile*

Surrealist activities in Santiago de Chile grew around the literary magazine *Mandrágora*. It ran for seven numbers from December 1938 to 1943, first edited by the poets Braulio Arenas, Teófilo Cid (1914–1965) and Enrique

---

[55] Emilio Adolfo Westphalen, 'Contra las entrevistas', *Diario 16. Culturas* (27 May 1989), 16.

[56] Emilio Adolfo Westphalen, *Escritos varios: sobre arte y poesía* (México: Fondo de Cultura Económica) and *Bajo zarpas de la quimera: Poemas 1930–1988* (Madrid: Alianza, 1991).

[57] E. A. Westphalen, 'Poetas en la Lima de los años treinta', *Dos soledades* (Lima: Instituto Nacional de Cultura, 1974), 44.

Gómez Correa (1915–1995), and then joined by the younger ballet dancer, poet and painter Jorge Cáceres (1923–1949) and Gonzalo Rojas (1917– ). These were turbulent times in Chile, with the Popular Front in power, the Spanish Civil War raging, and Pablo Neruda dominating poetry and politics. From the first number, it was evident that Arenas was an orthodox follower of Breton's, publishing a collage poem, and praising Breton's *L'Amour fou* as ratifying his adhesion to 'poetry, revolution and love'.[58] The whole of number 4 (July 1940) of this surrealist magazine insulted Pablo Neruda who had set up the Alianza de Intelectuales, the 'Salvation army of cretins who want to save themselves saving shit' in Huidobro's words. The Alianza was run by the Chilean Communist Party and its 'jumble of uncouth police informers'. Pablo Neruda was referred to as an 'opaque fish', a 'cod' sowing hate and slander. Neruda's plagiarism of a Tagore poem, passing it off as poem 16 in *Veinte poemas de amor*, featured prominently. Arenas also recounted how he interrupted and ripped up a speech that Neruda (mocked as don Neftalí Reyes Cordero [Lamb]) was to have given on having been appointed Consul General to Chile in Mexico (July 1940). Neruda's reaction was portrayed thus: 'From the back of the trousers of the author of "Twenty Poems by Tagore and a desperate Sabat Ercasty" came a terrible stink of I smell a rat' [*gato encerrado*]. Arenas was beaten up by Neruda's 'thugs' (Neruda, however, ignored this incident in his memoirs).[59]

If Neruda was the enemy, Huidobro was the group's mentor, the 'master' in Gonzalo Rojas's words.[60] Huidobro had freed, according to the editors, Chilean poetry from 'baseness', rhetoric and prison, to make it pure and active. This yoking of Huidobro and Surrealism was curious given Huidobro's earlier dissidence from Breton. By the last number of *Mandrágora*, Enrique Gómez Correa had taken over. He dismissed his former friends Arenas and Cáceres for being nominalists, Huidobro for lacking ethical values, and Breton for thinking that Lorca was a true poet. Later, Gómez Correa lived for three years in Paris from 1949, and Magritte and Hérold illustrated his books. Just before his 'suicide' in 1949, Jorge Cáceres met Breton in Paris, and published in the surrealist review *Néon* in May 1948. Arenas edited the *Boletín surrealista* in 1941 and a further surrealist magazine, *Revista Leitmotiv*, for two numbers in 1942. He summarised this period as one where the group lived intensely, but slightly 'alejados' [distant] from their environment, trying to write a new kind of poetry.[61]

---

[58] Luis G. De Mussy, *Mandrágora. La raíz de la protesta o el refugio inconcluso* (Santiago de Chile: Universidad Finis Terrae, 2001), 135. I would like to thank Luis for giving me a copy of his work.

[59] De Mussy, 174–5.

[60] Gonzalo Rojas, 'La palabra', in Alfonso Calderón (ed.), *Antología de la poesía chilena contemporánea* (Santiago: Editorial Universitaria, 1970), 315.

[61] Braulio Arenas, 'Trayectoria de una poesía', in Alfonso Calderón, 287–90.

Klaus Meyer-Minnemann and Sergio Vergara Alarcón have studied *Mandrágora*'s role and the manifestos on 'poesía negra' written by Arenas and Gómez-Correa. They clearly establish the links with Bretonian Surrealism (dreams, the surrealist tradition, chance, automatic writing, Freud etc.), as well as their break with the Stalinist left, and all nationalist politics.[62] In 2001, Luis de Mussy published a detailed historical account of the Chilean surrealist group, and a facsimile edition of all the numbers of *Mandrágora*, and *Leitmotif*, with an excellent bibliography.

The Chilean surrealist group appeared collectively in André Breton's New York exile magazine *VVV. Almanac for 1943* in their 'Letter from Chile', with a chronology of their surrealist activities, including the surrealist exhibition of 1941 in Santiago, organised by Arenas and Cáceres, who both signed the collective *La parole est à Péret*. Arenas defined Surrealism as a 'moral passion'.[63]

Gonzalo Rojas, who published in *Mandrágora*, has emerged from that period as one of Chile's finest poets. He published *Miseria del hombre*, 1948, and then *Contra la muerte*, 1964. Over this period he lived in the desert north of Chile, inheriting the surrealist dream of fusing life and work and changing the world. He discovered the Romantic / surrealist tradition (Blake, Novalis, Rimbaud, Lautréamont etc.). But he rejected the *Mandrágora* group for being too 'afrancesado' [Frenchified], admitting that their lack of inhibition initiated him into the freedom that poetry grants.[64] In conversation, Rojas praised the *Mandrágora* group's 'anti-village' energy; that they were a seed, 'something boiling and cheeky, quite uncompromising', but they remained too 'bookish'.[65] Rojas's poetic credo reflects the inner world: 'Vamos sonámbulos / en el oficio ciego' [We sleepwalk / in the blind craft], or 'nadando en la marea del instinto' [swimming in the tide of instinct], or 'la madre de los sueños, donde empieza / toda sabiduría' [the mother of dreams where all wisdom begins]. Breton was one of Rojas's 'austere illumined prophets', according to Enrique Lihn.[66]

*Buenos Aires*

Graciela de Sola has studied the development of Surrealism in Buenos Aires from Aldo Pellegrini's two numbers of his surrealist magazine *Qué*, in 1928, to the 1940s, when surrealist ideas took root around the magazine *A partir de*

[62] Klaus Meyer-Minnemann and Sergio Vergara Alarcón, 'La revista *Mandrágora*: vanguardismo y contexto chielno en 1938', in Harald Wentzlaf-Eggebert (ed.), *Europäische Avantagarde im Lateinamerikanischen Kontext* (Frankfurt: Veruvert Verlag, 1991), 301–20.

[63] 'Letter from Chile', *VVV Almanac for 1943*, nos 2–3 (March 1943), 124–6.

[64] Marcelo Coddou, 'Gonzalo Rojas', *La Gaceta* (April 1998), 8–13.

[65] Juan Andrés Piña, *Conversaciones con la poesía chilena* (Santiago: Pehuén, 1990), 102–5.

[66] Gonzalo Rojas, *Oscuro* (Caracas: Monte Avila, 1977), 13, 59, 61. Enrique Lihn, *Vuelta* (February 1978), 16–22.

*cero* (1952–1956).[67] She outlined the *ultraísta* years, the aphorisms of Antonio Porchia (which Breton admired), and the influence of Oliverio Girondo. Three key figures emerge. The first was Aldo Pellegrini, indefatigable, with prologues, lectures, translations (Artaud, Lautréamont, Breton), magazines, his press (Argonauta) and his bookshop El Dragón. He organised surrealist exhibitions, prepared three anthologies, and wrote poetry, faithful to Breton's dictates. His 1966 *Antología de la poesía viva latinoamericana* alerted readers around the Spanish-speaking world to the enormous influence of Surrealism in the 1960s, and a continental surrealist tradition.[68] Pellegrini told Baciu that most of the new poets in Argentina had suffered a surrealist influence.[69] It is the late historical nature of this influence that is interesting. Recently, the poet Julio Llinás, commenting on the publication of Pellegrini's complete poetry, recalled his ferocity and scorn for the great Argentine writers, especially Borges, and the literary establishment around Victoria Ocampo's magazine *Sur*.[70] In 1974, José Viñals, in the catalogue to an exhibition in Pellegrini's memory, evoked Pellegrini's passion 'as not parochial' and 'anti-dogmatic'.[71] The poet Enrique Molina wrote in the same catalogue: 'I have known few people with his instinct for intellectual independence.' This breaking down of provincialism and being anti-dogmatic and free can be traced in Pellegrini's life-long defence of poetry, especially in his essays.

D.G. Helder has argued that Pellegrini was crucial in establishing a surrealist direction in Argentina in the 1950s and viewed his essays as a manual on 'surrealist ethics'.[72] In a lecture of 1950, Pellegrini argued that Surrealism was not 'dead' because it was a historical movement that tapped into 'a spiritual movement with deep roots in the past'.[73] So Surrealism's latish arrival in Buenos Aires was explained not in historical terms, but as part of a perennial search for value and art. Pellegrini's position was close to Octavio Paz's in Mexico in the 1950s. His summary of the 'Protean' nature of Surrealism was that its 'common strand' was 'its fervour for what is marvellous' (664). Pellegrini organised a show, 'El surrealismo en la Argentina' in the Instituto Torcuato di Tella in Buenos Aires in June 1967,

---

[67] Graciela de Sola (Maturo), *Proyecciones del surrealismo en la literatura argentina* (Buenos Aires: Ediciones Culturales Argentinas), 1967. See also Juan José Ceselli, *Poesía argentina de vanguardia, surrealismo e invencionismo* (Buenos Aires: Ministerio de Relaciones Exteriores, 1964), 17–25.

[68] Aldo Pellegrini, *Antología de la poesía viva latinoamericana* (Barcelona: Seix Barral, 1966).

[69] Stefan Baciu, *Surrealismo latinoamericano. Preguntas y respuestas* (Valparaíso: Ediciones Universitarias, 1979), 17.

[70] Julio Llinás, 'Ferocidad de un inconformista', *La Nación line*, 27.03.02.

[71] José Viñals, 'Aldo Pellegrini. In Memoriam', Galería Imagen, 1974.

[72] D.G. Helder, 'La presión del presente', *Diario de poesía*, no. 9 (Summer 1989), 24.

[73] Aldo Pellegrini, 'El Movimiento surrealista', *Cursos y conferencias*, no. 222 (September 1950), 297–315 and 641–4.

with a quirky catalogue, and wrote numerous reviews and books on contemporary Argentine art.

In 1953, Pellegrini edited *Letra y línea*, a general avant-garde newspaper-
format magazine, that was informative and critical, without abusing surrealist rhetoric, despite an attack in number 4 (July 1954) on Eduardo Mallea as
betraying himself in his fiction (Mallea was literary editor of *La Nación*,
friend of Borges and represented the status quo). Concurrent to this magazine,
was *A partir de cero*, edited by Enrique Molina (1910–1996), the second key
figure in Argentine Surrealism, in format an experimental and surrealist forum
with a subtitle of 'Revista de poesía y antipoesía' (before Nicanor Parra appropriated the term). The title suggests the *tabula rasa* that Surrealism intended,
abolishing the Judeo-Christian tradition, to start from zero again. The first
number (November 1952) has an editorial written by Molina that displays his
surrealist affinities by arguing that poetry is more than writing poems, it is a
'way of being' that has to be 'lived'. It fuses dreams and action, defies convention and defends love – 'the most intense of drugs' – that destroys all contradictions. Molina attacked Borges and his 'pernicious influence', with
Argentine poetry still tied to Spanish traditions, and formal concerns, rather
than burrowing into inner depths. Borges naturally stood for the conservative
*Sur* group, and was himself hostile to Surrealism, calling it a 'flirtation', with
surrealists faking disorder, and Breton as a 'businessman' and a charlatan.[74]
This first number of *A partir de cero* included poems by César Moro, Péret,
Molina himself, Pellegrini, Latorre and Llinás. The second number of *A partir de cero* opened with another Molina manifesto, defining authentic poetry,
based on 'automatism', followed by a homage to Paul Éluard and an interview
with Breton. The third and last number appeared in September 1956, with
another attack on Borges, by Pellegrini, who concluded that his kind of literature leads to 'complacent rapture' and 'sophisticated imbecilities', with life
being asphyxiated by 'literary sensations'. In his editorials, Molina's passionate language merged with that of many surrealist texts. It is as a poet that
he singularised himself.

From his first book, *Las cosas y el delirio*, 1941, Molina's Nerudan origins
are clear; a passionate relationship with matter through eroticised images and
lists. The sensuous surface of the earth was his territory. *Pasiones terrestres*,
1946, confirmed this turning the outer world erotic and vivid to the perceiv-
ing, transforming imagination. He was brought up in the Argentine provinces,
and travelled as a merchant sailor around South America, and the Caribbean.
His favourite areas are the open sea, tropical ports, cheap hotels, bars and
brothels, far removed from bourgeois respectability. His poetry has a 'tufo del
trópico' [stench of tropics] (74), the beauty he sought was 'marismas de

---

[74] See Jason Wilson, 'Jorge Luis Borges and the European Avant-garde', in Evelyn
Fishburn (ed.), *Borges and Europe Revisited* (London: Institute of Latin American Studies,
1998), 68–80.

prostíbulos y llamas / bajo las alas mórbidas del trópico' [swamps of brothels and flames / under the morbid wings of the tropics] (57). His poetic values relate to travel, nomadism, transience and exile, enjoying the sordid surroundings where surrealism's 'convulsive beauty', the 'belleza demoníaca del mundo' [the devilish beauty of the world] (71) is located. His enemies are home, family, urban tedium, sexual repression, imaginative sterility. He has also exhibited his surrealist collages. As a 'maldito', understanding happens through the senses, liberated from morality, 'what you see, touch, smell, hear and taste'; a return to primal sensations and paradise. Juan Gustavo Cobo Borda called this Molina's 'exaltation of the animal in man'.[75]

Molina's *Costumbres errantes o la redondez de la tierra*, 1951, was reviewed as an anti-bourgeois book (Molina's titles are manifestos), introducing dreams, characteristic of 'superrealismo'.[76] Molina's viewed this book as an orthodox surrealist text, written as automatic writing.[77] So in 1951, in Buenos Aires, Surrealism was still new. However, Molina's key text was *Amantes antípodas*, 1962, with its 'sudores de instintos' [sweat of instincts], and poems expressing his 'rabiosa voracidad de vivir' [raging voracity for life]. 'Alta marea', a love poem, reveals the poet's 'corazón hechizado por la amenaza tantálica del mundo' [heart spell-bound by the world's tantalic threat]. Much of this poetry, written from Buenos Aires, grapples with non-urban scenes like the tropics. His apparently semi-automatic texts turn memory into a mental present. As Julio Ortega noted, 'the present is the central tense in Molina', and the 'now' is the time of the senses and myth.[78]

The third surrealist figure in Buenos Aires was Francisco Madariaga (1927–2000), who developed a 'criollo' Surrealism as an ethical rejection of 'European' rationalism. His poetry explored his province of Corrientes, in a poetics of flashes of tropical intensities, mixing Guarani with Rimbaud, a blend of peasant and sophisticate that was unique. His first collection was *El pequeño patíbulo*, 1954, and his work was collected as *El tren casi fluvial*, in 1987. Madariaga adapted Surrealism as visionary energy, trapping intense sensations in words. The 1954 poem 'El verdadero país' summarises his poetics: 'Virtuoso bebedor del agua del diamante, tiéndete a bramar contra el enorme globo rojo de la idea. / Ese tambor de sangre es tu país' [Virtuous drinker of diamond water, lie down and roar against the huge red balloon of the idea. / That blood drum is your country]. 'El bosque', from 1963, captures his 'surrealismo criollo': 'Una olla hirviéndole / la sangre al invierno. / Comarca en que las

[75] Juan Gustavo Coba Borda, 'La poesía de Enrique Molina', *Eco*, no. 235 (June 1981), 127–38.

[76] César Rosales on Molina in *Sur*, no. 205 (November 1951), 70–7.

[77] José Luis Otero y Claudio Lomenzo, 'Reportaje a Enrique Molina', *La Guacha*, no. 16 (August 2002), 3.

[78] Enrique Molina, *Obra poética* (Caracas: Monte Avila, 1978). Julio Ortega, 'Notas sobre Enrique Molina', *Revista Iberoamericana*, no. 69 (Sept.–Dec. 1960), 532.

rojas putas / orinan al beber fuego' [A stew boiling / winter's blood / region where red whores / piss after drinking fire].[79] Madariaga remained grateful to Girondo's stimulation, and published in *A paritr de cero*.[80]

## Mexico City

As Ida Rodríguez Prampolini and Luis Mario Schneider have shown, Surrealism entered into debates about modernity in Mexico slowly, with hostile views emanating from nationalistic definitions of Mexico's post-revolutionary culture. Critics found Surrealism too dependent on Freud, and 'escapist'; the theory more interesting than the practice. The magazine *Contemporáneos* informed its readers from 1928 about Surrealism as part of a wider intellectual curiosity, with reviews of Breton's *Nadja*; and Jorge Cuesta's notes about Desnos, Éluard and Breton in Paris, so that Surrealism began to be taken more seriously. Schneider concluded that Artaud's trip to Mexico in 1936 remained unique to him, while Breton's in 1938 had lasting consequences.[81] Apart from drawing up his manifesto with Trotsky through Diego Rivera, and admiring Frida Kahlo's work, Breton mentioned Xavier Villaurutia, Agustín Lazo, and later promoted Rufino Tamayo. He also re-met César Moro.

Two moments define surrealist activity in Mexico City; the first around Moro, the second around Octavio Paz in the 1950s. With Breton's approval, Moro and the Austrian surrealist resident in Mexico, Wolfgang Paalen, organised the Surrealist Exhibition of January 1940. In the catalogue manifesto, Moro berated Aragon in Bretonian terms as the 'disgusting' traitor, who justified carnage (Stalin's purges); he mentions the Spanish conquest of America as 'barbarian', its shadow still persisting; he talks of the 'cretinization' of mankind by officials. Against all this, Surrealism placed the spectator 'in front of himself, and this is what few forgive'. So surrealist art lies beyond the market place, and social prestige; is allied with the gratuitous act, with 'amor-pasión', with suicide; it is dangerous, expressing 'absolute lack of conformity'. In 1940, Surrealism still provoked in Mexico.[82] However, Schneider documents the fashionable public at the show. Even Octavio Paz in 1940 thought that Surrealism prolonged Romanticism and had simply become literature, 'commonplaces'. Eight years later, Paz changed opinions and

[79] Francisco Madariaga, *El tren casi fluvial. Obra reunida* (Buenos Aires: Fondo de Cultura Económica, 1987), 41 & 99.

[80] See Javier Cofreces (ed.), *Siete surrealistas argentinos* (Buenos Aires: Editorial Leviatan, 2000), with poems by Ceselli, Latorre, Llinás, Madariaga, Molina, Pellegrini and Vasco.

[81] Schneider, *México y el surrealismo (1925–1950)* (México: Arte y Libros, 1978), 37–106 and 109–66; Prampolini, 53–80. See also 'Los surrealistas en México', special number of *México en el arte*, no. 14 (Autumn 1986).

[82] César Moro, 'Prólogo a la exposición internacional del surrealismo', in *La tortuga ecuestre y otros textos* (Caracas: Monte Avila, 1976), 107–9.

became a surrealist in Paris. In 1973, at the Surrealist Exhibition held at the Museo de Arte Moderno in Mexico City, Paz complained that Surrealism had been deformed, and withdrew his support for the show. But in 1940, Mexican reactions to 'foreign' Surrealism were negative; according to Prampolini, the show fell into a vacuum.[83]

Around Moro, and his close friendship with the poet and critic Xavier Villaurrutia and the painter Agustín Lazo, peripheral surrealist activities happened in magazines like *El hijo pródigo*, and *Letras de México*. Villaurrutia (who had exhibited in the 1940 surrealist show), for example, tried automatic writing, but remained outside orthodoxy.[84] The surrealist Benjamin Péret arrived in Mexico in 1942 and stayed with his surrealist painter wife Remedios Varo until 1948 (Péret later translated Paz's *Pierre de soleil*, 1962).[85] The foreign painters Leonora Carrington, Alice Paalen (who illustrated one of Moro's books) and her husband Wolfgang Paalen, who founded a quasi-surrealist magazine *Dyn* (1942–1944, with Moro publishing in each of the six numbers), continued to link Surrealism with Mexico, with little repercussion within Mexican culture.[86]

The second moment in Mexico centred on Paz's return to Mexico in 1952 as Breton's acolyte. In 1954, Paz gave a lecture arguing, with surrealist passion, that Surrealism was still alive, was not a school, but an exploration of the inner self. Paz saw Surrealism as dissidence to the state, the 'sacred disease of Western civilization'. Inevitably, Paz was attacked. Elías Nandino, in his magazine *Estaciones* in 1956, argued that Surrealism was dead, that Paz was a 'retrograde', that Surrealism was the enemy of 'mexicanidad' [Mexican identity]. Others joined in to elaborate on Paz's 'apotheosis of stupidity', his 'cheap conjuring tricks'; the best surrealist poets had long left Surrealism, that 'poisonous and tragic' movement. The mood was for realism, and exploring post-revolutionary Mexican identity, not hermetic, metaphorical inner adventures. The young poet José Emilio Pacheco summarised this rejection when he called Surrealism a 'contamination', though by 1971 he changed views, and called Paz a 'great' surrealist poet. He admitted that Surrealism had been a 'taboo' word.[87] From his Mexican perspective, Paz had turned Bretonian orthodoxy into a moral vision of dissidence, with poetry as a 'way of living' rejecting revolutionary nationalism in Mexico and Stalinism in the USSR. We come back to Breton's trinity of rotating signs, love, poetry and freedom. In 1974, Paz still evoked Surrealism as crucial, an 'osmotic' system that dissolved classifications, and blended ethics and aesthetics.

---

[83] Prampolini, 44.
[84] See Jason Wilson, 'Surrealism in Mexico', in *Octavio Paz. A Study of his Poetics* (Cambridge: Cambridge University Press, 1979), 20–7.
[85] See Fabienne Bradu, *Benjamin Péret y México* (México: Editorial Aldus, 1998).
[86] Schneider, 209.
[87] Wilson, 1979, 18–20.

To conclude, we have established that surrealist poetry in Spanish America varied from Moro's automatic texts to Paz's separation of the philosophy from the practice, but over the years of its reception in Latin America it stubbornly remained an international movement rigorously opposed to nationalism, provincialism and Stalinism. It exploited the inner world and allowed Spanish American poets to articulate an alternative tradition, based on pre-surrealist subversive writers and the rich mythic past; it fought for living poetry as an ethical attitude, based on erotic love, freedom of the imagination and poetry. It opposed a 'criollo' Surrealism to European rationalism. However, criticism of this delayed Surrealism centres on the manifestos about poetry being often more stimulating than the actual writing (even in Octavio Paz's case), on the consequent 'nominalism', the belief that words could carry these loaded meanings, and on Bretonian orthodoxy as not responding to local issues (for example, Enrique Lihn found Chilean Surrealism an 'exact replica').[88] Despite this criticism, Paz found, in 1954, that the 'corpse' was alive, intact in each person as a 'mysterious force'.[89] In 1973, he still defended Surrealism and attacked the 'pigs' who called Breton a 'pope'.[90] In 1994, Miguel Logroño summarised this surrealist tradition as 'alive, latent'.[91]

[88] Enrique Lihn, 'El surrealismo en Chile', *Nueva Atenea*, no. 423 (July–September 1970), 91–6.
[89] Octavio Paz, 'El surrealismo', *Las peras del olmo* (México: UNAM, 1965), 166.
[90] Octavio Paz, *In/mediaciones* (Barcelona: Editorial Seix Barral, 1979), 149.
[91] Miguel Logroño, 'La palabra surrealista' (Madrid: Museo Nacional Reina Sofia, 1994), 48.

# Select Bibliography

This bibliography is divided into three sections: works of general and theoretical interest on Surrealism; works on a specific author/figure; and works relating to Spanish American surrealists.

## Works of general and theoretical Interest on Surrealism

Adamowicz, Elza. *Surrealist Collage in Text and Image: Dissecting the exquisite Corpse*. Cambridge: Cambridge University Press, 1998

Alexandrian, Sarane. *Surrealist Art*. London: Thames & Hudson [1970], 1993

Aranda, Francisco. *El surrealismo español*. Barcelona: Lumen, 1981

Artaud, Antonin. *Selected Writings*, ed. Susan Sontag, trans. Helen Weaver. New York: Farrar, Strauss and Giroux, 1976

Balakian, Anna. *Surrealism. The Road to the Absolute*. London: Allen & Unwin, 1972

Bataille, Georges. *Eroticism*, trans. Mary Dalwood. San Francisco: City Lights Books, 1986

—— *The Accursed Share*, trans. Robert Hurley, II–III. New York: Zone Books, 1993

Bédouin, Jean-Louis. *La Poésie surréaliste*. Paris: Éditions Seghers, 1964

Bodini, Vittorio. *I Poeta Surrealisti Spagnoli*. Turín: Giulio Einaudi, 1963

—— *Poetas surrealistas españoles*. Barcelona: Diamante, 1982

Breton, André. *Entretiens 1913–1952*. Paris: Nouvelle Revue Française, 1952

—— *Manifestoes of Surrealism*, trans. Richard Seaver and Helen R. Lane. Ann Arbor: University of Michigan Press, 1969

—— *Surrealism and Painting*, trans. Simon Watson Taylor. New York: Harper & Row, 1972

Cernuda, Luis. *La invitación a la poesía*. Madrid: La Tentativa Poética, 1933

—— *Los poetas surrealistas españoles*. Barcelona: Tusquets, 1971

Chica, Francisco. 'Luis Cernuda y la tentación surrealista', in James Valender (ed.), *Entre la realidad y el deseo. Luis Cernuda (1902–1963)*. Madrid: Residencia de Estudiantes / Sociedad Estatal de Conmemoraciones Culturales, 2002, 211–233

Cirlot, J.E. *A Dictionary of Symbols*, trans. J. Sage. London: Routledge & Kegan Paul, 1962

Durán, Manuel. *El superrealismo en la poesía española contemporánea*. México D.F.: Universidad Nacional Autónoma de México, 1950

Durozoi, Gérard. *History of the Surrealist Movement*, trans. Alison Anderson. Chicago and London: University of Chicago Press, 2002

Finkelstein, Haim N. *Surrealism and the Crisis of the Object*. Ann Arbor: University of Michigan Press, 1979

Foucault, Michel. *The History of Sexuality*. New York: Vintage Books, 1990

Freeman, Judi (ed.). *The Dada & Surrealist Word-Image*. Cambridge, Mass.: MIT Press, 1989

*Gaceta Literaria, La*, reimpresión onastática. Vaduz: Topos Verlag, 1980

García de la Concha, V. *El surrealismo español*. Madrid: Taurus Ediciones, 1982

Gibson, Ian. *Lorca–Dalí. El Amor que no pudo ser*. Barcelona: Plaza y Janés, 1999

Guillén, Mercedes. *Conversaciones con los artistas españoles de la Escuela de París*. Madrid: Taurus, 1960

Harris, Derek. *Metal Butterflies and Poisonous Lights: The Language of Surrealism in Lorca, Alberti, Cernuda and Aleixandre*. Anstruther: La Sirena, 1998

—— (ed.). *Changing Times in Hispanic Culture*. Aberdeen: Centre for the Study of the Spanish Avant-Garde, 1996

Havard, Robert. *From Romanticism to Surrealism. Seven Spanish Poets*. Cardiff: University of Wales Press, 1988

—— *The Crucified Mind: Rafael Alberti and the Surrealist Ethos in Spain*. London: Tamesis, 2001

Higgins, Ian (ed.). *Surrealism and Language*. Edinburgh: Scottish Academic Press, 1986

Ilie, Paul. *The Surrealist Mode in Spanish Literature*. Ann Arbor: University of Michigan Press, 1968

—— *Los surrealistas españoles*. Madrid: Taurus, 1972

Lacan, Jacques. *The Four Fundamental Concepts of Psycho-Analysis*, trans. Alan Sheridan. New York: W. W. Norton, 1981

Morise, Max. 'Les yeux enchantés'. *La Révolution surréaliste* (Paris), 1 (December 1924)

Morris, C.B. *Surrealism and Spain 1920–1936*. Cambridge: Cambridge University Press, 1972

—— *This Loving Darkness: The Cinema and Spanish Writers 1920–1936*. Oxford: Oxford University Press, 1980

—— (ed.). *The Surrealist Adventure in Spain*. Ottawa: Dovehouse Editions, 1990

Mundy, Jennifer (ed.). *Surrealism: Desire Unbound*, exhibition catalogue. London: Tate Publishing, 2001

Nietzsche, Friedrich. *The Will to Power*, trans. W. Kaufmann and R.J. Hollingdale. New York: Random House, 1968

Passeron, René. *Phaidon Encyclopedia of Surrealism*, trans. John Griffiths. Oxford: Phaidon, 1978

Paz, Octavio. 'André Breton o la búsqueda del comienzo', in his *Corriente alterna*. México: Siglo XXI, 1967

—— *Los hijos del limo: del romanticismo a la vanguardia*. Barcelona: Barral, 1974

Riffaterre, Michael. 'Semantic Incompatibilities in Automatic Writing', in *About French Poetry from Dada to 'Tel Quel'. Text and Theory*, ed. Mary Ann Caws. Detroit: Wayne State University Press, 1974, 223–241

Sánchez Vidal, Agustín. *Buñuel, Lorca, Dalí: El enigma sin fin*. Barcelona: Planeta, 1988

Shattuck, Roger. *The Banquet Years. The Origins of the Avant-Garde in France: 1885 to World War I*, rev. edn. London: Cape, 1969

Waldberg, Patrick. *Surrealism*. London: Thames & Hudson, 1965

Wiser, William. *The Crazy Years: Paris in the Twenties*. London: Thames & Hudson [1983], 1990

Xuriguera, Gérard. *Pintores españoles de la Escuela de París*, trans. Antonio Urrutia. Madrid: Ibérico Europea de Ediciones, 1974


*Works on specific authors*

*Alberti, Rafael*

Alberti, Rafael. *The Lost Grove*, trans. Gabriel Burns. Berkeley, University of California Press; also *La arboleda perdida*. Buenos Aires: Losada, 1959; Madrid: Alianza, 1998

——— *Correspondencia a José María Cossío*, ed. R. Gómez de Tudanca and E. Mateos Miera. Madrid: Editorial Ayuso, 1973

——— *La arboleda perdida, Libros III y IV*. Barcelona: Seix Barral, 1984

——— *Obra completa, I, Poesía 1920–1938*. Madrid: Aguilar, 1988

Barthes, Roland. *Sade, Fourier, Loyola*, trans. R. Miller. London: Cape, 1977

Bowra, C.M. 'Rafael Alberti, *Sobre los ángeles*', in his *The Creative Experiment*. London: Macmillan, 1949, reprinted 1967

Chavarri, Raúl. *Mito y realidad en la escuela de Vallecas*. Madrid: Ibérico Europea, 1975

León, María Teresa. *Memoria de la melancolía*. Buenos Aires: Losada, 1970

Loyola, Saint Ignatius of. *Personal Writings*, trans., intro. and notes by Joseph A. Munitiz and Philip Endean. Harmondsworth: Penguin, 1996

Mallo, Maruja. *Maruja Mallo: 59 grabados en negro y 9 láminas en color (1928–1942)*, estudio preliminar por Ramón Gómez de la Serna. Buenos Aires: Losada, 1942

Popkin, Louise. *The Theatre of Rafael Alberti*. London: Tamesis, 1976


*Aleixandre, Vicente*

Aleixandre, Vicente. *Ambito*. Malaga: Litoral, 1928

——— *Espadas como labios*. Madrid: Espasa Calpe, 1932

——— *Pasión de la tierra*. México D.F.: Fábula, 1935

——— *Mundo a solas*. Madrid: Clan, 1950

——— *Poemas de la consumación*. Barcelona: Plaza y Janés, 1968

——— *Obras Completas*. Madrid: Plaza y Janés, 1968

——— *Poesía superrealista. Antología*. Barcelona: Barral Editores, 1971

——— *Espadas como labios. La destrucción o el amor*, edición de José Luis Cano. Madrid: Clásicos Castalia, 1972

——— *Diálogos del conocimiento*. Barcelona: Plaza y Janés, 1974

Aragon, Louis. *Une Vague de reves*. Paris: Gallimard, 1924

Cernuda, Luis. *Estudios sobre poesía española contemporánea*. Madrid: Gallimard, 1957

Morelli, Gabriele. 'La escritura surrealista de Vicente Aleixandre: nuevos datos y algunas reflexiones'. *Ínsula*, LI, no. 592 (April 1996), 20–22

## Buñuel, Luis

Aranda, Francisco. *Luis Buñuel: A Critical Biography*, trans. David Robinson. London: Secker and Warburg, 1975

Aub, Max. *Conversaciones con Buñuel*. Madrid: Aguilar, 1984

Babington, Bruce and Evans, Peter W. 'The Life of the Interior: Dreams in the Films of Luis Buñuel'. *Critical Quarterly*, XXVII (1985), 5–20

Baxter, John. *Buñuel*. London: Fourth Estate, 1994

Buache, Freddy. *The Cinema of Luis Buñuel*, trans. Peter Graham. London: Tantivy Press, 1973

Buñuel, Luis. *Luis Buñuel. Obra literaria*, introducción y notas de Agustín Sánchez Vidal. Zaragoza: Ediciones de Heraldo de Aragón, 1982

—— *Mon dernier soupir*. Paris: Editions Robert Laffont, 1982. *My Last Breath*, trans. Abigail Israel. London: Jonathan Cape, 1984

Durgnat, Raymond. *Luis Buñuel*. London: Studio Vista, 1967

Edwards, Gwynne. *The Discreet Art of Luis Buñuel: A Reading of his Films*. London: Marion Boyars, 1982

Evans, Peter W. *The Films of Luis Buñuel: Subjectivity and Desire*. Oxford: Clarendon Press, 1995

Higginbotham, Virginia. *Luis Buñuel*. Boston: Twayne Publishers, 1979

Ibarz, Mercè. *Buñuel documental: 'Tierra sin pan' y su tiempo*. Zaragoza: Prensas Universitarias, 1999

Kyrou, Ado. *Luis Buñuel*. Paris: Edition Seghers, 1962

Mellen, Joan (ed.). *The World of Luis Buñuel: Essays and Criticism*. New York: Oxford University Press, 1977

Pérez Turrent, Tomás, and José de la Colina. *Buñuel por Buñuel*. Madrid: Plot, 1993

Rucar de Buñuel, Jeanne. *Memorias de una mujer sin piano*, written by Marisol Martín del Campo. Madrid: Alianza Editorial, 1990

Sánchez Vidal, Agustín (ed.). *Luis Buñuel: obra literaria*. Zaragoza: Ediciones del Heraldo de Aragón, 1982

—— *Luis Buñuel: obra cinematográfica*. Madrid: Ediciones J.C., 1984

—— *El mundo de Buñuel*. Zaragoza: Caja de Ahorros de la Inmaculada de Aragón, 1993

White, G. *Hamlet* in *An Unspeakable Betrayal: Selected Writings of Luis Buñuel*. Berkeley: University of California Press, 2000


## Cernuda, Luis

Cernuda, Luis. *La invitación a la poesía*. Madrid: La Tentativa Poética, 1933

—— *Estudios sobre poesía española contemporánea*. Madrid: Guadarrama, 1957

—— *Prosa completa*, ed. Derek Harris and Luis Maristany. Barcelona: Barral, 1975

—— *Selected Poems*, trans. Reginald Gibbons. Berkeley: University of California Press, 1977

—— *Obra completa II. Prosa I y II*, ed. Derek Harris and Luis Maristany. Madrid: Siruela, 1994

—— *Un río, un amor / Los placeres prohibidos*, ed. Derek Harris. Madrid: Cátedra, 1999

Doce, Jordi. 'Pervivencias surrealistas en la poesía de Luis Cernuda'. *Ínsula* (Madrid), no. 669 (September 2002), 9–12

Edkins, Anthony and Derek Harris (eds). *The Poetry of Luis Cernuda*. New York: New York University Press, 1971

Ferraté, Juan. 'Luis Cernuda y el poder de las palabras', in Derek Harris (ed.), *Luis Cernuda*. Madrid: Taurus, El escritor y la crítica, 1977, 269–279

Morris, C.B. '*Un río, un amor* and the Evasive Subjectivity of Luis Cernuda', in Salvador Jiménez-Fajardo (ed.), *The Word and the Mirror. Critical Essays on the Poetry of Luis Cernuda*. Cranberry, N.J.: Associated University Presses, 1989, 44–57

Nerval, Gérard de. *Oeuvres*, I, ed. Albert Béguin and Jean Richer. Paris: Gallimard, 1960

Paz, Octavio. 'La palabra edificante', in Derek Harris (ed.), *Luis Cernuda*. Madrid: Taurus, El escritor y la crítica, 1977, 138–160

Sánchez Rodríguez, Alfonso. '1930: Salvador Dalí en Torremolinos. Cómo se frustra – y por qué – la aparición de una revista del surrealismo español en Málaga', in Gabriele Morelli (ed.), *Treinta años de vanguardia española*. Seville: Ediciones El Carro de la Nieve, 1991, 193–204

Valender, James. '*Los placeres prohibidos*: A Study of the Prose-Poems', in Salvador Jiménez-Fajardo (ed.), *The Word and the Mirror. Critical Essays on the Poetry of Luis Cernuda*. Cranberry, N.J.: Associated University Presses, 1989, 80–96

—— 'Lorca y Cernuda: el zumo amargo', in Laura Dolfi (ed.), *Federico García Lorca e il suo tempo*. Rome: Bulzoni Editore, 1999, 123–135

—— 'Emilio Prados y el surrealismo', in Francisco Chica (ed.), *Emilio Prados. Un hombre, un universo*. Málaga: Centro Cultural de la Generación del 27, 2000, 301–315

—— 'Luis Cernuda y el surrealismo: primeras lecturas (1925–1928)', in Renata Londero (ed.), *I mondi di Luis Cernuda*. Udine: Forum / Editrice Universitaria Udinese, 2002, 31–41


*Dalí, Salvador*

Ades, Dawn. *Dalí and Surrealism*. New York: Harper & Row, 1982

—— *Salvador Dalí: The Early Years*. London: South Bank Centre, 1994

Capasso, Nicholas J. 'Salvador Dalí and the Barren Plain: A Phenomenological Analysis of a Surrealist Landscape Environment'. *Arts Magazine*, no. 60 (June 1986)

Cowling, Elizabeth. ' "Proudly we claim him as one of us": Breton, Picasso and the surrealist movement'. *Art History*, 8, no. 1 (March 1985)

Dalí, Salvador. 'Nous limits de la pintura' [New limits of Painting]. *L'Amic de les Arts* (February, April, May 1928).

—— 'Objets surréalistes', in *Le Surréalisme au service de la revolution*, no. 3 (December 1931)

—— 'De la beauté terrifiante et comestible, de l'architecture Modern style'. *Minotaure* (Paris), no. 3–4 (12 December 1933)

—— *The Secret Life of Salvador Dalí*, trans. Haakon M. Chevalier. London: Vision Press, 1973

—— *The Unspeakable Confessions of Salvador Dalí*, trans. H.J. Salemson. London: Quartet Books, 1977

—— *Diary of a Genius*, trans. R. Howard. London: Hutchinson, 1990

Descharnes, Robert. *Salvador Dalí: The Paintings*. Cologne: Taschen, 1994

Finkelstein, Haim. *Salvador Dalí's Art and Writing 1927–1942: The Metamorphoses of Narcissus*. Cambridge and New York: Cambridge University Press, 1996

Foster, Hal. 'The Art of Fetishism: Notes on Dutch Still Life', in Emily Apter and William Pietz (eds), *Fetishism as Cultural Discourse*. Ithaca and London: Cornell University Press, 1993

—— (ed.). *Vision and Visuality*, Dia Art Foundation Discussions in Contemporary Culture no. 2. Seattle: Bay Press, 1988, 87–108

García de Carpi, Lucía. 'La respuesta española' [Itineraries of Surrealism in Spain]. *El Surrealismo en España*. Madrid: Museo Nacional Centro de Arte Reina Sofia, 1994–5

Gasch, Sebastià. 'Els Pintors Nous: Maria Mallo'. *L'Amic de les Arts*, no. 28 (31 September 1928 [*sic*])

—— 'Pintura i anti-pintura'. *La Veu de Catalunya* (13 June 1929)

Gibson, Ian. *The Shameful Life of Salvador Dalí*. London: Faber and Faber, 1997

Jeffett, William. *Dalí and Miró circa 1928*. St Petersburg, Florida: Salvador Museum Exhibition Series, 2003

Montanyà, Luis. 'Superrealisme'. *L'Amic de les Arts*, no. 10 (31 January 1927)

—— 'Panorama: punts de vista sobre el superrealisme'. *L'Amic de les Arts*, no. 25 (31 May 1928)

Rubin, William. *De Chirico*. New York: Museum of Modern Art, 1982

Santos Torroella, Rafael. *La miel es más dulce que la sangre: las épocas lorquiana y freudiana de Salvador Dalí*. Barcelona: Planeta, 1984


*García Lorca, Federico*

Allen, Rupert. *The Symbolic World of Federico García Lorca*. Albuquerque: University of New Mexico Press, 1972

—— 'A Commentary on Lorca's *El paseo de Buster Keaton*'. *Hispanófila*, no. 48 (May 1973)

Anderson, Andrew A. 'Lorca at the Crossroads: "Imaginación, inspiración, evasión" and the "novísimas estéticas"'. *Anales de la Literatura Española Contemporánea*, XVI (1991), 149–173

—— '*Et in Arcadia Ego*: Thematic Divergence and Convergence in Lorca's "Poema doble del lago Edén"'. *Bulletin of Hispanic Studies* (Glasgow), LXXIV (1997), 409–429

—— 'Sebastià Gasch y Federico García Lorca: influencias recíprocas y la construcción de una estética vanguardista', in *Federico García Lorca i Catalunya*, ed. Antonio Monegal and José María Micó. Barcelona: Universitat Pompeu Fabra-Institut Universitari de Cultura / Diputació de Barcelona – Area de Cultura, 2000, 93–110

Anderson, R. *Federico García Lorca*. London: Macmillan, 1984

Bergamín, José. 'Literatura y brújula'. *La Gaceta Literaria*, III, no. 51 (1 February 1929)

Blanco Aguinaga, Carlos. *Sobre el modernismo, desde la periferia*. Granada: Comares, 1998

Bonet, Juan Manuel. *Diccionario de las vanguardias en España (1907–1936)*. Madrid: Alianza, 1995

Dalí, Salvador. 'Sant Sebastià'. *L'Amic de les Arts*, II, no. 16 (31 July 1927), 52–54

—— Federico García Lorca: exposició de dibuixos colorits (Galeries Dalmau)'. *La Nova Revista*, III, no. 9 (September 1927), 84–85

—— 'Les arts. Joan Miró'. *L'Amic de les Arts*, III, no. 26 (30 June 1928), 202

—— 'Realidad y sobrerrealidad'. *La Gaceta Literaria*, II, no. 44 (15 October 1928), 7

—— *Salvador Dalí escribe a Federico García Lorca (1925–1936)*, ed. Rafael Santos Torroella. Special double number of *Poesía*, nos 27–28 (Winter–Spring 1987)

García Lorca, Federico. 'Santa Lucía y San Lázaro'. *Revista de Occidente*, XVIII, no. 53 (November 1927), 145–155

—— *Conferencias*, ed. Christopher Maurer, 2 vols. Madrid: Alianza, 1984

—— *Obras completas*, III: *Prosa. Dibujos*, ed. Arturo del Hoyo, 22nd edn. Madrid: Aguilar, 1986

—— *Manuscritos neoyorquinos. 'Poeta en Nueva York' y otras hojas y poemas*, ed. Mario Hernández. Madrid: Tabapress / Fundación Federico García Lorca, 1990

—— *Teatro inédito de juventud*, ed. A. Soria Olmedo. Madrid: Cátedra, 1996

—— *Epistolario completo*, ed. Andrew A. Anderson and Christopher Maurer. Madrid: Cátedra, 1997

—— *Poet in New York*, bilingual edn, ed. Christopher Maurer, trans. Greg Simon and Steven F. White, rev. edn. New York: The Noonday Press, 1998

—— *Poemas en prosa*, ed. Andrew A. Anderson. Granada: Comares, 2000

García-Posada, Miguel. *Lorca: interpretación de 'Poeta en Nueva York'*. Madrid: Akal, 1981

—— 'Lorca y el surrealismo: una relación conflictiva'. *Barcarola*, nos 54–55 (December 1997), 159–174

George, D. *The History of the Commedia dell'Arte in Modern Hispanic Literature with Special Attention to the Work of García Lorca*. Lampeter: Edwin Mellen Press, 1995

Gibson, Ian. *Federico García Lorca*, vols 1 and 2. Barcelona: Grijalbo, 1985, 1987

Harris, Derek. 'A la caza de la imagen surrealista en Lorca'. *Ínsula*, XXXII, nos 368–369 (July–August 1977), 19

—— Federico García Lorca: 'Poeta en Nueva York'. London: Tamesis / Grant & Cutler, 1978

—— 'La elaboración textual de *Poeta en Nueva York*: el salto mortal'. *Revista Canadiense de Estudios Hispánicos*, XVIII (1994), 309–315

—— '"Tierra y luna" de Federico García Lorca: un ejemplo de neorromanticismo surrealista'. *Donaire*, no. 5 (October 1995), 33–39

Hernández, Mario. 'García Lorca y Salvador Dalí: del ruiseñor lírico a los burros podridos (Poética y epistolario)', in *L''imposible/posible' di Federico García Lorca*, ed. Laura Dolfi. Naples: Edizioni Scientifiche Italiane, 1989, 267–319

Marco, Joaquín. 'Muerte o resurrección del surrealismo español (I) y (II)'. *Ínsula*, XXVIII, nos 316 & 317 (1973)

Martínez Nadal, Rafael.'*El público'. Amor y muerte en la obra de Federico García Lorca*, 3rd edn. Madrid: Hiperión, 1988

Masoliver, Juan Ramón. 'Possibilitats i hipocresia del surrealisme d'Espanya'. *Butlletí de l'Agrupament Escolar*, nos 7–9 (1930)

McMullan, Terence. 'Federico García Lorca's "Santa Lucía y San Lázaro" and the Aesthetics of Transition'. *Bulletin of Hispanic Studies*, LXVII (1990), 1–20

Monegal, Antonio. 'La "poesía nueva" de 1929: entre el álgebra de las metáforas y la revolución surrealista'. *Anales de la Literatura Española Contemporánea*, XVI (1991), 55–72

Oppenheimer, Helen. *Lorca, The Drawings: their relation to the poet's life and work*. London: Herbert Press, 1986

Rodríguez Herrera, José Luis. 'La coherencia de la imaginería surrealista en *Poeta en Nueva York'. Philologica Canariensia*, no. 1 (1995), 363–380

Salazar, Adolfo. 'In memoriam. Federico en La Habana', *Carteles*, 23 January 1938, 30–31

Wright, S. *The Trickster-Function in the Theatre of García Lorca*. London: Tamesis, 2000


### Giménez Caballero, Ernesto

Dennis, Nigel. 'Ernesto Giménez Caballero and Surrealism: a Reading of *Yo, inspector de alcantarillas* (1928)', in *The Surrealist Adventure in Spain*, ed. C.B. Morris. Ottawa: Dovehouse Editions, 1990, 80–100

•Giménez Caballero, Ernesto. 'Eoántropo: el hombre auroral del arte'. *Revista de Occidente*, XIX (1928), 309–342

—— *Yo, inspector de alcantarillas*. Madrid: Biblioteca Nueva, 1928

—— 'Por ejemplo: el superrealismo'. *La Gaceta Literaria*, LVIII (1929), 3

Hernando, Miguel A. 'Primigenia plasmación del superrealismo castellano: *Yo, inspector de alcantarillas'. Papeles de Son Armadans*, CCXXXVI–CCXXXVII (1975), 137–159


### Gómez de la Serna, Ramón

Cardona, Rodolfo. *Ramón: A Study of Gómez de la Serna and his Works*. New York: Torres, 1957

Gómez de la Serna, Ramón. *Obras completas*, ed. I. Zlotescu. Barcelona, Círculo de Lectores / Galaxia Gutenberg, 1996–

Hoyle, Alan. 'El problema de la greguería'. *Actas del IX Congreso de la Asociación Internacional de Hispanistas*, II, ed. S. Neumeister. Frankfurt: Vervuert, 1989, 283–292

—— *El humor ramoniano de vanguardia*. Manchester: Department of Spanish and Portuguese Publications, 1996

Morris, C.B. 'Ramón y la vanguardia', in Francisco Rico (ed.), *Historia y crítica de la literatura española. Epoca contemporánea: 1914–1939. Primer suplemento*, vol. 7/1, ed. A. Sánchez Vidal. Barcelona: Crítica, 1995, 132–146

Neruda, Pablo.'Ramón', prologue to Ramón Gómez de la Serna, *Obras selectas*, 2nd edn. Barcelona: AHR, 1971

Sánchez Vidal, Agustín. 'De Ramón al surrealismo'. *Ínsula*, no. 502 (October 1988), 13–14

Soldevila-Durante, Ignacio. 'Ramón Gómez de la Serna: *Superrealismo* and *Surrealismo*', in *The Surrealist Adventure in Spain*, ed. C.B. Morris. Ottawa: Dovehouse, 1991, 62–79

Umbral, Francisco. *Ramón y las vanguardias*. Madrid: Espasa-Calpe, 1978

Vela, Fernando. *El grano de pimienta*. Buenos Aires: Espasa-Calpe, 1950


*Hinojosa, José María*

Hinojosa, José María. *Epistolario*, ed. and intro. Julio Neira and Alfonso Sánchez Rodríguez. Seville: Fundación Genesian, 1997

—— *Obra completa (1923–1931)*, ed. and intro. Alfonso Sánchez Rodríguez. Seville: Fundación Genesian, 1998

Montanyà, Luis. 'Punts de vista sobre el superrealisme: *La Flor de California* de José María Hinojosa'. *L'Amic de les Arts*, no. 26 (30 June 1928), 198–200

Neira, Julio. 'José María Hinojosa: Vida y Obra'. Unpublished doctoral thesis. Cáceres: Universidad de Extremadura, 1981

—— *Viajero de soledades: estudios sobre José María Hinojosa*. Seville: Fundación Genesian, 1999

Sánchez Rodríguez, Alfonso. 'Una aproximación al "Caso Hinojosa"'. Unpublished thesis. Estudi General de Lleida, 1990

—— 'Donde arraigue el olvido, la *arriesgada* reivindicación del poeta surrealista José María Hinojosa'. *Palabras del 27* (Malaga) (5 December 1990), 25–26

—— (ed.). *Remolino de voces: La recepción de José María Hinojosa (1927–1929)*. Malaga: Centro Cultural de la Generación del 27, 1995


*Larrea, Juan*

Bary, D. *Larrea, Poesía y Transfiguración*. Madrid: Planeta / Universidad Complutense, 1976

—— '*Ilegible, hijo de flauta*: guión cinematográfico de Juan Larrea y Luis Buñuel', in his *Nuevos estudios sobre Huidobro y Larrea*. Valencia: Pre-Textos, 1984, 167–177

Diaz de Guereñu, J.M. *La poesía de Juan Larrea. Creación y sentido*. San Sebastian: Cuadernos Universitarios Mundaiz, 1988

Gurney, R. 'Juan Larrea, Unrecognised Father of Spanish Surrealism?' *Proceedings of the First Conference of Hispanists in Polytechnics and Other Colleges*, ed. R. Gurney. London: Middlesex Polytechnic / Instituto de España, 1978, 21–36

—— 'Larrea y la poesía francesa anterior al surrealismo (de Nerval à Valéry)', in *Al amor de Larrea*, ed. J.M. Diaz de Guereñu. Valencia: Pre-Textos, 1985, 11–38

—— *La poesía de Juan Larrea*. Bilbao: Servicio Editorial / Argitarapen, n.d.

Iglesia Lesteiro, M.-F. *Juan Larrea. Vida poesía*. Bilbao: Bibao-Vizcaya Kutxa, 1997

Laemmel-Serrano, S. *Juan Larrea ou Le suicide en poésie*. Berne: Peter Lang, 1995

Larrea, Juan. *Del surrealismo a Machupicchu*. Mexico: Editorial Joaquín Mortiz, 1967

—— '*Ilegible, hijo de flaut*a: complementos circunstanciales'. *Vuelta* (March 1980), 24–25

—— *Juan Larrea: Cartas a Gerardo Diego, 1916–1980*, Edición a cargo de E. Cordero de Ciria y J.M. Diaz de Guereñu. San Sebastián: Cuadernos Universitarios Mundaiz, 1986, 93

—— *Versión celeste*. Barcelona: Barral, 1970; Madrid: Cátedra, 1989

Sánchez Vidal, A. 'Juan Larrea y Luis Buñuel: Convergencias y divergencias en torno a *Ilegible, hijo de flauta*', in *Al Amor de Larrea*, ed. J.M. Diaz de Guereñu. Valencia: Pre-Textos, 1985, 121–144. *Actas de las Primeras Jornadas Internacionales Juan Larrea*, San Sebastian and Bilbao, July 1984

Sandry, G. and M. Carrère. *Dictionnaire de l'argot moderne*, cinquième édition, Paris: Au Quais de Paris, Editions du Dauphin, 1957


*Miró, Joan*

Adamowicz, Elza. 'Writing Miró: Blue Tales for Adults'. *New Comparison* (Lancaster), 31 (Spring 2001), 89–111

Burnett, David. 'The Poetics of the Paintings of Miró'. *Artscanada*, nos 238–239 (Dec. 1980–Jan. 1981), 6–11

Danto, Arthur C. 'Miró's "little miracles"'. *Art News*, 92, 8 (Oct. 1993), 138–143

Dupin, Jacques. *Joan Miró: Life and Work*, trans. Norbert Guterman. New York: Abrams, 1962

—— 'La transmutación', in *Joan Miró: Años 20. Mutación de la realidad*, exhibition catalogue. Madrid: Museo español de arte contemporáneo, 1983, 30–48

Foix, J.V. 'Presentació de Joan Miró'. *L'Amic de les Arts*, no. 26 (30 June 1928)

Gasch, Sebastià. 'L'obra actual del pintor Joan Miró'. *L'Amic de les Arts* (August 1926)

Meisler, Stanley. 'For Joan Miró, poetry and painting were the same'. *Smithsonian* (Washington, D.C.) (November 1993), 63–75

Mink, Janis. *Miró*. Cologne: Taschen, 2001

Miró, Joan. *Joan Miró: 1893–1993*, exhibition catalogue. Fundació Joan Miró. Boston, New York, Toronto and London: Bullfinch Press, 1993

Permanyer, Lluís. *Los años difíciles de Miró, Llorens Artigas, Fenosa, Dalí, Clavé, Tàpies*. Barcelona: Lumen, 1975

Raillard, Georges. *Conversaciones con Miró*. Barcelona: Granica, 1978

Rowell, Margit (ed.). *Joan Miró: Selected Writings and Interviews*. New York: Da Capo Press, 1992


*Works on Spanish American surrealists*

Aira, César. *Alejandra Pizarnik*. Rosario: Beatriz Viterbo, 1988

Baciu, Stefan. *Surrealismo latinoamericano. Preguntas y respuestas*. Valparaíso: Ediciones Universitarias, 1979

Bradu, Fabienne. *Benjamin Péret y México*. México: Editorial Aldus, 1998

Brotherston, Gordon. *Latin American Poetry. Origins and Presence*. Cambridge: Cambridge University Press, 1975

Calderón, Alfonso (ed.). *Antología de la poesía chilena contemporánea*. Santiago: Editorial Universitaria, 1970

Caracciolo Trejo, E. *La poesía de Vicente Huidobro y la vanguardia*. Madrid: Gredos, 1974

Ceselli, Juan José. *Poesía argentina de vanguardia, surrealismo e invencionismo*. Buenos Aires: Ministerio de Relaciones Exteriores, 1964

Cofreces, Javier (ed.). *Siete surrealistas argentinos*. Buenos Aires: Editorial Leviatan, 2000

Costa, René de. *En pos de Huidobro*. Santiago de Chile: Editorial Universitaria, 1978

Coyné, André. 'César Moro entre Lima, París y México', in Julio Ortega (ed.), *Textos en el aire*. Barcelona: Tusquets, 1974

Girondo, Oliverio. *Obras completas*. Buenos Aires: Losada, 1968

Graciela de Sola, Maturo. *Proyecciones del surrealismo en la literatura argentina*. Buenos Aires: Ediciones Culturales Argentinas, 1967

Hart, Stephen M. *César Vallejo: Autógrafos olvidados*. London: Tamesis, 2002

Huidobro, Vicente. *Obras completas*, 1. Santiago de Chile: Zig-Zag, 1964

Larrea, Juan. *El surrealismo entre viejo y nuevo mundo*. México: Ediciones Cuadernos Americanos, 1944

Madariaga, Francisco. *El tren casi fluvial. Obra reunida*. Buenos Aires: Fondo de Cultura Económica, 1987

Molina, Enrique. *Obra poética*. Caracas: Monte Avila, 1978

Moro, César. *Versiones del surrealismo*. Barcelona: Tusquets, 1974

Neruda, Pablo. *Obras completas, I*. Barcelona: Galaxia Gutenberg, 1999

Paz, Octavio. 'El surrealismo', in *Las peras del olmo*. México: UNAM, 1965

—— *Poemas (1935–1975)*. México: Editorial Seix Barral, 1979

—— *La llama doble. Amor y erotismo*. Barcelona: Seix Barral, 1993

—— *Itinerary*, trans. Jason Wilson. London: Menard Books, 1999

Pellegrini, Aldo. *Oliverio Girondo*. Buenos Aires: Ediciones Culturales Argentinas, 1964

—— *Antología de la poesía viva latinoamericana*. Barcelona: Seix Barral, 1966

Piña, Cristina. *Alejandra Pizarnik*. Buenos Aires: Planeta, 1991

Rodríguez Prampolini, Ida. *El surrealismo y el arte fantástico de México*. México: UNAM, 1969

Sucre, Guillermo. *La máscara, la transparencia*. Caracas: Monte Avila, 1975

Vallejo, César. *El arte y la revolución*. Lima: Mosca Azul, 1973

Westphalen, Emilio Adolfo. 'Poetas en la Lima de los años treinta'. *Dos soledades*. Lima: Instituto Nacional de Cultura, 1974

—— *Escritos varios: sobre arte y poesía* and *Bajo zarpas de la quimera: Poemas 1930–1988*. Madrid: Alianza, 1991

Wilson, Jasón. *Octavio Paz*. Boston: Twayne, 1986

—— 'Jorge Luis Borges and the European Avant-garde', in Evelyn Fishburn (ed.), *Borges and Europe Revisited*. London: Institute of Latin American Studies, 1998, 68–80

—— 'César Vallejo and "El bruto libre": Notes on the Burden of European Culture'. *Romance Quarterly*, 49, no. 3 (2002), 206–214

Yurkievich, Saúl, *Fundadores de la nueva poesía latinoaamericana*. Barcelona: Barral, 1973

# Index